What Others Are Saying About
Confessions of a Pickup Artist Chaser

"I lived and breathed the PUA world for years and I honestly thought I had seen everything. But Clarisse brought some fresh and interesting perspectives, which was really cool."
~ *From an interview with former pickup artist coach Mark Manson*

"Clarisse's analysis is as interesting, easy-to-follow and well-laid out as it is in all of her writing, but the most compelling thing in this book is not the analysis itself, but the way Clarisse uses memoir to supplement her analysis. Clarisse is a brilliant sex writer with what appears to be an unflinching ability to reveal personal information. That talent is highlighted here as Clarisse fleshes out scenes that create a parallel emotional and intellectual journey, allowing the reader to travel with her through the insights and frustration of her time on the fringes of the pick-up artist community. Her intelligent writing about S&M and polyamory help establish her presence in the text as someone with a subaltern point of view, and place pick-up artistry within the context of other sexual subcultures."
~ *From a review by Nebula award winner and feminist writer Rachel Swirsky*

"Insightful, thoughtful, engaging, and very well-balanced. Clarisse talks about all sides of the community — the positive, negative, and horrendous — and she draws larger lessons about society and human nature."
~ *From an interview with cognitive psychologist Scott Barry Kaufman*

"Clarisse's big strength in *Confessions* is her empathy. A lot of times people only understand their little corner of the gendersphere and have ideas that are at best strawmen and at worst outright lies about the other corners. But Clarisse understands why men might take up pickup, and how it would help them, and how it can become destructive. She understands the eroticism of power, both in vanilla and kinky sex. Clarisse Thorn understands that shit is complicated."
~ *From a review by feminist masculinity writer Ozy Frantz*

* * *

Confessions of a Pickup Artist Chaser:

Long Interviews with Hideous Men

* * *

Clarisse Thorn

* * *

clarissethorn.com
@ClarisseThorn

* * *

This book is copyright 2012 Clarisse Thorn, although I have mixed feelings about modern copyright law. Check out the Electronic Frontier Foundation at http://eff.org, a nonprofit that protects free speech on the Internet and does lots of awesome work around copyright issues.

Cover image copyright 2005 Beautiful Disasters Photography.

* * *

* * *

Notes and Acknowledgments

* * *

If you've read my blog a lot, you'll recognize some of this writing. Bonus points if you know every single post I quote or reference in this book. Triple bonus points if you can figure out my musical tastes from my music references, because honestly, my musical tastes don't make much sense even to me. The music references in this book are explicitly intended to assist with my social commentary, to give you a sense of the culture I'm describing, and to create a sense of ambiguity about my musical preferences.

This is Version 3.0 of *Confessions.* 2.0 included a new section in Chapter 6 that documents my meeting with the famous pickup artist Adam Lyons, which took place right after the initial USA release of this book. 3.0 includes edits that were done after I signed a German translation deal with Edel Germany GmbH; there is some rearrangement, especially in Chapter 3 and Chapter 12, and I stripped the infamous TL;DR sections. The last updates took place in January 2013.

Of course, I owe a huge debt to the beta readers, blog commenters, friends, and family members who shaped this book. Some of them are "characters" in my narrative, but most aren't. I thank them all from the bottom of my heart for their ideas, humor, and support.

All the events that I report in this story actually happened, but in order to protect the privacy of my friends and sources, some names and identifying details have been changed. When I use real names, it's either because I'm talking about stuff that's publicly known, or I have that person's consent.

Many many people read this first draft of this book; most of them were random friends, or readers who responded to a call that I put out on my blog. However, most of those folks did not want to be in the credits. A lot more men were okay with being publicly listed than women. I could provide a feminist analysis of that, but I'll just give you the credits. (Also, please note that none of the people below identify as pickup artists.)

Firstly, Brenda Errichiello is a guerrilla editor-for-hire. If you need editing for your self-published ebook (and you do), then you should totally contact her. Her website is [http://www.bee-editing.com/].

Other folks (alphabetical order by first name):
David Weasley [http://somefolks.blogspot.com]
Debbie Timmins
Ian K. Hagemann
Jesse Raber
Lance Hanson
Louis R. Evans
Mame Maloney
Master Arach [http://theeroticist.com]
Thomas MacAulay Millar [http://yesmeansyesblog.wordpress.com]
I'd also like to thank Beautiful Disasters Photography for giving me the cover image for this book.

* * *

* * *

THE FOLLOWING IS A TRUE STORY. It really happened. Men will deny it. Women will doubt it. But I present it to you here, naked, vulnerable, and disturbingly real. I beg you for your forgiveness in advance. Don't hate the player... hate the game.
~ Neil Strauss, *The Game*

* * *

I seem to be developing more of a sort of conscience [about falling in love]. Which a part of me finds terrifying, to be honest. ... I admit there's a kind of dread at the idea of having a conscience in this area, as if it seems as if it's going to take away all room to maneuver, somehow.
~ David Foster Wallace, *Brief Interviews With Hideous Men*

* * *

I'll just come out and say it: pickup artists rape women through coercion and manipulation. Full stop.
~ Female commenter on a feminist blog post

* * *

[Women] really are insipid, vapid airheads. If it wasn't for the pussy, there would be a bounty on them.
~ Male commenter on a pickup artist blog post

* * *

Love is a game that two can play and both win.
~ Thai fortune cookie

* * *

* * *

Table of Contents

* * *

Please note: there's a Glossary at the very end, page 304, Appendix H.

* * *

CHAPTER 1: **Come Jump In, Bimbo Friend** ... page 1

In this chapter, we meet the mysterious Clarisse Thorn, and we learn about her history as a nerd child with weird pets who eventually became a feminist sex activist. She loves S&M in a perfectly rational way, but her fixation on pickup artists (PUAs) was somewhat irrational. Plus: A History of Feminism, plus A History of Pickup Artistry, plus A Grand Taxonomy Of Pickup Artists. The chapter title is a lyric from the song "Barbie Girl," by Aqua.

* * *

CHAPTER 2: **You're A Good Soldier, Choosing Your Battles** ... 26

In which Clarisse ventures into the field, observing PUAs in their natural habitat. One PUA takes a special interest in her, and the resultant power struggle is tons of fun. Plus: a Theory of Adversarial Flirtation, plus a Theory of Strategic Ambiguity. The chapter title is from the song "Waka Waka (Time for Africa)," a collaboration by Shakira and Freshlyground.

* * *

CHAPTER 3: **Underground Communication** ... 39

In which Clarisse discusses what it means to be a respectful partner who creates a low-pressure sexual environment. She talks about how people communicate about sex in the S&M community, as well as the community around polyamory (i.e., people who choose to have radically honest open relationships). And she tells us all about some of the most disturbing seduction tactics: "Last Minute Resistance techniques," which PUAs developed for targets who resist having sex. The chapter title is after a song with the same name, by Bassnectar featuring Seasunz.

* * *

CHAPTER 4: **If You Knew How Much I Loved You, You Would Run Away** ... 64

In which Clarisse gets involved with Adam, a man she really likes. He's not a pickup artist, and he is a feminist... however, Clarisse analyzes their relationship in PUA terms from the start as part of her ongoing effort to understand the seduction process. Clarisse also discusses a book for ladies called The Rules, *which is sort of like* The Game *for women, and she describes some subtle ways of establishing social power, such as the tactic that PUAs call "compliance tests." Plus: a Theory of Emotional Escalation, also known as "the game of falling in love." The chapter title is from the song "Pretty When You Cry," by Vast.*

* * *

CHAPTER 5: **He's A Ghost, He's A God, He's A Man, He's A Guru** ... 88

In which Clarisse meets the uber-famous PUA guru Neil Strauss, author of The Game. *He turns out to be unexpectedly feminist-friendly, and as a result of his interview with Clarisse, he is attacked on the Internet by anti-feminist PUAs who can't decide whether he's an "ignorant fool or an opportunist liar." Plus: plenty of straight-up feminist theory, including the intersection of the feminist concepts "rape culture" and "enthusiastic consent" with both S&M and pickup artistry. The chapter title is from the song "Red Right Hand," by Nick Cave.*

* * *

CHAPTER 6: **Down the Rabbit Hole** ... 113

In which Clarisse dives wholeheartedly into the seduction community, and tells us about some of the different guys she found there. She also tells us about how her male friends and partners react to her PUA research. The chapter title is, of course, from Lewis Carroll's novel Alice in Wonderland. *The "rabbit hole" is probably the second most common metaphor used by PUAs to describe getting into the community, right after "taking the red pill" from the movie* The Matrix.

* * *

CHAPTER 7: **Tough Guy** ... 144

In which Clarisse sees Adam again, and her Field Report of emotional escalation continues. There's some confusion about what that means, though, because it's a long-distance polyamorous relationship and neither of them have extensive experience with that. There is also confusion because Clarisse and Adam engage in unexpectedly intense S&M, and the emotional fallout startles them both. Plus: a Theory of the Friend Zone and the Fuckbuddy Zone. The chapter title is after a song with the same name, by The Crystal Method.

* * *

CHAPTER 8: **Ladies And Their Sensitivities** ... 172

In which Clarisse re-establishes contact with the first PUA she ever met, and he gives her seduction advice. Clarisse also discusses the perspectives of various other women associated with the seduction community, including Playettes. Finally, there's the question of whether pickup artistry is aimed at all women, and whether it works better with some women than others. The chapter title is after a song with the same name from the Steven Sondheim musical, Sweeney Todd: The Demon Barber of Fleet Street.

* * *

CHAPTER 9: **A Disease of the Mind... It Can Control You** ... 185

In which the famous PUA Gunwitch attempts to seduce a girl at a party, and is rejected, and shoots her in the face. (Allegedly.) Gunwitch's teachings aren't even the most Darth Vader-esque that Clarisse has seen, though... and so Clarisse offers a whirlwind tour of an almost comically villainous PUA blog. The chapter title is from the song "Disturbia," by Rihanna.

* * *

CHAPTER 10: **I Want To Love But It Comes Out Wrong** ... 205

In which Clarisse becomes so anxious about PUAs that she mistakes a random guy at a party for an undercover PUA, has nightmares, and drunk-calls a guy she dated to accuse him of trying to use her for sex. Also, there's a total breakdown in strategic ambiguity with Adam, and the emotional escalation Field Report concludes. The chapter title is from the song "Blood and Roses," by The Smithereens.

* * *

CHAPTER 11: **The End Is The Beginning Is The End** ... 221

In which Clarisse is unexpectedly designated a "coach" by some PUA organizers. She gives a talk and offers "coaching services" at a PUA Dating Skills Convention in Chicago, and reports every detail from the depths of the rabbit hole. The chapter title is after a song with the same name, by the Smashing Pumpkins; Clarisse prefers the Stuck In The Middle With Fluke Vox Mix.

* * *

CHAPTER 12: **At Last I Am Free** ... 238

In which Clarisse presents her Grand Theory of The Ethical Game. The chapter title is after a song with the same name, by Pretty Lights.

* * *

About The Author ... 255

APPENDIX A: **Detrimental Attitudes You Can Pick Up Through The Seduction Community**, by Chris ... 257

APPENDIX B: **Towards My Personal Sex-Positive Feminist 101**, by Clarisse ... 267

APPENDIX C: **Mark Manson's PUA Taxonomy**, by Mark ... 277

APPENDIX D: **Interview with Neil Strauss**, by Clarisse ... 280

APPENDIX E: **Brian's Kiss-Close Routine**, by Brian ... 287

APPENDIX F: **The Much-Delayed Playette FAQ**, by Hitori ... 289

APPENDIX G: **Footnotes** ... 295

APPENDIX H: **Glossary** ... 304

* * *

* * *

CHAPTER 1:
Come Jump In, Bimbo Friend

In this chapter, we meet the mysterious Clarisse Thorn, and we learn about her history as a nerd child with weird pets who eventually became a feminist sex activist. She loves S&M in a perfectly rational way, but her fixation on pickup artists was somewhat irrational. Plus: A History of Feminism, plus A History of Pickup Artistry, plus A Grand Taxonomy Of Pickup Artists. The chapter title is a lyric from the song "Barbie Girl," by Aqua.

Always remember that there's a Glossary at the end!

This is version 3.0 of this book. If you're interested in details, check the Notes and Acknowledgments before the Table of Contents.

* * *

There's a huge subculture devoted to teaching men how to seduce women. Within the last half-decade or so, these underground "pickup artists" have burst into the popular consciousness, aided first and foremost by Neil Strauss's bestselling 2005 book *The Game*. Pickup artists are called "PUAs" for short, and the community is also known as the "seduction community." They exchange ideas in thousands of online fora, using extensive in-group jargon.

The pickup artist site PUALingo.com lists "over 715 terms, and counting." There are PUA meetups, clubs, and subculture celebrities all over the world. There are different ideological approaches and theoretical schools of seduction. Well-known PUA "gurus" can make millions of dollars per year: they may sell books; they may sell hours of "coaching"; they may organize training "bootcamps" or conventions with pricy tickets; they may run companies full of instructors trained in their methods. And although outsiders often believe that community members don't understand how weird it is, the community generates its own well-thought-out internal critiques. (I've included one of these internal critiques as Appendix A in this book, but there are lots of others from lots of perspectives.)

I guess you could say that I first got into pickup artistry when I was a 12-year-old scrawny nerd girl. Back then, I was known mostly for my weird pets, opaque sense of humor, and obsessive book-reading. I spent most of my time playing computer games. One day, I was sitting at the school lunch table with my 12-year-old girl friends, and a 12-year-old boy stopped by. I giggled at him from behind my round owl-glasses; we talked for a moment, and then he went somewhere else.

Swiftly, one of my girlfriends accused me of "flirting."

"I was *not*," I protested. "What do you mean? What exactly was I doing?"

"Come *on*," she said. "You were *flirting*."

It was impossible to get to the bottom of what she meant by "flirting," and the conversation freaked me out so much that I eventually decided to poll everyone I knew about the exact definition of "flirt." Responses were inconsistent. One person said, very definitely: "Giggling." Others cited examples such as "intense looks" or "making jokes." I compiled all the definitions, and was entertained to discover zero patterns or commonalities among them.

It seemed clear to me that no one actually knew what the word "flirt" meant; or at least, no one could explain it in terms of consistent behaviors. From what I could tell, flirting could only be explained in terms of invisible interpersonal dynamics.

I sent my list of "flirt" definitions out to a bunch of people I knew, but my fellow 12-year-olds didn't seem to find it as hilariously self-contradictory as I did. I sometimes wonder what would have happened if modern online PUA fora had existed back then, and I'd found them. This is a major facet of the PUA subculture: often, the discussions and the seminars and the meetups are one big group of people who break down seductive behaviors as precisely as they possibly can. And that's part of what sucked me in when I found them. Who else could ever understand my 12-year-old confusion when my friend insisted that I was "flirting," but no one would talk about what was actually going on?

Here's something else I started doing around age 12: I devised one-liners that I thought of as a kind of street game. I'd try my one-liners on random people, and see what happened. My best anecdote from this time occurred when I was 15. I was in a crowded subway station, and I turned to an older man waiting on the platform next to me and said: "Marmoset."

He was bemused. "What?"

"Marmoset," I repeated. (I can't believe I'm telling this story.)

"What's that mean?"

"It's a small South American mammal," I explained.

"Oh," he said.

There was a pause.

"You got really nice breasts," he said. "I was watching you come down the stairs."

"Er," I said, became flooded with anxiety, and moved away. That may have been the last time I played the random one-liner game.

In case you've been wondering why women typically do not start conversations with random men, you have your answer. Indeed, only an overprivileged white upper-middle-class girl like me who had never been assaulted or abused — who, in short, had felt safe my entire life — could possibly devise a game like that. And after Marmoset Guy pushed my boundaries, I stopped playing. I started keeping my head down as I walked around.

Age 15 may also have been when guys began shouting gross comments at me in the street, but I'm not sure. It was a few years before I started going to parties and clubs where some guys would approach and *refuse to leave me alone,* no matter how obvious I thought I made it that I wasn't interested. These experiences, among many others, contributed to the development of what a PUA would call my "bitch shield": my instinctive tendency to be cold and unfriendly during unexpected interactions with unfamiliar guys.

Many women have bitch shields to some degree — when we don't, we get a lot more "I've been watching you and your nice breasts" comments. PUAs devote a lot of mental energy to figuring out how to quickly convince women they're safe, friendly and/or entertaining enough to get around the bitch shield.

And PUAs have words for what I was doing with my one-liner experiments, too. A PUA would call my one-liners "openers," and would call my practice of talking to random people "sarging." Beginner PUAs often go out for the sole purpose of trying to approach women. They know that in order to reduce their anxiety about being rejected and learn not to get rejected, first they have to get rejected a lot. Some PUAs specifically tell themselves that they're *hoping to be rejected* a certain number of times, in order to inure themselves to the pain: they say things like, "The first thousand rejections don't count."

This makes complete sense to me. Rejection hurts. Sometimes, rejection hurts a lot. It would be nice if I could get to a point where rejection simply rolled off me like water off a duck's back, and I no longer felt any "approach anxiety" when approaching unfamiliar people.

Here's yet another tale from my teens, when I was a scrawny nerd girl with weird pets: I asked a boy to the dance, and he said that I could "shove one of those pets up [my] ass." I cried a lot, and resolved that I would never ask a man out again. This resolution lasted until my twenties, and it's not because I'm a shrinking violet. It's because I couldn't deal with the idea of getting that kind of reaction again.

Plus, these days, as a writer, my work is regularly rejected by editors and commentators. I need emotional strategies to deal with it, such as "The more rejection letters I get, the better!" So I totally sympathize with beginner PUAs who give themselves a crash course in coping with rejection by seeking it out.

Socially awkward PUAs also understand that if they want to learn to talk to people, they've got to practice talking to people "in the field." When I was a nerdling trying to learn the same thing, I saw "the field" as the whole wide world. PUAs often favor nightclubs and bars, because a huge proportion of women who go to nightclubs and bars are trying to meet people; but some PUAs sarge in bookstores, coffeeshops, the laundromat, wherever.

I guess that from one perspective, it's spooky to think about myself as a practice "target." (And make no mistake, a lot of PUAs refer to the women they want to bang as "targets.") But on the other hand, the marmoset story shows that I've done my share of sarging. Plus, imagining PUAs practicing gets less spooky after you watch them do it. I have stood in bars and watched beginner PUAs screw their courage to the sticking point, then try to start conversations with girls. I have watched the guys get ignored or shut down. It did not make me hate or fear them.

I have also watched master PUAs walk up to girls, start friendly conversations, and get phone numbers. That didn't make me hate or fear them, either.

Some PUAs don't just use openers; they have entire memorized "routines." They can get through a whole conversation without saying anything that's not pre-planned. (I'll tell you about having routines run on me later.) I read about routines long before I saw them in action, and when I was first learning about them, I felt very uncomfortable with how much "nerdy-but-nice" PUAs seemed to fake it. Much of the advice in the subculture seemed to be about memorizing canned lines: putting up a false front.

By the time I read about PUAs, I was in my mid-twenties, and I had a local reputation as a feminist sex educator. I'm still a nerd — I'll always be a nerd — but I get dates these days, too. I felt like I'd stuck to "being who I really am" and eventually started getting romantic attention. Why couldn't PUAs do the same? Why were they learning all the fake stuff? I knew plenty of nerdy guys who took the same route I did: unwanted in puberty, but romantically successful once they escaped high school.

I suspected that half the problem was that "nerdy-but-nice" PUA dudes felt entitled to some gorgeous blonde supermodel, and were ignoring nerd girls (like me!) because they wanted to prove their manliness by boning the hottest girl in the club. And although some PUAs are reasonable about respecting women's choices, there are plenty of typical asshole complaints in the PUA community about how women have "all the power." Also, "all women are always out to control men." The irony of these complaints in a community that's *training men how to manipulate women* is kind of amazing, and rarely acknowledged.

But... still... while I'm instinctively grossed out by fakery and entitlement, it became clear to me that some guys really are so shy and awkward that they can't get dates at all... not even with other nerds. There are definitely different "types" of PUAs. When I eventually got around to doing interviews, one PUA instructor estimated that 60-80% of guys in the community are mostly awkward... but 20-40% are gross misogynists with anger issues. He also noted, "I'd say at least 50% of guys in the community are just in it for accomplishment. As long as they get the dick in, they feel like they've got a notch on the bedpost." After which, of course, they move on to the next notch.

The worst PUAs are usually assholes who seek to hold 100% of the power in their interactions with women, perhaps because they're emotional wrecks. But the decent ones tend to be nerds who are trying to understand human social behavior. And in their journey to become less shy and anxious, it's hard to hate these guys for faking it till they make it. "Just be yourself" is terrible advice if you are naturally *unbelievably awkward.*

I became a lot less down on PUAs after I started acknowledging my own obsessive analyses of dating and interaction — and when I acknowledged times in the past when I've been super awkward, when I've faked it till I made it, or when I've taken an experimental approach to meeting people. Examples include my early-teens list of flirtatious behavior, and my one-liner opener game. Obviously, I'm really different from most PUAs, like for instance how I'm a lady. But I eventually realized that I had lots in common with some PUAs, too.

* * *

I discovered the seduction community in 2009, when I was 24. I was hanging out with my then-boyfriend and he asked: "Did you hear about the pickup artist?"

We hadn't been dating long. I'd met my boyfriend in the local Chicago S&M community. (Yes, there is a semi-underground community of sadomasochists. Because there are a lot of us.)

"Pickup artist?" I said.

"He came to one of the S&M meetups," my boyfriend said. "Everyone's been talking about it. I wasn't there, but apparently this guy is so smooth that the minute he entered the cafe, all the other guys put one arm around their girlfriends. Apparently this guy is a professional pickup artist. Apparently there's a whole underground community devoted to learning how to manipulate women. And this guy is a *master*. Men pay him hundreds of dollars to teach them how to seduce women."

As you can see, lots of people were gossiping about the pickup artist, but I didn't meet him myself until he attended a feminist sex education event I hosted. Afterwards, he introduced himself to me — James Amoureux — and I exclaimed, *"You're* the pickup artist!"

"That's me," James said, and smiled. "This is a great event. I wanted to compliment you on it."

I looked at him with interest. James was handsome, and he had long hair — I *love* long hair. He seemed charming enough. Still, my rush of attraction was over the top. *He makes a career of seducing women,* I thought. *Maybe he can get any girl he wants...* and I had to take a deep breath to steady myself.

"I feel a little weird about the pickup artist community, honestly," I told him.

"That's understandable," James said. "Talk about heteronormative!" My pulse jumped. I focused on him like a laser beam. "Heteronormative" is a term is used by gender theorists to describe the cultural expectations of "normal" heterosexual gender relations. I'm a sucker for a guy who can use that word intelligently in a sentence.

I probably made it too easy for James to get my cell phone number, but I couldn't help it! He was speaking my language. After he took my digits, he told me he'd be sure to attend more of my events.

One of my flatmates at the time happened to be an ex-boyfriend. (Listen to me, please listen to me: *Never live with your ex if you can possibly avoid it.*) My ex was making food in the kitchen that night when I got home. I sat thoughtfully at the dining room table, and described James to one of my female friends. "If I sleep with a pickup artist," I mused, "then do I win or do I lose?"

"You *lose!*" my ex shouted from the kitchen. He sounded agitated.

* * *

James the pickup artist attended one of my workshops several weeks later, and invited me out for coffee. He was in his late 30s, with a Masters in psychology and a recent divorce under his belt. Smart and unassuming, he fielded my confused questions with good grace.

"What you have to understand," he told me, "is that most guys who enter the pickup artist community are so shy and awkward, they've never had a girlfriend before. Many of them have no idea how to start a conversation with a woman. They've never had an opportunity to pick up basic social skills, and the community gives them that. At heart, what they really want is a long-term committed relationship, just like most people."

"Um," I said. "Is learning how to manipulate women *really* the best route to a long-term relationship?"

"Well, manipulation means different things to different people. Again, most of these guys are just trying to learn how to get along with people." James sighed. "Still," he admitted, "the community doesn't teach good relationship skills. In fact, these days, a lot of my money comes from community guys who ask me for help deprogramming their pickup artist attitudes. They seduce a girl they really like and they want to keep her around, but then they realize they don't know how to relate to her."

Misunderstood nerds looking for love, or merciless Casanovas looking to exploit women? Lacking further input, I suspended judgment. James himself seemed friendly, though controlled. He suggested that we might work on a project together sometime, like a sex advice column, and I had to tell him I planned to leave the U.S. to work abroad in a few months.

I probed after his experience with S&M, and was disappointed to discover that James's main interest was bondage (tying people up). Personally, I have very different S&M interests; I usually get bored by elaborate rope contraptions. The relationship I'd negotiated with the latest boyfriend was only half monogamous. We were both allowed to do S&M with people outside the relationship, but not have "vanilla" sex with them. So if James didn't share my S&M interests, that made him off-limits.

Not that James seemed interested in me, sexually or S&M-wise; I didn't pick up even the faintest flirtation from him. I worked hard not to feel offended. To soothe my ego, I told myself James might act more interested if I weren't dating someone else. And also about to leave the country.

"You'll never guess who came to my workshop," I said to my boyfriend later. I didn't normally feel like I had to tell him when I'd been hanging out with another guy... but a professional pickup artist felt different. Like I owed my boyfriend an explanation.

"Who?"

"The pickup artist!" I made my tone as jovial as possible.

"Really," my boyfriend said. His tone was so similar to the way my ex

had shouted, "You *lose!*" — I had to laugh.

"He's not trying to have sex with me," I reassured him. "He's not even an S&M match for me. Really."

"Hmm."

"He's an interesting guy," I said. "He uses words like 'heteronormative.' And he doesn't seem unethical."

"Well, that's what he would *want* you to think."

I laughed again. "Sure. I do wonder what his agenda is. He seems interested in my work; I wonder what he's trying to use me for. — At the same time, though, just by asking these questions I'm stereotyping him. And so are you."

"Hmm," my boyfriend said reluctantly. "You have a point."

* * *

Rumors spread that a fellow S&Mer had hooked up with James. I asked her about it when I ran into her.

"You have to realize," she said darkly, "that he will lie to you until he sleeps with you. And then he won't return your calls."

"How did you like him in bed?" I wanted to know. "Like, on a scale of 1-10."

She paused and sighed, then fluttered one hand away from her forehead in a dramatic gesture. "10."

I filed this away for consideration, and later sent James an email discussing some topics we'd covered over coffee. His response was tepid. I narrowed my eyes at the computer screen and considered my next move.

What did I want from him? I felt like I wanted *something* from this polished professor of seduction... and it was more than an interesting conversation, more than a shared sex education project, more than a notch in the bedpost (or flogging post). I wanted to know what was going on in his head. I wanted to make him react to me....

... but he clearly was not interested. I sighed and put aside my disappointment. Anyway, I was busy concluding my affairs, including a planned-and-foreseen-but-still-painful breakup with my boyfriend. A couple of months later, I moved to another country.

* * *

At age 24, I had just started writing about BDSM on the Internet. BDSM is a 6-for-4 acronym that covers Bondage, Discipline, Dominance, Submission, Sadism and Masochism; I often refer to it with the more colloquial term S&M. Others sometimes call it B&D, leather, or kink. I am what we call a "switch": I can go back and forth between the dominant role and the submissive role, though I'm more oriented towards submission.

I came into my own S&M identity when I was 20. Coming to terms with S&M was really hard for me, and the process was kick-started by a guy who picked me up at a party. He hurt me a lot; he had me beg for mercy. It was awesome, and it completely confused me. On the surface, my masochistic desires seemed completely at odds with being an independent, rational, feminist woman with self-esteem and integrity. But I instinctively recognized S&M as something I needed in my life. I knew that S&M is deeply and irrevocably intertwined with my sexuality. So I set out to reconcile myself with it.

I'm a writer; I've always coped with things by reading and writing. I spent a few years slowly pulling myself together, and writing incoherent private journal entries about my weird sexuality. Then I started looking for S&M writing on the Internet, and I discovered a fair amount of it. There were even feminists writing about feminist theory, their experiences with S&M, and the intersections of the two... and some of them were so smart it blew my mind. [1] I wanted in on the conversation, so I started my own blog.

I'd always considered myself a feminist, but I never specifically studied feminism when I was growing up. Getting into the blogosphere gave me a real crash course in the topic. It turns out that, within feminism, the topic of S&M is ridiculously controversial.

The history of feminism contains some amazing triumphs for human rights, including people working to win women's right to vote; people working to legalize abortion; people recognizing, discussing, and working against all kinds of gender-related double standards. The history of feminism also contains some really awful failures. For instance, there have been a lot of terribly racist things said and done by white feminists. And many feminists have said and done terrible things to harm and ostracize sexual minorities such as sex workers, transgendered people, and... S&Mers.

There are zillions of examples of feminist difficulty with S&M, including:

* An editrix during the early days of iconic feminist magazine "Ms." threatened to retire if the magazine published an essay by a woman about her S&M desires. Thus, she successfully buried the topic. [2]

* In the 1980s, a group of radical feminists went to a lesbian S&M club and non-consensually used crowbars to destroy much of the club and attack attendees. [3]

* And in 2009, a radical feminist blogger published an article stating that S&M sadists should either repress their sexuality or kill themselves. [4]

The "Feminist Sex Wars" started in the 1970s — seriously, people call them that and they have their own Wikipedia entry. The Wars have mostly been about whether porn can ever be okay with feminists, but they also include battles about whether S&M can ever be okay with feminists. Many feminists claim that, at best, a woman who's into S&M has deep-seated self-esteem issues and is being abused. And some feminists claim that a woman who's into S&M is selling out to The Enemy; these are of course the same feminists who are likely to describe men as The Enemy. As the famous German feminist Alice Schwarzer once said: "Female masochism is collaboration!" [5]

From this infighting developed a strand of the movement that we call "sex-positive feminism," a strand that includes me. Feminism is a diverse movement, and I don't feel totally comfortable in the "sex-positive" box, but it's the subgroup where I tend to fit in best. I included an attempted Sex-Positive Feminist 101 as Appendix B in this book.

Over the years, there has also been feminist controversy over men's place in feminism. Obviously, feminism isn't really about men, except for how it's a movement that resists men's societal dominance. But is there more to feminism than resistance? What does it mean to be a man who's supportive of women and wants to work towards gender equality? Are men who support women's rights always feminists, and if not, why not

Different feminists can give very different answers to these questions, and sex-positive feminists have often been sympathetic to discussions of masculinity. Sex-positive feminists are not always into S&M, but we often are... and sometimes I wonder if we're more open to talking about men's issues because we have a nuanced understanding of power. If I've learned anything from S&M, I've learned that power is rarely a one-way street.

But I don't mean to imply that *only* sex-positive feminists care about men. In 1963, Betty Friedan wrote in her classic book *The Feminine Mystique* that: "Men weren't really the enemy — they were fellow victims suffering from an outmoded masculine mystique that made them feel unnecessarily inadequate when there were no bears to kill." For the next 49 years, feminists have continued trying to explain that anti-feminists are lying when they say that every single feminist is a man-hater. Other feminists have specifically tried to take on the stereotype of the "man-hating feminist," such as bell hooks in her 2000 book *Feminism Is For Everybody*. Does anyone listen to us? Of course not. [6]

Or maybe they do listen. In 2005, Betty Friedan's bit about masculinity and bears was quoted in a *New York Times* bestseller written by an actual man. The man was Neil Strauss. The book was *The Game: Penetrating the Secret Society of Pickup Artists.* I'll tell you more about my interview with Neil Strauss, and what he said to me about feminism, later in this book.

While the actual term "feminist" may be too much for a lot of people, and while feminists may argue about whether men (or S&Mers) get to call themselves "feminists," it's obvious that feminist theory is spreading in many directions. On the down side, it's being co-opted by non-feminists and even anti-feminists. On the up side, it's benefiting a huge number of different people. While researching PUAs, I was endlessly fascinated by the places where their ideologies overlapped with feminist ideologies.

bell hooks defines feminism as "a movement to end sexism, sexist exploitation, and oppression." If that's feminism, then men can totally be feminists. And so can I, despite being a wicked kinky pervert. I'm not sure whether Neil Strauss would claim feminism. He kind of evaded the question when I asked him.

* * *

Women's sexuality has been greatly contested territory in the Feminist Sex Wars; men's sexuality has been less discussed. Again, a lot of feminism is based in resistance to men's social dominance — not to mention men's non-consensual, violent dominance. Rape Trauma Syndrome (a type of Post-Traumatic Stress Disorder that affects rape survivors) was first identified by feminists in the 1970s; it may sound incredible, but before that, an enormous number of people didn't even recognize rape as traumatic.

I once spoke to a 65-year-old woman who was violently raped by a man who invaded her home in 1970. She told me that she finally sought help from a therapist in 1974 because of the sleepless nights, flashbacks, panic attacks, and other ill effects. When she told the therapist her rape story, he looked at her over his glasses and said: "Do you really think that's important?"

Seriously, that actually happened. So with that kind of historical context, it makes sense that most feminists wouldn't be particularly interested in discussing male sexuality — especially given that many feminists have survived just that kind of attack from violent men. It has been crucial to prioritize and explore the female experiences that were dismissed as "unimportant" for so long.

But through the years have come intimations that, perhaps, discussing male sexuality is not mutually exclusive with doing anti-rape work.

(Especially given that some survivors of rape and abuse are, in fact, men.) Or that discussing men's experience is not mutually exclusive with feminism. Or that perhaps gender-related issues are all intertwined, and that ignoring some avenues of inquiry will just limit our truth. Thoughtful discussions of male sexuality are becoming more and more common, especially among feminists.

The biggest recurring theme of these thoughtful discussions is how limited our social standards around male sexuality are. For men, sex is "supposed" to be about maximum consumption and accomplishment and insatiability and violence: *how big is your dick, how hot a girl can you score, how many chicks can you bang....* That's a shallow, incomplete picture of most men's desires.

This shallow, incomplete picture is central to pickup artist culture, and it is exploited by pickup artist marketing. Although different PUAs can have different tastes in women, the majority of them express preferences that hew close to typical standards of beauty. Some PUA assholes — and indeed, lots of non-PUA assholes — will tell you that this is because all men want the same thing in women. They'll tell you that men have zero interest in women with personality or brains; that it's only about youth and slenderness and whiteness; that all men who claim that they're attracted to, say, older women are lying because "they can't score anything better."

While this may be true for some men, it's certainly not true for all men. (Ironically, it also expresses a fairly misanthropic view of men in general. This is the dirty little secret of woman-hating — *it usually goes hand-in-hand with man-hating.)*

Don't just take my word for it, though. Take the word of John Devore, who spent years working for a men's magazine — and chasing models mostly because he thought it was what was expected of him:

Beauty is in the eye of the beholder, and so are boners. ... Does Megan Fox cause my eyes to pop out of their sockets, cartoon-style? Sure. But it's an almost Pavlovian response. Conditioned. There is a profound disconnect between what we're told to think is sexy, and what it is that we actually think is sexy, between glamour groupthink and the sanctity of the individual kink. Our blush-worthy little perversions are too often hijacked by flesh merchants and the noise of the hive. Not all dudes want to go home with vampy, bikini-clad beauty queens. In fact, most men will probably agree with me that what satisfies their touch and tongue cannot be communicated in two dimensions. That while the pack howls for sexpots built to factory specifications, we're all still lone wolves hunting our lust's lonely prey. The difference between a boy and a man is simple: a man knows what he wants and doesn't apologize for it. The right "type" is whoever he says it is. He owns it and rolls hard.

... There was a time when maybe I cared too much what the studio audience thought, pursued and dated women as if I was packing someone else's penis. Those women deserved a man who was more secure and didn't need to advertise to the world, "Look Who I Can Bang!" ... I remember going out with a knockout, so smoking my friends would high-five me whenever her back was turned. She was, and remains, a remarkable woman of depth and awesomeness. And for some reason, she was really attracted to me. Anyway, we were making out, and there just wasn't that desire on my part. But she was into it, and her abandon surprised her. It turns out she normally went for the athletic type, with gelled hair, abs, and a superhero jaw. Basically, the anti-moi. But recently, she was really into my type. Which I found out was, more or less, dumpy, plump, sarcastic dork. No wonder I hadn't been paraded around to her more shallow friends for approval — I was of no value to them. But I was to her, and clearly she was arriving at conclusions I would shortly thereafter share.

It took a woman who loved bravely to teach me a liberating lesson. Life is too few breaths, and it's wise not to waste them on romantic fool's errands. [7]

As near as I can tell, women featured in PUA materials are *always* young, thin, white (occasionally Asian), cisgendered, able-bodied... you know the drill. ("Cisgendered" is a term that means "not transgendered." [8] For example, I am a cis woman or a cisgendered woman.)

In PUA vocabulary, an HB is a "hot bitch" (for PUAs who make no bones about hating women) or a "hot babe" (for those who try not to). HB is often accompanied by a 1-10 numerical rating: e.g., an HB5 is average, an HB8 is very hot, while an HB10 is maximally hot. "Hot bitch" is negative, but it's incredibly mild compared to the words many PUAs use for women who are considered unattractive ("warpig," for example).

PUALingo.com, a popular index of PUA definitions, offers this under the entry for "fatty":

PUAs that have laid fatties (many of us have in the practice of game) will feel a sudden feeling of disgust during sex as he stares down his perfect abs and sees the flab of the fatty. On a positive note, fatties are extremely grateful and generally give very good blowjobs.

In other words, fat women are good only for a quick fuck, and fat women's feelings are irrelevant except inasmuch as those feelings make them better in bed. That website, by the way, is fairly sanitized. Plenty of PUA writers say much worse things. So, in case you've ever wondered what feminists are complaining about when we discuss "objectification"? Exhibit A.

Also. For the record? Most PUAs do not have "perfect abs." (You rate women's bodies, I'll rate yours backatcha, assholes.)

This focus on stereotypical hotness creates a vicious circle. While many men are attracted to pickup artistry because they're shy nerds with nowhere else to turn, many other men are attracted to it because they want to bang as many stereotypically "hot" chicks as possible. And since the community norms revolve around doing that, dudes who want something different tend to be quiet about their preferences. They're less likely to get heavily involved in the community... or at least, they're less likely to be involved for a long period of time. And they rarely challenge PUAs who claim that "all men want the same thing."

So the community norms stay in place, and continue to scare off men who don't fit in.

Interestingly, some PUAs oppose the number system, and they do it because they want to avoid setting a standard for what's hot. They know that social expectations for men's desires are very narrow and that many individual men feel limited by them. Those PUAs are more likely to use a descriptor system: actual examples include "HBGreatAss" or "HBYoga." Other PUAs will say things like, "She was an HB8 *for me,*" in an effort to show that preferences are individual.

But there are plenty of PUAs who deny that these concerns are legitimate, and who viciously mock other men who dare express attractions outside what they call "normal." As an S&Mer, I was particularly struck by one nasty online PUA who found a photograph that looked like a submissive man, and wrote: "If it's a fetish, then this is proof that some fetishes are the domain of losers." [9]

Maybe saying stuff like, "She was an HB8 *for me"* is a step in the right direction... but while this may be good for helping PUAs differentiate their own desires from each other's, it's still pretty dehumanizing for their targets.

Also, I have rarely seen conversations by PUAs where they talked sympathetically about women who don't meet their standards. Even if they acknowledge that different men's attractions can be different... and even if they aren't complete assholes... many PUAs will still describe less-hot women as nothing more than pawns (or "obstacles") in the game to pick up the hotties.

And lots of PUAs take unwholesome glee in mocking fatties and warpigs. The irony is incredible, given that this comes from a community of men who are struggling to be more attractive. I am hardly the only person to notice this. As one male commenter observed while analyzing PUAs on a blog I read:

While I like the "helping conventionally unattractive men find their sexual confidence" bit, I don't much like the absence of any apparent sympathy toward conventionally unattractive women. You'd think suffering through it yourself would give you perspective.... It strikes me as very hypocritical. [10]

I don't have much interest in shaming other individuals for their sexual desires, especially given that my own are so unconventional. But I have a big problem with how so many people — not just PUAs — define "all men's desires" in an incredibly narrow way. I have a big problem with people who treat their sexual partners as less than human. And I have a big problem with how narrow standards of beauty hurt women... not just in the dating world but everywhere, from college to the workplace. (For example, a 2010 study found that blonde women make 7% more money than women with other hair colors. [11] A 2011 study found that thin women make more, too. Women who are "very thin" earn nearly $22,000 more than their "average weight counterparts." [12])

I've become more interested in conventional fashion as I got older. When I was younger, I felt deeply uncomfortable merely with wearing makeup (unless it was stagey goth makeup). I wanted to be beautiful. I was *desperate* to be beautiful. But I wanted it on my own terms. Growing older, and becoming more willing to do "mainstream beauty things," sometimes feels like I'm losing an epic battle for my self.

I've dated guys who didn't seem concerned about my appearance one way or the other. I've also dated guys who made it clear that they respected me more because, while they thought I was hot, they also thought I was not "superficial." And simultaneously, one of the boyfriends I've loved most told me that I'm "very focused on my appearance"... while making it clear that he judged me for it.

I loathe the tightrope-walk of knowing that my appearance matters, and hating it. Wanting to be pretty, feeling joy when I feel pretty, but hating it. Being smart, and knowing that half the time, my intelligence doesn't matter nearly as much as my appearance. And it especially hurts when I talk to men who seem perfectly capable of *both* being attracted to me, *and* hating me because they're attracted.

I loathe the terror that comes with gaining weight or aging. I can't quite repress that terror, no matter how much I tell myself that I've got intelligence and skill and plenty of other sterling qualities. I loathe this terror, and I don't just loathe feeling it; I loathe myself *because* I feel it. Part of me fears that *merely being scared about "losing my looks"* makes me "fake," "manipulative," and "shallow."

Hanging out with PUAs did not improve my feelings about this.

I never had the guts to ask PUA acquaintances to rate me on the number scale. Just thinking about it makes me feel queasy and anxious. I've joked once or twice about estimating myself as an HBX; but it's a weird joke. It's an attempt to dissipate the tension I feel, more than something I think is actually funny.

The closest I got to direct feedback about this was when a PUA coach said to me, "I like it when you sarge with us. You're hot. You've got this Anne Hathaway thing going on." I changed the subject fast.

When most men tell me they respect my perspective or intelligence, I can frequently convince myself that my appearance is not the central factor. With PUAs, I never had this luxury. Even when I had fun flirting with them, even when I liked them, I couldn't help also hating PUAs a little bit. There was only so much I could hear terms like fatty, and warpig, and HB1-10, before I became depressed and angry. Let alone the other horrible things many of them say about women.

Now, I don't mind if a guy tells me honestly that I look good. It's kinda nice. Especially in bed. What's horrible is *being reduced to my appearance.* What's horrible is *being informed that nothing matters but my appearance.*

Even the PUAs who I felt sure respected my opinion: I tried to believe that they would still listen if I weren't... for example... thin. Let alone white, cisgendered, able-bodied, etc. I could never quite convince myself.

Maybe there were some PUAs who talked about fatties and warpigs and hot bitches more because that was the subculture's social standard, and less because they thought that was a reasonable way to discuss actual people. But I couldn't help it; I disliked them for it nonetheless.

There were a few guys in the PUA subculture who I liked — who I even *trusted* — who never used the worst PUA language and never tripped my misogyny-meter. Those guys were rare, though. I was more liable to trust blog friends with an interest in PUA theory. I've met some of my blog commenters in person, but I always hang out with them online first, where only text mediates the relationship. The fact that I'm a sex writer may have an effect, of course. But when a guy leaves hundreds of thoughtful comments on my blog, and we both know that we'll probably never meet, then I can feel pretty sure that our relationship is more about the theory than it is about my body.

Of course, I can't deny that I myself pay more attention to hot men. I certainly laugh more at their jokes. Women may generally care less about physical hotness than men, but in all honesty, I'm not generally attracted to fat dudes. I've got some serious physical turn-ons, like the long hair thing. Everyone, of all genders, judges everyone else at least a little bit based on physical sexual attraction. And within the dating arena, it has to be reasonable to judge a *potential physical partner* based on physical attraction!

The important question, I suppose, is less what we personally find attractive, and more how we talk about and deal with it. You're not attracted to fat people? Fine. But that's no reason to treat them badly! And it's no reason to claim that no one in the world is attracted to fat people. Or to be an asshole about their bodies. And for God's sake, it's no reason to not hire fat people when they're more qualified for a job than thin people.

There's one last thing I have to admit. It's kinda creepy. You've probably already figured it out:

I can't deny that I *wanted* PUAs' approval. Of course I did. I was an ugly duckling who grew up wanting to be a swan. Even when I fetishized them, it was never *just* about PUAs being hot; it was also about *wanting to feel hot myself.* I wanted to feel the judgment of men who spend all their time judging women's fuckability. Accordingly, while I was researching PUAs, my self-consciousness about my appearance reached a record high. Some of them obviously thought I was pretty, but it was equally obvious that I could never *possibly* be pretty *enough.*

These guys were desperate for a certain kind of validation from women, and I was depressingly like them. There's something horribly twisted about the fact that part of my interactions with PUAs was my own desire for validation. Horribly twisted... and I felt gross as soon as I realized it. Horribly twisted... and maybe it's an inevitable result of a culture that constantly tells us a woman's worth is best measured by her appearance. Horribly twisted, but there it is.

* * *

When I first heard of pickup artistry, I imagined them all as flawless Casanovas. After all, they do call themselves "pickup artists" and the "seduction" community. In reality, however, there are different "types" of PUAs. The decent ones tend to be nerds who are trying to understand human behavior. The really bad ones are usually assholes who seek to be 100% in power; they are unbelievably controlling in all their interactions with women — sometimes because they're emotional wrecks, but that's no excuse. Other types fall in between, and I'll give you a full Taxonomy Of PUAs in a moment here.

The seduction community got its start with techniques that are very controlling, such as hypnosis and Neuro-Linguistic Programming (NLP). NLP practitioners claim to be able to control human targets via precise gestures and word choices.

Lots of current PUA ideas originated in NLP, such as "frame theory." A "frame" is a paradigm, or a way of thinking about the world. For example: the difference between how Fox News talks about an event, versus how National Public Radio talks about an event, is a matter of different frames. The way you present yourself to your family, versus how you present yourself when talking to your boss, is often a matter of different frames.

Many PUA conceptions of social interactions center around frames. In some ways this is cool, because it's obviously important to recognize that everyone's perspective is different... and we all have to communicate from our own frames into different frames, all the time.

This also offers insight into flirting, because a lot of flirting is about "reframing" or "stealing the frame." If I say, "Are you a pickup artist?" and the guy says, "Whoa girl, you think I'm trying to pick you up? You move too fast for me," he's stealing the frame. And also being hilarious.

Yet frame theory can get very aggressive, very fast, when it starts talking about "frame control." The idea of "frame control" is that each individual has their own frame; no one wants to change their own frame. Everyone wants *their* frame to dominate interactions.

So, the theory goes, a socially strong person will control the frames of people around them. Their ideas will influence everyone else, and they set the terms of all interactions. Your social strength depends on your ability to keep your own frame intact... and dominate other peoples' frames.

There is a lot of truth to this, but I have mixed feelings about the way it's, well, framed. Of course I try to convince others to see things my way; most people do. But I can't help wondering: how adversarial do we want our interactions to be? Does this always have to be about staying in control of the interaction? Wouldn't it be better to think about this in terms of "merging frames," or "understanding frames," instead of "frame control"?

As you can see, Neuro-Linguistic Programming can be a little freaky to talk about for those of us who are sensitive to power dynamics. Here's another example: one of the big NLP tenets is that the meaning of our speech is never actually in what we say; it's in *how others react to our words*. Now, obviously the way people react to our words should always be a major factor in how we speak (or write). "Know your audience," as the maxim goes. But there's a lot more going on with language than the reaction we can get by using words.

I've read NLP resources that emphasize connection, that talk about how you can make other people feel great using NLP... even when they're discussing gestures that automatically elicit certain reactions, or word choices that are likely to get a certain response. A few NLP resources even give tips on how to express *your own* honest thoughts, feelings and desires (what an idea!). Still. Treating communication only, or even primarily, as *a tool for getting a specific reaction* is a rather aggressive frame.

Some PUAs claim that NLP and hypnosis don't work, so they aren't worth learning. Other PUAs claim that these disciplines *do* work, but they're more complicated and harder to master than basic social skills. And given that so many guys in the community start out as very socially incompetent... well, let's just say they've got a ways to go before they get into NLP.

I've certainly seen some NLP tactics work; as a very basic example, try talking to someone in a normal tone while nodding. Your target will almost always start nodding along with you. Interesting trick, right? NLP as a whole has never gotten much popular or scientific validation, though. It should be noted that NLP is promoted in all kinds of contexts, not just pickup artistry; for instance, there are NLP courses for salesmen.

Pickup artistry has developed into more of a general "social skills discussion group" within the last ten years or so. Hypnosis and NLP have become less popular in current PUA discussions, although they still come up a lot, and their influence on the PUA-verse cannot be denied. As one PUA guru said to me, "Of course there are problems with pickup artistry. What do you expect from a community that has its roots in NLP?"

It might seem obvious, but social mores around sex, romance, and dating have changed enormously in recent decades. Although there are still plenty of norms out there, most social expectations and etiquette have become less rigid. For example: "serial monogamy" is still the norm across the Western world, but divorce is common and accepted, and open relationships are becoming more and more accepted. Also, women (and gender minorities) have gained newfound power over our destinies.

Many people are scrambling to deal with the implications of these changes. They're trying to find new guidelines for an age where *everything* is questioned, from abortion rights, to gender identity, to the meaning of marriage. Arguably, PUAs are one natural result of this situation.

When there's no standard etiquette or well-understood social channels for how to meet women, then it seems obvious that a bunch of dudes would start getting together trying to figure out how to do that. And in fact, some anti-feminists criticize PUAs because they believe that PUAs *are too concerned with women's feelings;* they believe that PUAs are actually *catering to women in a problematic way.* For example, here's a blog post quotation from an anti-feminist writer:

The seduction community never or rarely addresses those things that women are doing wrong. It's like a child who throws a tantrum and instead of disciplining him or her you take the position that you have to find out what it is they want and give it to them. There's this intense fear that if you call out women on their misbehaviour you are a chump or weak or unable to take it like a man. So rather than do that many guys prefer to just take the "spoil the child" approach to getting laid. Game is basically a coping strategy for women's rotten behaviour. If a woman has attitude and is unresponsive god forbid you tell her to open up. It's your job to figure out what buttons to push. [13]

I have a large number of serious problems with that post. Examples include comparing women to children, claiming that women need "disciplining" in order to be reasonable, and refusing to think about why women might be engaging in what this person describes as "rotten behavior." (I bet that this guy's list of women's so-called "rotten behavior" starts with "refusing to have sex with me," especially given that he's mad about women being "unresponsive.") But it's interesting, because it outlines an argument that PUAs care *too much* about women, or that PUAs are misguidedly rewarding women who are snippy and cruel.

Of all the people I met in the PUA subculture, I especially loved talking to guys who — much like myself — saw pickup artistry as another tool for understanding gender and sexuality. Often, the most thoughtful guys preferred not to label themselves "pickup artists" at all, because they saw the community as just one influence on their lives, rather than an identity they wanted to adopt.

Towards the beginning, I encountered a blogger who went by the handle Hugh Ristik, who was a textbook example. Hugh Ristik started as a shy, awkward nerd who got into pickup artistry because he couldn't get a single date. He was also ridiculously smart and analytical, and had a genuine interest in morality. He'd taken more gender studies classes in college than I ever did. His blogger name was a pun on the semi-obscure psychological term "heuristic," which indicates an experience-based method of making quick decisions. It took me an embarrassingly long time to recognize the pun, but once I did, I was hooked.

Hugh Ristik was especially interesting because he didn't want to buy into America's ideas about masculinity — yet he was afraid he might have to be heteronormative *in order to get a girlfriend.* He didn't want to be a manly man. He wanted to *bust gender stereotypes and still be hot.* He asked questions like, "What is the minimum level of masculinity I have to perform in order to attract women?"

Here's a typical example of Hugh Ristik's writing:
I think there are many questions we need to ask about the seduction community:

* What is it? What are its practices and assumptions?
* What drives men towards it? What are the experiences of these men? How do they see the world? What are their goals?
* To what degree do the practices advocated by the community work with women? And what does "work" mean?
* Is the seduction community damaging or sexist towards women? Does it have positive impacts on women?
* Is the seduction community damaging or sexist towards men? Does it have positive impacts on men?
* What is the relationship between the community and gender political movements [like feminism]? What are the areas of conflict, or overlap?
* Are the practices of the community ethical?
I put the last question last for a reason: although it's the question people like to jump to immediately, I think all the previous questions must be answered or at least considered before this one can be approached intelligently. [14]

I admired Hugh Ristik's analytical approach, and often sought his opinion while writing this book.

At one point, I tried to develop a Grand Taxonomy Of Pickup Artists on my own. It came out looking like this; please note that people can belong to more than one category:

TYPE 1: THE ANALYSTS. *Questioning Gender.* Like Hugh Ristik, a few guys who look at PUA materials are deconstructing them. They see the whole PUA community as a bunch of data to help them understand sex and gender.

TYPE 2: THE FREAKS AND GEEKS. *"Average Frustrated Chumps."* "Average Frustrated Chump" (AFC for short) is a PUA term used to describe dudes who rarely get laid and haven't bought into PUA theory. PUAs also talk about "below-Average Frustrated Chumps" (bAFCs) — guys so shy and awkward that they've never had a single date. The Freaks and Geeks are AFCs and bAFCs who are learning social skills that men in their peer group learned earlier than they did. Some of these guys also find good friends and social support among the other men in the community.

TYPE 3: THE HEDONISTS. *Seeking Pleasure.* Some folks got into pickup, or stayed in the community, because they thought it was just plain fun. Those folks weren't always guys; I've heard that groupie girls exist, though I never met any (unless I count myself). Like any type of pleasure-seeker, PUA Hedonists can be as harmless as a casual wine-drinker. But they become harmful when they value their pleasure over other people's boundaries.

TYPE 4: THE LEADERS. *Community Organizers.* Along with AFC and bAFC, there's the term rAFC: "reformed Average Frustrated Chump." Every once in a while, a guy who is "saved" by pickup artistry will turn into a kind of PUA evangelist. Other Leaders were never AFCs in the first place, but they find other value in becoming community organizers. They may simply enjoy having high status among PUAs. Or they may have moral feelings; for instance, one such gentleman told me that his goal was to "make men better men through pickup."

TYPE 5: THE SHARKS. *Out To Make A Buck.* Most organizers in the seduction community aren't paid for the work they do. But as the seduction community has gotten bigger, it's also become quite commercialized, with lots of guys (and a few women) selling their services as dating coaches or event marketers. Some of these folks seemed nice enough when I met them; others struck me as rather predatory.

TYPE 6: THE DARTH VADERS. *Seeking Power and Revenge.* The worst PUAs make it obvious that they mostly feel resentment, contempt, and distrust for women (although of course they still want to bang us). Not just that — they often belittle other men a whole lot, too.

One of the weird things about this typology is that these people are all usually coming together and debating tactics on the same message boards and in the same community groups. And they all use the same vocabulary, which can get... strange.

For example, one widely-discussed PUA idea is the "neg" tactic. "Neg" is short for "negative hit," and one site defines a neg as "a remark, sometimes humorous, used to point out a woman's flaws." [15] Like many terms, the deeper meanings and usage vary from PUA to PUA, but it's an especially dramatic range of meanings with "neg."

Some PUAs see negs as friendly teasing: a way to show that he's paying attention to the target, without appearing needy or overeager. Here's cute example from my life. I was sitting in a cafe with a former PUA, and he gazed deep into my eyes.

"Wait a minute," he said slowly. "Are your glasses held together by epoxy? It looks like you had to repair them at the corners."

"Yeah," I admitted.

He grinned. "Everything about you just screams 'starving artist,' doesn't it."

This made me laugh for a long time. I think it worked because he understood that I have chosen (for now) to be a broke writer, but he also recognized the tension I feel about that choice. So this gentleman was demonstrating that he correctly discerned my priorities, that he doesn't mind a choice that makes me feel self-conscious, and that he's confident enough to tease me.

Also, at a moment when I thought he might compliment my eyes, the former PUA shook up my expectations by breaking the romantic pattern. Often, effective flirting involves offering the right mixture of confidence plus novelty plus paying attention.

I'd put that guy in the "Type 3: Hedonist" category; he was in it for fun. (He was also nerdy, so I think he might have been in the "Type 2: Freaks and Geeks" category too. But I didn't know him when he was younger, so I couldn't say for sure.)

Some PUAs see negs more strategically, as a way of passing the target's "tests" or breaching her indifference (a way to get past her bitch shield). They argue that this is necessary for targets who are very high-status, very beautiful, etc. Most PUAs only advocate using negs on girls who are at least HB7 or higher. Neil Strauss, author of *The Game,* once wrote that:

When you give a woman who's often hit on a generic compliment, she will usually either ignore the remark or assume you're saying it because you want to sleep with her.

When you tease her and show her that you're unaffected by her beauty and demonstrate that you're out of her league — and THEN let her work to win you over and ultimately REWARD her with your approval, she will leave that night feeling good about herself. Like something special happened and she connected with somebody who appreciates her for who she REALLY is.

In short, a neg will buy you the credibility you need to sincerely compliment her later.

That said, I don't necessarily advocate negs; they are in many ways a temporary patch to stick onto your personality while you learn to possess real confidence and strength of character. [16]

Manipulative? Sure. But how harmful is it? Aren't we all trying to pretend we don't care about what other people think? Aren't we all trying to be taken seriously by people we like? Additionally, for many people, flirting involves a certain amount of strategic ambiguity and plausible deniability, and negs are a useful tactic for that kind of game.

I'd put Neil Strauss first and foremost in the "Type 1: Analyst" category, although he fits plenty of others, too.

So in some cases, negs aren't a bad thing, right? But this is all cute and mild compared to how some PUAs talk about negs: some cite the neg *specifically as a tactic to make the target feel bad.*

One well-known PUA who goes by the name Tyler Durden wrote that: "You use self-esteem negs to lower the target's self-esteem, and crave your attention to re-validate herself." [17] Similarly, an especially pitiless PUA blogger writes:

The best negs are those which are conceivably meant as compliments, but which linger in her psyche for hours afterward, undermining her self-conception and encouraging her to qualify herself to you [i.e. encouraging her to explain why she's worth your time].... [A neg] infiltrates a girl's subconscious so that she spends more mental energy analyzing her worth than she does analyzing yours. [18]

One commenter adds to the above blogger's words that: "So long as you have a woman auditioning for you, power remains where it belongs — squarely in your pocket."

In other words, if you make the target feel anxious and unworthy, she'll be easier to control. Congratulations, guys: you have learned the same lesson as thousands of people in abusive relationships.

I see that blogger as leading the charge in the "Type 6: Darth Vader" category.

While my Taxonomy Of PUAs is Grand, it arguably is not definitive or authoritative. For example, I emailed my taxonomy to one PUA coach who I like and admire, Mark Manson. I discovered Mark's work towards the end of my PUA research, when I came upon him through the blogosphere. He's super-analytical too, and he makes a real effort to keep his mind open, up to and including asking me for feminist book recommendations. He ultimately decided that he doesn't want to call himself a feminist, but he said that he learned a lot, and I was glad that he made the effort to engage.

When we first encountered each other, Mark left a comment on my blog about PUA market research:

Market surveys done by myself, other coaches and large forums find a few things consistently:

— Something like 60% of the guys who read this stuff only read it to address one very specific problem (i.e., how to ask the cute girl in class for her number, etc.)

— Like 80% of the guys, once they experience some success (they get laid a couple times, they get a girlfriend), they're never heard from again.

[Much of] the marketing is laid out [with claims that it will teach you to get ANY woman] because that casts the widest net. Whether you want to get a date with a girl you know, or whether you want to fuck 1000 girls, if I tell you I can help you get "ANY GIRL" then both of you will buy.

The point I'm making I guess, is don't mistake the marketing message of a minority of the companies, with the intentions and motivations of 80% of the actual guys out doing this stuff. [19]

When he received my taxonomy, he wrote back:

Well, I have to say, it's interesting as hell to read these. I spend so much time "in the trenches" so to speak, that it's rare I get to see the industry as perceived by others who think about it critically.

With that said, a lot of these groups exist, but I see them as either being quite tiny, or there's so much overlap, that it's hard to tease them out individually. I honestly don't even know where to start with a taxonomy. In my eyes, the industry is way too varied and complex. But if I had to start....

Mark then provided his own taxonomy; it's a bit long, but you can read it in Appendix C if you like. (Incidentally, he does sell his own PUA curriculum, which is called *Models: A Comprehensive Guide to Attracting Women*. I haven't read it. Sorry Mark.) Personally, however, I still think in terms of my own taxonomy. It's not as complicated as real life, but it's the method I find most helpful to explain the seduction community to people who don't have much experience with it.

* * *

My time in the seduction community was extremely weird, and I want to tell you everything. But so many things happened while I was running about among pickup artists, and I had so many thoughts, that I could never possibly cover everything in one book. Also: I tangentially discuss feminism, S&M, and open relationships in this book, but I could talk about those topics for days and I'd still have more to say. If you want more once you're done here, you should totally check out my site at clarissethorn.com; many of my thoughts get posted there eventually. You can also follow me on Twitter @ClarisseThorn.

* * *

CHAPTER 2:
You're A Good Soldier, Choosing Your Battles

In which Clarisse ventures into the field, observing PUAs in their natural habitat. One PUA takes a special interest in her, and the resultant power struggle is tons of fun. Plus: a Theory of Adversarial Flirtation, plus a Theory of Strategic Ambiguity. The chapter title is from the song "Waka Waka (Time for Africa)," a collaboration by Shakira and Freshlyground.

* * *

Remember how I met the pickup artist James Amoureux right when I was leaving the country? Well, I didn't forget PUAs while I was gone. During my year abroad, I spent a lot of time reading about PUAs on the Internet. I was kinda grossed out, but my fascination remained.

When I got back, I decided to investigate pickup artistry in person. After all, I didn't want to be a "keyboard jockey": the PUA term for someone who reads theory online and then acts like he knows what he's talking about, but never puts anything into practice. I wanted *more*.

My months of field research took place in my home city of Chicago and my soul city of San Francisco. And when I talk about how I did "field research," I mean that I experienced "some crossover of having fun and going out of my gourd." The blogger Hugh Ristik put me in touch with some contacts; I found others through James Amoureux, others via online scouting, and others when mentioning pickup in my everyday life.

Through sheer chance, my first meeting with a group of PUAs was scheduled for a goth night. I was delighted; I'm good at goth nights. It was *on*. Excitement thrummed across my nerves as I tied myself into a corset and black boots. There was something intoxicating about the thought of a game, a contest, on the battleground of a nightclub. About competing over who toyed with who. I felt like I had license to kill.

I didn't yet recognize that I was doing exactly what feminists complain PUAs do to women: viewing these guys primarily as objects.

* * *

Contrast is a powerful thing. There's the old adage, "Opposites attract." When I'm doing S&M and my partner hurts me — say he scratches my skin hard enough to leave marks — then it's unbelievably intense if he touches me lightly, right afterwards, on top of the scratches.

Unpredictability is powerful, too; why else would people enjoy roller coaster rides? In an S&M context, I find it really hot when I'm not sure whether a partner will kiss me or hurt me.

And novelty is perennially sought by most humans. Philosophers have often discussed this, but Real Scientists have lately decided that they wanted to Really Demonstrate how novelty affects romance. A 2008 *New York Times* article outlined some relevant experiments by Dr. Arthur Aron, including:

In one set of experiments, some couples are assigned a mundane task that involves simply walking back and forth across a room. Other couples, however, take part in a more challenging exercise — their wrists and ankles are bound together as they crawl back and forth pushing a ball.

Before and after the exercise, the couples were asked things like, "How bored are you with your current relationship?" The couples who took part in the more challenging and novel activity showed bigger increases in love and satisfaction scores, while couples performing the mundane task showed no meaningful changes. [1]

Contrast, challenge, unpredictability, novelty: these things clearly hook into deep-rooted human urges. It seems that maintaining a level of uncertainty can be hot. PUAs talk a lot about the importance of "plausible deniability," or the pretense that nothing is going on. A lot of PUAs (and people in general) prefer to go through the whole flirtation process without ever acknowledging aloud that sex is on the horizon... although of course, during a successful seduction, the endpoint eventually becomes obvious.

But most humans want to feel safe, too. Too much contrast, too much unpredictability, too much challenge, or too much novelty: these things are usually dealbreakers. It's interesting to meet a person who offers a new perspective, but if you meet someone who speaks a totally different language, then you can't communicate with them at all. I may be into S&M, but even I don't want to be hurt too much.

There's a PUA distinction between two strands of the game: "direct game" and "indirect game." Indirect game is basically plausible deniability on steroids. It's like a romantic comedy: no one explicitly acknowledges what's up, or makes any overt statements about their attraction, until the couple lip-locks and tumbles into bed. On the other hand, direct game means giving explicit signals from the start, such as an obvious Statement of Intent: "By the way, I think you're sexy." Some PUA gurus specialize in direct game, some in indirect game, and some bridge the "gap."

Arguably, though, the distinction between direct vs. indirect game is often more a continuum than a binary; arguably, there is no gap. I'd venture to say that successful seducers always mix the two. But some people tend towards one more than the other. Personally, I wish I could say that direct game is my favorite thing ever, because I believe that honesty is important. And make no mistake: I put a huge amount of effort into communicating straightforwardly with people I date. But there's something very compelling for me about the indirect game, too.

During my analysis of pickup artistry, and also my entire romantic life, I came up with a phrase for something that seems to attract me (and lots of other people): *strategic ambiguity.* It's a version of contrast, challenge, unpredictability, novelty that often comes up in dating.

One way of creating strategic ambiguity is through mildly adversarial flirting. Pickup artistry contains the best theories I have ever seen on how to engage in this type of mutual game. Negs, which I discussed in the previous chapter, are one example of mildly adversarial flirting. Another example is a concept called "shit tests."

I have huge problems with how PUAs conceptualize "shit tests." Most PUAs describe this phenomenon by claiming that "all women" are give men a hard time *just to see if the men will react in a dominant way.* Supposedly women are *constantly* issuing "shit tests," and if a man fails to react in a properly dominant manner, he basically loses the game. Yes, *constantly:* I've seen PUAs describe example shit tests ranging from

* "You're not too smart," to
* "Are you a player?" to
* "What are you taking at school?" or "What do you do for a living?" to
* "Sorry I missed your call, I was in the shower," to
* "What are you thinking?" to
* "I don't want to have sex with you."

PUAs usually encourage each other to ignore shit tests, to verbally smack the girl down, or to reframe what she said in a hilarious, unexpected and/or cocky way. For example, if she says, "You're too young," then he might say, "Don't worry so much, I'm totally legal." If she says, "I don't want to have sex with you," then he might ignore her and continue with his seduction process.

There are obvious issues here, and I'll talk more about those soon. However, there's also definitely something to the shit test theory. Continuous reframes are used by comedians of all genders, because reframes are frequently hilarious. But even for non-comedians, responding to a target like she's shit testing can create fun faux-adversarial flirting. Banter is fun. Back-and-forth is fun. Push-pull is fun. Lots of people like being snarky, lots of people like being kept on our toes, as long as the situation's not too serious.

If I say, "You're not too smart," then I'm probably flirting; if he responds with something like, "I'm smart enough to ignore your BS," I'll laugh. If I ask a guy I just met, "Are you a player?" then I'm probably flirting; if he responds with something like, "Yes, and I think you might do for my harem," I'll laugh. (An especially great reframing tactic for shit tests is to "agree and amplify." The "harem" example fits this profile: agree with the target, then intensify what she said to the point of ridiculousness.)

I know plenty of women (and people of other genders) who don't flirt like that at all. And even I don't always flirt like this. I try to keep an eye out for guys who seem into it. And I wouldn't describe myself as "testing dominance" when I do it. In fact, when I sat down and thought about my dating history, I realized that I used to do a whole lot more adversarial flirting when I was younger, before I got into S&M. Now that I do S&M a lot, I specifically seek men who seem able to play serious power games with me... *and yet I do less adversarial flirting.* (In fact, before I got into the seduction community, I wrote a blog post in which I theorized that some of my aggressive social tendencies had always been about S&M. [2])

It's almost like I *replaced* adversarial flirtation with S&M. Or, perhaps: now that I know how to get the S&M I want, I prioritize men who mostly communicate in a *safe* way over men who mostly communicate in an *exciting* way... because I know that good S&M (much like good sex) requires careful, safe communication. And because I know that good S&M can generate plenty of excitement on its own. (Of course, nothing is a binary. My ideal man would do some adversarial flirting, but he'd be good at straightforward mediation, too.)

This leads me to suspect that adversarial flirtation and S&M deal with some of the same deep-rooted human urges. Perhaps the two phenomena can sometimes create the same energy. Strategic ambiguity: sometimes, it can be intoxicating to feel unsure exactly what a man thinks of me. Sometimes, it can be intoxicating to feel unsure whether he's about to hurt me or kiss me.

I'm sure people have individual preferences here, as people tend to do. I'm probably more into S&M-strategic ambiguity than most people; my S&M preferences go really deep. I'm pretty sure that I could never entirely replace S&M with anything else, even if it was really strategically ambiguous and fun. Still, I think there are enough commonalities that these differently ambiguous urges can be viewed as overlapping or related, and one type of excitement can go a long way towards filling the urge for another.

There's an important aspect of non-verbal communication here, too. Part of my Theory of Strategic Ambiguity is that when some people engage in verbal ambiguity, they are sometimes testing each other's non-verbal communication skills. *This is not always true.* But, for example, let's suppose a guy recognizes that when I say, "Are you a player?" I'm initiating a conversational game, and answers with something like, "Yes, and I think you might do for my harem." Then he's showing that he knows how to read my non-verbal conversational signals.

The problem is, some PUAs label any pushback or questions as shit tests. It's not cool when a PUA won't answer or respect anything I say. And a girl who asks, "Are you a player?" might not be flirting. She might be insecure. She might feel confused about why such a fun guy is bothering to talk with her. She might feel like she's "not hot enough" for him, and imagine that he *must* be playing her.

An even better so-called "shit test" is: "What are you thinking?" Most people see this question as an attempt to connect with another human. But one Darth Vader-type PUA suggests:

Answer with "thoughts are sacred" and change the subject so it doesn't seem like you're trying to be profound. I stole that from a Fellini film. Have used it on a few different types of girls and it works like a charm. [3]

(On that article, a girl commenter asks, "What if... *HE* asks you what you're thinking?" A male commenter responds, "If he asks you what you're thinking, he's gay. So... your boyfriend is gay.")

And it's important to note that if a person ignores or overrides *every boundary a partner sets or every disagreement they express...* then that's a map to an abusive relationship. A person who never lets you talk honestly about your disagreements is not an emotionally safe or respectful person. People who research abuse have found that a very common abusive tactic is to both *minimize* and *deny* the victim's reactions and feelings... or to *blame the victim.* [4] Abusers will often tell their targets that "it wasn't that bad," that "it never happened"... or that "it was your own fault."

In other words: abusers will reframe and ignore and smack down "shit tests," in their own way.

So if your partner treats *everything you say* like a shit test, I advise you to run far away as fast as you can. Period.

The blogger Hugh Ristik once wrote that "every critique of the PUA community was made by a PUA first." PUA coach Mark Manson has a blog post called "Shit Test Paranoia":

80% of the time, what guys perceive as shit tests aren't actually shit tests at all. ... I think it's another PUA concept that ends up hurting more than it helps. ... As with most PUA concepts, the idea of the shit test creates a defensive mindset in the guy, the idea that this is some obstacle that must be overcome and defeated rather than accepted and connected with. [5]

In another of Mark's posts, called "5 Ways to Deal With Women's Tests," item #5 is "Never be afraid to admit to a mistake. If you legitimately fucked up, say it. Never be afraid to say, 'I'm sorry' if it's warranted." [6] In other words, Mark thinks a woman who honestly tries to express frustration about bad behavior deserves an apology, rather than to be ignored. It's nice to see this acknowledgment... although it's kind of depressing that my standards are so low. It's depressing that I get excited when a PUA merely acknowledges that women sometimes deserve apologies.

Having established all this, however, I have to acknowledge another problem. If a person is very new to adversarial flirtation, then teaching that person the difference between a "shit test" that's part of adversarial flirtation, as opposed to a "shit test" that's a real question or boundary, is actually kinda difficult. This is part of the reason every single PUA I've met emphasized field experience.

The best PUAs go out and observe nightclub life for hours and hours every week, and then they analyze their experiences with their PUA friends for more hours. They have vocabulary words for various types of non-verbal communication; for example, there's an entire PUA field of inquiry called "kino escalation," which is about how to hit on a person with body language. But although they discuss these things extensively with words, observation really is the best way to learn these non-verbal communication skills.

So my advice to the hopeful seeker is this: go forth, and practice thy adversarial flirtation... gently. Remember that plenty of people aren't shit testing, and be ready to apologize. And this is especially important with "shit tests" such as "I don't want to have sex with you."

Now here's the thing: notwithstanding the fact that I am a psycho feminist, I'm willing to buy that a *minority* of people say no to sex and mean yes. In fact, one study put the percentage of USA people who frequently do this around 15%. [7] What that means, however, is that *85% of people generally mean no when they say no.* Perhaps there's a higher percentage of that behavior in some settings, such as nightclubs, and that's why PUAs are convinced it's so common. But the problems of instructing men to consistently ignore women saying "no" are obvious, *even if a minority of people usually say no and mean yes.*

* * *

My dress was bright red. My corset was black. I was wearing fishnet stockings, elbow-length opera gloves, and an obscene amount of eyeliner, and I was standing in a goth club amongst many PUAs.

They were a mixed group. One was a square-jawed, typically masculine dude who was forced to borrow goth clothes to fit in at the club. Another was a gorgeous, cross-dressing, elaborately-made-up male submissive wearing a skimpy miniskirt and platform heels. I felt rabidly curious about their different perspectives — but just like when I met James Amoureux, the attraction was more than that. My blood seethed as I was introduced around.

I realized quickly that I was dialing up both my excitement, and my snideness. I realized just as quickly that they loved it. These guys *wanted* women to be dramatic; and if that was what they wanted, no wonder they loved concepts like "shit tests."

When one PUA said after a short conversation, "I'm going to go dance," I tossed my head and said, "Good, I won't miss you." "You're mean," he said, and laughed, and stayed to talk some more. So who tested who?

So many PUAs claim that they only learn the game because women require it. But I suspect that *most PUAs want women who play the game*. I wonder how much PUAs even notice women who don't play the game. And I wonder how many women learn to shit test *because it makes guys more attracted to us.*

Eventually, I told that dude to go dance. Then I headed for the bar, where a PUA instructor named David joined me. He, too, lacked proper attire for a goth club, but rather than borrow black clothes he sported a lavender rhinestone-studded suit. (PUAs refer to ostentatious clothing as "peacocking," a tactic primarily promoted by the Mystery Method and The Game. Snakeskin suits and platform boots are par for the course while peacocking.)

David wasn't my type, but he was somewhat experienced as a PUA, and the fact that he'd run workshops on seduction made me really want to talk to him. When he tried to usher me away from the bar so we could sit upstairs, I said: "One of my friends owes me a drink, but he hasn't come over yet." This was, in fact, true. "I'd ask you to buy me one," I added, "but I know PUAs aren't supposed to do that."

"It's not that..." David started. "That is, we aren't... oh, never mind, it's complicated. What kind of drink do you want?"

One thing I like about PUA rules is that most of them are flexible. The point of the "no buying drinks" rule isn't that you never buy drinks. The point is that you make sure the girl actually likes you before you buy her a drink; you make sure the girl *isn't just using you for drinks*. It's part of a broader strategy whereby PUAs try to avoid neediness, or "supplication" — i.e., being desperate for attention. Offering too many compliments and buying drinks just so a girl will talk to you are examples of supplication.

I ended up in a corner upstairs with four PUAs, sipping rum-and-coke and people-watching while I asked endless questions about workshops and techniques and experiences. One of my non-PUA acquaintances spotted me, took me aside, and asked what the hell I was up to.

"Interviewing pickup artists!" I said happily.

He cracked up. "None of that stuff works. You know it's total bullshit, right?"

"Is it?" I asked.

"And they're trying to manipulate you. But maybe that's what you want. Do you want to be manipulated?"

I smiled. "What do you think?"

"It depends on who's doing the manipulating," he said, and I nodded. "You're too easy," he said scornfully, and grinned.

If pickup artistry doesn't work, why'd you just neg me? I considered asking, but I laughed instead and lightly touched his arm. "I should get back to them," I said.

The square-jawed, fish-out-of-water PUA was sitting a little apart from the others. I sat next to him. "Not your kind of place?"

"Not really," he admitted.

"Could you still get phone numbers here?" I asked mischievously.

"Totally," he bristled.

"Could you get the phone number of any girl in the club?"

"Yes."

"How about that girl?" I indicated a girl who was making out with some guy in the corner.

"No fair," he protested.

"You did say *anyone.*" I tried pretending to be disappointed, but I couldn't help laughing. This night was turning out *awesome*. "Okay. How about that one?" The blonde in question was standing and talking to a couple of people about a piece of art.

"Definitely," he said.

"Well, now you have to do it," I said, and he got up. I moved to sit with David. "Your friend says he can get the number of any girl in this club," I said.

"Bad idea," David said. "I wouldn't claim that."

"Oh?"

"No. Not every girl in the club is going to like you. Some girls will have something on their mind, or they'll be loyal to some other guy, or you won't be their type. It's important to keep an eye out for girls who react well to you, and game *them*. Otherwise it's a waste of time."

Another PUA leaned over us to pick up his jacket. "Already?" I cried, and grabbed his hands. "Are you leaving me already? Don't go! I haven't even talked to you!"

He laughed. "What do you want to know?"

I tried to think of a good question quickly. "Why are you into pickup artistry?"

"Pickup lets me express who I am," he said seriously. *Damn,* I thought. *I'll be pondering that answer for a while.* I released his hands. David and I watched him go.

"He's a really nice guy," David said softly. "One of my former students. I think I failed with him, though. You want to create a balance of niceness and asshole when you're creating a new PUA. I didn't make him enough of an asshole."

"I like him," I said. "Based on what he just said, I wish I'd been talking to him more."

David didn't say anything. After a moment, I got up to dance, and he joined me.

* * *

The square-jawed PUA failed to get the blonde's number. He confessed this to me with a hangdog expression; I gave him mine. He never called.

Most of the PUAs departed around 1 AM, except for David, still hilariously out of place in his sparkly suit. We hit the dance floor again until David asked, "Want to go get something to eat?"

"Sure," I said, and left the club with him. On our way out we ran into one of my non-PUA friends, who gave David a sharp look. "You get her home safe," said my friend.

"Of course," David said amiably.

We jumped into David's car, and within ten minutes we were driving through an area that was *definitely not* the 24-hour-diner district. "Where are we going to eat?" I asked, and then my circumstances caught up to me. "Are you taking me to your apartment?" I demanded.

"Yep," he said, and laughed.

I couldn't help it... I laughed too. "I've *read* that you guys do stuff like this," I said, "but I can't believe you decided to take me to your apartment *without even asking.* You know that I read PUA materials, right? Look, I'm not going to have sex with you, okay?"

David waved one hand airily. "There are so many different definitions of 'sex,'" he said.

He thinks I'm shit testing him, I realized. *He's trying to reframe what I'm saying.* "Seriously," I insisted, "I'm not going to have sex with you."

He changed the subject. I couldn't tell if he still thought I was shit testing. I took a quick mental inventory: I felt alert and not-drugged. One of my friends had seen me leave with David. David seemed pushy, but I didn't feel threatened. My internal safety warning bells weren't going off, even though he *was* a pickup artist. Still... "I don't know if I should trust you," I said aloud.

"You were referred to me by a good friend," he pointed out. "I wouldn't mess with you."

Social proof, I thought. PUAs often prioritize building or exploiting "social proof." "Social proof" is originally a broad sociological term; PUAs use it narrowly to mean, "Having other people demonstrate that I'm safe, fun and/or hot." For example, when I first started hearing about James, my boyfriend unintentionally gave James social proof by telling me how smooth James was. James also received social proof when my fellow S&Mer rated him a "10" in bed. If I was hanging out with James at an event and lots of people greeted him or came to chat with him, then he would have a lot of social proof.

For this reason, PUAs often work to get the good opinion of the target's friends before engaging the target. Sometimes this means a master PUA will deliberately, callously flirt with ugly warpigs in order to land a gorgeous HB8, which is pretty insensitive. But sometimes it means he'll be the life of the party and charm everybody he meets, which is pretty awesome.

David is reminding me that he's trusted by someone I already know... and, well, that does happen to be true, I concluded. *Let's go home with him and see how he acts.* I felt like an old-time anthropologist venturing into the jungle.

David's apartment was a masterpiece of PUA layout. "We can't sit in the living room," he said as soon as we got there, "because my roommate's asleep and if we talk, we'll wake him up." Of course, the only other available room was his bedroom. Where there was nowhere to sit except the king-size bed.

"I thought we were going to eat something," I said.

"Oh, yeah," said David, and rummaged around until he found a half-eaten chocolate bar.

Seriously? I thought. It was so sleazy, but I was more entertained than appalled. David sprawled on one side of the bed. I perched on the other edge, as far away from him as possible, and kept my spine ramrod-straight.

"Tell me PUA stories?" I said, and he did.

In general, most PUAs describe a framework of seduction with a number of stages. Different PUAs promote slightly different frameworks, but common stages include:

PHASE 1) Attraction — Make the girl attracted to you, or at least respect you.

PHASE 2) Qualification — Make her feel like she's earning your attention, and make her think you like her for more than her looks.

PHASE 3) Comfort — Make her feel like she can trust you.

A PUA's main goal is to get the target's attention, generate some basic attraction, and then move into the Qualification phase. Once he has her attention, she will start trying to prove that she's "qualified"; she'll try to prove that she's worth his attention. Non-PUAs might see this stage as the point when the flirting becomes mutual.

Within this framework, one might say that David entirely missed the Attraction stage with me. He didn't make me Qualify myself, either: if anything, I made him Qualify himself to me. On the other hand, he apparently succeeded at Comfort, or at least he succeeded enough to get me to sit on his bed listening to PUA stories.

David told me many a tale that night. My personal favorite anecdote involved his roommate. Apparently, at one point the roommate brought home a girl and had sex with her. Afterwards, the roommate decided to leave the apartment for a cigarette, so he and the girl came out into the living room and chatted with David. Five minutes into the conversation, the roommate addressed David in German (which they knew she didn't speak): "Dude, I think she's into you."

"Do you mind?" David asked in the same language.

"Not at all," said the roommate, and departed to smoke his cigarette, leaving David to seduce the girl.

"It didn't take much effort," David told me cheerfully. "She was totally into it."

I complimented him on some candles. "Oh, do you like them?" he asked. "I have a giant box of them. You can have some! This one girl followed me home one night, and she had this big box of candles. She accidentally left them behind in the morning."

"Why didn't you call her to give them back?"

"I didn't have her number." In a more serious tone, he added, "I never take a girl's number unless I plan to call her."

I got the impression that this was an ethical boundary for him. In one way, it made sense: taking a girl's number without the intent to call could be seen as leading her on. On the other hand, sleeping with someone and then never speaking to them again seemed harsh. I wondered if this girl had left the candles behind in an attempt to get him to track her down. (Yes, I took some candles home with me. My mom *loved* them.)

Then there was the tale of the girl who attended a PUA lecture and slept with three PUAs the same night. I had to admit, David was fun to talk to. Within an hour, I was tired of sitting up on the edge of the mattress, so I took the chance of lying down... still keeping three feet of real estate between us. Regardless, he was on me in a moment.

"Stop that," I said, and he pulled back. "Look," I said, "I really am not going to have sex with you. I just want to talk. Also," I added, "I should go home soon. It's late."

"You're totally sleeping over," David said firmly. "I'll drive you home in the morning."

"No, I'm going home tonight," I said.

Again, he changed the subject. I wondered if it was wise to let him do that, but it didn't seem like I could say any words he would take seriously.

We talked until 5 or 6 AM. He continued lying next to me. I continued to rebuff his advances. Every time I said I would go home, he said I should sleep over. Finally I said, "I'm just going to walk."

"That'll take you hours!" he protested.

"Watch me," I said. "I'm pretty sure I know how to get there from here. Plus, we can't be far from public transit."

"No, okay, I'll take you home."

The sun came up as we drove across the city. The conversation shifted to my writing and my thoughts about sex and sexuality. I talk about sex a lot in a cerebral, non-hot way; I'm used to discussing my own sexual desires that way, too. This is what we do in the S&M subculture, and sex writers do it a lot, too.

But David made it clear that for him, the conversation was extremely hot. I hadn't meant to tease him — really — but as we pulled up to the corner near my apartment, I looked at David thoughtfully. His voice had gone husky. He gazed at me meaningfully.

I didn't feel attracted to him. I had no intention of having sex with him. If he hadn't been a PUA, I would have continued to keep him at arm's length. But there was something so incredibly hot about pickup artistry in general...

... I leaned over and kissed him, and he groaned.

I realized that the thrill I felt was a power trip. I'm the first to admit that I fetishize power; and I knew, in that moment, that my feelings about interacting with PUAs really *were* similar to S&M feelings. Except that the difference was this: if I were playing S&M mind games, I'd discuss it explicitly. I would try to respect everyone's emotions. If I were looking for a real relationship, then I would try very hard to be honest and honorable.

In contrast, I stepped out of David's car without a word. In that moment, I felt zero compunctions about messing with his head in a completely non-negotiated way.

He was a PUA, right? He'd spent the whole night pushing my boundaries and trying to manipulate me. I dreaded to imagine how well his tactics could have worked on a younger, more naive, more insecure version of myself.

This was *war*.

And besides, it wasn't like PUAs had *feelings* or anything.

This may have been my first omen that learning about PUAs was making me more cynical and manipulative, and encouraging negative attitudes about men. Alas, I paid it no mind.

* * *

***

CHAPTER 3:
Underground Communication

In which Clarisse discusses what it means to be a respectful partner who creates a low-pressure sexual environment. She talks about how people communicate about sex in the S&M community, as well as the community around polyamory (i.e., people who choose to have radically honest open relationships). And she tells us all about some of the most disturbing seduction tactics: "Last Minute Resistance techniques," which PUAs developed for targets who resist having sex. The chapter title is after a song with the same name, by Bassnectar featuring Seasunz.

***

You're going to read a lot about my sex life in the pages to come, and I've got a somewhat unusual sex life. To set the stage, let me tell you about the two communities that taught me the most about sex and relationships: the S&M community, and the polyamory community.

Polyamory is a form of consensual non-monogamy in which people have multiple lovers, and are honest with each other about it. Every person has individual preferences; each relationship has its own texture; and different polyamorous relationships have their own textures, too. Some people have lots of loving sexual relationships. Some people have only one or two sexual connections that involve emotions, while others are purely sexual.

A lot of poly people (though not all) talk about "primary relationships," "secondary relationships" and so on. A "primary relationship" usually indicates a relationship with more commitment and expectations than other relationships. For example, a primary relationship might be one where the participants live together and/or are married.

I've been reading about polyamory and I've had polyamorous friends since I was a teenager. Still, I spent years dating monogamously. My longest relationship lasted about six years, but I've had other long ones too. I generally like my exes. I have great memories, and I wish them well. For a while, it was very important to me to be monogamous, and I'm glad I had those relationships.

But in my last few monogamous relationships, I thought about negotiating polyamory and was discouraged by my boyfriends' reactions. So when I returned from abroad, I decided to make polyamory a clear priority in all my relationships from day one. No more getting involved with people and then — oops! — ending up monogamous. If I'm ever monogamous again, I hope it will be after trying polyamory for a long time, and deciding it's not for me. Right now, my goal is to have some ongoing polyamorous relationships... and to eventually end up in a polyamorous marriage where I can have kids with my primary partner.

Polyamory relies on open, explicit communication. The polyamory subculture has a huge emphasis on talking things through. A lot of PUAs (and hipsters) have co-opted the term "polyamory." Indeed, in some circles polyamory is a fashionable term to drop. Alas, most people just learn the word. They don't familiarize themselves with the polyamory community, or with the radical honesty and open communication encouraged within it.

As polyamory educator Raven Kaldera puts it:

If you can't yet bring yourself to communicate honestly with your partner about everything that goes wrong... and don't wait too long after it goes wrong, and don't lay on guilt when you bring it up, then don't do polyamory. Stay monogamous. Polyamory is not the place to work out your neuroses, any more than running a marathon is the best way to exercise your recently-broken and healing ankle. [1]

Another well-known polyamory educator, Tristan Taormino, has said that the five pillars of polyamory are "communication, responsibility, honesty, negotiation, and patience." [2]

Pro tip: if you think a person might just be using "polyamory" to mean "I do whatever I want and I don't respect my partner's emotions or boundaries," then don't blame the concept of polyamory. Blame *that individual person.*

Personally, I am much more experienced with S&M than I am with polyamory. I am an S&M switch: I can go back and forth between the dominant role and the submissive role, though I'm more oriented towards submission. As I mentioned in Chapter 1, I've been writing and thinking about S&M for years, ever since I came into my own S&M identity around age 20. Coming to terms with S&M was really hard for me, and the process was kick-started by a guy who picked me up at a party.

Our first encounter was brief; it started and ended at the party. During my second encounter with that guy, we were in private, and he hurt me enough that I started crying. "Are you okay?" he asked when he saw the tears. I told him that I was fine, that I wanted to continue.

Soon after that, I started instinctively fighting back and saying "no." So my partner stopped, and he said gently, "Can we clarify something? Do you really want me to stop when you say no?"

In that moment, I realized that I didn't: I wanted him to keep going. The realization shocked me so much that I started crying so hard I couldn't even talk. He said, "We should take a break," and got me a glass of water. Afterwards, once I'd calmed down, we talked about safewords: we arranged a word that I could say when I *really* wanted him to stop.

The point of this type of discussion — and the point of safewords — is that even if one partner wants to be screaming "no," *both partners can still be involved in the negotiation process.* In S&M, it's understood that if your partner wants to say no and mean yes, *they will tell you ahead of time.*

The experienced S&Mers I know also usually discuss what we want to do, ahead of time. We tell stories about our previous encounters, and ask our new partners questions like:

* "What do you have experience with?"
* "Could you go into that more?"
* "What do you like?"
* "Is there anything new you want to try?"
* "What makes that fun for you?"
* "Is there anything you really don't want me to do?"

Only after we feel like we have a good handle on our partner's boundaries do we go for the S&M.

I have some experience with various S&M relationships, but back when I was starting out, it took a while to learn how to talk straightforwardly about my desires. Although I've always been somewhat blunt and brazen, learning to ask for S&M directly was not easy. Talking about sexual desires makes most people feel vulnerable and anxious, especially if those desires are unusual.

But I *had to* learn how to talk about it, because it was obvious that talking about it was the only way I could get what I wanted. I had to learn how to ask, and I had to learn how to be clear. It was hard, but I had to learn it. Sometimes I still have trouble communicating clearly, but I like to think that I get better and better.

Now my S&M encounters usually look something like this:

STEP 1) Initial, flirtatious conversation in which mutual S&M interest is established and a meeting time is set.

STEP 2) A more serious conversation in which we discuss what we like. Sometimes, this conversation is short and casual. The submissive's side might look like this: "You want to flog me? Great! Please don't hit my right shoulder, because it's got an old injury. My safeword is 'red.' Let's go."

Sometimes the conversation is longer and more nuanced: "I want to be flogged until I cry. If you want to call me a bitch or a slut while you do it, I'd like that, but please don't call me a whore. You can keep going after I start crying if you like, but please, don't feel pressured to keep going if you don't want to. My safeword is 'red'; if I want you to slow down or do something different, I'll say 'yellow,' and if I want you to hit me harder I'll say 'green.' My right shoulder can't take hard sensation, but if you want to touch it lightly, that's okay."

An even more nuanced conversation might stretch over multiple meetings, and include many anecdotes and questions about our previous experiences.

STEP 3) The actual encounter.

STEP 4) Afterwards, it's common practice for partners to give each other "aftercare": a cool-down period that usually involves cuddling and reassurance, and often includes a follow-up discussion of how things went. Not everyone does this, but in my experience, most people prefer it. The best aftercare feels unbelievably intimate, and can build an intense relationship very quickly. It's especially important to do aftercare if I plan to see the other person again. If we're seeing each other again, then we both need to know what went well; what wasn't good; and what might be worth trying next time.

This is the most communicative, feminist framework for sex that I have ever seen. It's feminist because it's communicative; it's feminist because of the immense emphasis on getting consent every step of the way. To me, it's rather ironic that S&M has always been so controversial in feminist circles. Even though rape fantasies might look like rape, implementing a rape fantasy is *the opposite of rape* — and I'd think feminists would want to jump on that bandwagon.

I should add some disclaimers:

* A lot of people do S&M, and not all of them use careful communication tactics.

* Despite the community's emphasis on verbal communication, there's still a lot of non-verbal communication that goes into S&M.

* Just as there are predators in the mainstream, there are predators within S&M communities across the world: people who honestly don't care about their partners' boundaries.

* And of course, there are misogynists in the S&M community, too. Some people even *put S&M itself in sexist terms,* like with claims that "all women are naturally submissive." That shit pisses me off.

Still, most people I've encountered in the S&M community prioritize talking about sexual needs in an honest and sensitive way.

Can polyamory and S&M attitudes be incorporated into pickup artistry, or vice versa? As I dove deeper and deeper into pickup artistry, I wasn't sure. PUA materials rarely talk about what actually happens during sex. Or about how to honestly conduct a relationship. Or about how to facilitate a loving and egalitarian dynamic rather than fighting to control the frame at all times. For example, the landmark curriculum *The Mystery Method* offers over two hundred pages of advice and theory about how to get a target into bed. Then, under the header "Sex" on page 205, there's no advice at all... just a picture of two people having sex.

On the other hand, S&M and polyamorous materials rarely talk about how to flirt, construct sexual tension, and build attraction. You'll notice that in my list of steps above, I put the entire "initial, flirtatious conversation" into Step 1... but that's a *big* step.

Some PUA gurus teach physical sexual technique, or sexual communication, but the vast majority of conversations and materials have nothing to do with it. The notch in the bedpost strikes again: too many PUAs don't care much about a mutual experience. (This is another factor that can vary by misogyny level, though. Some PUAs promote maxims like "Always leave her better than you found her," but many speak with incredible harshness about "using" women for a "pump and dump".)

As James Amoureux told me: "A lot of my money comes from community guys who ask me for help deprogramming their pickup artist attitudes. They seduce a girl they really like and they want to keep her around, but they realize they don't know how to relate to her." Tactics like negging and responding to so-called shit tests can be fun, but even when they're done in a non-evil way, how much can they possibly facilitate honest and intimate communication?

The Game contains a striking moment when author Neil Strauss is hanging out with a bunch of smart PUAs: Strauss realizes that while they've all got women at their beck and call, none of them have girlfriends. I heard similar tales from PUAs (and former PUAs) in person.

Hypothetically, PUA advice could fill the gaps left by S&M and polyamorous advice. But generally speaking, typical PUA writings emphasize manipulation and objectification and unspoken communication, whereas typical S&M and polyamory writings emphasize straightforwardness and mutuality and direct verbal communication.

Eventually, I developed the Theory of Strategic Ambiguity that I gave you in Chapter 2. That helped me feel like I was starting to resolve these questions. But for a long time, trying to shift back and forth between a feminist, S&M, polyamorous perspective and a PUA perspective felt like a continuous migraine. Especially when I dealt with aggressive, arguably non-consensual PUA tactics that directly oppose the ideals I seek with my feminist, polyamorous S&M.

* * *

Some PUA theory is weirdly feminist-friendly. For example, some PUAs talk about how women live with the threat of male violence. They encourage men to imagine what life would be like if they were usually attracted to people who could beat them up. Another example: PUAs often discuss "Anti-Slut Defense" (ASD). ASD theory is based on the idea that women face massive social pressure not to be so-called "sluts," and that women are often shamed for exploring their sexuality.

In other words, some PUAs encourage men to have sympathy for some common women's fears.

However... another part of ASD theory is that, supposedly, women are so ashamed about wanting sex that *all of us* have been socially programmed to resist having sex even when we want to do it. Which is just not true. I think many feminists would agree that women are socially influenced to feel ashamed about wanting sex. Feminists would *not* agree that all women who resist having sex secretly want to have sex.

My personal feminist analysis looks more like this: women are commonly perceived as "losing" (or becoming "sluts") if we have sex, whereas men are perceived as "winning" (or becoming "players") if they have sex. Therefore, women are less likely to seek out sex than men. In other words, as long as people see sex as an "accomplishment" for men but not for women, then men will have a higher "demand" for sex than women do in the sexual "marketplace." This is especially true for casual sex: since women are typically expected to "trade" sex for a relationship, most women will be even less interested in casual sex, because casual sex doesn't give women what society tells us to want from the "transaction."

In case it wasn't obvious: all the words that I put in quote marks above are concepts that I consider incredibly problematic. I'll explore more of that later, in the chapter about feminism.

So anyway, many PUAs have decided that Anti-Slut Defense is the only important factor in female sexual hesitation. And when women resist having sex after a night of flirtation, PUAs call their behavior "Last Minute Resistance" (LMR for short). Many PUAs use the theory of Anti-Slut Defense to justify an array of manipulations called "Last Minute Resistance techniques" (LMR techniques). The theory of Anti-Slut Defense implies that all women secretly want it, and are just scared of being perceived as sluts if we admit it. Which can justify almost any tactic designed to have sex with a target after she's tried to prevent it from happening.

When PUAs are processing their field experience, they often go home and write "Field Reports" (FRs)... or if they've had sex, they write "Lay Reports" (LRs). They share these reports on PUA fora. Together, they seek patterns and critique each other's tactics. (Ostensibly, anyway. A lot of the discussion is less sharing and more bragging.)

Like everything in the seduction community, Last Minute Resistance discussions are a mixed bag. They're probably my least favorite set of tactics. Occasionally, Lay Reports that describe LMR techniques sound harmless or entertaining. But sometimes, as a woman and as a feminist, reading about LMR techniques makes me want to throw up. There are some in the middle ground, too: some Lay Reports sound pushy or creepy, but probably not non-consensual.

For example, here's an excerpt from a Lay Report in which a woman has been making out with the PUA. She has just told the PUA that she doesn't want to go back to his place because she's supposed to stay at her dad's place. The PUA reports:

I continue kissing and eventually I ask again "You can't tell your dad you're sleeping over at a friend's house tonight?"
"I could"
"k do it"
"but..."
"hurry, we need to make the last tram to my place. call him now."
She takes out her phone and starts dialing. I grab her hand and lead her towards the subway station. [3]

The woman is hesitant, the guy is pushy. It's gross that he acknowledges not actually caring about anything she says: he writes that, "While she talks I keep that learned 'mesmerized' look on my face." And it's grosser that the guy writes about how, before he starts kissing her, he determines that she has low self-esteem: "She begins to show me her self conscious side. She has an extremely low self esteem, makes me feel pity," he writes.

On the other hand, it seems that he didn't lie to her or coerce her. It could be much worse. And indeed, there are some LMR Lay Reports that sound like date rape. Some PUAs will outright post about how a girl said "no" and looked upset, but they kept going; they'll *brag* about it. It's horrible to read.

One Lay Report on the biggest PUA forum describes a sexual encounter thusly:

I suggest that she comes to my place and she refuses. ... I suggest that I

45

drive her back to her place and she agrees. [They take public transit to his place, because his car is there.] We get to my home, and come up stairs to my room. She suddenly says, "No!" I ask her why and she says that she's "worried that I'll close the door." I assure her that I won't; she comes in.

Now this chick did not verbally coalesce in the least. I tried to take her pants off, "Take me home." I tried to kiss her, "Take me home." I'm rubbing her tits, "Take me home."

So, in short, she said she didn't want to go home with him; he tricked her into coming home with him anyway. She expressed discomfort while coming upstairs with him; he told her that he wouldn't close the door... but then he must have closed the door, because next thing we know he's having sex with her. At every step of the sexual interaction, she asked him to take her home; *he continued having sex with her anyway.*

This does not sound like so-called Anti-Slut Defense. This sounds like he ignored her objections and had sex with her anyway.

Afterwards, the PUA writes about how he tried to talk to her after having sex:

There is nothing to say here because she simply didn't say anything, tell me anything when asked about this. Something about her was just so soft, subtle, and... unreachable, ungraspable. I can only describe her as though she's evaporated into emptiness/emptied herself of all thought/concern/trouble.

The reaction he is describing is *extremely consistent* with a person who has been raped. A lot of people freeze up while being raped because they don't know how to react, or are afraid of violence if they resist. When a person is being raped, their body is not a pleasant place to be, and thus, many people dissociate from their bodies during a rape. A person who has been raped may, therefore, seem spacey. Or "unreachable" and "empty."

The PUA concludes that she's quiet and doesn't want to talk after sex because she's "a true Buddhist." Um. Wow.

Then he writes:

She, even to the very end did not tell me why she came over. I asked her twice: "Why did you come to my house" and she said, "Because you said you would drive me home." [4]

Apparently, the PUA can report this *and yet he doesn't think he raped her.* To me, this looks like total delusion — *at best.* And it's aided and abetted by the ways PUAs frame concepts such as "Anti-Slut Defense" and "Last Minute Resistance."

It's worth noting that another PUA on the forum responds to this Lay Report by saying:

Dude, you should really elaborate on how she was ACTIVELY DOING things that let you know she really wanted to be fucked, because from what your Field Report says right now it sounds like you were raping her.

Right now it doesn't sound like a pick-up at all. Not saying it wasn't, but you need to elaborate on the actions SHE took to let you know she was inviting/enjoying the seduction.

Read Maniac's Lay Reports [i.e., the Lay Reports of another PUA] to see how he talks about clear signals he gets, even when he's seeing resistance. [5]

The first PUA responds merely with:

It may sound that way; I will read Maniac's lay reports to figure out how to write this shit up. [6]

The blogger Hugh Ristik sent me that Lay Report. He mentioned that he hesitated before sending it to me, because he knew I might tell the world about it, and he didn't want to give the impression that most PUAs are out there raping people. But he added that:

That Lay Report was hard for me to read. Usually, when you are reading a Field Report, you really want to be on the guy's side. So it's really tough when you read one that gives you doubts about consent. You want to give the benefit of the doubt. After all, he was there, you were not, so maybe he had good reasons to believe in consent that he simply didn't mention. I've only seen a few outright rapey LRs like the one I sent you, but PUAs need to know that there are other PUAs going out and doing stuff that they might not agree with.

I wouldn't say that the "ignore her when she says no" theme comes up constantly in PUA writings... but it's too common, and some instructors reinforce it. "The first two 'no's don't mean much, and should be expected," advises one PUA. [7] Others talk a lot about the "agree and continue" tactic, whereby the target says something like "We should stop," and the PUA says, "Yes we should"... and then keeps going.

There are other Lay Reports that make me feel anxious, too, although they don't describe ignoring a girl when she says "No." Instead, they describe coldly manipulating her into sex that she clearly doesn't feel ready for. Here's some LMR advice from a popular PUA manual by Love Systems. It describes what grade school kids would call the "silent treatment," and what PUAs occasionally call the "freeze-out":

When you reach a point that she doesn't want to cross, and persistence didn't work, then stop. Say "I understand" with not even the slightest hint of disappointment or annoyance and remove the romantic/sexual frame. Candles, incense, dim lights, mood music — all gone. You're not punishing her, you're just doing something else. After all, you like her and you enjoy her company. Let her know this. Then do something else — ideally something boring. Check your email. Play "go fish" with a deck of cards. She will likely re-initiate physical/sexual contact (if she doesn't, do it yourself in a few minutes). When she does, re-establish the mood with what candles, incense, lights, music, or whatever you were using to begin with. Then proceed slowly to the resistance point, taking your time. If you hit it, or any other resistance point, say "I understand" and repeat the process — wait longer this time if it's you who re-initiates the physical/sexual contact. [8]

What gets me about this passage is how much trouble the author goes to to convince the audience — and, probably, to convince *himself* — that he's not being diabolical. "You're not punishing her, you're just doing something else"... really? When he acts intimate, romantic, and friendly *only until* she tries to set a boundary, at which point he specifically *withdraws* all those positive things and acts cold and distant... he really expects us to see it as "just doing something else"?

Besides, if you genuinely "like her and enjoy her company," then *why are you checking your email rather than talking to her?* If this hypothetical PUA genuinely liked her and enjoyed her company, then he'd do something that she would enjoy too.

Some of this might be decent advice in a different context. For example, if a PUA genuinely likes her and enjoys her company, then there's nothing wrong with telling her that. The problem is that it's bundled with other advice that tells him to act suddenly less interested, remove romantic signals, and then persist later even though she's put on the brakes.

Freeze-outs are social punishments. (Many PUAs also list freeze-outs as a response to intense shit tests.) Grade-school kids punish each other by giving the "silent treatment"; some cultures, such as certain religious groups, punish people by "shunning" them. These social tactics are famously effective... and harsh.

Women are inundated with social messages that guys won't like us unless we have sex with them. Many women are trained to expect that we must trade sex for affection. Using a freeze-out as an LMR tactic may work, but it seems more likely to capitalize on those complexes than to turn the target on or make her feel sexy. (And of course, it's just going to piss her off or bore her if she sees through the manipulation, or if she doesn't care much about the guy's affection.)

Years ago, I attended an S&M discussion group where we talked about how to deal with it when you're in the middle of an S&M encounter and things go terribly awry. Obviously, at such times, you end the encounter and have a conversation with your partner... or you take some space to think about it, then have the conversation later. But there's more to it than that. What you want is a situation where your partner feels like the S&M is over, but simultaneously does not feel abandoned. You want to withdraw sex, but you don't want to withdraw intimacy.

Here are a few tactics for withdrawing sex without withdrawing intimacy:
* Reassuring the person that you care about how they feel.
* Taking the pressure off and making it clear that whatever happens now, you're happy.
* Maintaining non-sexual physical contact, like hand-holding.
* And, of course, speaking calmly and kindly.

That's the key to setting a positive, mutual boundary rather than freezing someone out: *don't withdraw intimacy.*

Some of the guys I talked to in the seduction community described themselves as using "freeze-outs"... but a lot of them acted in a more pressure-free way than most freeze-out descriptions. They told me that when a girl starts giving LMR, they would do something like:
* offer to get her a glass of water,
* suggest that they go grab a snack together,
* or just call it a night.

Which all sounds completely reasonable to me! I'm not sure why they called these activities freeze-outs. I guess it's just because the activities can look superficially similar from the outside, and the guys didn't have any words to describe actually *respecting* a target's LMR. They had no words to talk about setting boundaries while maintaining intimacy.

It's worth noting that PUAs can't claim copyright on any of their tactics (though they can and do copyright clever names for those tactics). PUAs have learned from experimenting and observing men who are naturally good at picking up girls, or they are men who are naturally good at the game, who boiled their approach down into a curriculum.

As the blogger Hugh Ristik once asked me: "Do you *really* think there aren't non-PUA men out there using LMR tactics on their own? Or that there aren't plenty of heterosexual women who try to get past male resistance to sex?" He later added, "Most PUAs learned their techniques by copying what socially and sexually active people were already doing. Pickup is a barometer of what's fucked up in wider society."

So perhaps PUA descriptions of the worst LMR techniques can be valuable because they show us, step by step, how fucked up mainstream cultural approaches to sex can be.

* * *

I'm a feminist sex-positive activist. For me, that means that I try to raise awareness of social problems around sexuality. And I try to give people mental, social and emotional tools to deal with sexual issues. I run sexual communication workshops when I can, and I write about these topics constantly.

We live in a world where people of all genders feel a huge number of different sexual pressures. The Last Minute Resistance techniques that I've described are a marvelous and terrible showcase of how some men use those pressures against women.

LMR techniques make me particularly angry because I believe that one of the most generous, important things we can do for our sexual partners is relieve that pressure whenever we can. I can remember, for example, that when I was younger I had an especially hard time setting boundaries once any kind of sexual interaction had started. (Because setting a boundary after you've started is being a "tease," right? And women who tease men are horrible bitches, right? Once you start a sexual interaction, you're "committed," right? Argh.)

This meant that I would get really nervous about rejecting a guy sexually if I was already making out with him. So I clearly remember the first time a guy quietly *asked* how far I wanted to go, after kissing me.

I said, "I'd rather not have sex tonight..." and then I faltered, overwhelmed by anxiety. I added awkwardly, "I don't know, I can't explain it...."

"It's okay," he said in a completely friendly, no-nonsense way. "You don't have to explain it. Of course I don't want to do anything you don't want to do." He didn't move away, kept his hands on me, maintained intimacy while respecting my boundaries. I was stunned at the flood of relief that went through me *just because he hadn't acted put out.* I felt relieved *entirely because he didn't seem bothered.* I felt so relieved, it made me dizzy.

It was such a simple thing, such an *obvious* way to act. But on the other hand, if he'd acted frustrated or cold, I might have felt terrible and guilt tripped myself into doing things I didn't want to do.

I directly trace moments like that, *moments where I felt specifically and mindfully un-pressured by my partners,* to the development of my ability to trust and explore while setting limits with partners today. That man was one of the first people to show me what "no pressure" looked like, which helped me see ways that I'd been pressured in the past, and helped me walk away from partners who tried to do it later. Men like him were proof that, as opposed to stereotypes, men might not always try to push me further than I felt okay with.

Those interactions *enabled me to feel safe with men...* and therefore *enabled me to explore sexuality further with men, later in life.* And, of course, those interactions are perfect examples of withdrawing sex without withdrawing intimacy.

So aggressive Last Minute Resistance techniques have interpersonal problems — but they also have cultural problems. The techniques that I've described create the opposite of the pressure-free environment that's so important for sexual realization. They can potentially damage a target's potential for positive sexual development: they can contribute to future issues.

I don't think the man I just described deserves a cookie for how he acted. I think that how he acted *ought to be expected, assumed behavior.* In fact, those moments should be expected and assumed from people of all genders. Men are not the only ones who can pressure people to be sexual in ways they don't feel comfortable with.

Those interactions didn't just teach me about my own boundaries. Those interactions also helped me learn how not to pressure other people. I felt incredibly thrilled as I started getting chances to "pay forward" the lessons I'd learned. One particular example comes to mind: a heavy S&M encounter with a submissive gentleman. It was my first time with him, and I had ripped him to shreds with delightful metal claws.

His eyes were closed — I had ordered him to keep them closed — and I was sitting in his lap, my whole body wrapped around him. We were both shirtless. His back was covered in my harsh marks. We were breathing hard, stunned, riding our bodies through the S&M charge we'd both experienced.

As we slowly came down from the S&M headspace, I wasn't sure what to do next. I wondered what it might be like to have sex with him, so I asked idly, "Do you want me?"

His muscles tensed. I was amazed at how much he tensed. And he averted his face from me, even though his eyes were closed. "Yes," he said haltingly, "yes, I do want you, but I don't want to have intercourse... it's just one of my boundaries, it's...." and I saw the same terrible anxiety that I'd once felt. I saw his fear that he would drive me away by refusing sex.

I think he may have been afraid in a different way from how I'd been afraid. While women often feel as though we "should" act like stereotypical nymphos in order to keep a guy's attention and confirm our attractiveness, men tend to feel as though they "should" want to have sex in order to be "properly" virile, or to reassure a woman that she's attractive. (These are tendencies I've noticed, of course, and not even close to immutable facts of the universe; in particular, I need to reiterate that I'm heterosexual. There could doubtless be a whole nother book on pressures in the queer community.)

Still. No matter why my ex was anxious, the important thing was that he was anxious about not having sex, and I knew exactly how to calm him. I covered his mouth with one hand as he stumbled over his words. "Shh. It's totally fine," I told him, "you don't have to explain it." And kept my arms around him. And meant it.

Relief poured off him. His trust in me skyrocketed. We made out without intercourse until 5 AM, and it was *awesome*. (And later in the relationship, we did indeed have intercourse once he felt ready for it.)

I won't lie, though: specifically and mindfully keeping the pressure off partners can be genuinely difficult. Keeping a long-term relationship completely pressure-free is especially hard because there are so many factors involved, and the stakes can be high. If one or both parties are helplessly in love, if they are married, if they have children, if they live together... then it becomes very hard to keep everything, including the sexual arena, pressure-free.

A husband who is afraid his wife might leave him is more likely to do sexual things on her behalf that make him uncomfortable because he wants her to stay, *even if she doesn't ask him to*. A girl who is totally in love with her boyfriend is more likely to acquiesce to sex that she's not really into, because of course she wants to please him, but *she is simultaneously unlikely to tell him outright that she's not into it.*

These situations can be especially hard to figure out because there can be fault on both sides. People must learn how to set boundaries as much as they must respect boundaries. It's important to take responsibility for what's going on in your own head, to learn how to watch out for yourself, to say "no" when you mean "no" (and to say "I'm not sure" when you mean "I'm not sure").

It's just as important to speak directly and explicitly to our partners, as it is to create space for them to speak to us.

Indeed, setting boundaries can look a lot like respecting boundaries. When I made a list of ways to set boundaries, I thought it looked a lot like the list I already made of how to respect resistance:

* Maintaining intimacy while setting the boundary. Depending on your situation, examples might include touching your partner gently, or putting your arms around them, while saying you don't want to do something.

* Suggesting a mutually fun alternative: "I'd rather not go down on you. Can we use a toy this time instead?"

* Suggesting a concrete alternate time: "I don't feel up for it tonight, but let's do it over the weekend."

Yet even while I acknowledge that setting boundaries is important, I really wish people would take more responsibility for *not creating pressure against setting boundaries.*

Of course, there's also the fact that what feels like "pressure" for each person will be different depending on that person's triggers, the relationship, and the time in their life. Today, I usually feel comfortable setting limits and clearly telling my partner "no" if he asks me to do something I don't want to do... but it wasn't so long ago that I'd feel anxiety-inducing pressure to do something if my boyfriend merely mentioned that he liked it. (Because obviously the whole point of my existence as a woman is to please my man, am I right? And obviously no man will tolerate a relationship with me if I'm not serving his every sexual whim, am I right? Women *pay* men for relationships using sex, right? Argh.)

Which brings me to my last pressure-related thought: there can be a confusingly fine line between sharing and pressure. One must be careful when bringing up one's own preferences and desires, which isn't to say one shouldn't bring them up! It's just that it's important to recognize that these are difficult topics. When we discuss these things with people we love or admire, there's lots of potential for accidental anxious pressure.

It's important to emphasize from the start of any new sexual interaction that, "This is something I'm interested in, but it's not a requirement and I don't want you to do it if you're not into it." In fact, it might help to begin by saying those exact words.

One of my favorite exercises along these lines came from a workshop led by the S&M writer Laura Antoniou. She suggested that if you want to bring up a particularly weird, gross, or dramatic sexual fantasy with your partner, and if you're nervous about it, you go out and buy some ice cream. Actually, as a vegan, I recommend that you obtain the frozen dessert Coconut Bliss instead. The chocolate flavor is obscenely delicious.

Once you have the Coconut Bliss, then sit down with your partner. Put the Coconut Bliss in front of you, and describe your fantasy clearly but briefly. Then say, "Let's have some Bliss while you process that!"... and talk about something completely different while you eat.

I think this exercise is brilliant because everyone gets Coconut Bliss, and also because it takes the pressure off both parties. Both people can use the unrelated, friendly conversation to reaffirm their connection and reassure themselves. The person with the fantasy can feel reassured that the other person isn't going to be appalled and reject them wholesale; the person who heard the fantasy can calm down, if the description triggered strong feelings. Then they can pick up the thread again later and figure out how they actually want to deal with the fantasy, once everyone feels more settled. Ideally, anyway.

I have plenty of sympathy for people who feel pressured to engage sexually in ways that don't work for them. But I also have a lot of sympathy for people with socially unacceptable sexual preferences, who are scared to bring up those needs with their partners. I've been in both positions, and both positions are dark and difficult.

I don't want to come off as saying that sexual needs aren't important. *I believe that sexuality is very important.* As long as a sexual desire can be fulfilled consensually, then it seems wrong to put it on the back burner indefinitely. If you have sexual needs that are being routinely ignored, or can't be fulfilled, by your partner, then it's obviously no good to keep gently saying: "Don't worry, I can do without this."

This unfortunately brings us into ultimatum territory. For example, you may be tempted to say: "If you can't participate in my sexual desires, then I need an open relationship so I can find someone who can, or else we have to break up." If this must happen, then it's best to state the ultimatum gently, to emphasize that this is difficult for you because you care about your partner, and then steel yourself to act quickly and thoroughly in case you have to go through with your ultimatum. (And if you're not sure you can go through with it, then *don't issue an ultimatum!)*

Sadly, pressure can sometimes be unavoidable. In that case, the best we can do is be mindful, understanding, and prepared to deal carefully with the consequences.

* * *

Now, the same way I accept that I enjoy participating in S&M scenarios where I say no and scream and beg for mercy... I accept that *it's conceivable* that aggressive LMR techniques might be part of a great sexual encounter for *some* people. I would identify those people as closeted S&Mers. And I think their situation would be easier and safer for everyone concerned if those folks could learn how to talk clearly about their sexual desires, and learn how to use a safeword.

Here's a standup bit from the comedian Louis C.K.:

I remember one night I was with a girl, I was about 20 years old.... We're making out, and she's into it, she's like, humping me. So I start putting my hand up her shirt, and she stops me. I'm like hmm, ok, so then we're making out more, so then I put my hand on her ass, and she stops me. So after a while she went home. Nothing happened.

The next night I saw her in the club, and she said, "Hey, what happened last night?" I was like, "What?" And she's like, "How come we didn't have sex?" I was like, "Cause you didn't want to." She was like, "Yes I did, I was really into it." I was like, "Well, why did you keep stopping me?" She goes, "Cause I wanted you to just go for it." I was like, "What does that mean?" She says, "I'm kinda weird, I get turned on when a guy holds me down and just fucks me." I said, "You should have told me, I happily would have done that for you." And she says, "No, it has to feel real, and dangerous." And I said, "What? Are you out of your fucking mind? You think I'm just going to rape you on the off chance that hopefully you're into that shit?" [9]

I've talked to a lot of straight guys — PUAs and non-PUAs — with stories like that.

Remember that study I mentioned about people who say no when they mean yes (or, in other words, put up "token resistance")? [10] Again, the study found that 15% of people *of both genders* do this regularly. Here's another interesting tidbit: a previous study had already "found that women who had at least once said no when meaning yes, compared to women who had not, were more likely to endorse attitudes or beliefs such as romantic relationships are often adversarial, men are entitled to use force to get what they want, women like forceful men, and token resistance is common."

In other words: women who are likely to say no when meaning yes are also likely to *tell you that other women act the same way they do.* But, and this is important, *the fact that those women tell you this does not mean they are correct.*

This is important because it's a common theme among the straight guys who told me these stories. These guys tell me there's a woman in their past who was always saying no, who later told them she really wanted to have sex... who then informed them that "women always do that." But *those women were wrong.*

Let's make another thing crystal clear: confusion about boundaries, and the "no means yes" problem, is not unique to women. People of other genders do it too, like my ex-boyfriend Mr. Chastity.

I call him Mr. Chastity because he observed chastity before marriage. I dated him for a long time, and I was cool with the chastity thing, because he had no problem with heavy make-outs and giving me orgasms by... ahem... alternative means. In fact, after a while I was able to feel like it was *ridiculously hot* that Mr. Chastity wouldn't have sex with me. I made up a whole constellation of S&M fantasies about how he was so contemptuous, controlled, and in charge of the situation that he felt no need to fuck me.

Indeed, I had a conversation with one hardcore S&M submissive where I told her my boyfriend refused to fuck me, and she got *incredibly jealous.*

Don't get me wrong: it would have been awesome to have sex with Mr. Chastity. But these fantasies helped fill the gap, for sure.

In general, Mr. Chastity was incredibly happy that I respected his boundaries. He told me he'd never had another girlfriend who didn't push him further than he felt comfortable... or worse, take it as a personal insult that he wouldn't have sex with her.

So Mr. Chastity was grateful to me for respecting him. Initially. But after a while, he told me that he actually kinda *wanted* me to push harder. He said he thought it was hot.

He told me this while expressing concerns about the way we were dealing with sex already. In fact, he even said that sometimes he felt like we should stop having any kind of sexual contact whatsoever. Not even kissing.

He was giving me mixed signals and putting me in a double bind, and I didn't like it *at all*. I freaked out on him, and I insisted that his consent was super important to me. I told him that I *never* push explicit boundaries unless those boundaries are explicitly withdrawn first. I told him that I *certainly* would never initiate any kind of sex unless I felt *sure* he'd feel okay about it the next day.

At which point he was clearly *very disappointed.*

So, obviously, a few people seek out situations in which they want to have mixed-signal sex that they haven't discussed ahead of time. But it's not clear how common those people are. And that's a big burden for those people to put on their partners.

And certainly, when *I* say "no" or "stop," then I don't want to have sex, and I *really* don't want to be pressured about it. Maybe, for other people, "no" doesn't always mean no. With me, *no means no* (unless I have a safeword). Plus, here's another thing I know for sure: I am not alone. Many other people *of all genders* are like me. I know this from talking about sex with lots of people, and from working with rape survivors.

Another important point is that even if you do read someone perfectly, and even if the person really does want to fuck while saying "no"... if you don't have a safeword, then you're creating a situation where you're responsible for reading your partner flawlessly in the future, and they won't have any surefire way to call things off.

In other words, you're setting the frame so that your partner's "no" is always subject to your interpretation. And I know *I* sure as hell wouldn't want to be in that situation, on either end. Maybe it would be okay if I'd known the guy for a while and I was certain that our non-verbal communication was rock-solid, but even then, I'd want to be careful. After all, men expect me to read their minds enough as it is! I don't want to encourage that crap.

Also! The best way to train people to not say "no" when they mean "yes"? Is by *treating their no like a no.* If you want your partner to mean "no" when they say "no," then you should take them seriously when they say "no." Most people won't keep doing something that doesn't work. It might take a while, but people will learn to ask and talk directly if they understand that it's serious enough. After all, that's what happened to me: once I determined that I had to communicate directly in order to get my S&M urges fulfilled, I put a whole lot of effort into learning how to communicate directly.

I'm not saying you should be pulling freeze-outs and ignoring your partner until they say yes. In fact, I encourage the opposite. If your partner says "no" to sex but enjoys making out, then your best strategy is to continue turning them on by making out. Even if they say "no" all through the night, they'll go to bed hungry. And they'll want you more next time.

* * *

If PUAs were usually more concerned with their partners' experience than with notches in the bedpost, then there would be more PUA discussion of the potential problems with LMR techniques. A few targets may be into it, but what about other targets who would feel manipulated or coerced? Even Neil Strauss, at the end of *The Game,* acknowledges that his eventual serious girlfriend did not fall for LMR techniques. In fact, a lot of his PUA tactics pissed her off, and he almost lost her by trying them.

Reasonable non-misogynists are often discomfited when they examine aggressive LMR techniques. This includes some men who appreciate many PUA ideas, who feel that the seduction community changed their lives, and who believe PUAs can meet a high standard of ethics. As the blogger Hugh Ristik wrote to me by email,

I do have problems with a lot of the ideas in LMR tactics, and I actually see them as contradicting certain other ideas in pickup. What I like about pickup and seduction is that they teach you to raise the chances of someone wanting to be sexual with you out of their own free will, for reason of desire. That's the overarching principle I see behind most of what pickup artists teach. There are certain ideas in LMR tactics that seem counter to that principle, in practice or in theory.

A rare few PUAs actively write against aggressive LMR techniques. The coach Mark Manson writes:

In [an LMR situation], there's always a fork in the road: you can do

the typical freeze-out / high-pressure PUA bullshit to try to manipulate her or annoy her into giving up the resistance. Or you can be honest about the situation and resign yourself to accepting the fact that you may not have sex tonight.

Guys, listen. Always, always, always go with the second option. It may sound counter-intuitive, but you have to go with the second option. Not only because it's the right thing to do. Not only because it's what any respectful human being should do. But because if you make it clear that there is absolutely no pressure for her to sleep with you, if you show her that you can be trusted and that you're OK with whatever she decides (and by the way, you do need to be OK with whatever she decides), then she's going to become ten times more comfortable with you, and therefore is actually more likely to WANT to have sex with you. You are in bed with her half-naked after all, it's not a question of want, it's a question of trust and comfort.

Besides, sex with girls who aren't excited to have sex with you is fucking awful. It's worse than masturbating. I never get LMR and from now on, neither should you. Stop pressuring these girls. Let them know you're OK without having sex and do actually be OK with it. Most of them will soften up and it'll end up happening naturally and it will be a far more pleasant experience for both of you. [11]

Here's another perspective from guru David Shade (who often describes himself as specializing less in pickup than in "what comes after pickup"):

Do not push against last minute resistance. You will be like all the other guys who objectify women and do not respect her as a real person. And it will reek of desperation.

Instead, defer your own gratification for the big goal. The big goal is to bring out that ruthlessly expressive sexual creature in her. It's going to take a little time before she becomes your very naughty horny little cum slut fuck bitch.

In fact, move things along just slightly slower than she'd like it. Make her wait. It builds that sexual tension, and it makes her think. When she is away from you, she is going to think about it a lot. [12]

Backing up my point, David Shade emphasizes that respecting LMR will encourage the target's sexual expressiveness later. Shade is saying exactly what I'm saying, about how providing a more pressure-free sexual environment makes people feel safer to explore sexuality... although admittedly he's doing it with very different, very controlling words.

Some LMR techniques aren't as bad as ignoring "no" or using freeze-outs. Indeed, some PUAs give much friendlier tips, like "make sure she's very turned on with lots of foreplay" and "make sure she knows you like and respect her as a person." Which is perfectly reasonable advice! Here, I'll break it down into steps:

STEP 1. Ensure that the target wants to have sex with you.

STEP 2. Ensure that the target thinks you're not an asshole.

STEP 3: If the above things are true, then the target probably won't resist if you try to have sex. And if they do, they'll have a good reason (such as, "I'm in a monogamous marriage with someone else!").

The blogger Hugh Ristik, who provided me with most of my material about PUAs and ethics, once emailed me about Dave Riker's 3 Rules. These Rules were developed by a 1990s seduction guru who told PUAs that if they encounter LMR, they should make three things clear to the woman right away:

a. I always use a condom.

b. I want this to be something that you (the woman) want to do.

c. I want this to be something that you (the woman) will look back upon and be happy about. [13]

Riker claims that when he sincerely tells women those three things, it usually works, which doesn't surprise me. As long as she felt that the man was being honest, those statements would reassure most women very thoroughly. As I wrote earlier in this chapter, a pressure-free environment is really important for open sexuality; and what Riker says here is a lot like what my early partners said to me, when they were trying to help me feel comfortable about setting boundaries.

Other PUAs advise identifying *why* the target is giving LMR. This is the saving grace of LMR discussions; this is the reason I don't think that all LMR techniques are awful. For example: occasional Lay Reports describe a girl giving LMR, and then when the PUA actually *talks to her* about what's up, it turns out that the girl is on her period and feels self-conscious. In these cases, PUAs often advise each other to reassure the girl that he's not grossed out, and offer tips on how to minimize the mess.

I tell you, men: most of my period-related sexual anxiety stems from dudes who have freaked out on me. Or dudes who have decided that since I'm on my period, I should totally blow them while they refuse to touch my naughty bits with a ten-foot pole. I testify that these past experiences made it hard for me to believe dudes will be reasonable about period sex.

Yes indeed, I have given plenty of menstruation-related LMR in my time... and dudes who convince me they're not freaked out by periods can sometimes blast my LMR.

I reckon there are two categories for LMR techniques: "mutual" ones, and "aggressive" ones. Mutual LMR techniques are the ones where the

PUA is most concerned about creating a mutual experience, like by using awesome foreplay, or by figuring out why she's objecting to sex. Aggressive LMR techniques are the ones where the PUA basically steamrolls her objections and ignores her reality.

Here are some more reasons a woman might give Last Minute Resistance: she might be self-conscious about her body. She might be thinking about her ex-boyfriend. Or she might be a cheater, and be thinking about the person she's betraying.

Something else to keep in mind is that women usually deal with very different potential costs for sex than men do. Men can catch Sexually Transmitted Infections. Men can also end up paying child support, which is not a small consequence. But due to our physiology, women have a higher risk of catching STIs. For example, a man with HIV is *eight times more likely* to give it to a female partner than a woman with HIV is to give it to a male partner. [14] And we women are obviously the ones who would actually have to deal with an unwanted pregnancy.

Another factor in women's hesitation about casual sex is that women fear more physical danger from men than men do from women... especially strangers. A 2011 study found that, when confronted with a random stranger offering sex, straight ladies were quite likely to rate male strangers as potentially dangerous, while straight dudes were *not* likely to rate female strangers as potentially dangerous. [15] When we women go home alone with men, we believe we're taking a much bigger risk than the men do.

A third extremely important factor is that *women are much less likely to actually enjoy sex with a new partner than men are.* For one thing, surveys show that women are more likely to feel that emotional connection is crucial for sexual enjoyment than men are, and an emotional connection is obviously less likely with a new partner than an established one. [16] For another thing, the same 2011 study I mentioned above found that women usually anticipated that sex with a random man would be kinda bad, whereas men usually anticipated that sex with a random woman would be average.

This is unsurprising because historically, sex has usually been defined in terms of two things: (a) reproduction, and (b) the sexual pleasure of stereotypical men. Cultural sexual standards are based on these things.

For example, the sexual "base system" (commonly discussed among USA schoolchildren) describes kissing as "first base," groping as "second base," oral sex as "third base" and penis-in-vagina sex as "home base." Why should this metaphor exist? It only makes sense if we think of sex as being centered around reproduction. If we think of sex as being about pleasure and open exploration in ways that are different for everyone, then having a "home base" — a standardized goal — makes zero sense.

Another example: penis-in-vagina sex is often seen as "real" sex or "actual" sex, and all other sex is considered "less real." How many arguments have you had over the course of your lifetime about whether oral sex "counts" as sex? Hint: more than the subject deserves. (Remember Bill Clinton telling the world, "I did not have sexual relations with that woman.")

For a more recent example, there's the Kink.com virgin shoot. In 2011, the S&M porn site Kink.com created a live event wherein a porn model publicly "lost her virginity"... despite the fact that she'd already had plenty of oral and anal sex on camera for years. [17] She'd never had vaginal sex, though, and so she was still viewed as a "virgin."

As for sex being defined by the pleasure of stereotypical men: one example is how people usually think about orgasms. In my experience and that of people I talk to, and in the vast majority of porn, it seems commonly accepted that sexual activity ends with a man's orgasm. Whereas women are commonly expected to continue engaging in sex after having an orgasm, *despite the fact that many women seem just as tired and less-interested in sex post-orgasm as many men.*

In part, this goes back to defining sex in terms of reproduction: men (usually) have to orgasm in order for reproduction to happen, so men's orgasms must (supposedly) be central to sex. It's all influenced by these other social ideas, like how penis-in-vagina sex is "real" sex, or "home base": many people are confused by the idea that you'd shift sexual gears "backwards" to oral sex or whatever if you've already "made it to home base."

But this also arises from centering stereotypical men's desires. It arises from a culture that generally perceives men's sexuality as more important, more driving, and more necessary than women's. Note that it's quite unusual for women to achieve orgasm from penis-in-vagina sex in itself... and many women report feeling *terrible* about that, *as if there's something wrong with the woman herself rather than the social standard!* For example, here's a heartbreaking letter written by a 17-year-old girl to the sex education website Scarleteen:

I have no idea what is wrong with me and I am desperate to find out because it is destroying mine and my boyfriend's sex lives. I can orgasm through clitoral stimulation but that is it and I do not know what else I can do. Please help me because I don't know what is wrong with me.

The woman who runs the website, the brilliant educator Heather Corinna, responds that:

> *We get this kind of question so much, that if it was about something being wrong with women's bodies, it'd have to mean something is wrong with MOST women's bodies. But since most women, through history, have NEVER been able to reach orgasm through intercourse, or only do very infrequently, it doesn't make sense to think something is wrong with us, just as we are.* [18]

As is often the case with broken gender norms, this social standard can be bad for non-women, too. Gay men are considered "pansies," or they're viewed as "not real men," because they don't have penis-in-vagina sex. But of course, straight men aren't immune to masculine anxiety. Every time a straight man declines to be dominant, to be sexually insatiable, or to have a large penis, he risks being viewed as a failure.

And I've spoken to lots of dudes who don't even see orgasms as the most exciting part of sex. Some dudes even wish that they weren't under so much *pressure* to have an orgasm, and think sex is more fun with fewer orgasms! I once wrote a blog post about how orgasms aren't my favorite part of sex, and *almost all the comments on it came from men who said that it was true for them, too.* For example, here's the first comment on the post:

> *I wanted to support this idea of orgasms not being absolutely necessary to "sex." As a guy, I often feel as though it is expected that I will come at some point. But I just don't care much for it much of the time. The hottest sexual encounters I've experienced involved no such thing. Coming can be very nice, but it's not necessary to have fun.* [19]

Well, anyway. When I was younger, I thought that the high cost of casual sex for women was obvious. That was before I started encountering men who resented women for "being able to get sex whenever." I met men like this before I started talking to PUAs, but it's a particularly epidemic type of resentment within the PUA subculture. It never fails to stun me. These guys say things like, "It's not fair! Women can walk into bars and get laid, whenever they want," and they seem blind to how dangerous and unpleasant most of us ladies believe random sex could get.

These guys are jealous because they think it's easy for women to get laid. Which is probably true for many women. Not *all,* but *some.* Yet if women's so-called "easy sex" is likely to be bad and dangerous, *why should we want it?*

If women could rely on sex — even casual sex — being safe and fun, then I suspect that women would go for it more. Indeed, in the USA, women's sexuality has become more understood and accepted. Women have more orgasms during sex in the modern era, and women fear violence less than we did in the bad old days. We also have access to much better birth control than ever before in history. As a result, women are *much* more likely to have casual sex than we used to be. But casual sex for ladies is still not reliably safe and fun, and we still pay higher potential costs.

You'd think these factors might lead men to, say, volunteer with anti-rape initiatives more than they do. That would be a great way to help lower the potential costs and dangers around sex for women! Yet instead of doing something productive, lots of dudes prefer to hate women, because they think we have "easy access" to something they want.

* * *

***

CHAPTER 4:
If You Knew How Much I Loved You, You Would Run Away

In which Clarisse gets involved with a man she really likes. He's not a pickup artist, and he is a feminist... however, Clarisse analyzes their relationship in PUA terms from the start as part of her ongoing effort to understand the seduction process. Clarisse also discusses a book for ladies called The Rules, *which is sort of like* The Game *for women, and she describes some subtle ways of establishing social power, such as the tactic that PUAs call "compliance tests." Plus: a Theory of Emotional Escalation, also known as "the game of falling in love." The chapter title is from the song "Pretty When You Cry," by Vast.*

***

I wasn't just out flirting with PUAs. After being out of the country, I had some serious *urges*. I prowled the S&M community seeking androgynous men in black, and I tried new things with friends I'd known for years. I was looking both for short-term adventures and longer-term arrangements.

I hooked up with another sex writer. (I have a theory that all sex writers secretly want to sleep with other sex writers.) It was fun, and I liked the way he communicated. Still, the spark didn't overwhelm either of us.

A handsome survivalist invited me to stay with him in the woods. Alas, nothing romantic happened. Perhaps I didn't shit test enough.

I had a brief and pleasant affair with an old friend, but he felt unsure about polyamory and ultimately decided that his goal was a monogamous marriage. Of course it stung... for both of us, I think. I really liked him. But we only dated for a couple of months, and we already had a solid friendship; I think that's why we were able to end it without drama. We're still friends, and I sincerely hope that he finds a monogamous wife who's worthy of him.

My most hilarious dating interaction went something like this:
1) Spotted a long-haired, glasses-wearing, slender man at an S&M

club. He had a beautifully wry mouth. I wanted him immediately.

2) Walked up to him and introduced myself.

3) Ended the conversation by asking for his information.

4) Messaged him on Facebook to suggest that we go out to dinner.

5) After dinner and a nightclub, offered to go home with him and was rejected. He didn't say anything else, or ask to see me again; he just turned me down.

6) Therefore, I figured he wasn't interested in me romantically or sexually.

7) Soon afterwards, I encountered him again at another club, at which point he insisted that he was indeed interested. We ended up passionately making out in his car, but I refused to go home with him because I had too many things to do the next day.

8) Aaand when I said, "Dude, I don't get it, I totally figured you weren't into me when you didn't want to take me home last time," the gentleman replied, "I'm going to feel like an idiot if you're serious about that." He later added, with perfect sincerity: "I'm offended that you assumed I'd have sex on the first date!"

The irony was not lost on me.

* * *

In USA culture, men are expected to initiate sexual encounters. Men are also expected to escalate sexual encounters: in other words, men are expected to take charge and "run the fuck." Men often complain about this. Men claim that they would love it if women would sexually initiate more. But in practice, many men get confused and weirded out by women who try to run the fuck. Assertive sexual women are often labeled "sluts," judged harshly, treated as disposable, or just plain seen as confusing. In fact, they're often treated that way *even by men who claim they want assertive sexual women.*

Indeed, when men are polled about why they call women sluts, they give a variety of reasons from "she dressed trashy" to "she slept with multiple men at one time." But the most fascinating reason men call women sluts is this: *some men state that they would call a girl a slut if she slept with him on the first date.* As one male writer observes in a whole article about this topic: "Guys, if you'd sleep with her, you can't call her a slut." [1]

Let me be fair: not all men engage in this absurd hypocrisy. Just most men.

And there are certainly exceptions to the initiation rules. I've certainly been known to ask men out and attempted to run the interaction, as you can see from my story above. What I'm describing are cultural norms and stereotypes, and there will always be exceptions to those.

PUAs understand this. After all, they talk about Anti-Slut Defense, which I described last chapter. The idea of Anti-Slut Defense is that women resist having sex because we're so often socially attacked for our sexual desires. For all my problems with the concept of Anti-Slut Defense, PUAs are approaching important truths there. More women would be comfortable acting overtly sexual if we weren't shamed for it, and PUAs work this knowledge into their strategies for sexual escalation.

I came up with the phrase "emotional escalation" to parallel the "sexual escalation" PUAs learn. Emotional escalation is "the game of falling in love." While men are typically handed the role of sexual escalation, women are typically handed the role of emotional escalation. Men are expected to game women into bed, and make it look effortless. Women are expected to game men into falling in love with us, and make it look effortless. (The Genesis song "Invisible Touch" is arguably an example of a man praising a woman who does this.)

This isn't to say men don't *want* to fall in love. I'm sure there are plenty of men who want to fall in love, just like there are plenty of women who want to have sex. It's just that many men who want to fall in love *also* want women to "do all the work."

Of course there are exceptions. Some men are more interested in love than sex, the same way some women are more interested in sex than love. Indeed, one might argue that most men are interested in intimacy, but *there's a lot of social pressure against men admitting that they want intimacy.* After all, any dude who wants to be in love with a monogamous girlfriend rather than seeking to bang as many chicks as possible is a total pansy and probably he's actually gay... am I right, guys?

Perhaps, within a theory of emotional escalation, men can be described as having Anti-Relationship Defense similar to the PUA concept of women's Anti-Slut Defense.

* * *

A frequent and obvious comparison to *The Game* is the 1995 book *The Rules: Time-Tested Secrets for Capturing the Heart of Mr. Right,* by Ellen Fein and Sherrie Schneider. It's a guide for women on how to get a relationship and, eventually, a marriage proposal out of a man. Some of it is definitely good advice, like "don't date a married man" (the assumption here is that the man is in a monogamous marriage, of course).

But *The Rules* also includes strategies like "don't call him and rarely return his calls" and "don't meet him halfway or go Dutch on a date," because this is not about compromising or building a mutual relationship. It's about setting up a challenge that he has to overcome; it's about *gaming him into it.* It's about keeping the power as much on the woman's side as possible. It's about circumventing his Anti-Relationship Defense just enough to snag the big diamond ring.

Here's what the brilliantly sarcastic feminist writer Kate Harding says about *The Rules:*

[The principles of The Rules *are that] every lonely adult would be happily married right now if slightly dim, marriage-obsessed harpies (i.e., women) were only more skilled at manipulating slightly dim, chest-pounding horndogs (i.e., men). That infernal book spawned not only umpteen follow-ups and countless knockoffs, but a freakin' multimedia empire for the authors, whose sole qualification to write the original was having husbands, and whose success barely hit a speed bump when Fein broke up with hers just as* The Rules for Marriage: Time-Tested Secrets for Making Your Marriage Work *came out. In fact, they are now in the business of training other people as "relationship experts." People like Jag Carrao, who wants you to know that you can be engaged by Christmas, ladies — as long as you've had an exclusive boyfriend for at least nine months, and you haven't fucked it all up by letting him really get to know you.*

Carrao offers a few tips for women looking to orchestrate a holiday engagement — without doing anything so stupid and Rule-breaking as proposing themselves, of course — and they do contain a single nugget of good advice, which probably partially explains the enduring popularity of The Rules. *That is: "Stop making excuses for him... [D]on't let him snooker you into pretending that marriage isn't important or doesn't matter IF it IS important to YOU and DOES matter to YOU." Fair enough. The argument in favor of* The Rules *has always been that the advice is fundamentally about self-respect and boundary-setting, about teaching women to stand up for their needs, ditch opportunistic losers, and hold out for guys who really treat them well and have similar goals. These are all good things! The problem is all the other advice, which encourages you to scheme, lie, dumb yourself down, squelch your instincts, and make incredibly unflattering generalizations about men. And which also reinforces the idea not only that you're doing something wrong if you haven't yet earned the coveted ring, but that there must be something wrong with you if you're not desperate to get engaged this holiday season. Says Carrao, "NOTHING could be more natural than for a woman in love with hopes for marriage and possibly children to wish to see her dreams reciprocated during a season centering around family, tradition, and reflections on the year behind and that ahead." NOTHING. Do you hear me? NOTHING!* [2]

Scheme and make incredibly unflattering generalizations... yep, *The Rules* sounds similar to lots of PUA advice. The webcomic XKCD has a great take on this, called "Beautiful Dream." It depicts one character saying to another, "I just woke up from the most beautiful dream.... All the women who read and follow *The Rules* and all the guys who swear by the techniques in *The Game* paired off with each other and left the rest of us alone forever." [3]

And yet while the advice in *The Rules* is often problematic, much of it works. At least, it "works" if your goal is to emotionally escalate a partner and convince him to do what you want without regard for honesty, genuine mutuality, or your partner's deeper personal preferences.

Sound familiar?

There's another famous volume, similar to *The Rules,* called *He's Just Not That Into You,* by Greg Behrendt and Liz Tuccillo. This book contains sentences written by a man that include: "Don't let him trick you into asking him out. When men want you, they do the work. I know it sounds old school, but when men like women, they ask them out." Also: "Men, for the most part, like to pursue women. We like not knowing if we can catch you. We feel rewarded when we do." [4]

While building attraction, PUAs look for "Indicators of Interest" (IOIs). These can be anything from a target playing with her hair, to a target giving a compliment. If we adopt the PUA framework, and agree that women offer men sexual Indicators of Interest when we want them to take the sexual initiative, then perhaps we could also say that men give women *emotional* IOIs when they want us to take the emotional initiative. We could say that men work for our attention once they're into us, the same way women start working for a man's attention during the Qualification stage of seduction.

In this context, *He's Just Not That Into You* could be seen as a manual for seeking a man's emotional Indicators of Interest. It's a manual about how to not "fall for it" if you really like a guy, yet he won't work for your attention and thereby show that he's open to your game.

"I know it's an infuriating concept," writes the male author of *He's Just Not That Into You,* "that men like to chase and you have to let us chase you. I know. It's insulting. It's frustrating. It's unfortunately the truth. My belief is that if you have to be the aggressor, if you have to pursue, if you have to do the asking out, nine times out of ten, he's just not that into you."

The exhortations of *He's Just Not That Into You* are incredibly heteronormative, and I disagree with them in a lot of ways. But I see what the authors are trying to do: they're trying to keep women from putting too much effort into men who aren't open to their emotional escalation game. PUAs do something similar with a lot of their advice: they try to keep men from putting too much effort into women who aren't into them sexually.

PUAs develop their tactics by trying to understand how sexual encounters are *stereotypically expected* to go. They recognize that men are expected to "take charge" sexually and women are shamed out of "taking charge." And if men are expected to "do all the work," when it comes to sexual escalation, then PUAs may complain, but they'll still focus on learning how to "take charge" and "do all the work."

The blogger Hugh Ristik has written that "my project is either to reform the pickup artist community, or to take what is positive from it and leave the rest." Something similar could be said for stereotypically "girly" emotional escalation tactics like *The Rules*. Is it possible to boil down emotional escalation tactics the same way PUAs think about sexual escalation tactics? Is it possible to take what's positive from those tactics, and leave the rest?

It didn't take long for me to obsess about it.

* * *

Power is at the heart of most PUA tactical discussions. Sometimes, their tactical breakdowns are ridiculous and paranoid. But sometimes they're... yes, I'm going to admit it!... sometimes they're accurate.

In Chapter 1, I talked about "frame theory." (Recap: a "frame" is a paradigm, or a way of thinking about the world. PUAs theorize that socially dominant people set the terms of social interactions by "controlling the frame." A person can take control of a social interaction by "reframing" it to their advantage.)

In Chapter 2, I talked about "shit tests." (Recap: most PUAs describe this phenomenon by claiming that "all women" are give men a hard time *just to see if the men will react in a dominant way.* Supposedly women are *constantly* issuing "shit tests," and if a man fails to be properly dominant in response, he basically loses the game. Example shit tests include, "Are you a player?" or, "I don't want to have sex with you." PUAs usually encourage each other to ignore shit tests, to verbally smack the girl down, or to reframe what she said in a hilarious, unexpected and/or cocky way.)

Related to shit tests are "compliance tests." Some PUAs fold compliance tests into shit tests, and indeed, there are many commonalities between the two concepts. But there are important differences, too.

Compliance tests are one of the single most useful concepts I picked up from the seduction community. It took me a while to get it, though, because compliance tests are usually described in a way that made me instinctively furious. As usual, most PUAs frame the idea of "compliance tests" in a way that's hostile to women.

Many PUAs claim that women are always trying to get as much compliance out of a man as possible, but that a woman loses respect for a man who actually fulfills her requests. (Here's a compliance test some PUAs describe as an example: "Could you hold my drink while I get something from my purse?") Many PUAs claim that the response to compliance tests is the same as the response to shit tests: ignore, smack down or reframe. (Don't hold her drink... or take it, and drink the whole thing.) The general idea is that if you allow the woman to control the frame so that you're doing her favors, you'll lose social power.

In contrast, a PUA may offer a compliance test to gauge her interest ("Give me your hands, I'll show you a magic trick": if she does this without hesitation, then she's comfortable and up for more; if she doesn't, or if she hesitates, then more verbal game is necessary). This is more how I would personally use the "could you hold my drink" test: as a way of showing interest and figuring out how much he wants to interact. Assuming I would even use it as a test, rather than... you know... *actually trying to get something from my purse.*

In short: compliance tests are viewed as entitled and demanding when women do them, but as tactical and flirtatious when PUAs do them. Some PUAs also refer to compliance tests as part of "hoop theory." If you guessed from the name that "hoop theory" is all about ladies forcing dudes to jump through hoops, then you were right!

As one site says:
A Compliance Test when used by a women is a small request or series of requests to shift the power in the interaction onto her side. But when used by us PUAs is a test for her compliance and overall attraction to you. [5]

As usual, the moral of the story is that women are power-hungry bitches, but PUAs are just playing the game.

Like shit testy adversarial flirting, I can see this kind of thing being entertaining when it's not too serious. But the thing is, *sometimes people actually need to know whether we can rely on each other.* I once heard a story about the band Van Halen. Van Halen was famous for being finicky about stupid things. For example, the band demanded that when they were backstage, there should be a bowl of M&M candies with all the brown ones picked out. If they arrived at the venue and found a single brown

M&M, then the band refused to go onstage.

People often complained that Van Halen was composed of capricious prima donnas. But it turns out that when this band went on tour, they would use ridiculous special effects in their shows: pyrotechnics, explosions, God knows what. And so, in his autobiography, the lead singer explained:

Van Halen was the first band to take huge productions into tertiary, third-level markets. We'd pull up with nine eighteen-wheeler trucks, full of gear, where the standard was three trucks, max. And there were many, many technical errors — whether it was the girders couldn't support the weight, or the flooring would sink in, or the doors weren't big enough to move the gear through.

The contract rider read like a version of the Chinese Yellow Pages because there was so much equipment, and so many human beings to make it function. So just as a little test, in the technical aspect of the rider, it would say "Article 148: There will be fifteen amperage voltage sockets at twenty-foot spaces, evenly, providing nineteen amperes..." This kind of thing. And article number 126, in the middle of nowhere, was: "There will be no brown M&Ms in the backstage area, upon pain of forfeiture of the show, with full compensation."

So, when I would walk backstage, if I saw brown M&Ms in that bowl... well, line-check the entire production. Guaranteed you're going to arrive at a technical error. They didn't read the contract. Guaranteed you'd run into a problem. Sometimes it would threaten to just destroy the whole show. Something like, literally, life-threatening. [6]

In other words, Van Halen made the ridiculous demand about brown M&Ms *entirely because they were testing to see whether venues read their contract.* If Van Halen saw brown M&Ms backstage, they knew that the venue hadn't read the contract, which meant that the venue also didn't know about the difficult technical tasks in the show. Which meant that the show couldn't go on, because the people in Van Halen might be killed in some completely preventable accident.

You know what else is, in many ways, a difficult technical task? A relationship. When you're in a relationship, you need to know whether you can rely on your partner. If he screws up a compliance test, what else will he screw up?

People live socially complex, interwoven lives, and we have to be able to count on each other. I believe that "compliance test" is often a reasonable description of behavior that's used by all humans. When used by any human, compliance tests can be *both* a way of measuring the target's interest and reliability *and* a way of shifting social power. In fact, they can be both those things *and also* they can sometimes be a genuine request for assistance. And, sometimes, *there's nothing wrong with that.*

On the other hand...

During my PUA research, I was also re-establishing contact with an ex-boyfriend. We'd been out of touch for quite a while. The relationship got disrupted because one of us moved away, and we had no real closure. I still liked him, and I felt really attracted to him. After all, he was cute and smart and he was into S&M and he knew lots of feminist theory. What's not to like?

We were both highly interested in resuming the relationship. Even better, we both currently identified as polyamorous. There was one complication: his feelings for me were stronger than mine for him. He felt hurt by things I'd done in the past. He needed to feel reassured that I cared about him. He needed to feel that I was committed to working things out.

This was fine with me... at first. I did care about him, and I did feel committed. But after a while, I started feeling uneasy about the ways he made me jump through hoops. Or, if you prefer: I disliked his compliance tests.

For example, we lived across the city from each other; the trip was two hours by public transit or half an hour by car. My ex had a car, and I didn't. He asked me to meet him for coffee in his area anyway.

"I know it's out of your way," he said, "but it would just mean a lot to me. Please."

Okay, I thought. *If this is what you need to feel like you can trust me.* So I did it. We talked, and stayed up late talking some more. He drove me home, which kinda made up for the fact that he'd insisted that I make a 2-hour journey to see him.

We met again. And again. He's a somewhat dramatic guy... and he's always been dramatic, so I watched his reactions carefully. But although he was as emotional as ever, my ex also seemed secure and stable. We didn't even kiss, but as we spent time together our sexual chemistry got more and more intense. I left the ball in his court, waiting for him to make a move when he felt safe... but believe me, I was itching to put my hands on him.

Then one day I emailed him with a random question, and he told me he refused to answer it because he was too upset. "Also, I am never reading your blog again," he wrote. "You keep writing things that hurt me." He informed me that after he read my last blog post, he'd been unable to sleep all night and unable to concentrate at work all day. He added that he absolutely *wouldn't* tell me what exactly upset him, because he was too upset.

I blinked. I reviewed my blog.

I hadn't written about my ex in a long time. My most recent blog post wasn't about him. In fact, my most recent blog post wasn't even about my life. In fact, my most recent blog post *had not even been written by me.* My most recent blog post was a long quotation from the book *Speaking Sex To Power* by the awesome sexuality writer, Pat Califia.

I couldn't figure out what upset my ex, so I carefully wrote back asking which post he was referring to. He told me that it was the book quotation. Then my ex added, once again, that he refused to actually look at my blog in order to give me details. He *refused to even glance at my blog in order to tell me what hurt his feelings.*

And then he compared his feelings to being hit by a car.

Wow, I thought. What was my ex trying to do? To me, it felt like he was just creating random drama. I guessed that what he really wanted might be some kind of reassurance or emotional display on my part. Maybe on some level, he sought to force me to "prove" how much I cared, by begging his forgiveness even though I didn't feel like I'd done a single thing wrong.

But if that was true, then he was doing exactly the wrong thing to get what he wanted. I wasn't about to reward him for freaking out apparently at random, and then refusing to communicate about it.

I thought: *If my ex is so upset about a blog entry that I didn't write myself, which has nothing to do with him... and he's refusing to even explain what got him upset... then if we have a relationship, it's bound to go up in flames.*

I was angry at myself. After all, I'd already known that my ex was dramatic. I'd spotted his hoops, but I jumped through them anyway. Should I have seen this coming? Had I been naive to think it could work? Had I allowed him to set the frame of our relationship such that drama like this was inevitable?

With a mix of extreme frustration and regret, I emailed my best girlfriend for advice. I wrote:

If this is what happens when he and I are flirtatious friends, then we can't have a relationship, and we either need to stop flirting or stop being friends altogether. Advice on how to cut it off in the gentlest possible way is welcome... it will really suck for me, not just because I'm losing him and I care about him, but because it will make things more complicated in our mutual social circles. But I don't think there's another option.

She responded:

At this point, I hate to say it, but I think maybe you don't want to go for letting him go gently. You might want to go for letting him down decisively. Not coldly or cruelly, obviously, and yes respectfully, but I think your priorities should be (a) maintaining — or opening the door for a future — cordiality so you can socially coexist and (b) making your intentions toward him (or lack thereof) utterly clear.

She was right. I elected to cut him off completely, and say that maybe we could be friends in the distant future.

It wasn't fun. In fact, it hurt. I missed him, and I had to resist his attempts to engage me in further discussion. When I saw him at an event several months later, it was hard to quell the urge to talk to him. I kept watching him out of the corner of my eye and having wistful thoughts like, *Damn he looks good,* and *Maybe there was a better way for me to handle that relationship, but I'm damned if I know what it was.*

Later, I encountered my ex's behavior in a PUA blog post about "shit tests" in long-term relationships. Said post was written by Athol Kay, one of the smarter and less evil PUA bloggers I've discovered. Don't get me wrong: I'm often un-thrilled by how Athol Kay writes about women. However, he could be much worse, and he's written posts where he explicitly warns readers away from "the dark side of game." His wife sounds happy enough when she contributes her perspective to his blog. Kay's main topic is using the game to improve one's marriage. In my PUA Typology, I think he counts as Type 1: Analyst, but he also fits into the Leader and Shark categories, because he dispenses advice and sells products.

Athol Kay seems to believe that shit tests and compliance tests are basically the same thing. The post in question offers a list of such tests, but notes that sometimes they aren't "just" tests. Behold the relevant passages:

The Badly Inconveniencing You Request Test — *This is where she asks you to do something that would cost her little of her time, but costs you a lot of yours. So "can you pick up the girls from school today" when school is five minutes round trip from home on a work from home day for her, while you have to leave work early to get to the school on time. That's a big test. Just say no.*

The Badly Inconveniencing You Request Non Test — *This is when yes indeed this is going to screw your day, but if you don't help out she is going to be royally screwed. So today the kid is sick so someone has to stay home, but today she has that presentation thing and that meeting with her boss. So you save her with your best smile.*

Apparently, I should have just said no when my ex asked me to take that two-hour trip... a trip that would have cost him half an hour. Maybe that's true; I'm not sure myself. One might argue that when I walked into his frame, and took the two-hour trip, I allowed him to set the frame such that he could throw stupider tests at me in the future. But I was trying to show him that I was committed to making him feel loved.

Also:

The I'm Getting Emotional About This Test — *As soon as a woman finds out her tears are your Kryptonite you're in deep dodo. Don't respond to her drama and hysteria over minor things. Sometimes this is tied into her menstrual cycle, but typically the women that reach for this tool use it an awful lot. After a while the entire relationship gets run based on her minute to minute mood. She is unhappy about X so you must do something about X right now. Now she's unhappy about Y, why can't you fix Y? Z also displeases her. The more you cater to her the worse it gets until eventually she becomes the unhappiest woman in the world and you are near death from exhaustion.*

The I'm Getting Emotional About This Non Test — *This is when something really does happen that isn't trivial or minor and she's upset. Everyone has a crappy day once in a while, as long as she's not making a lifestyle of it, you should be standing in, standing up, or standing with her during these moments. The key here is not to try and bail her out of a bad situation and solve her problem for her, but to be present and available to her to aid in solving it herself. Sometimes you just gotta let them cry it out for a bit.* [7]

Menstrual cycle, eh? Fascinating. So, do you suppose my ex's emotional reaction to my blog was tied to his hormones? You know, I've read a lot about testosterone, and it *totally does* make men irrational and whiny....

Really, ladies, why do we allow those hysterical creatures to vote?

But seriously, folks, let's leave aside the fact that *people of all genders can be drama queens,* regardless of menstrual cycle (or whatever other sexist excuse is available). Let's talk instead about how I could have dealt with my ex.

Let's suppose I had taken the recommended PUA route. When my ex freaked out about a random blog post, and then refused to talk about it, then I could have treated his drama as a compliance test and ignored his emotional reaction. I could also have smacked him down verbally, or reframed the exchange with something hilarious and unexpected and cocky. And I'm pretty sure that this strategy could have "worked." And by "worked," I mean I could have kept the relationship going. I could even have gotten him into bed.

But acting that way would have required me to not care about his emotions. Or, at the very least, it would have required me to *not communicate about his emotions.* It would have meant creating a frame where I treated his emotions like they were irrelevant. Why would I want a relationship with someone, if I have to ignore his emotions for the relationship to function?

I think that describing my ex's behavior in terms of "compliance tests" is kinda... accurate. However, it seems to me that any mutual, egalitarian relationship requires both partners to occasionally accede to each other's compliance tests. Such a relationship also requires both parties to have a sense of proportion about the compliance tests they give. That's the difference between thinking in terms of "merging frames" or "sharing frames," rather than "frame control."

Plus, I think there was more to my ex's behavior than "testing." Most PUAs claim that "shit tests" (sometimes including compliance tests) arise from women looking for a dominant partner; they claim that she's "testing for dominance." I don't pretend to understand all women, so maybe this is actually true for some. But the more I examine what PUAs often call "shit tests," the more I think that a lot of so-called shit tests arise from confusion, or not knowing what to do, or genuine frustration, or insecurity.

Among PUAs and in PUA discussions, you'll occasionally find women who say that they recognize "tests for dominance" in their own behavior. These women claim that they're testing men for dominance all the time. Maybe that's true for them. Again, I don't pretend that I can speak for all women. (And again, I'll admit that I love strategic ambiguity and adversarial flirtation.) But maybe, sometimes, it's easier to believe that you're purposefully testing a man than it is to believe that you're scared, or insecure, or don't know yourself, or don't know how to ask for what you want.

* * *

I reckon that, like so many other social tactics, there are good and bad versions of compliance tests. For example, if a woman who goes to bars and gets men to buy her drinks, and then ignores those men, then she's issuing bad compliance tests. She has no respect for the men, and she doesn't want a conversation; she only wants the drinks. (Yes, some women do this. It's not okay.) Another example might be a woman who asks her boyfriend to buy her something expensive, not because she actually wants it, but because she wants to show that she can make him buy her things.

In other words: a negative compliance test is given by a person who has little or no respect for the target. A negative compliance test is done entirely to gain power, to set the frame that the target fulfills such tests on command, or to gain some benefit that has little to do with a mutual relationship. (I can see these kinds of power-seeking tests being an S&M-

ish headgame, but I would hope that all parties would be aware and okay with the fact that it's a headgame. Did you know that some submissive men have an actual fetish for handing cash to random women who are very rude to them, and give them nothing in return? Now you do. Some guys are really into "high-maintenance" women.)

On the other hand, positive compliance tests are issued by a person who actually cares about their target and wants a relationship... or who genuinely needs help. She may be trying to set the frame such that the two of them help each other when it's important. So for example, if a woman is genuinely having trouble trying to get something out of her purse while holding a drink, then if she asks for help, that's a positive compliance test. In that case, if a PUA takes her drink and downs the whole thing, then it might be funny, but it's also unnecessary. And if she asks for something more important, and he refuses, then he's actively being an asshole. An example would be Athol Kay's "Badly Inconveniencing You Request *Non* Test" above: that's a positive compliance test.

PUAs recognize that a person who is 100% reliable is often a predictable and boring person. Strategic ambiguity: most humans like *some* novelty and unpredictability and challenge. A partner who often ignores or reframes compliance tests will be full of surprises, and frequently entertaining, and probably seductive for those reasons.

Plus, a partner who often ignores or reframes compliance tests is probably showing confidence. After all, if he doesn't cave to your compliance tests easily, then he probably won't cave to bad compliance tests easily... from anyone. If he doesn't cave to compliance tests easily, then he might be seen as having good boundaries and personal integrity.

In short, a person who wants to appear fun and independent might choose to ignore and reframe a lot of compliance tests. But a person who wants to appear trustworthy might choose not to do that. So if you want to appear trustworthy, yet fun and independent, then you need a middle path between "helping out whenever someone has a request" and "ignoring or reframing all compliance tests."

Also, for a person who is uncertain about how to strike the middle path, then it could be argued that the powerful option is to err on the side of ignoring and reframing. If a person concedes too many compliance tests, then they'll definitely be seen as "too nice" or a pushover. Yet if a person ignores and reframes too many compliance tests, then they may be seen as an asshole... but at least they'll be seen as a confident and independent asshole. So in other words, if you're looking for power and you come across something that looks like a compliance test, then the safe option is to ignore and reframe, rather than being friendly and helpful.

But I also think that once you get to the point of reading all interactions in terms of *power* rather than *sharing,* you'll be in a very sad place. Er, I mean that *if* you get to that point, you'll be in a sad place. Not once. If. More on this later.

* * *

In the midst of all this, I met Adam at an activist event in San Francisco. I was hanging out with a group of friends when he walked up, and one of them said, "Ah, Clarisse, I've been meaning to introduce you to Adam."

Adam and I didn't chat long because I was on my way out. But between the social proof from my friend and talking about some projects he'd worked on, Adam quickly demonstrated that he was interesting and worth making friends with... maybe dating. Plus, he had long hair.

(PUAs would refer to Adam's apparent coolness as his "Demonstrations of Higher Value." For example: since I'm an activist chick, Adam Demonstrated Higher Value by showing that he'd worked on awesome activist projects. Typical dude DHVs would include talking about one's job or car. PUAs would also refer to the way we met as "Social Circle Game." Predictably, some PUAs take these things too far. They brag, make up accomplishments, and run themselves ragged maintaining a presence in an inhuman number of social circles. But other PUAs simply get good at making friends and doing cool things. Actually, Social Circle Game is how I meet almost all my partners. It's probably how you meet your partners, too.)

Here's how I gave Adam my email address: I was in a rush and didn't want to bother marking it down. So I told him to get it from a mutual friend. Arguably, I gave Adam a little tiny compliance test.

Adam could have reframed my test and expressed dominance by simply handing me his phone as I spoke, and telling me to enter my contact information.

Or here's another hypothesis: Adam *passed* my compliance test by playing by the arbitrary rule I'd set. By getting the info later from our friend, he showed that he was chill and cooperative. He showed that he liked me enough to deal with a mild inconvenience.

Or... I wasn't testing, I just wanted to get out of there.

Remember how I mentioned in Chapter 2 that PUAs often discuss two types of game: "direct game," and "indirect game"? Direct game involves being very straightforward about one's sexual intentions. Indirect game involves lots of beating around the bush (heh). This is a frequently-discussed philosophical distinction in the community. Of course, the reality is that everyone uses some of both, although most guys tend towards one or the other.

There's another philosophical distinction that can be useful, too: "natural game" vs. "synthetic game." Some guys are instinctively good at the game, and PUAs refer to those guys as "naturals." But the difference between natural game and synthetic game is also one of approach. It's like the difference between improv theatre, and scripted theatre. It's like the difference between musicians doing a jam session, and playing a pre-written piece. It's like the difference between a basketball player running a set piece, and a basketball player just running out onto the court and using his skills. (That last metaphor came from a guy friend. I don't know anything about sports.)

When a PUA uses synthetic game, he'll learn openers and routines; he'll study lists of shit tests and memorize responses to them. When a PUA uses natural game, he'll try to understand the underlying principles of social interaction, like by learning frame theory, or learning to identify shit tests on his own. Of course, once again, the reality is that everyone uses some of both, including "normal people." For example, most human beings use routines known as "anecdotes," whereby they retell stories from their actual lives so often that it becomes practically scripted.

Part of learning PUA theory meant slotting my own behavior into their frameworks. To understand what they were talking about, I had to learn to see the world in their terms. This included examining my own behavior.

How much of what I did was small unconscious manipulations: maneuvers that a PUA might call my "natural game"? I've always been theoretical about relationships, but was I starting to get ridiculously Machiavellian about them? Was I playing the game, or was I doing things for neutral, non-game reasons? There's an old saying that comes up often in PUA critiques: "When all you have is a hammer, everything looks like a nail."

I couldn't tell. As I walked out of the activist event where I met Adam, the thought that I'd just compliance-tested him crossed my mind. Then I thought: *Really?*

I really couldn't tell.

* * *

One of the major ways PUAs share information is by writing Field Reports that discuss their experiences. These Field Reports can be meticulously detailed, boringly long, self-indulgent, and somewhat voyeuristic. The same applies to the typical lady practice of discussing our relationships with each other. I have done my best to write about my relationships in a way that makes it clear, at every step, why I am telling you these things. I try to make it obvious what meaning I find in my experiences, and what theories I am illustrating. But I know that according to some tastes, I will still occasionally end up being overly detailed, long, boring, and voyeuristic. As Neil Strauss says, "I beg you for your forgiveness in advance."

I confess: I felt satisfied that I was so busy, Adam and I had trouble scheduling dinner. He had to contact me multiple times, and at one point he said, "That's what I get for not booking your time sooner." I didn't do this on purpose, but it *is* what *The Rules* say to do: if he wants to see you on a Saturday, he better get in touch before Wednesday, because otherwise you tell him you're busy whether it's true or not. If you're a Rules Girl, that is. Which I'm not. I'm genuinely busy.

Besides, I reckon showing that I'm busy is a Demonstration of Higher Value, not a Rule.

After we finally met for dinner, we hung out for several hours afterwards, first in a park and then at a bar. (A PUA might call these venue changes over a short period "time dilation." The idea is that you can make it feel like you've spent more time together than you actually have, if you switch environments a lot.)

I liked Adam. He was smart and unassuming and nerdy, an excellent conversationalist, had an ironic sense of humor, had done some interesting activism, read lots of science fiction, *and* his feminist politics were rock-solid. You know what's even hotter than a man who intelligently uses "heteronormative" in a sentence? A man who can use both "heteronormative" *and* "cisgendered."

I gave Adam fairly obvious Indicators of Interest, and he returned them. He'd dropped references to S&M, and I knew he'd read some of my S&M writing. Adam also dropped references to a lady friend... but he seemed familiar with polyamory. It didn't sound like he knew as much about polyamory as I did, but I figured that he might be experimenting with it.

As the hour got later, I debated with myself whether I should go out to my favorite club night, or make a move. I mentally reviewed the evening and decided I needed more information.

"I'm thinking I might go out to a club," I said first, to cover my bases.

(Some PUAs might call this a "false time constraint." I usually use false time constraints because it gives me a graceful way out if I need one. It also encourages my partner to make his move, if he plans to. PUAs often frame them differently, though: false time constraints are used to mask his intentions of picking her up. They may also make the PUA seem like a challenge, like he's "in high demand." In some cases this seems fine. I mean, if a guy chats me up in a bar while pretending he's only got five minutes... well, whatever. But some PUAs promote false time constraints as a way to get a woman alone when she doesn't want to have sex. In that case, the PUA says something like, "We're not having sex tonight because I have to be somewhere in 15 minutes," and she'll feel safe going with him *because she thinks he won't put the moves on her.* And then he puts the moves on her. Which is creepy. You can see this in the classic movie *Groundhog Day,* where the tactic ultimately fails and the female target slaps Bill Murray across the face. I obviously feel fine about false time constraints when they're used as an escape hatch or as light flirtation, but using them to get a reluctant partner alone is sketchy as hell.)

So anyway, since I'd established that I might leave soon, I added: "You mentioned being involved with someone. What's up with that?"

Turned out, Adam didn't have other established relationships to check in on. If he had, then I would have asked about those other partners and what their boundaries were. It's common for open relationships to involve restrictions, like for example: "we can make out with other people as long as we don't have oral sex or intercourse."

Next I said, "You also mentioned S&M. What kind of experience do you have with that?"

"Mostly playful," Adam said. "Nothing really intense." I waited for him to add more, but he was done.

That was his whole answer? He hadn't even told me whether he was dominant, submissive, sadistic, masochistic.... I sighed internally. This is always the risk of hooking up with guys outside the S&M community. To me, Adam's answer sounded like code for something light. Maybe something like: "My partners and I have tied each other up with silk scarves and tickled each other with feathers." Not that there's anything wrong with that, but it's not what I'm into.

It also sounded like Adam might not have the experience to enable a more elaborate conversation: an explicit talk about sensations and desires and boundaries.

Vanilla sex can be fun, I consoled myself. *And sometimes people surprise me.*

I thought about it and looked at him: Adam was attentive, but seemed relaxed. I got the feeling that he really would be cool with things no matter what, which is always attractive. I knew he lived nearby. (Tacticians take note. Always schedule the date near a venue for sex.)

"Why don't you show me your apartment," I said, "before I go out." Worst came to worst, I had the nightclub escape hatch.

Turned out, I didn't need it.

Like I said: sometimes people surprise me. Once we ended up in Adam's apartment, we talked briefly, and then he kissed me, and then he bit my shoulder. The bite was gentle by my standards, but hard by vanilla standards. At which point I thought, *That's interesting... and he seems like a good communicator, let's try it,* so I moved into a typical S&M communication frame. We talked for 5 minutes about my biting preferences, and then Adam went for it.

And he was incredible.

We were into S&M headgames within minutes. S&M can be reduced to the whips and chains, the physical pain and pleasure. For a lot of people, that's all they want. For some of us, though, there's a big head-trip element to S&M.

Some folks enjoy being called terrible names. Others enjoy role-play situations like rape, slavery, or interrogation fantasies. One of my favorite S&M phrases is "predicament bondage": in a predicament scenario, the goal is to create a situation where the submissive partner "can't win." For example, I've heard about a game in which the submissive partner stands next to a wall, and holds two coins against the wall — one in each hand. The dominant then hurts the submissive in ways that make it hard for the submissive to continue holding the coins. If the submissive drops the coins, then the feeling of failure will be painful, and there may be a painful physical punishment as well. But if the submissive continues holding the coins, then the current administration of physical pain continues.

I don't always like taking orders from my S&M partners. It depends on the person and the energy. But some guys can get me into that headspace really fast. And once I'm there, sometimes I can't obey certain orders, no matter how hard I try. My partner may order me not to move, for example, when I can't help moving. If I were in the above scenario with the coins, I'm not confident that I wouldn't drop them.

It's a scary feeling, especially if I love him, because then all the emotions are multiplied. But even if I'm not in love... as long as he's got me in the right mental space, then if I fail, I will say "I'm sorry" over and over. I'll be terrified of his anger. I'll feel like I deserve punishment, and if he doesn't keep hurting me I'll feel abandoned.

The more I fail, the more it hurts — more than physical pain ever could. Slamming up against my own limits makes me feel terribly inadequate. It's intense and compelling, but it's dangerous; it can rip me apart. At times like that, I often need my partner to tell me after we're done: "I still like you and think you're a good person."

And sometimes I need to hear that especially if I safeword out of the encounter, because sometimes — not always, but sometimes — calling my safeword can feel like the worst failure of all.

Adam had a knack for this type of strategic ambiguity. His sensitivity was extraordinary... or maybe we had good chemistry. "You told me you'd done *nothing intense!"* I said, when I had a chance to catch my breath. "You are *not* an amateur."

He seemed equally dazed. "I've never done anything like this before," he insisted. "Similar things, and I've watched some S&M porn, but not like *this."*

Adam needed a lot of breaks to deal with what was going on, and I had to give him careful feedback. I defined some S&M terms for him; I tried to explain how everything felt for me; I offered basic advice. I reassured him that feeling weird about S&M is completely normal. I warned him that he might require extensive processing. It was a kind of basic step-by-step guidance that can sometimes be frustrating, but with him, the time flew.

Rules Girls aren't supposed to go beyond casual kissing on the first date. Good thing I'm not a Rules Girl.

I shelved my own processing during the encounter, but after we'd finished and split up and I had time to think, I realized my emotions were a mess. I was able to pull myself together (mostly), but I could barely keep track of how fast Adam had gone from "interesting guy" to "guy I like" to "guy I like so much it scares me."

* * *

The first thing I did was find our mutual friend.

"I need to know *everything you know about Adam,"* I said.

Our friend laughed. "What happened?"

"Nothing," I said. "I mean, we went on a date. I mean... just tell me everything you know, okay?"

I grilled him for half an hour. It was a positive report, with one exception: one of Adam's exes said he gave a lot of mixed signals. I filed this away for consideration, but didn't take it seriously yet.

The second thing I did was try to take a thorough inventory of my feelings. I reminded myself that I hadn't experienced such an intense S&M encounter for over a year: *of course* I was going to feel wild. I knew that if I'd learned anything from my previous relationships, it was that I should give myself time to calm down.

Plus, I was trying to compensate for New Relationship Energy. This term originated in the polyamory community, but PUAs use it too. New Relationship Energy is exactly what it sounds like: the high you get when you've just gotten involved with someone you really like, during which you are apt to be obsessive and irrational about that person.

I felt euphoric and ridiculous. I rode the wave, and reminded myself that I barely knew him.

The third thing I did was follow up with Adam. In the S&M community, "aftercare" is an important expectation: emotional processing after the encounter. A lot of aftercare involves helping your partner calm down immediately after you're done, but some people include morning-after phone calls under the heading of "aftercare." Personally, I felt an extra obligation to follow up with Adam because he was inexperienced.

I had to fight my feelings as I thought about following up, though. Part of me was dying to talk to Adam, and part of me wanted to stay away until I got a grip. I barely knew him, and I wasn't sure I could trust him.

Since then, I've concluded that it would be wise for me to avoid S&M before I know someone well enough to trust them. This is less out of concern for my physical safety, and more out of concern for my emotional safety: S&M can have such a powerful effect on me that it can be very hard for me to be reasonable about that person, and that's not good with a brand-new partner. Back then, though, I wasn't nearly as careful about it.

So the day after we had dinner, I sent Adam a short email thanking him for my spectacular mood. I told him that I knew this stuff was new to him, and that I could meet to talk about it if he needed to. Adam's reply thanked me back, said he was "AOK" and that he would see me at our date next week.

I observed my own reaction to his response: I felt a mix of relief and disappointment. How much had I been offering aftercare, and how much had I been measuring his emotional escalation potential? That seemed to be part of my motivation, I realized. If Adam had wanted to see me again right away, then I would have known that he was both into me and easy to escalate.

His reply looked similar to the emails I usually sent new guys: a tone of "that was fun, see you soon." A PUA might call it "managing expectations." He didn't want me to get the wrong idea, and was keeping his distance.

What if Adam had emailed me first, implying that he wanted to see me right away? I thought about it. Normally I'd keep my distance, but with this guy? I wasn't sure.

I wasn't sure. Which meant I already ran the risk of being way more into him than he was into me. Scarily, un-strategically into him.

On the one hand, I had a plane ticket out of San Francisco scheduled in a few weeks. Because Adam didn't live in Chicago, he wasn't going to be a super-major relationship no matter what.

On the other hand....

Be careful, I thought to myself. *Be careful, careful, careful.*

In yet another corner of my mind, I hoped Adam was wise enough to talk to someone else about S&M. If he was trying to avoid showing emotional escalation potential, then it might be a good idea not to see me... but he probably needed S&M processing.

* * *

Adam's need for better S&M processing became obvious when he canceled our third date. We'd had a decent second date, not as intense as the first, and when I texted to finalize our third meeting, he suggested that we only meet for drinks and catch up. I sucked in my breath, sighed with regret, and measured how stung I felt: I didn't want to see him again if I was going to feel like I had to prove something the whole time.

Also, if his goal was to turn this into a tacit we're-sleeping-together-but-pretending-that's-not-what-we're-doing arrangement, then I wanted nothing to do with it.

I decided I wasn't too stung. If I saw him, then I didn't think I'd feel desperate to prove anything. But I still felt wary of Adam's intentions. So I texted back that I was open to getting drinks, but that I wanted to understand his motives better before doing so.

I wasn't thinking in PUA terms at the time, but this is a perfect illustration of frame control. Basically, I was afraid that Adam was trying to make the framework of our relationship into one where we were sleeping together, but weren't admitting that was going on. (In mainstream terminology, this arrangement might be called "fuckbuddies.") Instinctively, I wasn't cool with that. And so I made it clear to Adam that I wouldn't see him unless we were either explicitly sleeping together... or explicitly *not* sleeping together.

One thing I concluded towards the end of my PUA research is that most people have an instinct for some actual patterns and strategies that PUAs have pointed out. But when people don't have an explicit vocabulary or framework for those strategies and patterns, then a lot of the time, those instincts manifest as discomfort and confusion... or drama.

After I texted him, I asked Adam to respond by email or text rather than a phone call, and his answer arrived that afternoon:

So my text was not really well-considered. ... I'm just feeling intimidated and uncertain about our kinkiness. On one hand I've been feeling "aaa this is weird, run away". But I'm also feeling like this is fun and new and hot and fascinating, and I should get over my bs and try it again. So if you can forgive my impulsive text and my erratic emotions.... I'm free on your free nights this week.

And if I've spooked you or your schedule has filled up, then I would be disappointed... but I'd understand. Sorry about the drama. I'm usually drama-free, I swear.

"Usually drama-free." *Are you?* I thought.

I'm not convinced that anyone in the world is genuinely "drama-free." The real question is, how do they deal with drama when it comes up?

People who are new to intense S&M typically have a lot of thinking to do, and some freaking out to do. It wasn't Adam's fault, it was the fault of social stigma. I felt a lot of sympathy. Exploring S&M isn't always a fun wild ride. It can also be an exciting journey through the fucked-up attitudes most people internalize about sex and power.

Unless Adam was using the S&M thing to cover up an attempt to create a tacit we're-sleeping-together-but-pretending-that's-not-what-we're-doing arrangement. Unless he'd been throwing up a barrier to check me for weakness. Unless he was testing to see how socially dominant I was.... He might not even be aware that he was doing these things; he might just have natural game.

Was I running up against Adam's Anti-Relationship Defense? Had I just dominated an emotional escalation shit test? Were we basically jockeying for power in the relationship?

Stop being paranoid. Take him at his word, I scolded myself.

Adam wasn't flawless, and if I wanted to concentrate on his flaws, I could convince myself to cut bait now. But there were limits to how cautious I wanted to be with someone I liked so much.

* * *

The third date was great. My favorite part was when Adam made a joke about "a natural 20." This is a *Dungeons and Dragons* reference. Yes, I am that much of a nerd.

Or maybe my favorite part was the conversation we had about words used in S&M encounters. "I guess a lot of straight male doms use the word 'slut' when they feel dominant," Adam said reflectively, "but it usually makes me feel submissive. I think it's because out in the real world, men usually call women sluts when men feel powerless."

Combining S&M analysis with feminist sensibilities? Baby, you had me at hello.

I noticed we were both gently ensuring that the other person didn't anticipate too much contact: managing each other's expectations. We both knew I was heading out, and it was clear neither of us wanted to keep closely in touch. When we bid each other farewell in the morning, we confirmed that we'd see each other again sometime, and left it at that.

I was pleased and relieved: Adam seemed a lot more relaxed. I thought I, too, felt relaxed until I ran into him on the street the day before I left town.

It was Halloween. San Francisco was full of costumes and musicians and people out of their heads, like me. I'd been out dancing all night, I was quite intoxicated, and I was rampaging about the city with intoxicated friends. I insisted that we go trick-or-treating at the crumbling antique armory that houses the S&M porn company Kink.com, and I felt somewhat disappointed that we didn't get into the building. (The man who answered the door grinned and said, "Sorry, girls, I wish I had some candy for you. I really do.")

Adam passed us as we watched a street performance. We chatted for a few minutes, and he went on his way.

My friends liked him, and said so. I had an unreasonable moment of panic and over-analysis, and said so.

"How did that *go?*" I demanded of them.

"It went fine."

"This is the last time I'm going to see him for a while. I have to make sure he's got a positive final image of me," I insisted.

They reassured me.

"Oh my God, I'm freaking out just from running into him in the street," I said. "Okay. I know I'm kinda messed up right now, but I might be freaking out even if I were sober. Oh my God, what does this *mean?*"

One of my friends grabbed my hand. "It's okay, hon," she said. "Sometimes you just freak out about people. It doesn't mean you're in love with them."

* * *

***

CHAPTER 5:
He's A Ghost, He's A God, He's A Man, He's A Guru

In which Clarisse meets the uber-famous PUA guru Neil Strauss, author of The Game. *He turns out to be unexpectedly feminist-friendly, and as a result of his interview with Clarisse, he is attacked on the Internet by anti-feminist PUAs who can't decide whether he's an "ignorant fool or an opportunist liar." Plus: plenty of straight-up feminist theory, including the intersection of the feminist concepts "rape culture" and "enthusiastic consent" with both S&M and pickup artistry. The chapter title is from the song "Red Right Hand," by Nick Cave.*

***

    Neil Strauss, author of *The Game,* published a new book about celebrity interviews during my PUA research. His book tour took him through Chicago; I heard about it the day before his event. I was inspired to request an interview on behalf of *Time Out Chicago,* where I was employed as a freelance blogger. Neil's publicist agreed. (You can read the interview in its original form in Appendix D of this book.)
    Neil was scheduled to read aloud and answer questions at 7 PM Saturday at a local bookstore. I was slated to chat with him for about 15 minutes before the reading. Then Neil himself texted me and suggested that the interview take place *after* the reading, instead. I agreed immediately, of course, because I knew it would give me a lot more time.
    I also had pre-existing plans to meet a partner at an S&M party around 11.30 PM. I'll admit it: I thought about canceling those plans. But I didn't want to flake out at the last minute, and besides, it seemed so arrogant to think that *Neil Strauss* would want to hang out with me late into the night. Even though he'd sent the signal of rescheduling the interview for after his reading, I didn't want to read too much into that. I figured the interview would be over long before I was scheduled to see my partner.
    I don't usually do interviews, and I had certainly never interviewed someone so famous before. One factor I didn't reckon with was Neil's enormous, dedicated fan base. When I made it to the bookstore, the place was like a mosh pit. I literally couldn't get in the door, so I hovered at the

door-crack along with a number of nice young men, listening to Neil from afar. The crowd was at least 95% male, and they all looked extremely mainstream. The scent of excessive hair gel made me dizzy.

Notwithstanding the fact that Neil was there to promote a different book, most of the audience questions were about *The Game*. Many guys brought their copies of *The Game* to be autographed along with the new book.

Allow me to take this moment to rhapsodize about *The Game*. The book was powerfully recommended to me by a straight feminist dude friend, who insisted that it's so hilarious and absurd that I'd never get over it. He was right. The same friend later pointed out, "At heart, *The Game* is as much a critique of PUA culture as a chronicle of it." He was right about that, too.

The Game describes Neil Strauss's meteoric rise to fame and fortune at the side of Mystery, a famous PUA coach. Mystery comes off as a kind of mad genius; he eventually starred in VH1's reality show *The Pickup Artist*. Neil, who went by the name "Style" among PUAs, was a rock-and-roll writer who became obsessed with pickup artistry. He went on:

* to be voted the world's best PUA;
* to live in a Hollywood mansion rent-free for months, doing little besides chasing girls;
* to pick up Courtney Love, Britney Spears, and others;
* and to write a *New York Times* bestseller about the experience.

I could write a cultural studies treatise on *The Game's* layout. The book is bound in fake black leather, with gold-edged pages. The title is stamped in gold on the cover, along with gold-stamped silhouettes of hot chicks. Basically, this book belongs in a manly library that smells of tobacco and is lined with overstuffed brass-studded dark red armchairs.

But *that's not all!* Open the book and you're introduced to a whole new world of desperate manliness. Each chapter title is accompanied by a comic-style drawing of Neil, plus at least one stone fox. My personal favorite is the one that depicts Neil pulling himself out of a swimming pool with a hunting knife between his teeth; he's facing a woman's spread pair of legs, complete with glamorous high heels. Or maybe my favorite is the chapter called "Blast Last Minute Resistance," featuring Neil with a lady on one arm and a handgun pointed towards the reader. I am not making this up.

One of the first pages says in ginormous type, "THE FOLLOWING IS A TRUE STORY. It really happened. Men will deny it. Women will doubt it. But I present it to you here, naked, vulnerable, and disturbingly real. I beg you for your forgiveness in advance. Don't hate the player... hate the game."

A male friend of mine says that "Don't hate the player, hate the game" is directly quoted from an Ice-T song about dealing drugs in the 'hood. My friend adds: "I should note that I'm *not* endorsing Ice-T's clear misogyny and lack of reflectivity, but I *do* think that he's voicing a lot of things that men are actually thinking." I wouldn't know about that.

I do know, however, that *The Game* is widely criticized by experienced PUAs. Some of them say things like, "That whole book is made up." Neil insists that it's all true, but that he uses writerly tactics to disguise some characters because their real-life analogues didn't want to be in the book. (Incidentally, the same is true of this thing you're reading right now.)

Other PUAs claim that Neil's characterizations of some PUAs are unfair. And others call him Neil $trau$$; they criticize him as a relentless self-promoter. When I met Neil in Chicago, he seemed low-key and authentic, but I suppose that's just what he'd *want* me to think, right?

What's really amazing about *The Game* is the critique. Neil uses the freeze-out, and some other tactics that make me shiver. Nevertheless, he generally comes across as a decent, shy guy who wants to make sense of the ridiculous world around him. And there are aspects of pickup artistry that Neil is clearly ambivalent about. In fact, by the end of the book, epic betrayals litter the landscape. Mystery has multiple emotional breakdowns... well, I won't ruin it for you, but it's a wild ride.

During Neil's reading in Chicago, he was incredibly gracious to everyone. It was lovely to watch. And his awesome sparkly purple tie was *very* lovely to watch. By the time he was done signing everyone's books, it was already 10.45. So I texted my dungeon partner, and I told him that I would be really late because of an interview. He texted back that I shouldn't worry and should take my time.

The interview ended up happening in a Mexican restaurant, surrounded by about 20 of Neil's fans, as well as some of his family members. It was quite an environment, and Neil had to manage a lot of interactions, but he stayed friendly to everyone. I couldn't help liking him. He seemed to have authentic humility.

If he negged me, I didn't notice.

It would have been easy to critique everything Neil said... and, when I published the interview, many feminists did. [1] Still, while many of Neil's words could use more analysis, I was more interested in the positive things he said about feminism.

Smart PUAs usually find common ground with feminism, although the *way* they find it can be very different for different PUAs. For example, the feminist movement and other factors have liberated women to explore our sexuality more than most women have historically been able to. Obviously, this is great for straight dudes who want lots of sex.

Misogynist, Darth Vader-esque PUAs will acknowledge this and stop there. They talk about how awesome it is that women are "easier" in more feminist societies, then they'll go right on to denigrate women's intelligence. They'll complain about women who have too many independent ideas, or women who have jobs, or women with the audacity to vote. (We're *such* bitches, aren't we?)

Less misogynist PUAs usually have more nuanced and surprising views. For instance, during my interview with him, Neil Strauss outright stated that "we still are a patriarchal society; men are dominant," which is an admission most PUAs can't handle. (They're too busy claiming that all women want is control.) He even said that men who hate feminism "are scared of powerful women."

If you read *The Game* carefully, you can spot Neil's feminist sympathies from the start. For example, on page 227 he talks about how getting obsessed with pickup artistry was leading him to ignore his career and non-PUA friends. He writes, "All the sarging was beginning to scramble my brain.... In the process of dehumanizing the opposite sex, I had also been dehumanizing myself."

More strikingly, each chapter of The Game begins with a quotation from a famous feminist. The selection for Chapter 1 is from Betty Friedan's 1960 classic, *The Feminine Mystique:* "Men weren't really the enemy — they were fellow victims suffering from an outmoded masculine mystique that made them feel unnecessarily inadequate when there were no bears to kill."

When I first read *The Game* and saw that Strauss had included those quotations, I immediately started laughing. I thought he was being ironic. Yet as I read further, I saw that the quotations were very well-chosen, and I had to admit he'd done some serious feminist reading. Then, when I interviewed him in person, Neil seemed far from ironic. I asked him about the feminist bits, and he said:

I felt like the main problem with the book, as I was putting it together, was that it needed more female characters. I couldn't invent another female character because there weren't any women giving advice in the community. So I thought, why don't I put in a female voice through these quotes.

This seems completely reasonable to me. I confess, however, that I had trouble containing my reaction when Neil compared *The Game* to a classic 1950s pre-feminist tome: *The Second Sex,* by Simone de Beauvoir.

There's a lot to *The Second Sex,* but the main idea is that in Western culture, history is framed around male heroes; most powerful politicians are male; and most media has been made by men. In such a society, men and men's typical desires have generally been considered "normal" and "ideal." And if men — and men's typical desires — are seen as normal and ideal, then women will feel and be treated like we're "abnormal" or second-class citizens. The truth is merely that, in many ways, women are different from men. We're not worse (or better), we're just different.

After he compared *The Game* to *The Second Sex,* Neil Strauss went on to say:

On some levels male sexuality is everywhere in society, but on the other hand it's completely repressed: men are afraid to show it because it will make them socially unacceptable as well as less sexually desirable. I wanted to write something that was honest about male sexuality, not like "Maxim" magazine or the billboards. The Second Sex *is obviously a different book and much more philosophical than* The Game, *but my goal really was to do something like that.*

It definitely took me a while to digest this analysis. It's a very unusual comparison. But the bottom line here is that Neil Strauss *intentionally took some cues from feminism.* (That, or he went to an awful lot of effort to make it seem like he did.)

After I published my interview with Neil, a lot of feminists got angry about his words. They missed the fact that, from a PUA perspective, Neil Strauss is *way on our side.* Anti-feminists sure didn't miss it, though. Anti-feminist sites, including some PUA writers, quickly launched enraged attacks... up to and including misogynist insults like "mangina." Yes indeed, they called *Neil Strauss* a mangina. I don't even know where to start with that one.

Really though, here's the best quotation:

Whether Strauss is an ignorant fool or an opportunist liar who wants to appease feminists in order to avoid negative feedback is anyone's guess, but if his words are anything to go by, we can safely assume that the best-known public advocates of Game are perfectly OK with parroting feminist dogma. [2]

I'm tempted to laugh hysterically at the thought that anyone would claim Neil Strauss "parrots feminist dogma." But there are a couple of useful points buried in that weirdness. Here's the first: it's easier for some people to believe that famous PUAs are "opportunist liars" or "ignorant fools"... than it is for those people to believe that *anyone* who looks carefully at gender dynamics *will inevitably conclude that feminists say important things.* Some PUAs feel such anger at women and feminism that they'll throw out their own gurus for the slightest association with us.

The second important point is this. Consider how Neil Strauss, one of the most famous PUAs in the world, was viciously derided for saying slightly-feminist things. Now imagine what would happen to a PUA with less cred, who did the same thing. And then you understand why many PUAs might feel anxious about discussing feminism in a positive way, or why they might be outright unwilling to do it.

When feminists discussed my Neil Strauss interview, one feminist commented: "Clarisse, I don't understand why you're not more critical of this guy." This, my friends, is why: because Neil took a huge step by supporting feminism *at all* in a public interview.

But how compatible are PUA tactics and attitudes with feminism, *really?* Even if some PUAs are smart and analytical and interested in gender liberation... can there ever be such a thing as a feminist PUA? To discuss this further, I'm going to have to describe some important feminist concepts; I'm sure you can grasp them, even if you're a PUA.

(Read my last sentence again. Pop quiz: did I shit test my PUA readers, or neg them?)

Although people are currently enabled to explore our sexuality in ways that would have been unthinkable a hundred years ago, there remain serious problems with how our society thinks about sexuality. As the male, heterosexual, feminist lawyer Thomas MacAulay Millar writes in his brilliant essay, "Towards A Performance Model Of Sex":

We live in a culture where sex is not so much an act as a thing: a substance that can be given, bought, sold, or stolen, that has a value and a supply-and-demand curve. In this "commodity model," sex is like a ticket; women have it and men try to get it. Women may give it away or may trade it for something valuable, but either way it's a transaction. This puts women in the position of not only seller, but also guardian or gatekeeper.... Women are guardians of the tickets; men apply for access to them. This model pervades casual conversation about sex: women "give it up," men "get some." [3]

In my Sex-Positive Feminist 101, which I included as Appendix B in this book, I write that:

Women are expected to trade sex to men in exchange for support or romance. Women who don't get a "good trade" (e.g. women who don't receive a certain level of financial support or romance "in exchange for" sex) are seen as sluts. Men who don't get a "good trade" (e.g. men who don't receive a certain amount of sex "in exchange for" a relationship) are seen as pussies. (Yes, "pussies"... don't you just love that a word for female genitalia is a commonly used insult against so-called "weak" men?)

I could rant all day about how much I hate the "commodity model."

For example, it makes some people feel that women who have been raped have "lost value." The commodity model is also one factor instructing people to "save" our sexuality, as if sex isn't something that gets better with experience.

The commodity model makes it harder for men and women to negotiate a mutually pleasurable sexual encounter. When women are pressured to feel like we "trade" sex for affection or love or commitment or support... or when men are pressured to think of sex as a thing that they get, rather than a mutual experience to enjoy... then it becomes hard to ask for pleasure, or to explore our desires in an open-ended way.

The commodity model also feeds into what feminists describe as "rape culture." Another male, heterosexual feminist who goes by the Internet name Ampersand has defined rape culture thus:

A culture in which rape is prevalent and is maintained through fundamental attitudes and beliefs about gender, sexuality, and violence. [4]

I'm citing male heterosexual feminists, rather than feminists of other genders, partly because I want to show that straight feminist dudes exist. It seems appropriate in a book about PUAs.

One way of thinking about this is that rape culture is *a culture that often excuses or disguises rape.* For one thing, most sexual assaults are never reported to the police, because there are so many excuses and community pressures around rape. [5] (And by the way, men comprise an estimated 10% of rape survivors, although statistics are hard to be sure of with such a crime. Some people argue that men are less likely to report being assaulted than women because of unrealistic cultural standards around manliness. [6])

Different feminists approach the "rape culture" framework in very different ways, and reasonable feminists can disagree about what exactly constitutes rape culture. For example, some feminists feel that because S&M involves sexual power dynamics (and sometimes includes rape fantasies), S&M is therefore a facet of rape culture. Other feminists argue that S&M actually *subverts* rape culture by attempting to describe sexual power dynamics. S&M puts those dynamics out in the open, especially when S&M acts are clearly negotiated and discussed ahead of time by the people involved. You can guess which camp I fall into.

Nevertheless, here are some ideas that many feminists agree are wrapped up in rape culture:

RAPE CULTURE IDEA #1: *Rape myths.* Rape myths are cultural memes that make it harder to recognize, prosecute, and heal from rape. For example, many people believe that sexual assault usually occurs between strangers. However, by most estimates, 66% - 90% of sexual assaults are committed by someone the victim knows. Many people believe that rape usually happens to young, "hot" women. However, interviews with rapists show that they usually prioritize targets based on how vulnerable they are, rather than how "hot" they are.

RAPE CULTURE IDEA #2: *The commodity model.* If sex is seen as an exchange, then sometimes people are seen as "owing" other people sex. If a couple is married, then they're "supposed" to be having sex; they "owe it" to each other. If a guy pays for enough dates with a girl, or offers enough emotional support, then a lot of guys feel like eventually she's "supposed to" have sex with him. This can lead to people having sex they don't really like, because they feel like they should... or it can lead to people being pressured (or raped) by partners who think they're "entitled" to sex.

RAPE CULTURE IDEA #3: *Blaming the victim.* If a person is raped, many people assume that the victim created the situation. Rape culture includes telling a woman that because she wore a short skirt, it's "her own fault" she was raped. Other reasons people might consider it to be "her own fault" that she got raped might include "because she was out after dark" or perhaps "because she got drunk." Often, the same people who obsessively analyze the behavior of the person who was raped will ignore the fact that somebody else *chose to commit rape.* In short, blaming the victim means talking more about the behavior of a rape survivor than about the real problem: the behavior of the rapist.

RAPE CULTURE IDEA #4: *Adversarial gender roles.* Men and women are viewed as fundamentally opposed. There are plenty of cultural attitudes about how men and women are deeply, inherently different ("men are from Mars, women are from Venus"). There are also plenty of cultural attitudes about how men and women are out to take advantage of each other. Men hate marriage, right? And women are marriage-obsessed gold-diggers, right? Plus, women hate sex and men are sex-obsessed satyrs, right? Well, wrong. The truth is that everyone is different, and that many individual men and women have more in common with *each other* than with stereotypes of their gender. If people saw cross-gender relationships as more mutual than oppositional, then people would expect sex to be more mutual than oppositional. Instead, most people expect aggression and trickery to be part of sexuality... and it's a very short jump from aggression and trickery to coercion and rape.

PUAs rarely use feminist words. In fact, PUAs are rarely aware of feminist words. I have literally never met a PUA who accepts the overarching feminist idea of rape culture.

Yet in many ways, PUAs deal frequently with the rape culture concepts I outlined above. For example, PUAs have their own problems with the commodity model, because they don't like the idea that a guy should have to offer something, whether it's financial support or a relationship, in exchange for sex. Many PUA tactics implicitly question the commodity model, like the way they discourage buying drinks for women. I even spoke to one PUA who chooses to own a shitty car and live in an apartment that's less expensive than he can afford, *because he doesn't want women judging him for his money.*

On the other hand, most PUAs fail to consider other ways the commodity model affects their own thinking. Sometimes PUAs even come off as cheerleaders for the commodity model. Here's another quotation from Millar's "Towards a Performance Model of Sex":

Buying into the commodity model also means buying into its internal valuation method: that value derives from scarcity, so that any woman who expresses her sexuality by actually having sex partners is devalued. One [PUA on a PUA forum] wrote:

"Recently, as soon as I hook up with a girl, I start to resent her, because it was SO easy to seduce her. My skills have gotten pretty good, and I've seduced two girls this past week, and immediately after it happened, I wasn't attracted to them anymore. I feel like, how can she be a high-value female if she was THAT easy to get in to bed."

A forum moderator responded, "Too bad she's still a depreciating and often damaged asset."

These men openly adopt the commodity model... because a better world is not in their perceived self-interest.

This may match something another PUA told me in the field. He explained that he'd gotten good at snaring women, but he had trouble dating them long-term because: "After a while, with every girl, I'll be in bed with her, and I'll suddenly start thinking that she's a whore. And then I have to dump her."

A Vader-type PUA blogger writes that:

My default opinion of any girl I meet is "worthless dirty whore until proven otherwise." When so many girls have opened their legs up for me so quickly and easily, it's hard for me to respect them (and their opinions or ideas) like I would a family member or close friend. [7]

Calling women "worthless" and treating them with disrespect just because they've had sex *only makes sense if sex is seen as "decreasing a woman's value."* (And by the way, why is "whore" such an insult? What's immoral about consensual sex work? But this is a whole nother topic....)

Then there's blaming the victim. This is interesting, because most PUAs are prone to claiming that they're in charge of a given interaction. If something goes wrong, it's usually viewed as *the PUA's failure to "run the game" properly.* So you might think PUAs wouldn't be prone to blaming the victim.

However, one aspect of the PUA framework consistently sounds like blaming the victim. This is the common PUA insistence that women are always illogical and unreliable, and that we can never be trusted to know what we want. One popular PUA line: "You can't change a woman's mind; you can only change her mood." Here's another, much creepier one: "The first rule of women is, never listen to what they say." It's all best summarized with: "Women don't know what they want."

Now, I'd agree that most people — of all genders — don't have a solid idea of what they want. And I can understand why men would want to get each other's advice on how to flirt with women. It's the same principle behind me asking other women for advice on how to apply eyeliner, rather than asking straight dudes. I mean, most straight dudes *can't even tell* when I'm wearing eyeliner, although they might say something like, "You look really nice today." So why would I ask the average, non-goth straight guy for eyeliner tips? And why would a guy ask a girl for flirting tips?

But regardless, this doesn't mean that what people say they want should be ignored. *If what a person says is ignored or overridden, how will they ever learn to talk openly?*

Aggressive Last Minute Resistance tactics, which I thoroughly discussed in Chapter 3, are especially problematic in the context of rape culture. "She said no, but she secretly wanted it" is a victim-blaming pattern that feminists have been fighting since the beginning of the anti-rape movement. There's a reason "no means no" is a feminist slogan.

There's another PUA concept that's just as troubling as aggressive LMR techniques: the concept is called "buyer's remorse." "Buyer's remorse" is the catch-all PUA phrase to cover situations where a girl feels bad after having sex with a PUA.

The very phrase "buyer's remorse" ties strikingly into the commodity model, of course, but there's a lot more to it than that. Here's a quotation from a Field Report where the writer complains of buyer's remorse:

So I take it very slow knowing she's that sort of person, and at the end of the night take her by the hand and go up stairs to sleep as it's now 3:30 am. So being very careful I begin by snuggling then I slowly tilt her head and make-out with her... no sex though (felt that was way too fast for her). And after some comfy makkin' we dose off. Next morning, I wake up and I notice that she's all distant silent now, and I'm thinking "FUCK!!" and think of what I may have done.

... So now I'm at school with her and she's all nervous, withdrawn and

silent with me. I know there's attraction still because she always looks at me when I enter a room, and I when she enters a room. And from here I don't know what to do, and I'm not giving up on my challenge. So, any suggestions on how I should go about this and smash though this thick sheet of ice between us and line-up some attraction again? [8]

There are a huge number of potential reads on this situation, and it's dangerous to umbrella all of those reads under the single phrase "buyer's remorse."

* The girl might not have enjoyed making out very much, for example.

* Or the girl might have something else going on in her life, like a boyfriend she's cheating on. If she's a cheater, then the PUA got used by an unethical person, and I feel sorry for him.

* Or she might really like the PUA, but feel afraid that he doesn't like her as much. She might feel afraid that he used her.

* Or, in fact, the girl might feel like this guy pushed her into it. She might feel violated. On the limited description from this PUA, it seems totally possible that she feels hurt and confused. She might look at him every time he enters the room, not because she feels attracted to him... but rather because she feels anxious about him.

You'd think that it might be a good idea to *ask her how she's feeling*, especially since there are so many possibilities, and this guy obviously *cares*. Just as obviously, no PUAs on the forum gave him that advice. (The lone respondent told the guy to do more routines during the Comfort phase, next time.)

I feel especially unnerved by the conceptual structures some PUAs build to explain buyer's remorse, while they acknowledge *none of the above* potential reasons for it. For example, at one PUA lecture, the instructor described buyer's remorse as arising from "biological" factors. Women, he explained, have been "programmed" by years of evolution: supposedly, women have a "negative biological response" to having sex "too soon." He further explained that a man can get around this "biological response" by doing a good job with the Comfort phase before having sex with her.

While it's clearly good that PUAs advise building comfort with a woman before sex, I was floored when that speaker shoehorned all the different potential reasons behind "buyer's remorse" into a vague appeal to "biology." Not only does it send the message that all women are the same (again), it also reinforces a more subtle and horrible PUA tendency: ignoring women's *entire psychological reality*, and treating us like biological machines that yield the desired result when the correct routine is applied.

In some cases, the idea of "biological" "buyer's remorse" probably saves the PUA's ego. *Don't worry man, you weren't terrible in bed, it's just her biology! That's why she won't call you back!* In other cases, it strikes me as a Shiny And Exciting New Way to blame the victim. *Don't worry man, it's not like you hurt her emotionally by being so pushy and aggressive. If only women didn't have crazy biology, everything would be fine!*

It's important to acknowledge that PUAs see buyer's remorse as a sign of less-than-solid game. My old friend PUALingo.com avoids using scary words like "rape" and "consent" when telling me:

Buyer's remorse happens when the game was not played properly, such as skipping comfort, gaming a drunk girl, or doing something that would otherwise jeopardize the long term sexual relationship with the girl beyond a one-night stand.

PUAs generally consider buyer's remorse bad game, as the goal should be to create a long term sexual relationship with the target.

While many PUAs aren't looking for girlfriends or monogamy, most are interested in long-term fuckbuddies or even "real relationships" if the girl is "high quality" enough. But what this also means is that buyer's remorse is considered more acceptable when "lower-quality" women feel it. When the above instructor discussed it, he added that you mostly want to avoid buyer's remorse with women you really like. The implication here is that with girls you don't care about, it's okay if they feel awful in the morning.

When I hear quotes like that, it's hard to avoid thinking that PUAs don't care about how women actually *feel,* just how women *act.* It makes it sound like the priority is not a partner who feels okay; rather, the priority is an object that provides an orgasm. In this framework, it seems like the PUA priorities are the cold and practical questions of (a) how difficult it will be to convince hot girls to fuck you again, and (b) how best to get your rocks off with non-hot, disposable chicks.

But the same instructor used a common anti-misogyny PUA catchphrase: "Leave her better than you found her." He suggested that the best way to imagine any interaction is to think of it as having fun, as having a good time *together,* rather than regarding everything as a step on the Path To Vagina. Indeed, in some ways, this PUA coach sought to undermine adversarial gender roles.

Yet are adversarial gender roles *intrinsic* to pickup artistry? From the way most PUAs discuss "the game," it sounds like an adversarial contest. It's a struggle to reframe it as a cooperative game instead.

Metaphors have an undeniable effect on how we think about the world.

In early 2011, I was excited to see Real Scientists demonstrate this. Here's a quote from "Discover" Magazine's science coverage:

In a series of five experiments, Paul Thibodeau and Lera Boroditsky from Stanford University have shown how influential metaphors can be. They can change the way we try to solve big problems like crime. They can shift the sources that we turn to for information. They can polarise our opinions to a far greater extent than, say, our political leanings. And most of all, they do it under our noses. Writers know how powerful metaphors can be, but it seems that most of us fail to realise their influence in our everyday lives.

First, Thibodeau and Boroditsky asked 1,482 students to read one of two reports about crime in the City of Addison. Later, they had to suggest solutions for the problem. In the first report, crime was described as a "wild beast preying on the city" and "lurking in neighbourhoods". After reading these words, 75% of the students put forward solutions that involved enforcement or punishment, such as calling in the National Guard or building more jails. Only 25% suggested social reforms such as fixing the economy, improving education or providing better health care.

The second report was exactly the same, except it described crime as a "virus infecting the city" and "plaguing" neighbourhoods. After reading this version, only 56% opted for more enforcement, while 44% suggested social reforms. The metaphors affected how the students saw the problem, and how they proposed to fix it.

And very few of them realised what was going on. The two reports both contained the same "shocking" statistics about Addison's crime rates. When Thibodeau and Boroditsky asked the students to say which bits of text had most influenced their decisions, the vast majority circled the numbers. Only 3% noted the metaphors. [9]

Philosophers, linguists, writers and feminists have made arguments like these for many years. Unfortunately, it has always been difficult to measure *how much* language influences people's thoughts, but we *know* that language influences our thoughts at least *a bit*.

Given that we know how influential metaphors can be, there are plenty of worrying metaphors that are emphasized in the seduction community. The commodity model is a particularly important example. It's worth noting, however, that the commodity model is generally prevalent in the mainstream. It's not like PUAs made it up.

* * *

Ideally, feminists want to build a better world, and that's what a lot of feminist theory is working towards: a more equal, egalitarian world for people of all genders. One feminist goal, in criticizing established power structures, is to think of *a better replacement.* The goal is to create systems that involve less rape for all genders, equal opportunities for all genders, and fewer unrealistic expectations for all genders.

Pickup artistry, on the other hand, is all about being effective within our current world: getting laid *tonight,* getting a relationship ASAP, improving social skills this year, et cetera. Both feminists and PUAs are analyzing gender issues. Yet while most feminists talk about the long term, most PUAs are thinking in the short term.

Another big difference between feminist priorities and PUA priorities is that PUAs tend to focus on *behavior,* while feminists tend to focus on *experience.* Of course there are exceptions, but while PUAs spend most of their time breaking down their observations about people's *actions,* feminists spend most of our time talking about people's *emotions.*

When looking at these differences between feminists and PUAs, the most important feminist concept to understand is "enthusiastic consent." The basic idea is simple: don't initiate sex unless you have your partner's *enthusiastic* consent.

Enthusiastic consent does *not* mean a partner who says, "Okay, I guess," in a bored tone, but doesn't actively say, "No." It also does *not* mean a partner who is silent and non-reactive, but doesn't actively stop you when you start having sex with them. Nor does it mean a partner who seems hesitant, or anxious, or confused. Enthusiastic consent means an enthusiastic partner: one who is responding passionately, kissing you back, saying things like "Oh my God, don't stop"... or a partner who talks to you ahead of time about what to do, like the S&M discussions I described in Chapter 3, and who knows how to safeword out of the situation if you do something they don't like.

Any PUA tactic that involves ignoring a target who clearly communicates that she wants to stop is just plain nonconsensual, of course. The word "enthusiastic" doesn't even come into a situation like that. But freeze-outs, for example, fail the "enthusiastic consent" test, because if you have to give someone the silent treatment to get their consent to sex, then your partner is *clearly not* enthusiastic about it. Their *actions* might include sex, but their *emotions* are less likely to include feeling sexy.

A common objection against the "enthusiastic consent" standard is that if everyone insists on enthusiastic consent, rather than mere "well, okay, I guess..." consent, then people will get laid less. This is true, at least in the short term. On the other hand, if people regularly followed the enthusiastic consent standard, then all sex would involve partners who are definitely psyched about having sex with each other.

So here's the selfish argument: if everyone lived in a world where they could always assume that their partners cared about both their pleasure and their consent, then more people would want to have sex. As one unusual PUA commented in a Lay Report:

I identify as a feminist which is KEY in getting me laid. Really, guys. I read a book titled Yes Means Yes: Visions of Female Sexual Power and A World Without Rape *[a well-known and important feminist anthology from 2009]... I swear I've used that book several times over to help me get laid.... I haven't dealt with LMR from the last six or seven girls ever since I started telling girls I'm a feminist, that I'm super cautious about consent, etc.* [10]

So maybe if we encourage enthusiastic consent, people will eventually start getting laid *more.*

Maybe that PUA is exaggerating his feminism in order to get into girls' pants? I hope not. Even if he is, I'll at least give him props for encouraging other PUAs to read *Yes Means Yes.* It's a challenging book for a lot of people, and I don't expect everyone to agree with every word in it, but it's packed full of important ideas.

Enthusiastic consent is an idealistic concept. It assumes that people are capable of caring as much about a partner's experience as about their own. It assumes that people are genuinely willing to go the distance to ensure that a partner's sexual experience is really good.

It also assumes that people have a stake in taking down rape culture: *enthusiastic consent is as much a long-term strategy as a short-term one.* Enthusiastic consent involves trying to change broad social standards, and set positive examples that might take a long time to be widely adopted. It means being willing to say: "I really want to get off right now, but I'll do my level best not to pressure you about it, because I believe that refusing to pressure you will contribute to a better world."

Also, it means acknowledging that if you really want to get off right now, you can always go to the bathroom and take care of it yourself. I've masturbated myself into calmness during moments of sexual frustration, and a lot of men I know have done the same. As one of my ex-partners used to say, "I want a much more interesting and mutual experience out of sex than just an orgasm. If I only wanted an orgasm, I could do *that* on my own."

But although I have little patience with people who attack the enthusiastic consent idea from outside feminism, it's worth noting that there are critiques *within feminism* of the concept of enthusiastic consent. For example, some feminist sex workers point out that when they have sex for money, their consent is not exactly "enthusiastic," but they still feel that their consent is real consent, and that their choices must be respected. The same goes for some asexual people. Asexuality is commonly defined as "not feeling sexual attraction to others," but some asexual people have romantic relationships with other people in which they have sex entirely to satisfy their partner, and some of them have said that they don't feel included by feminist discussions of enthusiastic consent. [11]

Hey, even some of my so-called "normal" friends have problems with the idea that they aren't "really" consenting unless they're super-enthusiastic about the sexual act at hand. A married friend once commented wryly that if she and her husband always demanded 100% enthusiastic consent from each other, then the marriage would fall apart. But as we continued to discuss it, she and her husband both agreed that they have zero problem with the situation as it stands.

I don't want to sweep those critiques under the rug. Yet, all this having been said: the concept of enthusiastic consent has been very helpful for me personally. I know that it's also been helpful for an enormous number of other people who are trying to understand boundaries in their sexual relationships. In fact, the PUA coach Mark Manson once emailed me to say:

You might be interested to hear how your influence on me has produced new behavior recently. I got into bed with a girl a few weeks ago and felt incredibly uncomfortable being there with her. I didn't want to have sex despite a large expectation that that's what we were going to do. In the past, in these situations, I'd more or less chastise myself for being a pussy and force myself to go through with it and terrible sex would ensue, which I may or may not regret the next day. But this time, I suddenly had a moment of "My consent matters; and my consent should be an enthusiastic yes. And right now it's not." So I worked up the nerve to tell her I didn't want to have sex... something I don't think I've ever done with a random before in my life. She actually took it well.

Ironically, Mark later wrote a blog post about why he's not a feminist, in which he spent several paragraphs talking about how much he hates the concept of rape culture. [12] Personally, I would argue that in the above anecdote, rape culture is expressed in the very expectation that he "ought to" have sex with this girl and "force himself" to go through with it. Such expectations are rape myths when they happen to people of all genders, not just women. But I guess if Mark buys enthusiastic consent but not rape culture, that's still a 50% win.

There are valid objections to holding everyone to the "enthusiastic consent standard," yet its actual impact seems largely positive, and it has even benefited PUAs like Mark.

In order to promote enthusiastic consent, feminists tend to teach explicit, straightforward verbal sexual communication. This contrasts with pickup artists, who typically teach non-verbal or playfully tacit sexual communication. Like feminists, S&Mers also teach explicit, straightforward verbal sexual communication. I've mentioned safewords a lot, because they're the most famous and high-profile example of careful S&M communication tactics.

Safewords are obviously very useful in a context where one partner might want to scream "No!" or "Please don't!" or "Mercy!" with no intention of actually stopping the action. But safewords serve another, stealthier, equally important function: they bring home the idea that consent is a continuously changing process. Consent is part of an ongoing sexual negotiation that takes place between two people. Here, S&M consent ideas overlap heavily with feminist consent ideas. For example, one article by high-profile feminist Jaclyn Friedman pushes back against dominant conceptions of consent by stating that "consent is not a lightswitch." As Friedman writes:

Sexual consent isn't like a lightswitch, which can be either "on," or "off." It's not like there's this one thing called "sex" you can consent to anyhow. "Sex" is an evolving series of actions and interactions. You have to have the enthusiastic consent of your partner for all of them. And even if you have your partner's consent for a particular activity, you have to be prepared for it to change. [13]

Safewords are, effectively, a constant reminder that "you have to be prepared for [consent] to change."

For S&Mers and feminists, the sexual consent territory continues to overlap after safewords. Huge factions within both groups have concluded that the best way to encourage consent is not merely to encourage people to understand that they can withdraw consent at any point, but to encourage open communication and self-knowledge about sex.

Among feminists, an example of this approach is Jaclyn Friedman's brand-new book *What You Really, Really Want: The Smart Girl's Shame-Free Guide to Sex and Safety.* The writer Tracy Clark-Flory at *Salon* notes that, "The book is filled with writing exercises that prompt readers to reflect on everything from body image to sexual assault. It's essentially a guide to writing one's own personal sexual manifesto." [14]

Among S&Mers, an example of this approach is long, multi-page checklists of sexual acts that partners review together. Each act on the checklist looks something like this:

FLOGGING — GIVING _____ O O O O O

FLOGGING — RECEIVING _____ O O O O O

Each partner rates each entry by filling out 1-5 bubbles, with 1 darkened bubble meaning "Not interested" and 5 bubbles meaning "I crave this!" Seriously, people do this! And it often works amazingly well.

This type of explicit communication is both an excellent way to help partners understand each other's desires, and to help partners understand each other's boundaries. They're concrete examples of enthusiastic consent in action, and I try to teach those tactics in my writing and workshops.

During my PUA research, as I started developing ideas about strategic ambiguity, I began thinking deeply about how strategic ambiguity intersects with direct communication and enthusiastic consent.

Strategic ambiguity: contrast, challenge, novelty, unpredictability. If lots of people seek strategic ambiguity from their sex and relationships, then where is the line where strategic ambiguity becomes non-consensual or cruel? What are the "bad" types of strategic ambiguity, as opposed to "good" ones that work better for consent? Addressing those questions became a major goal of this book.

Some PUAs talk about something that looks a lot like enthusiastic consent, like the guy whose Lay Report I quoted above, and the guru I quoted when I wrote about Last Minute Resistance who says: "If you make it clear that there is absolutely no pressure for her to sleep with you, if you show her that you can be trusted and that you're OK with whatever she decides (and by the way, you do need to be OK with whatever she decides), then she's going to become ten times more comfortable with you, and therefore is actually more likely to WANT to have sex with you."

Unfortunately, other relevant feminist concepts are usually much harder to sell to PUAs than enthusiastic consent. Thinking about rape culture means confronting some difficult ideas for everyone, and arguably more so for PUAs. It means recognizing that some social systems PUAs exploit, and the ways PUAs often measure or insult women, are not awesome for anyone of any gender, *including PUAs.*

A PUA who grasps the extent of the commodity model and wants to avoid propping it up wouldn't call women "depreciating and often damaged assets," for example. But try telling the guy who wrote those words that they come from *the exact same social structure* that makes men feel like they must have a nice car, or buy drinks, in exchange for a woman's attention. Seriously, you try it. I'd bet a rum-and-coke that he won't listen to me.

While debating on a feminist blog about PUAs, I met a woman who went by the Internet name of AnneBonney. She has spent years chatting with PUAs on various fora, and I was fascinated to see how closely her thoughts mirrored mine. At one point, she wrote to me by email that:

My perspective as a woman changed a lot over the time that I spent dialoguing with these guys and reading more about the community. When I started, if someone asked me if I was feminist I would have answered "of course!", but I hadn't spent much time investigating what that meant for me.... It was actually my involvement with PUAs that caused me to broaden and deepen my understanding of contemporary feminist thought, because the issues that these guys were raising — sexual double standards, the variety of pressures put on men, and sometimes issues with divorce and child rearing — did really speak to me, and were troubling to how I understood gender relations.

But the answers that they often settled on — essentially that the trappings of hegemonic femininity were women's ways of hurting men, instead of things that many of us also really aren't keen on either — seemed really wrong, from my experience. So I went back and learned more about feminism, started reading more blogs and books, getting into conversations with my friends about gender. A lot of the things that were bugging me about the PUA community started to make sense in light of the new vocabulary I was gaining, and I became convinced that we all were looking at the same problems with really really different solution sets. And I became increasingly concerned that their solutions really weren't meant to include answers for women's problems at all. That many were still seeing women themselves as the main obstacle.

... Personally, I've had to back away from the places I used to read as the misogyny has gotten worse and less called-out, because it honestly hurts to see these dudes double down on solutions that are really causes of their problems. I consider some of these guys friends, and I've learned a lot from them, and I really do think that a lot of their issues are feminist ones. But I have no idea how they would become feminist allies; most of them just won't hear it. Especially from a woman.

In fairness, many feminists are absolutely horrified by pickup artistry and are totally unwilling to interact with any PUAs whatsoever. Most feminists are way more horrified than I am, and you can tell that I'm not very comfortable with pickup artistry myself. When I wrote a post about PUAs on a major feminist blog, one feminist commented: "I'll just come out and say it: PUAs rape women through coercion and manipulation. Full stop. No amount of PUA whining, peacocking, and evolutionary psychology will change that." [15]

Personally, I reckon a few PUAs rape women, because statistics teach us that in any large group, some people will probably be rapists. I'm also sure that most PUAs don't rape women. A lot of PUAs are confused guys, trying to negotiate consensual relationships within the extremely loose modern framework for romance. However, although most PUAs aren't out there actively raping people, the philosophical underpinnings of the community include a lot of commodity model bullshit and adversarial gender roles.

But I keep coming back to what AnneBonney said about "looking at the same problems with really different solution sets." In a way, the gap between PUAs and feminists is more a cultural and stereotypical gap than a theoretical one. It's all about the metaphors. PUAs tend to see feminists as uptight bitches who don't want anyone to get laid, while many feminists view PUAs as the foot soldiers of rape culture.

* * *

Still, some PUAs do view themselves as activists. Kind of.

Many PUAs get into the community because they're depressed and want something better from their lives. For those dudes, the desire to score women is a kind of mental proxy for general dissatisfaction. Hopefully, they get in touch with that dissatisfaction over the course of learning the game, and learn to think proactively about changing their lives. The coach Mark Manson once said to me, "This is a giant self-help community in disguise." And Neil Strauss said he hoped *The Game* could become "the beginning of a men's self-help movement — because self-help isn't emasculating anymore if you're doing it to get laid."

And so, some of the guys who have used the community for self-help feel a kind of evangelical passion for giving that to other men. This is especially common among the PUAs who I label Type 4: Leaders, although it's also a strand of thinking among some Type 1: Analysts.

During my PUA research, I tangentially ran across a paper on social anxiety. [16] Turns out, lots of people with social phobia have excessively high standards for their social performance. The paper notes that social phobics may think things like, "I *must* not show any signs of weakness," or, "I *must* always sound intelligent and fluent."

Or perhaps some social phobics might think, "I *must* be attractive to all women."

Many people with social phobia also engage in what's described as "safety-seeking behaviors": basically, they overanalyze the social situation, and look for ways to categorize it. (Like classifying behaviors into "Indicators of Interest" and "shit tests," perhaps?) Social phobics try to think of actions that will protect them from some made-up social catastrophe. Then, if they make it through the encounter without catastrophe, they conclude that it was because of their safety-seeking behaviors. Witness:

Patients with social phobia who are worried that what they say may not make sense and will sound stupid, often report memorizing what they have said and comparing it with what they are about to say, while speaking. If everything goes well, patients are likely to think, "It only went well because I did all the memorizing and checking, if I had just been myself people would have realized how stupid I was."

Are you pondering openers and routines? Me too.

Here are some suggested treatments for social phobia:

* The patient can keep a log of successful social encounters in order to build up a positive self-image. (Field Reports. Lay Reports.)

* The patient can break some of the minor rules of social interaction, so they learn that breaking social rules isn't the end of the world. (Sarging could be viewed as deliberately breaking the rules. So could peacocking, when the PUA wears clothing that's deliberately out of place.)

* The patient is encouraged to deliberately avoid their safety-seeking behaviors. (Advanced PUAs often tell beginners that memorized routines are just a step in the process, and should eventually be abandoned.)

In other words, a lot of PUA methods look very much like classic behavioral treatments for social anxiety.

A word that comes up a lot in pickup conversations is "congruent." An action or statement is congruent when it matches how the person actually thinks or feels. For example, it would be incongruent for me to talk about "feminazi bitches," unless I was joking (and I often am). More to the point, a PUA who hates math, but who claims to be interested in math just because a hot girl is interested in math, would be incongruent.

Congruence goes beyond truth, though. Congruence is also about listening to oneself and acting in accordance with one's own actual desires. And it's about backing up one's words with one's actions.

PUAs theorize that human beings have excellent instincts for congruence. So being incongruent is not only bad for you, personally, because it makes you feel like you're not yourself; it's also bad for your game, because your target is likely to sense that you're incongruent.

Memorized routines initially seem incongruent, but they're one path to learning congruent social skills. As a newbie PUA practices the routine, he will become more socially calibrated; he'll add his own twists and turns into the routine. Eventually, he can deliver it well because he's taken it into himself, or he will abandon it altogether and use it as a springboard for creating something more congruent. At least, that's the ideal trajectory, especially for guys with a high degree of social phobia who believe that they need social crutches like routines.

Is this the *best* way to learn congruent social skills? Maybe not, but it works for a lot of people. The blogger Hugh Ristik observed among the feminist comments on my Neil Strauss interview:

Right now, the best hope for many socially inept or anxious men (who don't understand dating norms and what preferences different sort of women may have) is to study pickup to get some social experience with women and confidence... and then study how to undo some of the mechanistic attitudes that they needed to get there. That's a highly circuitous route that takes years to traverse.

Can this route be shortened? I believe it can. But I would caution anyone who hasn't gone from socially inept to successfully dating women from making too many assumptions about alternative routes. If there was an easy shortcut, the seduction community wouldn't exist in the first place.

Pretty much everyone has gone through periods of incongruence while learning a new skill, integrating into a new job, and so on. The more dramatic the change of environment, the more incongruent the new person may seem as they struggle to adjust. When people move to new cultures, we call this culture shock, and one of the primary symptoms of culture shock is "not feeling like yourself." Perhaps the subcultures of the Western world have become different enough that when people want to switch between them, there's some very mild culture shock. Such as, for example, when a nerdy guy learns how to navigate the mainstream dating world.

As Neil Strauss told me, "I think one of the many misconceptions about the game is somehow that guys are being taught to be fake — I know I'm more real and more honest than I ever was before the game, when I was too shy to really express myself. People go through a process of not being themselves. It's part of the journey. Through anything you have to struggle and get dirty in the mud and get to the other side and become yourself, and that's part of the process."

So by now it's overwhelmingly obvious that pickup artistry is sometimes a social phobic support group. The problem is that sometimes, it's *also* a misogyny support group.

Many feminists think that viewing pickup artistry as therapy is ridiculous — or, worse, immoral. A feminist acquaintance, who goes by Kristen J. on various feminist websites, observed that:

They chose PUA over therapy because it is more socially acceptable. I think that says something about them as people and their ability to be allies to women. Anti-oppression work is not a cakewalk, and this is not the last emotional double bind they will have to navigate. If not being able to get "Hot Bitches" is where they resort to misogyny, then what happens when they have to unpack bigger pieces of their privilege and social programming?

Actually, "the game" is not unlike advertising. Ad agencies understand the effects of problematic norms on women, and they use those norms to sell their products. Society telling you that you're too old? Yeah, you are, have some goop to put on your face that will make you look younger. Society telling you that you're too fat? Yeah, you are, try this New and Improved Weight Loss Program!

Society telling you that you're worthless without male appreciation? Yeah, you are... so let me become a PUA and steer you around like a little car to meet my needs, and I'll give you only as much approval as is required to keep you from dumping my ass.

The thing is, advertising isn't just a consequence of problematic norms... it's a creator of them, too. And these dudes aren't just working with the hand the universe dealt them, they're reinforcing those norms through their exploitative behavior. If you want to try to drag them to enlightenment, I'm all for it, but I'm still going to think that PUA culture is deeply misogynistic and they acted like little shits for participating in it.

If they can't or won't seek psychological help, then Kristen recommends that socially anxious guys read a book called *The Language of Emotional Intelligence* by Jeanne Segal, instead of PUA materials.

I can see her point, and I agree with what she's saying in many ways. And yet, to me, there's something almost cruel about expecting men who get into the seduction community to have it all figured out from the start, especially if they're struggling to overcome anxiety issues. Yes, I do believe that it is men's responsibility to be feminist allies, the same way I believe it is my responsibility as a white person to do anti-racist work when I can. But learning to understand all this social programming is a slow process, and people come to it in different ways.

In our culture, there is enormous pressure on men to be stoic and emotionless. It's part of the same complex of pressures that tell men they ought to bang as many chicks as possible, without caring about a relationship. Those pressures do two things: they drive many men towards pickup artistry, *and* they drive many men *away* from dealing carefully with their own emotions... or even *acknowledging that they want to deal carefully with their own emotions.*

In other words: for a PUA who is seeking self-help but doesn't know it yet, the thing that's blocking him off from seeking therapy is often *the very same problems of masculinity that push him towards the seduction community in the first place.*

On the topic of activism, there are also PUAs who offer analyses around race and racism. I do not feel qualified to judge their analysis, because I'm still learning how to be a good anti-racist ally, but it seems worth mentioning. For example, I attended one presentation by J.T. Tran, otherwise known as The Asian Playboy. He told the audience a story that went something like this: "The worst night of my life, I was out sarging and I approached this Asian girl. She had bleached blonde hair and blue eye contacts, and before I could even say anything, she snapped: 'I don't date Asians.' That kind of internalized racial self-hatred..." and, as I recall, he trailed off.

To be clear, J.T. Tran's lecture was focused on teaching guys how to get laid. But he also threw in notes about how Asian men are stereotyped in the workplace. After his lecture, I went out to a club with his posse, and on the way we talked about population-related gender issues in China. And for me, the most mind-blowing part of the evening was when someone at the club asked The Asian Playboy what he did for a living... and he answered: "I'm a lecturer in the Asian men's movement."

A feminist, Asian-American lady friend of mine who does a lot of work around racial justice told me later that she'd seen J.T. Tran on a list of important Asian-American leaders. She said she felt pretty conflicted about that.

* * *

After I published my interview with Neil Strauss, it didn't take long for people to claim that he only said slightly-feminist things because he wanted to sleep with me. Which gives me too much credit, don't you think? I mean, really. As if a world-famous PUA would have to lie about feminism in order to fuck a glasses-wearing, less-than-10 brunette. As if a world-famous PUA would *bother* with a glasses-wearing, less-than-10 brunette.

But seriously, folks, Neil seemed unexpectedly interested in talking to me. When we were done with the interview, he said that he'd read some of my previous work and that he wanted to hear more of my thoughts on S&M and polyamory.

I checked my watch. I was already 40 minutes late to meet my dungeon partner, but then again, my partner *had* told me to take my time. "Of course," I said.

I talked to Neil about writing and sexuality for quite a while. I felt torn the whole time. I hate flaking out on people at the last minute, but... I mean... this was *Neil Strauss.* Maybe my partner would understand.

50 minutes late.

65 minutes late.

It was a fun conversation, and I wanted to keep talking, but I just couldn't bring myself to flake. So finally I told Neil that I was expected at this party, and invited him along. Neil said he'd come after he was done talking with everyone else.

It was a risky maneuver. It would have been much more solid game to stay at the restaurant, because at the restaurant there was no way I'd lose track of Neil. Which was exactly what happened, due to a text message mix-up.

I felt out-of-sorts the whole next day. Then I was confused about why I felt out-of-sorts.

Weirdly, I felt as though I should have made more of a play for Neil Strauss. Except I couldn't figure out whether I genuinely wanted to sleep with him, or *why* I would want to. Maybe I was a status-obsessed, gold-digging whore who would jump on the cock of any available high-status man. After all, this is what Darth Vader PUAs claim all women are. And obviously PUAs are more likely to know what I'm thinking than I am, right?

Or maybe I was just curious.

Or maybe I'd originally entered the seduction community feeling like a huntress, and now I felt weird because I'd missed the greatest prey. I was like Captain Ahab: "Moby-Dick seeks thee not. It is thou, thou, that madly seekest him!" Except that I'd met the great white whale without trying to harpoon it.

I should have made more of an emotional play, I thought. *Hung out with him all night without having sex. Sought an actual bond.* But was I actually into bonding with Neil, or did he just pique my interest as an emotional escalation challenge?

I felt gross thinking about it, and I recognized that I was totally objectifying Neil Strauss. *It's just as well it didn't work out,* I concluded.

* * *

* * *

CHAPTER 6:
Down The Rabbit Hole

In which Clarisse dives wholeheartedly into the seduction community, and tells us about some of the different guys she found there. She also tells us about how her male friends and partners react to her PUA research. The chapter title is, of course, from Lewis Carroll's novel Alice in Wonderland. *The "rabbit hole" is probably the second most common metaphor used by PUAs to describe getting into the community, right after "taking the red pill" from the movie* The Matrix.

* * *

Most of my in-person conversations with PUAs took place in nightclubs or coffee shops. Our conversations were always polite, sometimes warm and friendly, sometimes flirtatious... and sometimes strained. I met so many PUAs that I lost count, but I should note that most of them knew I'm a feminist writer, and they didn't flip out about it. If I were a more responsible "researcher," I presumably would have sought to interview anti-feminist PUAs who I consider very misogynist, so that I'd have a more balanced perspective. But it was hard enough relating to some guys I was already talking to. The flashes of rage were already intense, and I didn't want any blood on my hands.

Occasionally, I'd meet a PUA who had a good idea of where I was coming from. They usually fit into the Type 1: Analyst category, like the blogger Hugh Ristik. I could express myself straightforwardly to those guys. When the conversation got heated, we'd both come away having learned something.

Still, I frequently had to prevent myself from expressing a feminist perspective. Sometimes, when chatting with a PUA, I opted to just piss him off and see where the conversation went. (For maximum fun, make an offhand joke about "the patriarchy" to PUAs. Watch their discomfort.) More often, I avoided speaking my mind, or I phrased my critiques as questions.

People — especially women — can go a long way when we phrase objections as questions. I'd rather live in a world where women can be assertive without being labeled bitches, but sometimes it's fun to see how many feminist concepts I can get into a conversation by stealth.

I flatter myself that I changed some perspectives. I especially enjoyed getting comments like: "Huh. I guess that judging you for the 'feminist' label is like when people judge me for the 'pickup artist' label."

In one conversation, I mentioned a typical feminist critique of street harassment: I was saying that street harassment is often used as a weapon to intimidate women. In many contexts, catcalls are more about trying to freak the target out than they are about expressing genuine attraction. This seems unbearably obvious to me, but maybe that's just because I've experienced it a lot. When I described some of my experiences to one PUA coach, he rewarded me with a measuring, respectful look. "Wow," he said, "that's really insightful."

I resisted the urge to grab him by the shoulders and shout: *Feminists have been saying this stuff for decades. Maybe you should fucking start listening!* Instead, I smiled. "Wait until I get started," I said.

It was funny what helped me gain some PUAs' respect. My favorite was the guy in an upscale club who insisted that women never, ever do cold approaches. "I approach guys first sometimes," I protested. "It's harder for women, though, because we're never expected to approach first."

(As a PUA coach once told me:

I'm not surprised that women don't make the first move. They have so much to lose. There's judgment from their girlfriends — "oh my God, she's such a slut to hit on that guy." And she risks judgment from the guy she approaches — "oh my God, she approached me, must be a slut, I'll just fuck her and dump her." [1]

And the blogger Hugh Ristik, after many conversations with me, once wrote that:

As far as I can tell, for most people who aren't highly extraverted or dominant, initiating sucks. When women try initiating, they often run into the same challenges that men do. I think there are also a couple gender specific wrinkles that women deal with. [For example], some men don't like it when women initiate. ... [And] some men are just so surprised and flabbergasted when women initiate that they don't know how to respond. It just doesn't compute. [2])

"Still," I told Upscale Club Guy, "I totally do cold approaches. Just not often."

"Whatever," he said, "women never do that."

"I do," I said.

"Do it right now," he said.

I sighed in exasperation and looked around the club. It wasn't my scene. All the men had short, excessively gelled hair. I didn't see anyone who instantly appealed to me, and besides, I'd been working on a super smart guy who was currently in the bathroom.

"I don't..." I started, then sighed again. Maybe this guy was compliance-testing, just to see if he could grab some power over me. Or maybe he wanted to feel like I was in the game with him for real. Maybe he wanted a sense of solidarity. "Okay," I said. "Help me pick someone and I'll do it."

"How about that dude over there?" said Upscale Club Guy, and I did it. I was paying no attention to the man I approached, and by the time I was standing next to my target, I realized I had no idea what to say. My opener was completely synthetic: I used the classic PUA standby, "Hey, did you see those two strippers in a hair-pulling fight outside? Yeah, it was totally wild." I felt silly, and I had no interest in a conversation, so I quickly fled.

By the time I made it back to Upscale Club Guy, he thought I was the greatest thing in the world. He shook my hand and later introduced me excitedly to others by saying, "I've seen her do cold approaches!"

Yup, I bonded with that PUA via objectifying some random dude. Guilty as charged.

The more I interacted with PUAs and read PUA material, the more I had to remind myself: "When all you have is a hammer, everything looks like a nail." I wasn't only watching my own behavior, either. It's easy to see every interaction in the whole world as game.

PUAs themselves were rarely helpful with this paranoia. One gentleman told me, "I hate how I have to game my female friends just so they'll be good friends."

I asked what he meant.

"I've got this one friend, for example," he said. "She's incredibly flaky. It's annoying. So finally, I made plans with her, then canceled on her at the last minute. Canceling is incredibly powerful. After that, she was definitely less flaky." He sighed. "It sucks, but I guess that's how women are."

I pondered whether I should use similar tactics on my flaky friends (many of whom are, incidentally, male). In the past, I've usually categorized people as "flaky" or "unflaky" based on their behavior, then attempted to avoid relying on the flaky ones. Was I behaving like an Average Frustrated Chick? (PUAs refer to non-PUA men with no "natural" game as Average Frustrated Chumps, or AFCs.)

I probably *was* acting like an AFC. I was letting flaky people define my behavior, rather than attempting to be in charge of those relationships. And if there's any concept central to pickup, it's ensuring that you're in charge of your interactions at all times. Plus, would my flaky friends continue to be flaky if I forced them to consider me "higher value"?

On the other hand, was it necessary to be in charge all the time? And how much did I *really* want the game bleeding into my *friendships?* I concluded that I didn't want the game affecting my view of friendship at all, and I think I was mostly successful at that. Pickup artistry colonized and colored my view of romantic relationships, sometimes in good ways and sometimes in bad ways. But I rarely put the situation in a PUA frame when I'm with my friends.

This seems like as good a time as any to tell you about my top 3 current routines. I didn't used to think of them as "routines"; I thought of them as "party questions," or simple strategies to revive a flagging conversation. But now that I've adopted a modified PUA mindset, it's quite clear to me that these are routines. And now that I'm telling them to you, I am fully prepared for these routines to start popping up all over town, which is what happened to Neil Strauss at the end of *The Game*. He became unable to use his own routines because he taught them to his followers. Eventually, all the women in Los Angeles had already heard his openers.

Which is to say: the next guy who comes up to me and asks whether I would eat human meat will fill me with ironic joy. I might even make out with him, just to close the circle.

CLARISSE THORN ROUTINE 1 (tm): "What surprised you most about this week / this month / your new job / the project you're working on / etc?" This question often opens people up and puts them in a good mood. I stole it from a guy I picked up on the public transit when I was 21.

CLARISSE THORN ROUTINE 2 (tm): "Would you eat human meat? You know, like, if you had the option to eat human meat. Would you?" I stole this routine from one of my favorite ex-boyfriends. Few people take this question seriously, but it freaks them out a little bit, which I like: it helps me detect whether they can handle me. Some guys suggest that we open a restaurant, which is always a winning response. My favorite response ever was the guy who hypothesized that we could use stem cells to grow the human meat. By the end of the evening, he and I had a name and logo for our restaurant. Yes, I did make out with that guy.

In case it needs to be said: Clarisse Thorn officially *does not advocate cannibalism.*

One of the focus groups who read the original draft of this book reported that the "human meat" question has been commandeered by OKCupid, a hipster dating site. Let that be a lesson to me.

CLARISSE THORN ROUTINE 3 (tm): "Describe yourself to me in 5 things you've done." I love this question because it not only gets the target talking about his life and activities; it also helps me figure out what his values are, and gives me plenty of places to jump in. Like, if a guy tells me he started a popular blog, then I can share my own thoughts and feelings about blogging.

This routine often gives you what PUAs would call an "open loop," which is a conversation that you can wander away from and return to during a later lull. For example, if some guy lists "thing #1" as "start a popular blog," and then we have a 30-minute conversation about blogging, and then we get distracted and go out for drinks... then even if several hours have passed, I can ask what "thing #2" is at any time. I stole this routine from one of my occasional partners.

I didn't really use my routines on any PUAs. I was too busy asking them questions about seduction. Plus, I was attracted to very few of them. Although I was sympathetic to the nicer PUAs, I rarely had any interest in dating them whatsoever. But there were exceptions....

* * *

Remember David, who got me to his apartment by sleight-of-hand and drove me home at daybreak? The guy I sort of unethically kissed? Yeah, that one. He called me the day after he drove me home. He also called me the day after that, which is against PUA rules... except that the second call was at 11 PM on a Saturday, so maybe it was a strategic attempt to grab me while I was out and about. You never know.

This Saturday happened to be the night before Folsom Street Fair, which is the biggest S&M event in the world.

"What's up, David?" I said into the phone. I would have missed the call if I hadn't been outside the dungeon, chatting up some smokers.

"I was just wondering if you were doing anything."

"David," I said, and laughed. "Really, David? It's the Saturday night before Folsom Street Fair. What are you doing calling a leathergirl?"

Kinda mean, right? So of course he called me again later. I'm telling you, most of these guys *love* snippy women. I suspect it's one of the big reasons they learn the game in the first place: they like the challenge factor. Which just makes it all the more ridiculous when PUAs complain about women being snippy. Guys, if you don't want snippy women, then *don't chase snippy women.*

Eventually, David took me out for a night on the town: my first opportunity to observe sarging at length. David and a couple other PUAs obligingly deconstructed themselves for me. It was super fun to watch.

They got some numbers, and they sometimes got shut down. But they were way better at reading women than I was. When David convinced me to try hitting on a girl, I made her very uncomfortable very fast. We talked for a while, but within two sentences after I moved on her, the girl turned mostly away from me, switched her gaze from my face to a spot just behind my head, and stammered. I felt guilty for making her so uncomfortable. I really didn't mean to.

The guys never got to that point, because they were more subtle. They read their targets' reactions much faster than I could; they were "well-calibrated." "Calibration" is how PUAs refer to a person's ability to read social cues and understanding of social nuance. Calling a person or action "uncalibrated" (or "miscalibrated") can be a pretty harsh PUA insult.

A famous PUA once told me that master PUAs discuss the "Terminator vision phenomenon," where they walk into any venue and instantly identify the best targets.

For all his calibration, though, I confused David a lot. In retrospect, I can see that he really liked me. Although I left him on a standoffish note, he was still texting me months after I departed from San Francisco. How did I emotionally escalate him? I'm not sure, but I think it had to do with showing genuine interest in his reality. Of course, teasing him played a role too.

Looking back on it, I feel kinda guilty. It's just that I had this image of David as a soulless PUA manipulator. I saw him as fair game. And he didn't help his case by pushing so hard the first night I met him. My first impression was that he was closest to Type 6: Darth Vader, but maybe he wasn't that bad.

There was something so *hot* about the idea of pickup... but at the same time, so many PUAs are so focused on using women, and I heard so much self-justification for ideas that made my skin crawl. I felt such satisfaction in "turning the tables" on that bullshit, I occasionally lost sight of the fact that PUAs are real people. Presumably, that's how misogynist PUAs feel about women.

Gotta love those adversarial gender roles.

* * *

At the goth club, one PUA was too involved in making out with his gorgeous girlfriend to talk to me. I still managed to get his number, though. He was on the scrawny end of slender, and he looked awesome in eyeliner. Five minutes of conversation showed me that he was an expert on feminism and polyamory, and he was an S&M switch just like me. His name was Brian.

A few days after the goth club outing, Brian and I started talking about meeting for drinks. We were both busy, though, and had to reschedule several times before we met. As we sized each other up, I tried to explain what drew me to PUAs like a moth to a flame.

"I don't know," I said, fumbling for words. "It's interesting from a feminist perspective, but it's more than that. It's like...." I looked away from him and thought about where else in my life I felt this intense, sexually-tinged fascination. "It's like a *fetish.*"

He started laughing. "You're a PUA chaser!" he cried, and I had to agree.

Brian double-booked me that night. He was scheduled to hang out with his girlfriend after he saw me. Remember, he was polyamorous: I knew he had a girlfriend, and I also knew it was legit for him to date multiple women. Yet when I discovered that he hadn't left the night open for us to hook up, I was hugely confused... and entertained. I thought I'd been obvious about my interest. Had I not been obvious *enough?* Or was Brian rejecting me?

Our conversation was both high-energy and theoretical. Brian was Type 1: Analyst *to the max.*

After a few hours, Brian said he had to head out. We stood up, and I found a penny on my seat. "Here," I said, and took his hand. Turning it palm-up, I put the penny in it and closed his fingers.

Brian dropped me off at a friend's place. As we paused outside, he gave me a hug. My blood leapt and clamored in my ears. We pulled apart slowly, and Brian pointed to his cheek. "Kiss?" he suggested.

What the hell is going on? I thought wildly. I was still confused about why he'd double-booked me. I felt like he had to be running a routine that I wasn't yet familiar with. I felt like a deer in the headlights. "Is this a trick?" I asked. Then I felt mad at myself, because I sounded like a breathless idiot.

"It's not a trick," Brian said. "It's a question... and you can answer it however you like."

I settled for a quick kiss and then breezed into my friend's apartment, sparkling. As it turned out later, Brian's actions were indeed a routine that he had developed very carefully, specifically including feminist concerns about enthusiastic consent. You can read his description of what he was doing in Appendix E.

"Where have you been?" said my friend. I told him. "So..." my friend said, "this guy Brian. He ditched you, and he left you feeling like *this?*"

I laughed and spun around in a circle, flinging out my arms. "Yes!"

"Must be some pickup artist," opined my friend.

It took a few meetings before Brian and I actually *talked* about our connection, which is hilarious, since we are both feminist-polyamorous-S&M people, and we agree that explicit verbal communication is very important. It seemed that we both had the same urge to keep our flirtation unspoken and uncertain for as long as we possibly could: we shared an urge towards strategic ambiguity. Finally, however, we puzzled each other so much that we were forced to discuss it openly.

"I had to double-book you that first night, because of all the rescheduling," Brian complained. "I hate to burst your PUA chaser fantasy, but sometimes I'm not acting with the strategic goal of ensnaring you in my devious, seductive web. Sometimes I'm being strategic, sometimes I'm acting automatically, sometimes I'm improvising, sometimes I'm being impulsive, and sometimes I don't know where you or I want the interaction to go, and I'm trying to figure it out. I couldn't tell how you were feeling when we met for drinks. You were so cerebral. It was only when you gave me the penny that I knew it was on."

"Would that be an Indicator of Interest?" I asked.

"Very good," he said. "An important lesson I learned from pickup is that just because someone was initially attracted to me, it doesn't necessarily mean they will be attracted later. And even when someone is attracted to me, it doesn't mean that I can assume they are ready to act on it now. I have to calibrate for the level of interest that someone is showing me in real time."

I swiftly discovered that Brian had way better fashion sense than I did, but there was more to him than impeccable eyeliner. In emails to me, Brian cited classic philosophers in his ethical analyses of pickup. He was able to debate the nuances of consent using feminist terminology. We'd go for walks in the park and talk about the game, or drink coffee and talk about the game, or dance in clubs and talk about the game.

Before you ask: my attraction to Brian settled down as I got more accustomed to hanging out with PUAs... but it never went away. Unfortunately, we are both busy people. Logistics between us are ridiculous, and constantly conspire against something more intense than kissing. On the other hand, I daresay that Brian is the PUA who I've most respected in the morning.

* * *

Josh was a cute-as-a-button, super-extraverted, incredibly warm guy. Once upon a time, he had felt very unsure about pickup artistry. "When I first looked at it," he said, "I was like, 'this is so sleazy and gross.' But I'd never had a girlfriend, and I kept telling myself, 'Dude, you are lonely and miserable and you don't want to die alone.'"

"Aww," I said. "I can relate. I couldn't get a date in high school."

"Yeah, I was the fat kid," he said.

Josh had done a little bit of instruction. Like many non-asshole PUA coaches, he screened his clients. "I'm known for being picky about who I'll work with. I turn down guys if I get a woman-hating vibe off them."

"What do you say to them?" I asked.

"I tell them I don't want to work with them."

"What if they ask why?"

"It's only happened a couple of times. In which case I tell them I feel a lot of anger from them, and I think they should work on that before getting into seduction."

David said something similar, in fact. He described directing excessively angry clients to groups that focus on personal development. The coach Mark Manson emailed me to explain his client interviews: "I screen my clients for attitude and general self-awareness. I'll take on 30-year-old virgins if they're good guys with healthy attitudes. But guys who are excessively angry or incapable of taking feedback, I tell them to get a therapist. Actually, I end up telling most guys to get a therapist anyway, hahaha. I think men in general are horrible at evaluating their own emotions."

PUAs get almost all their training in the field: sarging over and over for days, weeks, months. What this means is that many coaches' job boils down to standing around a bar, occasionally checking their watch, and not picking up girls themselves, because their role is to be an available advisor when the student needs one. Basically, a coach will hand-hold his client through a bunch of awkward social interactions, and then help his client analyze those same interactions.

Lots of coaches take video of PUA interactions and deconstruct it, too. Many of these videos are available on the Internet; you can Google them very easily if you like. Nicer PUAs bleep out the girl's name and blank out her face, but some Darth Vader types will leave the woman identifiable. Josh was the first to introduce me to how well these videos can work.

"I'll take video of the client interacting with a girl," he explained. "A lot of these guys have no idea how creepy they're being, but when I show it back to him, he'll learn. Like, I had this one guy whose eyes kept dropping down to girls' boobs. We watched the video, and I pointed out how the girl he was talking to turned away from him. Then she crossed her arms over her boobs, and then she got her jacket and put it on, all because he wouldn't stop glancing at her boobs. He just had no idea he was doing it. When I showed him, he was like 'Whoa!'"

There's no central authority in the PUA community that screens who gets to teach, and guys can set themselves up as instructors quite easily. A lot of the time, potential instructor cred is built within the community by writing good Field Reports; this factor often brings an even higher level of self-aggrandizement to FRs.

Many experienced PUAs complained to me about how the community has become centered on expensive classes and other forms of instruction. This includes Neil Strauss himself, who told me, "My big critique is that while once the community was a free flow of ideas, and — I'm partly to blame for this, with *The Game* and everything — now it's been commercialized. It's splintered into these niche markets — a guy gets in, he's like, 'What do I do? I only have so much money to spend.'"

There's no rating of instructional techniques, either. Very few PUA coaches are trained teachers. Lots of PUAs feel burnt out and disillusioned by various scams. Bootcamps, for instance: bootcamps are several-day intensive workshops with a bunch of attendees who pay fabulous sums to chill in a club with the coach. Positive reviews are often posted online by attendees, but bootcamps are a scattershot approach, and they often do more to showcase the instructor's charisma than teach. *The Game* implies that some bootcamp instructors use their social analysis skills specifically to convince students they've learned more than they actually have. One former bootcamp instructor told me that "bootcamps are just a shitty way to teach pickup."

All this having been said, pickup is a relatively new community, and the commercialization happened quickly and recently, so it's hardly reasonable to expect a Central Standards Bureau. I'm very curious to see if a bureau will pop up sometime in the next decade or so.

Anyway, I liked Josh, and he seemed like a good teacher. He was an interesting meld of my Typology of PUAs. He seemed like a little bit an Analyst, a little bit Freak and/or Geek, a little bit Hedonist, a little bit Leader, and a little bit Shark (since he was trying to make money within the industry). The only type that I couldn't see in him at all was Darth Vader. He seemed to feel zero anger or resentment towards women.

I liked Josh so much that I eventually suggested a fling. He turned me down. Perhaps I'm not hot enough. Or perhaps he sensed that I was still in my PUAs-are-fair-game-for-mindfucks frame, and wanted nothing to do with it. Or perhaps he couldn't handle being in the pursued position rather than the pursuer...

... but ostensibly, Josh was looking for something more serious than a fling.

Figures.

* * *

Ethan was a lean, angular gentleman who seemed philosophical and misanthropic. "It exploded my worldview when I first came upon the community," he said. "It threatened my manhood. Most guys are really uncomfortable when they first come across it."

When I drew him out, he talked about culturally accepted ideas of "becoming a man." The socially defined path to manhood emphasizes achievement: a good job, a good income. The socially defined path also implies that female attention *will come as a result of achievement.* Thus, many men feel cheated when they find that women are not the automatic reward of hard work. Unfortunately for them, women are independent humans with individual preferences and priorities.

Feminists have made these points before, given that this is yet another system that can harm both women and men. It harms men, because many men feel like their manhood is dependent on narrow and prescriptive career demands. It harms women, because we end up being treated like objects, and some guys feel entitled to our attention because of their salary. Ethan explained it in a PUA context thus: "When you buy into this step-by-step notion of manhood, with the job and everything, it's scary to realize that other guys get women without the buy-in."

We discussed media imagery. He told me that he hated how some movies show schlubby guys who get with beautiful, accomplished women: "The girl is *settling* for him. Guys are taught to hope that a girl will *settle* for us."

"I hate those movies too," I said, "but feminists usually talk about the opposite problem. About how in those movies, a guy who isn't smart or interesting is *still* seen as entitled to a talented and awesome girl."

"I see what you mean," Ethan conceded. "He's not really working on himself."

This led us into "inner game," one of the most fascinating concepts to emerge from the PUA subculture. Inner game is, essentially, genuine confidence and sense of purpose. (It contrasts with "outer game": i.e., the things a PUA says and does to attract women, plus how hot he looks.)

Successful PUAs usually reach a point where they realize that, in the words of one coach, "sport-fucking kinda sucks." They realize that it's time to pull back, figure out their priorities, and work on whatever else they want from life. Finding themselves in this way can be described as "inner game." Frequently, this includes a healthy dose of the self-help attitudes that I mentioned in the last chapter.

PUAs also realize that women respond well to genuine confidence and sense of purpose, and so a lot of PUAs will say that's why it's *really* worth figuring their shit out. Yes, it's true: notwithstanding the fact that it's about self-improvement and self-help, even the PUA concept of inner game is centered on banging chicks. I mean, it's even *called* "inner *game."*

In fairness to Ethan, his inner game goals didn't have much to do with women. He talked a lot about how he'd been thinking of going on retreat. He mused about joining a monastery. You'd be astonished how many PUAs think about this after a while in the community.

Or maybe you wouldn't. In a way, it seems like a natural conclusion, right? Boiling the game down to its essential elements can feel like a cold, soulless, inhuman process. Some people observe this and lose all hope about romance, since romance is "supposed" to be "easy" and "magical" and "natural." Why bother, if we're all just biological machines with learnable input-output algorithms?

Also, Ethan was a little bit of an Analyst, a little bit of a Freak/Geek... and a little bit of a Vader. He was nice enough and smart enough that he didn't buy into the worst PUA ideas about women, but I still felt a subtle undercurrent of resentment to his statements, like when he complained about the idea of women "settling" for men. It's possible that I was imagining it, but I don't think so; while researching PUAs, I became a pro at recognizing certain patterns of male resentment. It often takes the form of men thinking that women feel we're "too good for" men, or of men feeling angry because they "deserve" women and aren't "getting any," or of men dealing with a traumatic breakup (or divorce court) by blaming all women for their ex's cruelties.

Ethan seemed to feel at least two of the three above patterns of resentment. And when a person feels resentment towards the opposite sex, then maybe the kindest thing to do is to swear off dating for a while. It's the kindest thing to do for potential mates, and also for the self.

* * *

Kurt was an Asian scientist, with artistic ambitions that he'd been exploring since he discovered pickup. He explained that the seduction community helped him become much more social and much more ambitious. Even his mother noticed a big difference in his outlook. He'd always wanted to be an artist, but never saw himself reaching for it until now.

Most of Kurt's exposure to other PUAs came from books and Internet fora, because he hadn't checked out the local Lair. (I'd love to be able to say that the collective noun for PUAs is "lair," kind of like a "herd" of antelope or a "murder" of crows, but in fact a Lair is usually a physical location, or at least a website.) Kurt rarely posted on message boards. He and a few friends sarged and traded tips, but when Kurt wrote Field Reports, he kept them to himself for personal reference only. For him, this was an ethical boundary.

Ostensibly, I was interviewing Kurt, but like many PUAs, he started trying to pick me up right away. He took such a structured and synthetic approach that I kept asking, "So where'd you read about that line?" He was also probably the least experienced PUA I spoke to, which is why it was so obvious. But honestly, some of his stuff was great, and some wasn't even from PUA manuals. He showed me legitimately difficult geometric puzzles using bar straws. He read my palms.

After an hour or two, Kurt ran The Cube, a famous routine. By then, we'd reached a point where he wasn't even pretending to avoid pickup shtick. The conversation went something like this:

"Has anyone ever run The Cube on you?"

"Nope," I answered.

"No way! No one's ever run The Cube on you? I'm totally gonna run The Cube on you!"

"Sounds good."

The Cube involves conversational role-playing whereby the PUA draws out the target's answers to some hypothetical questions: "You're walking through the desert, and you see a cube. Describe the cube." Then he "analyzes" the results. I'd heard of it, but I didn't remember what anything meant when he ran it on me, so I figure my "results" were "genuine."

I hate to give you deep insight into my personality, but I'll tell you that my cube was small enough to fit in the palm of my hand; according to PUA fora, this indicates that that I feel insignificant. Kurt told me that I've got a confident exterior, but I'm uncertain on the inside.

Also, when I found a horse in the desert, I didn't care. I left the horse alone. However, when a storm came along, I ensured that the horse had shelter. Apparently, the horse is a symbol for my ideal lover, so this indicates that I won't chase my lovers... but I'll be there for them when they need me. Kurt told me it means I'm very independent.

It's like *magic,* right?

Kurt seemed crestfallen by how sarcastically I responded to his Cube reading, so I lightened up. Despite all the synthetic game, I couldn't help liking him. He struck me as a genuine example of a decent, kind guy who benefited from exposure to pickup. He was a classic example of Type 2: The Freaks and Geeks. And my misogyny-meter picked up nothing from him.

One thing Kurt appreciated about the community, he explained, was that it helped him engage with women... and also it helped him understand our reality a little better. For example, the idea of "bitch shields" helped Kurt grasp how much unwanted attention many women put up with. "Bitch shields" helped him frame bitchiness as a defense, rather than an offense.

I'd feel more positive about this if I felt like most information in the PUA community was reasonable (buyer's remorse, anyone?). But hey, with ideas like bitch shields and Anti-Slut Defense, PUAs are at least trying to describe some genuine phenomena.

I asked Kurt how he'd advise a newbie to the community, and he talked about self-improvement and inner game ideas. I asked how he'd critique the community, and he talked about how he wished there was more advice available for non-white men. He was considering attending a bootcamp by a guru who specialized in pickup artistry for racial minorities.

Towards the end of the interview, Kurt told me his most successful pickup story, which occurred in the very bar where we were sitting. After describing a couple hours of flirtation, he said, "I used the Evolution Phase-Shift on her. Has anyone ever done that to you?"

"I've read about it," I said, "though I don't remember how it goes. No one's done it to me."

"No way! Here, I'll show you," he said, and moved to sit close to me. If you want the entire Evolution Phase-Shift, you can Google it; it was developed by Neil Strauss and it's famous. It's a set of steps for initiating make-outs that involves a lot of specific physical body language (or what PUAs call "kino").

Hilariously, Kurt put the routine in the context of his previous seduction. For example, he said, "I started by telling her that she smelled good, and then I leaned in, brushed her hair aside *like this*. I sniffed her slowly, moving up from the shoulder to the ear, *like this*. Then I said: 'People don't pay enough attention to smell. But you'll notice how animals, before they mate, will always smell each other. Evolution has hard-wired us to respond to certain things. You are wired to respond when someone smells you.'"

In response to random assertions about evolutionary theory made by random dudes, I say: whatever. But there aren't many things more erotic than feeling someone's breath on my neck. Despite knowing the origins of the Evolution Phase-Shift... and despite the context, whereby Kurt explained each step as it applied to a previous seduction... I felt my hormones spike. Or maybe it was partly *because of the context.* Anyway, although it's not a magic spell to make the target 100% receptive, I understand why this routine works: the physical steps are well-designed.

Kurt could tell that I wasn't 100% receptive, if only because there's a step in the Evolution Phase-Shift that's designed to measure receptiveness. Late in the routine, the PUA says something like: "Do you know what the best thing in the world is? A bite... right... here," and points to his neck. A lot of girls will lean in to bite at that point, but I didn't. So the end was a confusing moment. We both looked at each other, then looked straight ahead, then looked at each other again.

"Do you want to kiss me?" he asked.

"I don't know," I said. It was true.

"Well," he said, "let's find out," and kissed me.

It was a fun kiss, but I couldn't help thinking about how a feminist guy who values enthusiastic consent would have responded. (I noticed with my partner Adam, for example, that if he asked a question and I said "I don't know" or "Maybe," he stopped completely or did something else.) If Kurt had said something like, "I'd rather you were sure," then I would have felt more comfortable with him. Nevertheless, it was a fun kiss.

And I must admit that he really had his routines down pat. I suspect that if I had said "No, I don't want to kiss you," then he would have said, "Well, I didn't say you could... you just looked like you were thinking about something." That's a famous one.

We wound the conversation down. I was expected elsewhere (for real). As we walked outside, laughing and chatting, Kurt twirled me around and threw me over his shoulder. Eventually he put me down, we prepared to split up, and he said, "Clarisse! You're the kind of girl who ruins PUAs. You get us into relationships!"

Oh no, I thought. *That's some fast emotional escalation.* My managing-expectations instincts perked up. I gave Kurt a slight smile and looked away. "Actually," I said aloud, "my ideal relationship includes watching my partner pick up other women."

He laughed and gave me a hug. I wondered if he understood that I was serious.

Kurt and I saw each other again, but ultimately we didn't have that much in common. For example, he had little experience with alternative sexuality, or activism, or the arts. And managing his expectations seemed like it could be troublesome. And also his apartment smelled like horrid socks.

I can't help wondering if Kurt will transcend the routines and become a master PUA, and what he'll be like if he does. Lots of guys never become a master, though. And perhaps most of them are happier that way.

* * *

Jonnie Walker — yes, that is his real name — had read my blog and had talked to me on the phone by the time I ran into him, randomly, at an event. He didn't know what I looked like, so I had to introduce myself. "You're Clarisse?" he said in surprise. "You're cuter than I thought you'd be."

Totally classic neg. I totally laughed.

Jonnie had a reputation for being smart and skilled, but he did less paid instruction than free community organizing. He was an archetypal Leader from my Typology of PUAs. In fact, we kinda bonded while talking about grassroots activism. When I mentioned some of the feminist volunteering I've done, Jonnie compared it to "teaching men to be better men through pickup."

"Any guy can get laid," he added. "The hard part is becoming a better man. There is a dark side to pickup artistry, and I try to encourage guys to stay on the light side."

So we traded tactics for organizing people, but I had difficulty discussing oppression with Jonnie. When we inevitably got on the topic of feminism, Jonnie said things like "I'm a feminist," but he didn't have a strong grounding in it. He was certainly willing to give critiques of feminism, though. Like the age-old idea that feminists are too combative and we're "looking for" things to get mad about. "Feminists need to be more socially tactical," he said. "Like PUAs."

I'm all for social tactics, but anti-oppression movements often have to say things people don't want to hear. I tried pointing out that injustice can't always be addressed in a happy, sunshiney, fun, non-awkward way. Where would we be if feminists were never "combative" about getting women the right to vote? Or, to shift the emphasis, where would the USA be if no one was ever "combative" about ending slavery?

Jonnie got my point. And he kept arguing, gently, which I respected even when it frustrated me. "If you put too much energy into an obstacle, you make it stronger," he said. "Freedoms and rights should always be fought for. But I'm not talking about that. I'm speaking directly about maturity and how the individual deals with those emotions that come with rejection and oppression. This is what makes great people great and the mediocre many.

"By sheer randomness and choices along the way," he continued, "we are where we are at in life. We could have it much worse or much better.

There is no entitlement. No one owes us anything. Complaining or wallowing in the sentiment of injustice — or rejection while dating — is a waste of time. The only real thing is getting past all that and getting down to the business of creating the change you want to see. All that negative emotion just gets in the way of creating what works in relationships and freedoms."

I thought I could understand where Jonnie was coming from, but eventually we hit a wall. The conversation culminated with Jonnie telling me, "I guess I just don't think life *should* be fair."

I looked at him: this attractive, white, American, straight, cisgendered man with a great education and an upper-middle-class job. Granted, Jonnie worked hard to get where he is... but really, why *would* he think life should be fair? I felt a headache coming on. I changed the subject.

Anyway, theoretical ramblings aside, I don't mean to give Jonnie a hard time. Notwithstanding our disagreements, he was open-minded and decent. He definitely made a real effort to discourage misogyny among PUAs he advised. In one conversation, we talked about how some PUAs act like women are all the same, and Jonnie agreed that it's bad, even for tactical reasons. "Learning how to deal differently with different women will help my game," he pointed out.

We also talked about the "women love assholes" trope, which made Jonnie shake his head. "I'm always trying to explain this to guys," he said. "Some women may appear to love assholes. But those women are not actually looking for assholes. They're looking for something that's *most closely approximated* by an asshole. Men don't have to be assholes to get girls, and they shouldn't. Men should figure out what assholes do right, and do that, without being assholes themselves."

Arguably, this is what the good PUAs are doing: they figure out what makes charming assholes charming, and then they seek to bestow that same charm upon non-assholes.

Later, after we'd known each other for a while, Jonnie and I shared insecurities. "Sometimes it hurts so much to hear PUAs talk about women," I said. "It makes me feel so... *disposable.*"

"Really?" said Jonnie. "I think about this all the time, because I feel so disposable. I always tell my guys: 'You're a beautiful snowflake... just like everyone else.' *Everyone* is disposable. So maybe you feel like men judge you for your looks. Maybe you feel like men can ditch you at any time for another pretty girl. But men, we contend with being judged for our wealth. There's always a richer guy. Gold-diggers make men disposable."

I guess that as much as women fear being used for sex, men fear being used for money.

I love it when references like "beautiful snowflake" come up in conversations about manliness. You've probably read Chuck Palahniuk's book *Fight Club* or seen the movie it spawned, featuring the actors Edward Norton and Brad Pitt. I've always asserted that *Fight Club* says a lot about how we think about men. "The first rule of Fight Club," my friends, "is that you don't talk about Fight Club"... because Real Men Are Strong And Silent, right? Note that Tyler Durden, the villain of *The Game,* took his PUA name from *Fight Club*. And don't forget that scene in *Fight Club* where Tyler says, "You are not a beautiful and unique snowflake. You are the same decaying organic matter as everyone else."

I usually saw Jonnie Walker at nightclubs during sarging expeditions. He knew I was constantly broke, so he always made sure I got drink tickets and drink deals. Late one evening, I sought him out to say goodnight, and he pulled me close. He seemed agitated.

"One of my long-term relationships is here," he said softly. "She's with another guy."

He directed my eyes to a lovely blonde, who was blatantly flirting with some dude. I thought about saying, *You're dating a ton of people yourself, Jonnie.* I thought about saying, *Don't you think you should talk to her about how you feel?*

I didn't know what their relationship was like. It seemed like she might be playing the game as much as Jonnie was. Besides, he was a PUA coach! I didn't feel qualified to advise him. Most of all, the hurt on his face was so stark. I held my peace.

So much for PUAs being cold, empty-hearted bastards.

"C'mon, dance with me," Jonnie said, and I put my arms around his neck. Always happy to provide social proof.

He looked down at me thoughtfully. "You really came out of nowhere," he said. "I mean, I didn't expect... you're like a *strafing run* out of nowhere."

I bet you say that to all the girls, I thought, *especially when you're trying to make someone jealous.* "That's sweet," I answered automatically, and danced a moment longer before going home.

* * *

When I was visiting my dad during the holidays, I discovered PUA material on his bookshelf. It was David DeAngelo's *Double Your Dating:* one of the most well-known curricula in the world. In *The Game,* Neil Strauss describes DeAngelo as a brilliant marketer. DeAngelo was, apparently, one of the driving forces that originally commercialized pickup artistry and made it into an industry as much as a community. Like a number of the wealthiest PUA marketers, DeAngelo stays away from seduction community jargon and events and focuses on reaching the mainstream, although the community has influenced him a lot.

"*Dad!*" I squawked. I immediately dropped everything and followed him around the apartment, peppering him with questions. First was, "Do you realize this comes from the same subculture I have been obsessing about and critiquing extensively from a feminist perspective? *This comes from the pickup artists!*"

My dad, incidentally, is one of the most ethical and feminist dudes I've had the good fortune to know. I mean, *he's* lectured *me* on rape culture.

"Er," Dad said, "I guess I didn't realize that. I got on some email list of DeAngelo's years ago, when your mother and I were getting divorced, and I thought it sounded interesting. I never listened to the whole tape, but it's not too bad. DeAngelo is a complete egomaniac, but he's not an idiot. He's not too much of a jerk, either."

"Not too much of a jerk?"

"Well, like I said, he's a complete egomaniac. But he's not a *complete* asshole." I'd chased Dad to his bedroom, where I hovered at the door, exploding with questions. He sat down with a sigh. "I've seen a fair amount of material where the guys were *such* assholes," he added. "I couldn't stand it."

"How much impact did pickup artistry have on your behavior?" I asked.

"I'm not sure. I didn't keep up with it. When I started dating again, I found that I was successful just being myself."

I'm not biased or anything, but my dad is quite smart and professionally established. He likes dating smart women his own age, and he doesn't chase his secretaries. I don't think it's hard for men like him to find partners. However, when he was young and awkward, I don't know how much action he got. Dad has great lady friends and exes, including my *extremely amazing* mom. Nevertheless....

"Do you think the advice would have helped when you were younger?" I asked.

"Maybe," he said thoughtfully. He looked down at his shoes, then back at me. I got the impression that he wanted to be honest, but that he felt somewhat embarrassed; I *am* his daughter, after all. "I'm not sure."

I decline to analyze where my dad falls in my Grand Typology of PUAs. He's my *dad*.

* * *

Lots of guys get into pickup artistry because they can't talk to girls. But some get into it *to improve their natural game.* One, a music promoter who's toured with tons of bands, told me: "Getting laid isn't hard. But I want to get laid with women I want to date."

In fact, I met one of the handsomest men I've ever seen on a sarging expedition. Seriously, heart-meltingly handsome. Also exceptionally smart, with an advanced degree from a prestigious university.

And his game was good. At one point, I watched a woman bump into him accidentally at the bar. He took a step back, smiled, and made a charming "surrender" gesture with his hands. His demeanor was an exquisite mix of friendly mischief, and he wasn't even trying; he was just being polite.

The woman laughed and went forward to join her friends. Then she leaned back to give him another chance to talk to her, and moved forward again. Then she glanced back at him and transparently batted her eyelashes.

She was pretty, too. At least I thought so. But, after his silent apology for the collision, he ignored her.

"Why are you even *here?"* I asked him. "You don't need any help."

"I guess I'm looking into this because I feel like I should," he said. "It seems like the next logical step." He explained that in relationships, he felt like he was "babysitting." He wanted to cast a wider net. He wanted a "better selection" of women.

"My problem," he confided morosely, "is that I'm picky. I want *both* beauty *and* intelligence."

I'm not sure how I'd categorize these guys within my Typology of PUAs. I guess they're sort of like Hedonists, or maybe the Freaks and Geeks: these guys aren't Average Frustrated Chumps to start with, but they still don't have the level of social skills they want. On the other hand, I do wonder about their standards. I wonder whether their perfect woman is too perfect to be real. Maybe their social skills *can't* be high enough, because the woman they want doesn't exist.

* * *

Carson was a African-American guy with an amazing smile and sweet man-jewelry. I slipped my finger under his necklace and played with it, then stood back and smiled at him. "Nice peacocking," I said.

This, my friends, is what PUAs call a "fake Indicator of Interest." Fake IOIs are often deployed by female waitresses, strippers, journalists, and other women whose tips depend on a man's satisfaction. However, I will point out that men do this too. I've totally been gamed by hot male salesmen, and Neil Strauss has written that his game made him a better celebrity-interviewer.

I caught myself delivering the fake IOI right after it happened. I swear to you, I was not deliberately pretending sexual interest in order to manipulate Carson. So here's the question. Where are the lines among flirting for fun, versus neutral friendly social interactions, versus cynical manipulation?

We were standing in the mist outside yet another club. Carson soon explained how he'd gotten into the PUA community: "I read *The Game*," he said, "and I knew that was *it.*"

I described *The Game* in the last chapter, but let's recap: the book chronicles Neil Strauss's development into an awesome pickup artist, but it contains a ridiculous amount of drama. So I'm always astonished to hear guys like Carson say, "I read *The Game*, and I knew that was *it.*" He knew *what* was *it*? The vomit-soaked mansion? The insincere sport-fucking? The breakdowns and backstabbing?

Except at the same time, I get it. Who doesn't want to be the focus of everyone's eyes when they enter the room? Who doesn't want to feel beautiful and charming and socially powerful? Who doesn't want to be a master of flirtation? Doesn't everyone want some strategic ambiguity in their life?

Or maybe not everyone is drawn so powerfully to those things. Maybe lots of PUAs have something twisted within them, and I've got the same thing twisted in me.

Carson was completing his first year in the community. A number of experienced PUAs have told me that there's a predictable PUA life-cycle. Some dudes are lifers, but the usual life-cycle goes for about a year. This year includes an extremely large amount of sarging. Eventually, the PUA starts getting laid regularly, and then the year typically ends with a sense of confusion, at which point the guy starts working on the rest of his life. Carson's PUA friends had reached this endpoint. He was the last one to think about his own business, other hobbies, etc.

His PUA friends mattered a lot to him. He talked about them more than he talked about women. Indeed, he exemplified a pattern I saw a lot: pickup artistry as a way of making dude friends. Carson said that he could recognize community guys simply by watching them pick up girls. He spoke of how he'd spot a guy working on a girl, and he'd say, "Hey, are you in the community?" The two guys would end up in a great conversation, as the girl wandered off, snubbed and forgotten.

Talking about relationships is a really great way to bond. Most women already do this with each other as a matter of course; men, much less so. So while a lot of PUAs seem surprised by the connections they make among each other, I'm not at all shocked that a community full of men who talk about relationships ends up generating intense friendships. And, of course, it also generates intense gossip and backstabbing. Lots of PUAs complained to me about all the shit-talking around the community. I encountered a few instances of this myself, but if you want a completely egregious example, read *The Game*.

In other words, the PUA community confirms that mean girls aren't mean because they're girls; mean girls are mean because they're mean. It turns out that when a person's social context involves a lot of social analysis and maneuvering, mean people use drama and backstabbing and shit-talking to get what they want. Even if they're men.

The mist was cold. Carson and I wrapped up the conversation, and he mentioned that some PUAs do sleazy things he doesn't like.

"Oh, definitely," I said. "You mean like some of those Last Minute Resistance tactics?"

"No, I mean like fucking really drunk girls," he said, and threw me a puzzled look. "LMR tactics? Everyone uses them."

"Everyone uses them"? Holy shit, I thought, *I've got to write that down on a cocktail napkin before I forget it.* I hoped that he was talking mutual LMR tactics, like turning a girl on with lots of foreplay, rather than aggressive LMR tactics like freeze-outs. I liked Carson. He struck me as a mix of Type 3 PUA, Hedonist, plus Type 2 PUA, one of the Freaks and Geeks. So I didn't like to imagine him pulling coldly manipulative moves in the bedroom, but maybe he does it all the time. I'll probably never know.

We wound our way through the crowd back into the club, and I smiled up at him. "Thanks so much," I said. "Really, this was great."

Carson gave me that million-dollar grin. "Anything for you," he said gallantly.

* * *

As my obsession with pickup artistry intensified, I brought it up with my friends a lot. This included my dude friends, and also guys I was dating. Sometimes, this got weird.

A lot of PUAs talk about how girls deliberately tease Average Frustrated Chumps. These PUAs claim that all girls are always seeking men to keep on a string. As a geek girl, I've always had a ton of dude friends. I've heard this line for years, and not just from PUAs. It makes me angry, especially when people ascribe intentions to me that I don't have. (Say it with me now: *"All women want is control!"*)

Let me be clear here: I've definitely encountered behavior from other women that makes me uncomfortable. For example, I once met a geek girl who told me that she convinces male platonic friends to buy her lingerie because she promises to model it for them. On the one hand, I feel like she's manipulating them. On the other hand, if these guys know that she has no romantic or sexual intentions, then they also know what they're getting into when they buy her lingerie. They know that they can see her in the lingerie, but they can't expect anything else.

I'm not going to treat those men like infants and assume they can't make their own decisions about that exchange.

And "treating men like infants" seems to be exactly what some guys expect me to do. Some guys tell me that all men *really* want is to fuck women, and no guys are ever "just friends" with women; PUAs are especially prone to saying this. I've heard men say things like, "The *definition of a bitch* is a woman who's friends with a man, when the man wants to sleep with her. The *definition of a bitch* is a woman *who knows that,* and who doesn't plan to sleep with him, but who hangs out with him anyway."

In the meantime, other guys tell me that there's absolutely no problem with men and women being friends. Other guys tell me that they have plenty of platonic female friends... even platonic female friends that they're attracted to.

What's especially irritating is that many dudes on both sides expect me to magically divine a man's intentions towards me. Not only am I expected to read dudes' minds; I am expected to figure out whether I'm attracted to a guy, and decide what will happen in our relationship immediately. Pro tip: sometimes attraction develops over time. Attraction doesn't always develop over time, but sometimes it does. I suspect that this is common for many women, if not for men.

And if a man is attracted to me and I'm not attracted in return, then I'm supposed to... um....

Well, that's the step I've never quite understood. If I suspect that a male friend is attracted to me, and I don't want to have sex with him, then what exactly am I expected to do? "Hey man, I can tell you want to have sex with me! But that will never happen, so I am hereby deciding on your behalf that we can't be friends, because you will feel sexually frustrated if we are friends."

Am I really supposed to say those words? I don't think so. A feminist might call that approach paternalistic, and I want nothing to do with it.

Supposedly, according to some guys, I'm being a manipulative bitch by staying friends with a guy who wants to fuck me, if I don't plan to fuck him anytime soon. But if I respect a guy enough to be friends with him, then shouldn't I respect him enough to let him make his own choices about interacting with me? If he chooses to stay friends with me while being attracted to me, and chooses not to talk to me about it, then *why is that my fault?*

I also don't want to assume that all men have zero interest in me besides fucking me, because that means assuming that men are incapable of relating to women without sex. And that's *really insulting* to men! I have interesting, thoughtful conversations with men all the time. Men aren't brainless horndogs, I promise.

And then there's the fact that some people are just confusing, *including men.*

My best dude friend these days is a total dude. He's probably less dudely than a lot of men, being as he cooks delicious food and lives in gender-bending San Francisco. However, he's dudely enough that I'll henceforth call him The Dude.

Sometimes I feel surprised that I'm such good friends with The Dude, being as he gets bored when I talk about feminism and social justice. But we talk about everything else, including relationships. The Dude has game, and I'm not always thrilled with how he treats his lady friends. A mutual friend once surmised that The Dude's real agenda has always been to get me into bed, after which The Dude will lose all respect for me.

In fairness, The Dude and I flirt a fair bit. Sometimes I wonder if we're going to do the romantic comedy thing and get married after some ridiculous incident in our thirties. But this is not my current plan, and I don't think he's just friends with me because he plans to seduce and abandon me. *Or is he?*

At one point while reading about PUAs, I freaked out so hard that I texted The Dude: "Are you just friends with me because you want to sleep with me? And would you be honest if the answer were yes?"

He texted back, "As I recall, you BEGGED to sleep with ME, but I was too much man for you."

I was composing an enraged, all-capital-letters text response when he called.

"You didn't answer my question!" I yelled into the phone. "And also you're flirting like a PUA!"

"Is that so?" he asked. He sounded amused.

"Yes! You're treating me like I'm shit testing you. You're reframing the exchange and acting cocky! You're even framing me as the sexual aggressor. Except that PUAs say you should never lie, and you're lying!"

"No way, man," he said cheerfully. "Remember, years ago, when we met, you and I were walking down University Avenue? And you said: 'Dude, you are so sexy! I totally want to fuck you this instant! Right on that sidewalk over there.' And I said: 'Sorry girl, I'm not into you like that, I hate to let you down.' It *totally* happened. I was there."

I found myself laughing. "Dude," I said, "come on, that never happened. Although I guess I have to give you PUA points. I was just reading a PUA blog post reminding me that a statement doesn't count as a lie if it's an obvious fabrication or an obvious joke. [3] So I guess this doesn't count as a lie. But anyway, quit making things up and...."

I stopped, because The Dude said something while I was ranting, and I couldn't quite hear it. But I was pretty sure he'd said, "Well, *obviously* I'm just friends with you because I want to sleep with you."

"What?!" I cried.

"Nothing," he said. I could still hear the smile in his voice. "Look, I'm going to continue drinking at this airport bar. You tell the guys on whatever PUA forum you're reading that men and women can definitely have platonic relationships. Because you and I are platonic. *Completely platonic.* Okay?"

I was laughing again. "Okay," I agreed.

This would be an example of mildly adversarial flirting. I can't explain why it's fun, but it is... for me, anyway.

It would make me angry if we had that conversation while I was trying to communicate something important and serious. But in response to a mild freakout that occurred while reading some ridiculous PUA forum? The Dude was hilarious. It would have been okay if he'd just said, "We're completely platonic, calm down." But instead, he chose to flirt while reassuring me, which was also okay. He put us right back in the "flirtatious friendly area" where we've been for years.

Does this interaction show that I'm a manipulative bitch? Maybe... but it doesn't sound like The Dude hates the situation. It's not like he's pining after me. On the other hand, what if I'm misreading things, and he's actually mocking me, and he feels zero attraction to me whatsoever? I guess I can't be sure of anything, because the mixed signals are thick on the ground here.

The real point is, I'm no more in control than The Dude. We've got a mutual situation, and it makes me no more a manipulative bitch than it makes him a manipulative asshole.

However, I would like to note that I think the "friend zone" is a real thing that really happens. Plus, the "fuckbuddy zone" is a similar thing that happens mostly to women. And I promise, I will analyze both of these things extensively in the next chapter.

* * *

Some male friends reacted to my discussions of pickup artistry with shrugs. One remarked, "It's weird that PUAs put so much effort into getting laid all the time, but I guess I get it. I mean, it's all about priorities, right? Those guys have their priorities, and I have mine."

Others felt sympathy, even pity. "It's hard for me to read PUA stuff," another guy told me. "Those guys' fears and insecurities are so painfully on display. It makes me feel bad for them, and it makes me self-conscious about my own insecurities."

Others were furious about it. A date almost jumped out of his chair with rage when I brought it up. "I *hate* that stuff," he said. "PUAs find tricks in human psychology, and manipulate those tricks to have sex with someone who doesn't really want to. It's not natural. As far as I'm concerned, it's rape."

"I dunno," I said cautiously. "I haven't seen any PUAs who seem capable of outright hypnotizing women. Some of them talk about hypnosis, but the majority, if not all of them, are just learning social tactics. And if they're just learning social tactics, then how is it different from having good pheromones? Or having a good body? Or otherwise being naturally attractive?"

"Or eating healthy food so that you have better pheromones and you stay in shape..." my date added thoughtfully. "Yeah, I see what you're saying. There are lots of social advantages you can gain by hard work, so why is this different?" He pondered for a moment, then smiled. "You got me," he admitted. "I don't know why it's different. Still, I don't like it. It's *cheating.*"

For plenty of men, the community's misogyny is the biggest problem, the same way it is for me. Recall, for example, that my father considered most PUAs to be assholes; he couldn't stand listening to most PUA curricula. Recall that Josh, the PUA instructor, told me he was appalled when he first saw the community because it was "so sleazy." Lots of other guys said things like "Reading PUA materials makes me so angry, because of the misogyny," or "I *can't even read* those fora because they're so misogynist."

One such gentleman was Adam, my long-haired activist partner in San Francisco. "I think one reason PUA stuff pisses me off," he remarked one evening, "is that I could really use advice like that. I just can't handle how they frame it in such a misogynist way."

"Really?" I asked. "You think you need advice?"

"Sure. I wish I got that kind of attention from women."

From where I was lying naked on his couch, I raised my eyebrows at him. He had the grace to laugh and look sheepish. "Well, I have no complaints right now," he said.

I grinned. "PUAs don't get laid all the time," I told him. "A lot of self-described PUAs probably get laid about as much as you do. And even the really good ones practiced a lot to get where they are. They go out and practice approaching women for hours at a time, multiple times per week. They learn tactics, and they gain experience, but they don't have a magic bullet."

"Okay...." He mulled it over. "I guess, if they practiced so much, then they earned it."

I obviously think it's great to critique the misogynist framing of pickup artistry. But I also think some people feel angry about PUAs because they believe PUAs have a special, evil charm that unlocks All Women In The World. The truth is, of course, that no PUA in the world can get "any woman." Even the experts fail with some girls, and most guys never get close to "expert level"... whether because they can't, or because they lose interest.

Most famous gurus promote themselves by claiming that they've got The Secret. Indeed, one of the most famous PUA ebooks is actually *called Magic Bullets*. But none of them really have The Secret. They've just got an assortment of tactics and attitudes.

Sometimes I think the books and workshops are practically superfluous. Guys might learn just as much about how to pick up girls if they did the hundreds of hours of practice, without being exposed to pickup theory. And despite all the jargon and self-promotion, PUAs recognize this. Every PUA I've ever met emphasized practice. I've mentioned this before, but it bears repeating: there are PUA maxims like, "The first thousand rejections don't count."

My goth-feminist-PUA friend Brian once told me: "People don't get how difficult it is, especially if you're starting from below-average social skills. They don't get that the first step is going out and trying to get numbers for several months. Then you finally start getting numbers, and women start flaking on you. After months of that, you get your first date... and then you whiff the kiss."

* * *

After I released this book, I was recruited for a panel about feminism and pickup artistry at the South-by-Southwest Interactive conference. It was a really interesting panel that included the famous PUA coach Adam Lyons. Naturally, I grabbed the chance to interview Adam Lyons so that I could add his perspective to this book. (Since the interview took place after this book's initial release, you know you're reading *Confessions* Version 2.0 if you're reading this sentence right now.)

We met in an apartment that Adam Lyons rents for PUA training courses. The place contained a hefty amount of booze, a bunch of leftover pizza, and some instructors who were all worn out after a weekend of teaching. The guys invited me to go play Lazer Tag after the interview, but I regretfully had to decline.

Adam Lyons is one of nine coaches listed as "significant figures" in the Wikipedia entry for the seduction community. Compared to some other top coaches, he's relatively new, but he got into the community when it was still pretty underground. "In maybe 2005 or 2006," he told me, *"The Game* had just come out. I was halfway through reading *The Game* and I knew I had to try this. So I managed to find this bootcamp company and get in touch with them. My contact was like, 'Come and meet me in a Chinese restaurant,' so I took an envelope full of cash and I met him in a Chinese restaurant. He took the cash and counted it, and told me to meet the group in a particular bar later that week."

"What did you learn?" I asked.

"In my first program, I learned the 'fall on the floor technique,' where you run up to a girl and you just fall on the floor. It was ridiculous."

I laughed. "That would totally work on me. I'd think it was hilarious."

"It can work surprisingly well," Adam Lyons acknowledged. "But I once introduced a guy to my wife who then kept falling out of his chair, and it was so terrible. Anyway, most of the other 'techniques' didn't work at all. For example, in that first program, they made me walk up to all these girls in the street and say, 'I'm the kissing bandit — now you have to kiss me!' It was so awkward."

Within a few months, Adam Lyons soaked up everything the community had to offer and had begun coaching for local PUA companies. Now he runs his own company along with his wife. We talked a lot about social phobia, and how some PUA techniques line up with treatments for social phobia. Adam Lyons echoed a point that I'd already heard from other PUAs, like Mark Manson: that social phobia techniques may be helpful for some guys, but not all guys... and more importantly, applying treatments for social phobia to men who aren't phobic will be utterly counterproductive.

"For people who genuinely have a clinical phobia, there are basically two ways of getting rid of it," said Adam Lyons. "One of them is 'flooding' and the other is 'systematic desensitization.' In systematic desensitization, you slowly expose a person to that stimulus until they're okay with it. So if they have a phobia of spiders, you might show them a photo of a spider, then show them videos, then put them in the same room with a spider in a tank, and then slowly put a spider on their hand. With 'flooding,' you'd do something like drop someone in a bath full of spiders.

"When picking up girls," he continued, "with 'flooding,' you force a guy to do a lot of approaches with a stupid routine or wearing a stupid outfit, until he's not scared of women anymore. So when a student who overcomes their phobia that way goes to teach someone else, they'll use the 'flooding' technique. But the other person might not actually have a phobia, they might just be a little scared, which isn't as bad and requires a different approach. So they're taking a technique, which is a proven psychological technique, and applying it to someone who doesn't need it. And any individual technique taught to the wrong person is going to give the wrong message. For example, the minute you tell a guy who's already confident that he should just say what he feels, then you've got a whole new problem coming up — he'll be over-aggressive. So that's my main issue with old-fashioned routine-based game. The right techniques, but only for certain people."

"You have other issues?" I asked.

"Probably thousands," he said ruefully, and we both laughed. "What most of these guys need is emotional help, not pickup artistry. But I think the community has really changed," he added. "Or rather, it's come to a tipping point. When I look at the Internet analytics for pickup, I see that pickup artistry as a topic isn't nearly as popular as it was a few years ago. But men are searching for dating advice now in a way that they never used to. Men are asking Google questions like 'How do I find a girlfriend?' — most men never used to do that. Dating advice for men has finally reached the point I've been waiting for, where it's really mainstream and acceptable. It's going to be a whole new landscape."

Again, all this was analysis I'd heard from other guys like Mark, but it was interesting to hear it from such a prominent PUA. Most of the top coaches aren't so interested in subverting the industry.

Adam Lyons also gave me one of the sweetest stories I've heard from a PUA coach, ever. It was about a man who came to his course in order to get his wife back. "We're doing this program," he told me, "and there's this guy turns up, he's totally built, and he's also nervous and quiet. He sits through the seminar silently and then asks to talk to me alone. Once we're in another room, he starts crying and he says: 'I'm not here to pick up a girl. I'm here to pick up my wife.'"

It turned out that this guy was a successful professional boxer, and this woman pursued him for years. Eventually he married her, but soon afterwards he decided that the boxing life wasn't good for him, so he quit and started a nonprofit for teaching kids how to box. She lost interest in him and eventually told him that either she wanted to be able to sleep with other people, or she wanted a divorce. He granted the exception to their monogamy because he was afraid of losing her, but he was miserable.

"So," said Adam Lyons, "I told this boxer: 'I'm going to teach you to get a girl. If it's your wife, that's great, but if it isn't then you'll have the skill set to find someone else.' I taught him a bunch of things, but ultimately we decided to re-create his lifestyle from when he was a pro boxer, in a different way. He started holding youth boxing championships. He didn't make much money by setting up the championships, but that was okay because he had another job, and he had this great social position with all these hot girls and young boxers who admire him. So his wife noticed this and she regained interest in him, and they renewed their vows."

(As it happens, the couple broke up for good a couple years later. But apparently the boxer felt a lot better about it when they did break up, and he reported feeling like he found himself through the whole process of creating the championships.)

Adam Lyons is himself married to a sultry and beautiful woman, Amanda Lyons, who helps a lot with his PUA training and marketing. Amanda is not known for her conversational restraint, nor for her empathy. At one point she had a big fight on Twitter with one of my feminist co-panelists, after she accused us of mentioning rape during the panel because it's a "feminist trump card."

Still, Amanda and I were able to get along, and she's certainly smart. It was interesting to watch the couple interact. When I came over to interview Adam Lyons, he was telling his wife a story about how he charmed a local baker into giving him pies for free — and deconstructing his tactics. It looked like a fun relationship: the two of them get to talk about social dynamics and manipulation all the time. And he clearly loves her exactly as she is.

"My wife's such a dude," Adam Lyons told me. "Amanda drinks beer, I drink wine. Amanda likes football, I don't. Out of the two of us, I try to be sympathetic to girls and issues that they have, but Amanda has no sympathy for girls really. Or boys, to be completely fair." He glanced over at where his wife was involved in her laptop. "Amanda is CEO of her own company — she's really dominated the pickup industry," he said fondly.

"She's a badass. She starts fights with feminists."

"How does it feel to be a prominent PUA who's married?" I asked.

"I crossed #1 PUA the day I got married," Adam Lyons said. "I was #1 worldwide within 3 months after I got married. Everywhere, every PUA site put me at #1 on every list."

Which tells us something about PUAs really want, doesn't it?

* * *

***

CHAPTER 7:
Tough Guy

In which Clarisse sees Adam again, and her Field Report of emotional escalation continues. There's some confusion about what that means, though, because it's a long-distance polyamorous relationship and neither of them have extensive experience with that. There is also confusion because Clarisse and Adam engage in unexpectedly intense S&M, and the emotional fallout startles them both. Plus: a Theory of the Friend Zone and the Fuckbuddy Zone. The chapter title is after a song with the same name, by The Crystal Method.

***

Unfortunately, since I just included a bit about Adam Lyons, there are too many Adams in this book, but I suppose that can't be helped. Anyway, the important Adam is my deliciously long-haired partner from San Francisco. I saw long-haired Adam again soon after leaving that fine city... but it was in a different city. We both happened to be passing through Atlanta at the same time.

I went in prepared, with a frisson of anxiety and excitement. I thought it might be pretty intense... and indeed, it was intense. He was interesting, he was smart, he made me laugh. And even though he kept claiming he was new to S&M, his instincts were *amazing*. I still recall some of the things he said to me, and shiver.

More importantly, he had brilliant instincts for S&M aftercare, too. After he hurt me until I cried, he knew exactly how to put his hands in my hair. He knew how to say my name, how to tell me it was safe to come back into my body. It was less crucial that he could shatter me in that way I like, than it was that he could help me pick up the pieces afterwards.

I'll tell you the thing Adam said that made me fall into terrifying trust. He said it as I lay next to him, head on his shoulder, blissed-out and calm after the S&M storm. "I keep getting the feeling," he said, "that, although I appear to be running the show... even when you aren't giving me obvious feedback, you're doing most of the work."

So many dominants think it's all about them, especially newbies. So many can't grasp how much is going on under the surface: the amount of emotional labor a submissive can end up doing. A dominant can have good instincts, and still *not quite get it*. But Adam got it.

There's a stereotype that S&M dominants "should" be distant and cold. In my experience, this couldn't be further from the truth. Sometimes it's sexy if the dominant can act distant and cold during an S&M encounter — I've done it myself — but it can be just as sexy for the dominant partner to act warm. And outside the S&M? I want a human being, not an iceberg. Adam's sensitivity was there in everything he said and did. Even when he talked about feeling burned out on activism, it was obvious how much he cared about it, too.

We ended up spending nearly 24 hours together. The sex was awesome, and the company was just as good. It was fun to trade rants about rape culture and activist problems.

Adam was clear about not wanting a "serious relationship," inasmuch as the idea of a "serious relationship" is clear. On the other hand, he was sure as hell giving what I later labeled "emotional Indicators of Interest." An important example was the I-Think-About-You-When-You're-Not-Around emotional IOI; he gave that one several times. (For instance: "I thought about you a lot, during this conversation with a friend about....")

And he tried to get that IOI back from me: at one point, he suggested that he'd been on my mind.

"What makes you think that?" I asked.

He smiled. "Well, it stands to reason."

I didn't confirm or deny. In fact, as I recall, I allowed a significant pause... then I changed the subject. Ignore or reframe: just like responding to a compliance test.

A PUA would say that if you play into a woman's compliance test, you appear weak. Maybe I was thinking something similar. Plus, strategic ambiguity!

By mid-morning the next day, I knew what the next step in my emotional game had to be. I had to give a straight-up emotional Statement of Intent. A lot of PUAs talk about Statements of Intent (SOIs) in a sexual sense: when a PUA gives an SOI, he says something like, "I'm trying so hard not to kiss you right now." SOIs are a big part of direct game, in which the PUA tries to be straightforward about his intentions from the start. But you don't want to give an SOI until the target has demonstrated that she's into you by giving Indicators of Interest, because otherwise you might freak her out.

A Statement of Interest clearly establishes the situation, and I can attest that this is often reassuring for the target. Uncertainty may be one of the keys to successful flirting, but it's important to leaven it with moments of total certainty. Plus, it's frustrating to flirt with a guy while trying to subtly figure out if he's available.

And an SOI is a high-risk but effective way to test whether the target is receptive. After all, if she's not receptive, then she won't respond positively to statements like "I'm trying so hard not to kiss you right now."

Also, from a feminist consent perspective, giving an SOI is great for ensuring that your partner is fully aware of and into what's going on.

I've given emotional SOIs any number of times. They can be as simple as saying, softly, "I'm falling for you"... or they can be as complicated as a long and impassioned letter. Obviously, people frequently give these signals without precise timing. Yet when you're playing for emotional escalation, then the timing can be just as tricky as during sexual escalation. If you give an emotional SOI too soon, the target thinks you're needy. Yet if you wait too long, the target might lose interest, or he might feel rejected and disengage, or he might badly misunderstand your agenda.

I wasn't thinking in PUA terms at the time. But, looking back on it, I reckon an emotional SOI has two main parts:

PART 1: Express emotional vulnerability and intent to escalate.
PART 2: Manage expectations... both mine, and his.

I couldn't figure out a way to talk about it in person, so I sent Adam an email later. Email can be a risky medium for relationship communication, but it usually works well for me, probably because I date smart nerds.

This was a delicate task. I've never before given an emotional SOI to someone with whom I *didn't* want a primary or monogamous relationship. Normally, I just have to show how much I like the guy, without supplicating; I have to be vulnerable in a non-needy way. This time, I had to do those things, and I *also* had to make it clear that I *still* didn't want a traditional, monogamous, or highly focused relationship.

Ultimately, I wrote to Adam that although I had no interest in changing anything between us — that I liked the way things were — I needed him to understand that I was developing feelings. I ended with:

I guess I'm not sure what you mean when you say things like how you don't want anything "serious" right now. On the one hand, I feel similarly. On the other hand, though... I'm not like, in love with you, but I'm really into you, and if you aren't comfortable with me feeling emotionally invested and attached, then I should probably reevaluate how I plan to interact with you in the future.

I added that he could take time to think about it before responding. He sent me an acknowledgment of the initial email, we chatted about music and politics for a while, and then he got back to me a week later with:

I'm AOK with some emotional attachment. I like you too. Just avoid counting on me to be especially on top of my shit. I'm happy that we have some mutual affection, but will be skittish if it starts to become complicated.

I'll do my best to communicate, but I should warn you that I'm emotionally exhausted and cagey right now. Does this make sense? Is this ok?

Notwithstanding the tacit positive signals, he wasn't giving me explicit positive feedback. In fact, he was warning me off. At the same time, though, he accepted my feelings, and seemed genuinely concerned about them. *And that's all I want from a non-primary relationship,* I thought. *Right?*

Back in my monogamous days, I would never have considered this guy to be relationship material. But it was long-distance, and we weren't monogamous....

I told him it was fine.

* * *

PUAs have a term, "one-itis," that they use a lot when talking to newbie Average Frustrated Chumps. "One-itis" basically indicates infatuation, or obsession, with one woman. When I started investigating PUAs, I thought "one-itis" was a reflection of their distaste for acknowledging emotions. Reasonable people might call it a crush... or, God forbid... *love.* Or so I believed at first.

The commonly recommended PUA strategy for dealing with one-itis is to GFTOW: Go Fuck Ten Other Women. Not coincidentally, the lady marriage-game guide *The Rules,* which I discussed in Chapter 4, prescribes something similar. *The Rules* tells us that if a girl is stuck on one man, there's no medicine like romantic attention from new suitors.

Since men draw cultural validation from having sex and women draw cultural validation from getting love, this makes sense. Finding something to boost your self-confidence is often a great way to deal with the pain of rejection. Unfortunately, there's sometimes a vengeful taste to those discussions. I really don't like that; it's important to not enter the dating scene seeking revenge on the so-called "opposite sex."

There's something deeper than self-confidence and revenge behind these strategies, though. The point when I understood that one-itis isn't love was when I understood that it's fundamentally about *scarcity.* One-itis usually indicates an infatuation that arises entirely from feeling unworthy, or afraid that "I'll never find someone else like this again."

Scarcity was one thing I worried about, at first, with Adam. I thought that because of the chemistry I felt with him, and because I hadn't experienced intense S&M while I was abroad... I thought I might be reacting to scarcity, not to Adam as a person. Maybe that's what my friend meant, on Halloween, when she saw me losing my mind over Adam and said: "Sometimes you just freak out about people. It doesn't mean you're in love with them."

Many S&Mers — and other fetishists — are prone to scarcity thinking. Since S&M is highly stigmatized and many people aren't willing to think about it, a lot of us grow up full of shame and repression. Simply meeting a partner who's into what we're into can feel overwhelming. I still remember, in an early S&M relationship, snuggling up to my lover and saying: "I just can't believe you love me *and* you want to hurt me like that. I'm so lucky."

And I caught my breath, I almost cried, when he said: *"I* just can't believe how much *you* want to feel it. I'm so lucky that you love me for it," and kissed me.

When that guy dumped me, I was devastated for a lot of reasons, but one of them was that I thought he was a lot more unusual than he actually was. Don't get me wrong; that guy is a beautiful and unique snowflake. But since then, I've found his S&M attitudes with other people. Knowing that other guys are up for shatteringly intense yet empathic S&M makes me a lot more resilient after breakups. Indeed, it makes me more resilient during relationships in progress.

In other words: while looking for relationships, many people value qualities that seem scarce to them. Of course there's nothing wrong with having standards or preferences, but in some cases, people value certain qualities so much that they become emotionally invested too quickly for caution. PUAs developed the term one-itis to describe how a lonely guy can get invested too quickly in a girl who shows interest, because he's not used to girls being interested.

Another relevant PUA concept is "outcome independence." It indicates not feeling obsessed with a goal; not being focused on an outcome. Outcome independence ties into avoiding neediness and desperation, but it also ties into inner game, which is all about developing genuine confidence and sense of purpose.

What's really amazing about outcome independence, though, is that it implies ignoring the game altogether. When you're outcome-independent, *you don't need to bang chicks to feel good about yourself.*

This, ironically, will make girls more comfortable with you... because one thing girls are trained to be anxious about, and to watch out for, is being "used for sex." Outcome independence is a powerful argument against the worst Last Minute Resistance techniques that I discussed in Chapter 3, because caring too much whether you get laid is needy, and pushing to get into a girl's pants means being obsessed with a goal.

One awkward thing about this is that even if you're the most outcome-independent person in the world, the outcome-independence starts going away once you're really into someone. When experienced PUAs confront this fact, they often talk about either pretending that they don't care, and thereby pretending to be outcome-independent... or simply letting go of the fear of being hurt. Actually, one of my non-PUA friends put it best: "Go into every relationship accepting that your heart may be broken, and you'll be fine." Being open to the ups and downs of a relationship is itself an important kind of outcome independence.

Another awkward thing about outcome independence is that it's tricky to train, especially for PUAs. After all, guys get into the PUA community because they're feeling highly dependent on a given outcome, right? PUA gurus sell outcomes: "Get laid tonight," "Get your ex-girlfriend back," "Fuck HB10s," "Double your dating," etc. And becoming an excellent PUA requires feeling dependent enough on an outcome that the guy is willing to go out for days and days of practice.

Lots of gurus sneak outcome independence into their stuff anyway, though. I've already mentioned an instructor who suggested that the best way to imagine any interaction is "just having fun together," rather than aiming to have sex with the girl at all times.

PUAs often tell each other that they must always be willing to "next" their partners: to walk away from the relationship. And again, *The Rules* says something similar. If you're always sure you can walk away, that's a big step in getting over the scarcity mentality. If you're always sure you can walk away, then you're outcome-independent. If you're always willing to next your partners, that makes you a lot less vulnerable.

"You always have to be willing to next people" can help someone break off a bad relationship. Sometimes you just have to dump a bad partner. But of course, "you always have to be willing to next people" can be a callous maxim. Taken to extremes, "you always have to be willing to next people" implies that everyone is interchangeable. That no one is worth caring about. That no relationship deserves any effort. The worst part of romantic outcome independence is potential heartlessness.

So the scarcity mentality is a real thing. One-itis is a real thing. It's true that these are phenomena that can be affected by feeling more attractive, by feeling like you have "options." These phenomena can be affected by feeling like you can go out and get laid, or get loved, if you want those things. Yet vulnerability isn't always a bad thing. Connection is a real thing. Personal compatibility is a real thing. And so is love.

* * *

    Throughout my research, I dated aggressively... more aggressively than I've ever dated before. Maybe part of me absorbed the frenetic PUA desire to "maximize" my corner of the so-called "dating market." Also, PUAs are often happy to remind you that women become hags once we pass a certain age. Every time a man talks about how older women are ugly, it increases my urge to savagely break hearts while I'm still in my 20s. I do my best to repress this urge. I don't want to harm any innocent bystanders.

    Anyway, I was busy "maximizing." During one memorable weekend, I sent the following text message to both my best girlfriend and Twitter: "I know I'm past the point of no return when a date with a porn star goes better than last night's date with a grad student."

    Gotta say, the porn star was a sweetheart, though he wasn't really into S&M. He met my mom once, and she liked him a lot. "He's got such a nice way about him," she said.

    Oh, and let me give you a free example of how to pass a feminist shit test. One of my activist friends visited me in Chicago. We didn't have a romantic history, but we'd always had fun together, and his sexual interest was tacitly obvious. At one point, I teased him about the flowery way he wrote his name: "Doesn't that make people question your masculinity?"

    He slanted his eyes at me, sideways, ironically. *"What* masculinity?"

    I cracked up and gave him a hug. He was super fun in bed.

    Adam was on my mind, though, and I was looking forward to seeing him again. Yet a curious thing happened as I planned my next trip to San Francisco. I arranged my schedule and I texted Adam the dates I'd be in the city, and he didn't get back to me for several days. And I freaked out.

    I don't normally freak out when guys take a while to get back to my texts, emails or calls. In fact, I'm usually the person who takes a while to get back to other people. So it was weird that when Adam took a long time to respond to my text about dates, I got upset. I got so upset that I had to specifically sit down and calm myself. I got so upset that I started thinking about how to break it off, and that was when I decided I was being unreasonable. *Or was I?*

    I remembered my freak-out moment in the street on Halloween. What was going on in my head? I've often thought that if I had a dollar for every relationship that ended because one partner felt too vulnerable, I'd be richer than Neil Strauss. So was it just that I really liked this guy, and that was making me feel vulnerable and scared? Or was this situation actually a *terrible idea?*

It was time to bring in the big guns. It was time for an evening consultation with my female best friend.

Good social networks are incredibly helpful for having good relationships. Counselors who work with people in abusive relationships have found that the first priority of most abusers is *to destroy their partner's social networks.* An abuser will try to gain complete control over their partner's social movements and activities, or will maneuver to ruin their relationships with their friends.

That's because our friends and family will hopefully share our values and care about our well-being. Therefore, they are often our best reality checks and emotional fallbacks. A person who wants total control over their romantic partner has to get rid of their partner's reality checks and emotional fallbacks if they want to succeed.

Women tend to have stronger social networks than men, in terms of discussing relationships and processing emotional issues. Obviously, both women and men have emotions, but women are stereotyped as "more emotional" than men. This has negative effects; for example, women are all-too-often unfairly dismissed as "hysterical" or labeled "illogical." Feminists often discuss how women in heteronormative relationships are expected to do subtle, invisible, thankless "emotional labor" on behalf of our partners. Also, I've been talking about how women are usually handed the social responsibility for emotional escalation in romantic relationships.

However, the positive effect is that most women receive lots of social support for showing and discussing our emotions. Emotional processing is a skill that many USA men miss out on because of our cultural environment. In fairness, I do believe that this problem was worse for my father's generation than mine, the same way many classic feminist problems were worse for my mother's generation than mine. In the modern world of newly-flexible gender roles, men are finding more and more ways to be open about their emotions and create their own emotional support networks. Unsurprisingly, PUAs often fill these relationship advisory roles for each other.

My social support networks are awesome, and I feel lucky to have them. I try to choose my friends carefully, and keep close with people who share my values. I have friends who are ethical, but not strategic. I have friends who are strategic, but not ethical. These days, my closest female friend is named Shannon, and she is socially observant and strategic... and highly ethical. When I explain PUA tactics to her, she immediately sees both the problems and the advantages in them. I couldn't possibly write a book like this without showing you one of our conversations about relationships. Also, she makes awesome vegan desserts.

Shannon has a test that applies to many situations, social and otherwise. It's called the Parking Brake Test. She developed the Parking Brake Test one day while she and her husband were parking in San Francisco. That city has a lot of hills, and some of the hills are incredibly steep. Her husband asked whether he should use the parking brake, and Shannon said, "Imagine if the car slips down the hill and there's an accident, and later you have to explain that you didn't use the parking brake *in San Francisco.* You'll feel like an idiot."

The way to apply the Parking Brake Test to other situations is this: if you will feel like an idiot explaining yourself later unless you take precautions now, then *you should take precautions right fucking now.*

And in relationships, sometimes "take precautions" means "break up."

"So, I'm freaking out about this one guy," I told Shannon as we cleaned up dinner and poured glasses of wine. She was baking cupcakes, which made my night. (I strongly recommend the book *Vegan Cupcakes Take Over The World,* by Isa Chandra Moskowitz and Terry Hope Romero.)

"How much are you freaking out?" Shannon asked.

"So, okay." I took a deep draught of wine. "The other day I sent him a text message, and he didn't get back to me for a while, and I got really upset. I couldn't concentrate on my work, I couldn't even read a book. Then I started fantasizing about seeing him again only once." I looked down at my glass, avoiding her eyes as I spoke. "I would be incredibly awesome, like, I would be on top of my game. I'd make sure that I was as charming as possible. And then I wouldn't return his calls or emails."

This is the kind of admission I can only make after chugging a glass of wine.

Shannon took a moment to think about this. "Why would you do that?" she eventually asked.

"Because if I do it right," I said, "that will get him very confused. If I do it *perfectly,* then he'll be obsessed with me. I'd be, like, this mythical mysterious figure. And then maybe I'll feel superior, so it doesn't hurt so much to walk away."

Interestingly, at the time, the term "freeze-out" didn't cross my mind.

Shannon laughed and clutched her head, then grabbed my shoulder. "No, no no no no *no.* That is not actually what you want! You said you haven't defined the relationship, but it sounds like a secondary relationship, not a primary one. Have you had any conversations about it at all?"

"Kind of," I said, and showed her some emails. "Also," I added, "after our second date, he freaked out on me and ended things. Then he took it back and apologized, and claimed he doesn't normally do that."

"I see why you're worried," she said, and frowned at my laptop screen. We prepared cupcakes while she pondered the situation.

"I mean, look," Shannon said, after we taste-tested some icing. "It sounds like you and Adam really enjoy each other. And he's doing things like taking you on semi-expensive 24-hour dates. He's paying, right?"

"Yes," I said, "but I'm only letting him pay because he makes so much more money than I do."

"Whatever," Shannon said. "He's still paying. Despite your postmodern feminist sensibilities, you know that means something. But it's hard to tell from these emails whether he feels anything strong... but maybe that's because *you're* being low-key. You've told him that this isn't a primary relationship for you, and even when you explain that you're vulnerable, you're writing about it coolly. You aren't exactly pouring your heart out.

"He might be receiving these emails, and having his own heart-flips. He might be warning you because he's super into you, but super afraid he'll let you down. He might walk on air every time you text message him, then act cool about it because he doesn't want to scare you off. Or he might not. Maybe he likes you, but he doesn't care very much. You don't know one way or the other.

"What's important is that he's telling you that you can't be sure of him, ever. Although he's being vague about *that*, too. Like, he says he'll be 'skittish' if things get 'complicated,' but what does 'skittish' mean? What does 'complicated' mean? As for you, you weren't much clearer. You said you want him to be 'comfortable' with emotional 'investment,' but what does 'comfortable' mean, and what does 'investment' mean? You guys haven't defined any actions, or parameters for your relationship. You could have played your cards a lot better here."

I couldn't help laughing. "Maybe you're right," I said. "So what do you think? Is this a parking brake situation? What precautions do I take?"

Shannon hesitated.

"I don't think there's anything to worry about right now," she said finally. "As long as you're sure you don't want a primary relationship with him. If part of you wants that, then you're doomed. But you are *sure* you don't want one. Right? You are *not* doing the stupid thing, and dating this guy as a secondary, while hoping he will realize he actually wants a primary relationship with you... despite the fact that *he clearly communicated that isn't what he wants. Right?"*

"Shannon. Do I *look* seventeen?"

"People are stupid at all ages. Okay. As long as you're not being stupid," she said, "you need to figure out what would make you feel more secure, and then you should have a clearer conversation when you see him again. Come on! *You already know this!* You yourself have told me this enough times."

"Yes yes, communication is awesome," I said. "But I have no idea what will make me feel more secure. And I don't want to start a conversation if I don't know what to ask for."

"Well," she said, "I mean, you've already told me one thing you want from him. You want to *not freak out when you send him a text message.* Maybe that means you talk about text messages, or maybe that means you discuss a stronger definition of the relationship."

"What with all the PUA research, I've been thinking a lot about indirect communication," I remarked. "PUAs like to escalate relationships via tacit or unspoken signals. And honestly, I'm not sure how much energy I have for Relationship Conversations. I know I'm always promoting super direct communication in relationships, but sometimes it feels like too much. Maybe Adam and I don't have to talk about things directly. Don't you think there are ways to communicate about this without having a direct conversation?"

Shannon gave me a look that said, *I can't believe I'm hearing this from you,* or possibly *You know better than that.* "If you can't have an actual conversation about your relationship?" She made a gesture as if pulling a lever. "Parking brake," she said flatly.

Maybe what I was really trying to ask was: "Shannon, how do I escalate this relationship without ruining the strategic ambiguity?" But I didn't have the vocabulary for that question yet. And in response, she told me that things were entirely *too* ambiguous; she told me that the strategic ambiguity was becoming non-strategic, at least on my end. She was right.

* * *

A while later, I showed up in San Francisco. I took a day to say hi to the city that owns my soul, and checked in with all my friends. Early the next afternoon, I walked into Adam's arms feeling both elated and unsettled.

Adam seemed pretty elated to see me, too. And that night, he pushed me pretty far, S&M-wise. Too far? I wasn't sure then, and I'm not sure now.

Let me me clear here... as clear as I can be without telling you exactly what happened, because, well, because I just won't. Even sex writers have boundaries. Besides, if I were to tell you what exactly he said and did, I feel like it wouldn't make sense to you.

I've said before that my favorite S&M encounters involve a kind of head-trip. Sometimes, that head-trip is intensely personal and won't make any sense to other people. Adam rarely used tools. He mostly used words. Men have made me bleed and hurt me less.

But let me be clear. Whatever-it-was that happened, I had never told Adam not to say what he said. I never explained how to avoid what happened. I didn't call my safeword on him, either. It was one of the things I liked about him: Adam had a sixth sense for words that ripped me up. It's just that, this time, he *really* hurt me. Partly because of what he said, and partly because I'd become so emotionally invested in him. Did he hurt me more than I wanted him to? I still don't know.

Sometimes, these things happen. One partner pushes a boundary, breaks it. Maybe the boundary was unspoken; maybe the dominant misreads signals; maybe the submissive didn't yet realize that the boundary was there. When it comes to S&M, these things can be so dramatic... yet sometimes they're nobody's fault. We find these mental and emotional blocks, and we call them landmines.

Adam didn't hit the landmine on purpose. He wasn't trying to push me as hard as he did. And I didn't warn him off. So the important question becomes: how does one deal with such a situation afterwards?

After we were done, I felt sick. My existing anxiety about Adam was multiplied, and I felt an overpowering urge to just *get the hell out of there*. I stayed quiet, I went into my head and tried to sort out my feelings. I'm sure it was blindingly obvious that something was *wrong*, and it made Adam anxious, too. Concern strained everything he said: even words as simple as, "Do you want a glass of water?"

He asked to talk about it, and I said to give me some time, so for at least half an hour he talked to me about unrelated things while I curled up by his side and pulled myself together. The concern was never far from his surface, though.

When I finally hauled in a deep breath and said, "Okay," Adam was right there with me.

"Okay?" he said.

I turned to him and buried my face in his chest. "Can you look at me?" he said, and tried to pull up my chin. I wouldn't let him. "All right," he said, "don't look at me, I guess," and laughed gently to show that it really was all right. Then he wrapped his arms around me. "Are you ready to talk about it yet?"

People who study abusive relationships have created lists of tactics that abusers frequently use. [1] One of the most important verbal tactics used by abusers is this: *minimizing, denying, and blaming.* Abusers *minimize* the pain they cause; they *deny* that they caused it; they *blame the victim* for what happened.

During aftercare, I look out for this: if the dominant partner ever minimizes my feelings, blames me for how I feel, or denies that he had a role in how I feel... that's a major warning sign. It's a warning sign so massive that if I think a partner is doing those things even a little bit, I seriously consider ending the relationship.

I can't remember a single moment when Adam used the tactic of minimizing, denying or blaming. Not a single one. In the end, that's what made it okay: seeing that he was *so* genuinely touched. That my confusion was hurting him, too, and that he needed to talk about it as much as I did.

I don't know how to describe how good aftercare can get. You'll just think I'm being melodramatic. And maybe I am. But. When an S&M encounter has been really brutal or intense, the intimacy afterwards... can match that intensity, if my partner and I are both open to it. If we *can be* open to it. This intimacy doesn't blow my mind every time I do S&M. Not even most times. But when it happens, it isn't like anything else.

Let me emphasize that *I don't think S&M is for everyone.* But for me, personally, I have never found anything else that can lay me open quite so bare. Yet at the same time, that vulnerability can be *so hard* to allow.

By the next morning, I was still a bit scared, and I felt like there was a lot left unsaid, but I didn't want to run anymore. Besides, my attraction was overwhelming. At the end of another 24 hours with Adam, my blood was still skipping with hormones. I knew I couldn't possibly keep him out of my head.

Not that I wanted to.

And yet. Yet. Adam and I still hadn't had what Shannon suggested: a careful conversation about our relationship. We were talking out the S&M, but we weren't talking about the bigger picture. Something within me resisted it.

Part of the problem was that I felt insecure. I wasn't sure how he would react if I brought it up. Part of the problem was that I was confused. I didn't quite know what I wanted from the relationship, myself. But... maybe I actually relished the chance to practice my tacit emotional escalation game. Maybe I was aiming less for a feeling of emotional security, and more for a feeling of emotional seduction.

The strategic ambiguity was compelling, and Adam's escalating signals felt like accomplishments. The whole situation fed my love of the game.

* * *

There are a few ladies who frequent PUA fora and conferences, and I'll talk more about them in the next chapter. For now, I want to quote the girl PUA I like best, who calls herself Hitori. I don't agree with Hitori about everything, but she's really smart. She wrote a "Playette FAQ" for the most popular PUA forum; in the FAQ, she advises women who want a relationship to avoid sleeping with a man unless the guy has already reached what she calls "emotional hookpoint." (PUA dudes define "hookpoint" as the point when a target is no longer merely being polite or amused, but is genuinely attracted and interested in what the PUA has to say.)

As she writes:

Emotional hookpoint is the intense, emotional, gut-level kind of attraction that most people think is required for a girl to spontaneously decide to fuck a guy. Guys feel this too — they just don't (usually) require it for sex. When guys are at emotional hookpoint, just like a girl in the same situation, they want to spend time around the person they're attracted to and have her think well of them and pay attention to them. EVEN IF THEY ARE PLAYERS.

... If you haven't hit emotional hookpoint yet AND YOU WANT IT, don't put yourself in a situation where sex can happen and then refuse to have sex — just try to keep subtle control of logistics such that the rate at which you approach a possible hookup roughly corresponds to the rate at which his emotional attraction is growing. If you can't think of a smooth, natural way to delay isolation until you've hit hookpoint, then you have to weigh your options and make a quick decision: would you rather bail on the interaction, or go for it and risk the possibility that you won't hit hookpoint at all? I'd like to stress gently, here, that no matter what there are no guarantees. Some guys can hit hookpoint after sex. Some will immediately before. And some, no matter how long you have with them, never will. In either case, a smooth interaction is key — smoothly bail, or smoothly go with it. In general, I would avoid any kind of "status of the hookup" talk or obviously artificial speedbump.

She prefaces the whole FAQ by saying:

To start with, any dude who you get involved with will either be open to the possibility of a relationship on some level — or not. **You cannot control this.** *Game affects how someone reacts emotionally to you, not their goals / values / personality.*

That said, you can get a guy to be your boyfriend by:

1) Finding a dude who is at least marginally open to the possibility of the kind of relationship you want, and

2) Gaming him right

I will add, at this juncture, that if you game a dude right who is not open to the idea of a formal relationship, you can often still end up with a de-facto boyfriend — a relationship in all but name / rules / exclusivity. In fact, I'll say this now because it's important: the practical reality of your situation, i.e. what you see in front of you, matters much more to your results than any "official designation" of relationship status.

I've included Hitori's "Playette FAQ" as Appendix F in this book. I do think it's good advice in many ways... but it leads naturally to the question of: how do I identify emotional hookpoint? I emailed Hitori about this and she wrote back, "A lot of that comes down to touchy-feely social intuition stuff — body language, behavior patterns — that I'm not, unfortunately, all that good at describing. Or I would have in the post." Oh, well.

Notwithstanding the vagueness, I'm pretty sure I know what Hitori means, and I'm not sure how to describe it either. If a target invites you out for non-sexytimes — e.g., a museum trip during the day — then that's a good indicator of emotional hookpoint. If a target invites you to meet his friends, that's a good indicator too. If a target remembers preferences or thoughts you expressed in passing, then that's a great indicator. For example, maybe you offhandedly mentioned that you love the cinema director Peter Greenaway and the target invites you to a Greenaway film. Basically, it's all about watching the target to see if he's genuinely interested in your reality.

These are *emotional Indicators of Interest: emotional IOIs.*

While I try to avoid using damaging economic metaphors for relationships, not every economic insight is evil, and some economic principles might be useful while describing emotional IOIs. Some emotional IOIs are more reliable and more valuable than other emotional IOIs. In other words, some romantic signals "mean more." *A valuable emotional IOI is one that costs more to give, or is harder to fake.*

Costs and fakery can be measured in obvious ways, like money or time; or in less-obvious ways, like the level of public exposure. For example, if a person puts weeks into finding the perfect gift for you, then that's a more valuable emotional IOI than if he picks one off the shelf at the first store he sees. If he spends a lot of money on the gift, then the IOI might be valuable... unless he's wealthy, in which case *the cost to him* is not high, and the emotional IOI is less valuable.

If a person calls you "sweetheart," then that's an okay emotional IOI... but it's least valuable if you are alone together. Calling you "sweetheart" becomes more valuable if he says it to you in front of his friends, because the two of you are then publicly linked. And it's even more valuable if he says it to you in front of his parents. The level of public exposure decreases the chances that he's faking, because if he offers fake IOIs in front of his friends and family, then he might stand to lose their trust as much as he stands to lose yours.

(This is an extremely basic analysis; I acknowledge that there are other factors that might affect a person's willingness to give or receive pet names in public. I also acknowledge that pet names aren't meaningful for everyone. Gifts mean different things in different cultures. Etc.)

However: *none of these emotional IOIs, in themselves, mean that a person is at emotional hookpoint. Even the valuable ones.* He could be faking. In the end, he could always be faking. That's the constant danger of the game. And if he's faking, then he may not even realize it; he may get swept up in the moment, and he may not understand that his feelings don't go very deep.

PUAs often say that flirtatious behaviors are usually unconscious. I think the same is true with people's behavior during emotional escalation.

Still, I suspect that if you want reliable emotional hookpoint, then the most reliable strategy is to seek valuable emotional IOIs: signals that cost a lot to give, or are hard to fake.

You may have heard of the dreaded "friend zone," which many people complain about bitterly, especially men. One way people talk about the "friend zone" is by claiming that once you're friends with someone you want to fuck, you'll be regarded as "just a friend" and you'll never be able to hook up with the target. This is bullshit. I, for one, have been seduced by a number of friends, including some I was friends with for years first. In fact, lots of people (not just women) say that it's best to date people you're friends with first. I've even heard PUA coaches say this.

However, I do think that there are people who use the friend zone to their advantage. Sometimes this is harmless, and sometimes it's not harmless. For example, I suspect that the friend zone can be a good strategy for people who prefer deeper emotional relationships and don't want to risk being "pumped and dumped." After all, if you've been friends with someone for a long time, then you can worry less about measuring emotional IOIs. The *mere fact that this person is a good friend* is a major emotional IOI, in itself.

As a romantic strategy, building tension while staying in the friend zone is hardly foolproof. For one thing, if you're in the friend zone with a person who prefers monogamy, then that person might be snatched up by someone else while you're just friends. But on the other hand, the nice thing about the friend zone is that *it doesn't have to be a strategy.* Again, I think that most friend-zoners don't do it on purpose. I think most people just like having friends, and most people don't mind being friends with people they're attracted to, even if it's ambiguous whether they'll hook up in the future or not.

I also think that there are some cruel, manipulative people who use the friend zone for power. You may recall that I mentioned "fake Indicators of Interest" earlier. PUAs describe fake IOIs as being strategically deployed by female waitresses, strippers, journalists, and other women whose tips depend on a man's satisfaction. The indicators are designed to make the man feel good, but they don't represent actual sexual interest.

I am sure that some women skillfully string men along in the "friend zone" with fake IOIs. (I suspect that there are men who do this to women, too. Maybe it even happens in queer relationships! Gasp!) I am also sure that this couldn't happen if those men had better boundaries and were willing to take some initiative. If they were willing to ask her out directly and deal with potential rejection, then they could never be strung along in the first place. Of course, that requires them to be outcome independent, and outcome independence is sometimes very difficult.

And this brings me to a concept that's very similar to the "friend zone," but is more often experienced by women than men: the "fuckbuddy zone."

Some people are totally cool with being "just fuckbuddies" with sexual partners, the same way some people are totally cool with being "just friends" with people they're attracted to. However, some people (not just women) can end up feeling locked into the "fuckbuddy zone" with folks they want a more emotional relationship with... the same way some people (not just men) may feel locked into the "friend zone" with folks they want a more sexual relationship with.

The same way there are some women who skillfully string men along with fake flirty IOIs, there are some men who skillfully string women along with fake *emotional* IOIs.

One thing that consistently makes me uneasy about PUAs is that many of them look for ways to capitalize on targets' desire for a stronger emotional relationship, *while refusing to offer that emotional relationship.* It's obviously okay if a person prefers not to offer a strong emotional connection; that's their boundary to set. But setting that boundary goes along with *making it clear to their partner.*

I have no problem with no-strings-attached sex when people treat each other honorably. What bothers me is this: when a PUA tells a target in words that he's not interested in a stronger emotional relationship, but then *learns how to fake the signals that imply emotional hookpoint.* Such a man knows that she wants a stronger emotional relationship, and he knows that the way she measures his interest is by seeking emotional IOIs. He knows that no matter what he says in words, *she's mostly watching the unspoken signals.* So he gives her those signals. And then he pretends to be surprised when she gets hurt.

Each emotional Indicator of Interest provides an impression of investment... or, if you prefer: it provides an impression of *leverage*. Each emotional IOI marks or strengthens one of the million tiny, implied agreements that sustain relationships. Faking emotional IOIs means faking investment, and faking leverage. Faking emotional IOIs means giving the impression that the faker is more emotionally reliable than he is.

This approach is obviously most common among the Darth Vader PUAs. Some of them are amazingly blunt about how they use emotional IOIs as poker chips. Those guys don't talk about this like I'm talking about it right now, because they don't have my "emotional escalation" framework. Still, I see examples all the time. One of my favorites comes from a PUA forum discussion in which the original poster asks for advice about a girl who recently got upset with him. The girl is figuring out that he has no non-sexual interest in her... but she likes him anyway, poor thing. She's asking questions like, "Why are you really interested in me?"

On the forum, the PUA wonders whether these questions are shit tests. In reality, of course, the girl is looking for more emotional IOIs. Other PUAs on the forum recognize this. Hence, they give advice such as:

Do that look. And get real close. Then tell her something like "I've never met anyone like you." [2]

I'd say that all socially calibrated people fake emotional reactions sometimes. Hell, I consistently pretend to pay attention to others when I'm really thinking about sex, or work, or something I saw on the Internet. Don't you? And most socially calibrated people have, at some point, accidentally given someone the wrong romantic impression. I certainly have.

Plus, there are many humans who have emotions but don't know how to express them, or who could learn to express them better. I have often given strategic consideration to how I wanted to express emotions *that were, nevertheless, real emotions*. In the past I've worried about this a lot, because I spend so much time thinking about consent and ethics in relationships. As I once wrote in a comment on my blog:

One thing I've noticed about myself that makes me a little uncomfortable is that I'll not only deploy true statements strategically, but I'll deploy the strategic true statements in a strategic way sometimes, e.g. I'll write something about how confused I am and write it in an extremely precisely calibrated, well-edited, confused way.... The ethics of this may be questionable.

The blogger Hugh Ristik responded:

I do this, too. Something I've learned is that if you are being honest and nobody notices, then nobody cares. What's important is not just being sincere, but being sincere in a way that other people recognize as you being sincere. *If you are being sincere, then you deserve to signal that you are being sincere, and get recognized for being sincere.* Juggler [a famous PUA coach] talks a lot about this.

Personally, if I was to "unlearn" everything I know about social influence, I'm not sure whether it would make me more ethical. But I am sure that it would make me less effective, especially less effective than people who are much less ethical than I am.

I am not convinced that being ineffective is ethical. You can't do any evil if you're ineffective, but you can't do any good, either. [3]

So, learning how to express real emotions carefully is okay. Fake IOIs can be okay, too: some people enjoy the game of flirting with a waitress or salesman who clearly doesn't mean it. But at some point, giving too many unspoken fake IOIs becomes the same thing as making a false promise, especially when it's designed to manipulate the target into the friend zone or the fuckbuddy zone.

I figure there are three potential solutions to these situations. Here you go, Clarisse Thorn's Official Advice If You Find Yourself in the Friend Zone and/or Fuckbuddy Zone:

CLARISSE THORN SOLUTION 1 (tm): You can become okay with the friend zone or fuckbuddy zone.

CLARISSE THORN SOLUTION 2 (tm): *If* you thought you were okay with that situation (e.g., "This guy is so hot and he gives me 500 orgasms per night, but he never calls, but I can deal with that," or "This girl is so hot and we always have such great conversations, but she's not attracted to me, but I can deal with that.")

... *but* then you realize you're not okay with it at all (e.g., "Oh shit, I suddenly appear to be crying in the bathroom or punching the wall in rage, because I saw 500-orgasm guy calling another partner with stars in his eyes," or "Oh shit, I suddenly appear to be crying in the bathroom or punching the wall in rage, because I saw great-conversation girl kissing her partner.")

... *then* you might consider an exit strategy.

CLARISSE THORN SOLUTION 3 (tm): If you want to have sex, you experiment obsessively to learn how to do well at sexual escalation, and if you want emotional connections, you experiment obsessively to learn how to do well at emotional escalation. Part of this game, also, is seeking people who have similar goals in the first place. As Hitori says in the Playette FAQ that I quoted earlier: "Any dude who you get involved with will either be open to the possibility of a relationship on some level — or not. **You cannot control this.** Game affects how someone reacts emotionally to you, not their goals / values / personality."

SECRET OPTION 4: Don't string people along when you don't really care about them.

* * *

After our difficult S&M encounter, I wasn't scheduled to see Adam again for a week. Which felt much too long. So a couple days later, when The Dude suggested that we head to a coffeeshop in Adam's area, I seized the chance to text Adam and let him know. I counted my breaths waiting for his response, and exhaled when he texted back offering to meet us.

Adam and I had never actually hung out in a non-date context before. *Emotional IOI,* I thought. I watched the social dynamics as Adam discussed work with The Dude; Adam and I talked social justice; we all chatted about random San Francisco things. It felt minimally awkward. I acted friendly and warm, but not very affectionate.

When Adam left a couple hours later, he paused at the door and looked back at me for a long moment. It was a vulnerable look... as if he wanted to say something but couldn't find the words. I know I've given guys that look before, but I wasn't sure how to react when Adam did it. So I pretended not to notice, and he walked out. *Major emotional IOI,* I thought.

"How'd that go?" I asked The Dude.

"Fine," said The Dude. "But you weren't giving him any Public Displays of Affection or anything. It was a little weird. ... I guess that's typical for a hookup, though."

"Yeah... you know I'm not usually into lots of PDA," I said. "Besides, Adam and I have discussed this, and he made it clear that *he* didn't want much PDA."

"I'm not sure he still feels that way," said The Dude. "Did you see how he stopped at the door and looked at you on his way out?"

I grinned. "Yes. I saw that. ... I *was* acting chilled-out, wasn't I? PUAs talk about using push-pull; I guess I'm doing a little bit of push right now." Today, I would translate the concept of push-pull as "the strategic ambiguity machine."

After a moment, I added: "I feel like I have a lot to talk about with Adam. We had a complicated night recently, and also, Shannon recently suggested we have an actual relationship conversation. What do you think?"

"Do you want anything to change?"

"No..." I said. "Well, nothing concrete. I just want to talk things over with him."

The Dude shook his head. "If you don't need a change, don't rock the boat," he said, very definitely.

Oh, Dude, I thought. *You are such a dude.*

Late that night, I rocked the boat. My pulse raced as I composed a precisely worded email to Adam. I thought a lot about what I wanted to say. I was working to give emotional IOIs, but to maintain a sense that I was outcome-independent. The message also contained the statement, "I'm confused," which was probably the first time I told him that outright.

If seduction includes a lot of strategic ambiguity, then maybe *telling someone he makes me uncertain* is a strong Indicator of Interest.

I included these sentences:

I feel like there are a lot of things unsaid, although I'm not sure what they are. I'm trying to keep distance between us, but managing that process feels more complicated to me right now than it did before. Would you rather keep our appointment later this week, and keep some distance until then? Or are you free sooner? It's cool if I can't see you before then, but I want to.

Adam got back to me fast. "Hanging out sooner sounds... real good," he wrote. "Give me a call." We discussed meeting at his apartment the next afternoon, but I figured that if we wanted a real conversation, we'd need a neutral location. We settled on Golden Gate Park.

* * *

In my experience, vulnerability is the greatest and most effective emotional escalation tactic in the world. But it has to be real. It has to be unforced, and it has to be open, and it has to be free of obligation. There should be few-to-no guilt trips in seduction. Everyone knows that guilt can be a very effective social weapon, but guilt is absolute poison to seduction.

When you're weaponizing your own vulnerability, it helps to be fearless, because your chances of getting hurt skyrocket. Good luck with *that.* It also helps to be eloquent: in words or in actions. With fearlessness and eloquence, a strong-but-vulnerable person can win almost everyone over.

Some PUAs talk about "vulnerability game," where the PUA shows calculated vulnerabilities as part of the seduction process. That's kinda like what I'm talking about, but only when the vulnerability is real and important. Some PUAs talk about "honesty game," which is also kinda like what I'm talking about. Some PUAs talk about "girl game," i.e. the game that clever women use, whether consciously or unconsciously. Those

PUAs measure women's gentleness, our sweetness, and this is also kinda like what I'm talking about.

Putting my heart on the line has worked for me a number of times... and when it does work, it works *spectacularly.* The resultant relationship can be mind-blowing. But weaponizing my vulnerability can hurt me, and it *has* hurt me in the past. I'm not always strong enough to do it properly. The costs are obvious. And I can't always convince myself to pay them.

A reasonable person might say exactly what I said above by advising, "Just be yourself," or "Try to stay open." A reasonable person might say, "You connect with people by being vulnerable." What do you think? Am I a reasonable person?

* * *

It was a gorgeous day. San Francisco always produces her best weather for me. I dressed in my favorite casual jeans and tank top so that I looked good... but I also seemed like I wasn't trying to look good. I did this instinctively, but when I remember it, it seems like Strategic Ambiguity: Step 1.

Adam found me at a park entrance. I was leaning forward with my elbows resting on a short cement wall. He ran his fingers gently down my arm, then rested his hand on the small of my back.

Ah, I thought. *Initiating minor Public Displays of Affection, are we? I'll leave that ball in your court, Adam.* I gleamed up at him, but I neither obviously objected to nor obviously encouraged the PDA. I did this instinctively, too... but when I remember it, it seems like Strategic Ambiguity: Step 2.

Here is a top emotional escalation strategy: always leave your target feeling good about himself. If you can consistently make your target feel good about himself, you *will* win him over. You might not win him as a lover, but he'll definitely care about you.

Tactically, the major challenge with this is that it's sometimes difficult to know how to make someone feel good about himself. People don't always believe compliments. Backhanded compliments — and negs — can be useful for making people feel good about themselves, because backhanded compliments and negs appear to be a highly sincere way of paying attention to the target. The problem is that some targets are genuinely hurt by them.

And anyway, the biggest problem is not tactical. The biggest problem is that if you're always trying to leave your target feeling good about himself, you might end up unable to discuss real problems in the relationship.

Initial chitchat was pleasant. The topic of blind dates came up. "One of my friends tried to set me up on a blind date, a few days ago," Adam remarked. "But it was for Thursday night" — the night I'd been scheduled to see him — "so I was like, 'I've got a date.' My friend said I should cancel because this girl was cute, and I was like, 'man, you don't understand, there's *no way* I'm canceling this date.'"

I'm uncancelable, I thought. *Is that an emotional IOI?* I classified it under "probably."

The real conversation started with a discussion of S&M: how things were going, and what happened last time we saw each other. "I'm sorry," he said. "I'm really sorry. I never want to do that to you again."

"It's okay," I said. "These things happen. But please do be careful. But don't worry...." I trailed off, trying to find words.

It's so hard to know how to talk about this, especially with people who aren't used to discussing S&M. When there's a fuckup, sometimes both sides feel betrayed. The submissive might think: *Maybe I didn't tell you exactly what to avoid, but sometimes it's too much to think about, sometimes it's hard to understand in the moment, sometimes I don't know ahead of time. Okay, so I pushed myself too hard, but I did it because I'm so into you. I did it because, in that moment, I lost track of myself. And anyway, I thought you could read me. I thought you understood me. I thought you knew. You've read me perfectly well before. Why not this time? Is it that you don't care?*

Whereas the dominant might think: *Maybe I went too far, but I thought I could trust you to stop me. I thought I could trust you to tell me. I don't want to harm you, I just want to push you; I want to break down walls with you. I want to see your eyes go deep and soft. It's not fair for me to feel like I fucked up, because you fucked up, too. I thought you could take care of yourself. I thought you knew. You've communicated perfectly well before. Why not this time? Can I rely on you?*

I tried to explain all this to Adam.

"You're much better at this than I am," he said.

"I'm more experienced," I corrected. "But I'm still learning, too. And I don't think you understand how good your instincts are. You're *awesome*. Look, I know you think I'm all on top of my shit... but this feels like a lot for me, too. It's a lot."

"I want you to be clear about your boundaries," he said. "I understand that you got blindsided, last time, but... I really need to know what I can and can't do." There was a sharp edge of real anxiety in his tone.

"I know," I said swiftly. "I know. I've been in your shoes before, when

I play the dominant role. And I've been in this position as a submissive before, too. I'm very familiar with this problem."

I paused, feeling inadequate. "I'll try to do better," I said. Inadequately. "Both of us will, I guess. But I mean... this is one of the things I really like about you, Adam. I love your sensitivity, and I'm glad that you're taking this seriously, but I also love your instinct to push me. I don't want to fuck that up."

There is nothing quite like wandering around in the sunshine with a crush. We were having a difficult conversation. I was managing and presenting my emotions very carefully. I was trying to preserve strategic ambiguity... trying to make him feel good about himself... trying not to come on too strong... *and* trying to actually explain what I wanted: it was a difficult balance. A gossamer tightrope.

Still, it felt good just to talk to Adam. It felt good just to look at him. He could merely glance at me and make me feel like I was blushing and overheated, though I'm sure my cheeks weren't pink at all.

Social psychologists have documented a phenomenon called "the illusion of transparency." You're likely to think that another person can read you much better than that person actually can. Especially if you've got an intimate relationship with that person! The chances that your partner knows what you're thinking are lower than you probably think they are.

And yet... there was a moment, when we paused under a tree facing each other, and Adam reached out and rested his hand on my hip. He drew me closer, but didn't embrace me. I was still a few inches away from him. By then, we'd shifted away from talking about S&M, and the conversation was much less intense. I was making a random observation about nothing important.

Don't stop talking, I told myself, *don't stop talking,* even as heat flared through my body from his touch. Even though I was not saying anything interesting. I don't know why I refused to stop mid-sentence. I guess I intuitively believed this was part of the game, too. Strategic Ambiguity: Step 3.

I thought my voice might shiver, so I lowered it. I looked away from Adam, casually, and forced myself to finish my sentence, even though I could barely track my own words.

He didn't say anything. I looked back at him. Met his gaze, and saw my desire reflected there. I felt as transparent as glass.

"This is why I wanted to meet in the park," I said softly. "We wouldn't have talked at all if I'd met you at home."

Adam grinned. "Well, we wouldn't have talked *as much.*"

If he'd put his arms around me, I would have gone for a full-on makeout session. I was past caring about blatant PDA. Besides, we were in San Francisco. Passerby would have cheered for us.

But Adam kept me at arm's-length, smiling, so I savored the moment instead. Savored the tension, the slow burn. The way my skin felt delicate, tissue-thin, sensitive as petals.

Maybe it's ridiculous to theoretically separate emotional escalation from sex. Sometimes, if I'm emotionally attached to a guy, I might do nothing more than walk through the park with him and still require a cold shower afterwards.

It didn't feel like much time passed before Adam and I kept walking. We resumed the conversation as if nothing had happened. Meandered, stopped a few times, meandered some more, and stopped again to watch a merry-go-round.

He remarked that he'd been discussing me with his friends. If I'd still been bothering to watch for emotional IOIs, then I would have noted this as a big one, but I was completely caught up in the moment. "I was talking to one of my friends about you," Adam said, "and she told me that this sounds like 'friends with benefits.'"

Something in his tone implied that he found her assessment incomplete.

"Yeah..." I said. "The other day, The Dude referred to you as a 'hookup.'"

We were standing side-by-side, angled towards each other. Adam moved close, so close that our bodies were touching all the way down. But he didn't look at me. He kept his eyes straight ahead, on the merry-go-round. "Well," he said slowly, "I guess we can let them think those things. Friends with benefits. Hookup." He smiled, but he still didn't look at me. "You and I both know it's more than that."

More than that? *He's not looking at me because he feels vulnerable,* I realized. And, of course, he probably felt uncertain.

I rubbed my cheek against Adam's shoulder. *You and I both know it's more than that....* Here was the conversation Shannon convinced me to have, delivered right into my lap. And I still didn't know what to do with it.

"If you had more experience with polyamory," I said carefully, "then I would call this a 'secondary relationship.'"

"Oh, interesting," Adam said. "Tell me more about that. I've often thought I should do poly, but I haven't read up on it or anything, so I'm not sure."

"Well..." I said, "sometimes it's a matter of debate in the poly community. Some people organize relationships into primary, secondary, et cetera. Some people don't like doing that; they say things like, 'How can one love be prioritized over another love?' I see primary relationships as relationships that have other big commitments involved, like living together, or getting married, or having children. I see secondary relationships as relationships that are still important, but don't involve those huge other commitments. Also, sometimes primary partners have veto power over secondary partners. Like, if I have a primary relationship with someone, and he wants to take on a certain secondary partner, then he might give me veto power over whether he can get involved with that specific woman."

Meandering again. By now, we were on our way out of the park; Adam was meeting a friend for an exercise date.

"But," I continued, "like I say, it's not as if secondary relationships aren't important. If a secondary partner had an emergency and needed me, I'd go see him, even if it was a night I was supposed to have dinner with a primary partner. And secondary relationships can evolve into primary relationships. So I understand why some poly people don't like to create the hierarchy in the first place."

"That makes sense," Adam said. "Thank you. It's interesting. Personally, I'm feeling burned out on traditional relationships." He sighed. "I'm just kinda tired of how emotional escalation always seems to be the name of the game."

What the hell do you think is going on right now, Adam? I thought. *Way to be a typical man, and make me do all the work. You don't think this is emotional escalation? Watch yourself when you look at me. Listen to yourself! You're adopting my vocabulary. You just said the words "emotional escalation"!* The whole thing tickled my sense of absurdity, and I had to smile.

Instinctively, I went for a Statement of Interest. Some part of me must have measured the moment as ripe. "Emotional escalation is the name of my game too, you know," I said cheerfully. "It's just that I'm not aiming for the stereotypical monogamous endgame."

Adam cast me a thoughtful look. "I guess I'm enjoying your emotional escalation," he said slowly.

The words warmed me more than sunlight. At some point, plausible deniability becomes implausible. Sometimes, ambiguity is key, but it has to be strategic; if you want a relationship to jump levels, then bits of certainty should also be deployed.

I walked Adam to the bus. "What are you doing for the rest of the day?" he asked.

"Oh," I said casually, and darted him a lowered-eyelashes smile. "My first order of business is to take a cold shower."

He laughed, with genuine delight. "I'll see you soon," he said.

* * *

I was not yet so far down the rabbit hole that I saw everything Adam did as an emotional shit test or compliance test. (That would come later.) But he was damn good at strategic ambiguity... though maybe it was more from insecurity, than because he was playing the game. I've often wondered how much of Adam's indirect tendencies are the game, and how much are sheer confusion.

All I know is what I saw: even when Adam gave intense emotional IOIs, he did it quickly and cagily. At one point, he called me "someone I *really* care about and *really* trust" right before he stepped out the door, so I didn't have a chance to respond.

I had to admit that in many ways, tacit emotional escalation was the most fun game ever. The side glances, the heart-flips, the scary unsure moments. The romantic-comedy flashes of vulnerability. The glimpses of unexpected significance. It's all so compelling.

Except that every once in a while, this game gets out of hand. A major problem with Adam was that our caginess made S&M more difficult. Feeling safe and certain is important to me when I do S&M. Perhaps I can only enjoy the strategic ambiguity of S&M within a reliable framework. And when I need aftercare, it's best if I can be blown open. It's best if I can show him my hand. It's best if I can allow total vulnerability.

If S&M and the game both tap into similar urges towards strategic ambiguity, then maybe too much ambiguity from the game can multiply the ambiguity of S&M. And maybe when these ambiguities multiply each other, they can become too much too fast. On one side of strategic ambiguity is total certainty, and on the other side is total uncertainty. While some people might tend more towards one or the other, neither extreme fits what anyone wants.

Still.... At the end of that trip, on my final morning with Adam, it was hard to walk away. I remember lying in his arms, trying to convince myself to get up. I counted seconds before I finally kissed him and said gently, "I'm heading out now."

His arms tightened around me. I watched his face, watched how his eyes darkened. He kept his voice artificially light, asked some final questions about our S&M interactions. I answered them thoroughly, keeping my voice gentle. I was as glad for the extra time as he was.

We parted outside on the street. His final smile, his final look, were so intense... like he was posing. He was managing our separation the same way I had, months before, when my friend said: "Sometimes you just freak out about people. It doesn't mean you're in love with them." Adam cared about the image I walked away with. He cared *a lot.*

Or maybe I was engaging in wishful thinking. Regardless, I texted Shannon that I was feeling a lot better about Adam.

"Good to know you're parking on flat ground," she texted back.

* * *

* * *

CHAPTER 8:
Ladies And Their Sensitivities

In which Clarisse re-establishes contact with the first PUA she ever met, and he gives her seduction advice. Clarisse also discusses the perspectives of various other women associated with the seduction community, including Playettes. Finally, there's the question of whether pickup artistry is aimed at all women, and whether it works better with some women than others. The chapter title is after a song with the same name from the Steven Sondheim musical, Sweeney Todd: The Demon Barber of Fleet Street.

* * *

James Amoureux, the first pickup artist I ever met, was still around Chicago. He was always posting interesting articles on Facebook, or changing his profile picture to better showcase his handsome self. I hadn't seen him in a long time. I knew a lot more about pickup artistry than I had when we met, but I was still learning. I invited him out for dinner and questions.

As we sat down across from each other, I examined him curiously. James was as hot and smart as ever, but I didn't feel nearly as attracted as I'd felt before. I took an inventory of my feelings, and realized that the sexy mystique of pickup artistry had dissipated. My "research" was no longer about fetishizing these guys... so what was it about?

I shelved that question for later, and asked what James had been up to. He explained that he'd been writing a new PUA curriculum called *How To Start a Kinky Relationship*. "I'd love your feedback," he said seriously. "Honestly, I've probably used some of your ideas already."

I perused the draft he set before me. It was long, and I was not the target audience, so I admit that I never finished reading it. Still, James covered a lot of ideas that I liked. He wrote about how to feel good about alternative desires. He wrote about how to respect sexual diversity, and not just S&M, but transgender and queer identities, too. He even had a section on feminist ideas of enthusiastic consent, although he avoided using the scary word "feminist" to describe them.

James framed certain concepts in ways I didn't enjoy, like aligning "dominant energy" with masculinity, and "submissive energy" with femininity. On the bright side, he at least included a short note acknowledging that some people would disagree with him. It's funny... you might expect that stuff to make me incoherently angry, but it usually just irritates me. I don't get nearly as angry about it as other people I know. Like the male submissives. Some — not all, but some — of those guys are *highly* masculine, and they will *fuck your shit up,* dude.

James struck me as a perfect split among Type 1: Analyst, Type 3: Hedonist, and Type 5: Shark. When I asked James for critiques of the community, his critiques were a lot like those of other smart PUAs. Notwithstanding the fact that he did paid coaching and was about to sell a book, he didn't like the commercialization. "I hate how they try to hurt men in order to sell their products," he said. "The same way TV commercials try to make you feel like a loser if you don't have a nice car, some gurus try to make you feel like a loser if you aren't fucking typical blondes 5 times a week. They know that if they just make men feel hurt enough, those men will buy."

Like me, he also thought a lot of PUA lingo could be problematic. "Jargon shows in-group status," he said, "and can quickly convey thoughts. But what the words tend to do is mask lack of immediate understanding and an absence of self-awareness by umbrellaing different experiences under the same term. A buddy of mine used to say things like, 'I was negging this HB8 and I went in to DHV...' and I'd be like, what the fuck? You were insulting a nice little girl who didn't even notice you, then you started bragging about your fucking used car. If you spent a year in the 'seduction community' to learn that, you should have just declared yourself a useless dickhead from the start and rolled with it. You'd be more congruent. Whatever 'congruent' means."

At the end of dinner, James told me about a club night he'd been attending lately. "They play music and they show vanilla porn, and they serve chicken," he said. "It's called Porn & Chicken. Seriously. [1] It's basically how vanilla mainstream people seek sexual adventure. It's like a trainwreck. You'll love it."

I tilted my head at him. He really didn't seem to be flirting. He wasn't giving a single Indicator of Interest... at least not that I could recognize. I'd been thinking about getting into the hipster Chicago club scene, and this way I could watch James in action.

"Okay," I said. "Let's go to Porn & Chicken. Sounds like fun."

* * *

One of my most entertaining moments with James in the next month was when he went out drinking with me and three of my sex worker friends. (Two were escorts, and one a professional dominatrix.) He spent much of the night explaining what it meant to be a PUA coach. My friends were fascinated.

"Whoa," one of them said. "You're totally stealing our clients! If you weren't training these guys, they might be paying for sex!"

"I know," James said. "I'm your competition."

Another time, James tried to tell me all about a spat he'd had with the Type 4: Leader PUA, Jonnie Walker. Jonnie Walker also tried to tell me his side of the story later. I don't remember any of the details, because it was a bewildering array of social references and defensive claims. I think there might have been a girl in the middle of it, but there also might not. The whole affair made me realize just how much PUAs can be like stereotypical high school Mean Girls. Best of all, the two men appeared to go back to being friends within a few months.

None of this happened at Porn & Chicken, however. Oh, yes, please *let me tell you* about Porn & Chicken. James was right: it was totally a bunch of vanilla kids seeking barely-controversial sexual adventure... although he seemed good at finding and picking up kinky 22-year-olds among the attendees. The porn was execrable.

I was less interested in the crowd than James was. Most of them were hipsters highly preoccupied with fashion. For hipsters, this means tattoos and stretched earlobes and skinny jeans and feathered hats. Personally, I'm more interested in the scruffy, vegan, bike-riding, awkward hipsters who like academic theory and social justice. But I do kind of love feathered hats. And I'll give the Porn & Chicken crowd this: they were cute.

One night, James said to me, "You should approach someone."

"What, in this crowd?" I said.

He grinned. "There has to be someone here who appeals to you."

At the edge of the dance floor, a slender boy danced atop a two-foot-by-two-foot box. He was wearing a white tank top upon which was handwritten: LOVE (much like the famous sculpture by Robert Indiana). The boy's skin glowed with youth, and his eyes hid behind preposterously large sunglasses. "That one's cute," I said.

"Go talk to him," James said.

I hesitated. I realized that I was feeling what a PUA would call "approach anxiety." *I'm a total Average Frustrated Chick,* I thought. "I can't," I said aloud. "I mean... he's so young."

James rolled his eyes. "You're just *practicing,*" he said. "You're not going home with him. Come on," and he turned away from me, working his way through the crowd towards the boy on the box. Once he got to the base of the box, he looked up at the boy and shouted over the music: "Is there room up there for two?"

Box Boy nodded. James gestured to me, and I climbed onto the box.

The DJ was playing Daft Punk, and it was deafening. I usually go to dance clubs to dance; I'm not optimized to meet people in places where I can't talk easily. Words are my chosen weapon. Also, I'm not good at dancing with people. I felt somewhat out of my comfort zone.

However, I'm not totally miscalibrated: I noticed that a pretty brunette below us on the dance floor kept batting her eyelashes at Box Boy. A girlfriend, perchance?

"Who's that girl?" I shouted at Box Boy.

"Never met her before in my life," he shouted back.

Hmm, I thought, but he seemed sincere. We danced through another few songs before I decided to try and have an actual conversation with him. I leaned in and started asking questions like his age... 22? Oh, not as bad as I thought, though he still made me feel old....

Next thing I knew, the pretty brunette leapt up and crowded onto the box with us.

It was a small box, and things were seriously awkward with the three of us there. She effectively disrupted the conversation. I asked myself if I was motivated enough to keep talking to Box Boy, with this girl insistent on interfering. The answer was no.

I found James outside. I wondered where *his* 22-year-old had gotten to. "Some girl just destroyed my game," I said, and told the whole story. "What would you recommend in cases like that?" I asked. "I know PUAs talk about Alpha Males on Guard. There are all kinds of routines for getting rid of AMOGs who interfere while you're gaming chicks, right?"

"Yeah," James said. "I try to stay away from using those terms... but one of the typical routines would be to say, 'You two look so great together. You should get married.' Then, 9 times out of 10, they react by saying 'No way' or laughing it off or something, so you've disrupted their couple energy. You're also implying that the guy is boring and safe by associating him with marriage. So, okay, with that girl on the box, you could say something to Box Boy such as: 'That girl's hot, and she's into you. I bet you could lay her tonight.' On the surface, you're being friendly, but really you're putting him in a position where he has to defend himself against the implications you're making. And plus, you're subtly insulting her: you're calling her easy. You're calling her a slut."

"Ick," I said. "I mean... I've encouraged my guys to flirt with other girls before, but it wasn't because I was trying to insult the other girls. At least I wasn't trying to do that on purpose. That's kinda awful. Besides, I don't believe in shaming women for their sexuality."

"It's not *you,*" James said. *"It's the game.* You know, one of the things I tell my clients is that they eventually want to get to a kind of higher mental place, a Zen outcome-independent state where they don't actually care what happens. But once they're in that mindset, they can still go down to lower mental places if they choose to. The point is, to play the game, sometimes you have to *perform* that catty, petty crap. Even if you don't believe in it."

He paused for thought. "Another thing you could have done with this girl," he added, "is make fun of her weight. Obviously, you wouldn't call her fat. But you could say something like, 'Wow, there's barely room for two on this box, let alone three. Not with those hips.' Then you look at her hips like you're grossed out."

"I don't want to be the kind of girl who makes other girls feel insecure about their weight!" I protested. "I don't want to appear like that to a guy I'm flirting with, either. I mean, I doubt I would even be attracted to a guy who wanted me to be like that."

James shook his head. "It's not you saying those things. It's not you," he said again. "It's the game."

* * *

The next day, I was startled to receive an email from Box Boy, because I hadn't given him my email address at the club. Upon reading, I learned that I already met him weeks before, when he attended one of my events. I'd thought he was cute back then, too. I'd had a whole conversation with him and found an excuse to give him my contact info, but I hadn't heard from him until now. He recognized me at the club, but I hadn't recognized him.

"I'm sorry we never got to say goodbye last night," Box Boy wrote. "I met the drunk girl who hopped up on the box at the end of the night, and found out I've met her once before, which is why she was kind of all over the place. She's much less crazy when she's not so drunk."

Upon receiving this email, I must have laughed for a good five minutes. *Wow,* I thought. *I may be unwilling to play the game enough to mock some girl's weight, but apparently I'm doing okay playing it my way.*

I lost touch with the guy, though. I answered his email, and he attended my next event, but I decided against asking him out directly, and he didn't contact me again, so there you go. It's just as well. I mean, 22.

* * *

It was James who first suggested that I give a talk at the Chicago Lair, and several PUA acquaintances tried to get me in there. (Many cities have "lairs," i.e. "PUA headquarters.") It was a no-go. The population of the Chicago Lair were even more distrustful of women than PUAs in other cities. In other cities, I'd heard that women could attend Lair talks for free, and that some guys brought their girlfriends and asked for their perspectives. In Chicago, however, there was just no way.

There was a story behind the rejection. Supposedly, many moons ago, a Chicago Lair guy left his computer open at a girlfriend's place. The girlfriend snooped. She found PUA fora and read his posts, as well as posts from his PUA buddies. Whatever she read appalled her, and she proceeded to find a bunch of those PUAs' girlfriends on Facebook and tell the girls everything.

Then, the story goes, the ladies banded together and made a bunch of posters that accused the guys of date rape. The ladies included photos of the PUAs and hung the posters all over town.

I don't know how much of this story is true. Being as it comes from PUAs, who often love to talk about women being "hysterical" and "dramatic," I am disinclined to trust it entirely. Presumably, however, it contains a kernel of truth. If the story contains a lot of truth, I'd like to know *what exactly the girl read* that led her to react that way. Sadly, it was impossible to track her down and ask for her perspective.

On the other hand, groupie girls are an established phenomenon among very successful PUAs. Seriously. I never met any, though (unless I count myself).

There are a few female PUA coaches. The most prominent is Erika Awakening, who seems heavily into New Age spirituality. She's written Field Reports about hooking up with other PUA gurus, and she flirts all over the Internet, which makes me wonder if she got into this for one of the same reasons I did: PUA fetishization. One PUA coach told me, "Erika is the big guru who does frou-frou emotional stuff. She can get guys really vulnerable, and get them to spill their guts to her... so even if she doesn't teach pickup very well, she'll be successful." There are plenty of rumors that she's hysterical and dramatic; maybe she is, or maybe she's being stereotyped in a hostile environment.

Another well-known female PUA coach is the gorgeous Kezia Noble. I have to hand it to her: PUA training videos made by a hot girl in a bathing suit? Brilliant idea. From what I can tell, though, Kezia's primary talent is repeating established PUA lessons.

Hitori, whose "Playette FAQ" I mentioned in the previous chapter and included in Appendix F, is a rare gem. She spends a lot of time analyzing the game and giving advice to men, but there are also sectors of some PUA message boards for "Playettes," where ladies can discuss "girl game" and engage in girl talk using PUA jargon. There, Hitori is a much-beloved poster. Sometimes, she even criticizes sexist bullshit from PUA dudes.

I don't always agree with Hitori, but I wish she would publish her own curriculum. Sadly, she has no interest in that. When I asked her some questions by email, she wrote to me that:

When I found the community, I was really just starting to come into my own as part of the social world outside the group I'd built for myself in high school. I mean, this isn't well known, but at the time when I wrote what's probably my most widely read community post ("Social Status / Women Explained"), I was 19 years old. It was hard enough to get them to believe I was a woman, though, so I didn't even bother mentioning my age.

I process things in an analytical way, and as I understand them I find myself wanting to talk about them. What I found, doing that, was that if you break down social behavior with no motive but to understand it then you'll quickly find yourself, purely by accident, forming conclusions that are subversive. And people tend to react very poorly to that, even if you're not analyzing them specifically.

So I found myself with all these thoughts and no one to share them with, when I stumbled over the seduction community. And these guys really don't care what you say, as long as it matches their experience and helps them get better at what they're trying to do. So I took my thoughts there.

I'm there to swap ideas, not make a name for myself. Unlike a lot of the posters on those boards I'm not looking to go commercial or win any popularity contests — so for me, the downsides of being outed in my general life would outweigh the upsides substantially. Had I realized my postings would end up as dispersed over the net as they have, I might never have started posting at all. I mean, my mom doesn't know I'm a seduction community demi-celebrity and neither does my boss. And that's just fine with me.

I asked her about feminism, and she said:

My reaction to feminism is quite mixed, in no small part because I am, and always have been, very into S&M and comfortable with that. Most women who argue mainstream feminist theory, in my experience, make no account for the possibility that our sexual interests may not always/ever be A) egalitarian and politically correct B) malleable or C) learned at all, so much as developmentally imprinted. This strikes me as at best an oversight and at worst frank intellectual dishonesty. When I read feminist blogs I tend to stumble over sexual shaming of people like me, which I don't like, so I leave.

That said, I realize feminism has a lot to offer analytical women who it doesn't accuse of deep-seated self-esteem issues, so as always — grain of salt.

You can see why I like Hitori. She probably has more in common with me than some feminists do.

* * *

After interacting with lots of PUAs, I started wondering what it would be like to talk to the women they slept with. From my observations, it was clear that PUAs were diverse in their approach. Some were at least somewhat concerned about the women they hooked up with ("Leave her better than you found her"); some weren't at all ("pump her and dump her"). Some wanted to get into a committed relationship; some wanted one-night-stands with all the HB10s in town. Some learned to give emotional Indicators of Interest because they wanted to trick the girl; some learned to do it because they wanted to show her how much they genuinely liked her.

From the Lay Reports I read and heard, it sounded like the majority of PUA sex was consensual. But how did PUA *relationships* usually go?

Most PUAs don't tell their girlfriends that they're PUAs. Some told stories about how a girl would find out he was a PUA, then get angry and dump him. Others said that a girlfriend might initially seem okay with the fact that he was a PUA, but then pull out the fact to use against him later, or cite it as a relevant factor during a breakup.

(Actually, the way PUAs talk about their relationships sometimes reminds me of how sex workers talk about their relationships. Sex workers — and retired sex workers — are often scared of revealing their job or past to their partners. Even when a partner seems cool with it, a sex worker can never be sure that a partner won't pull the "you're just a whore" card during a later conflict. Gotta say, though, I have a lot less sympathy for most PUAs than I do for most sex workers. Most sex workers are way more honorable than most PUAs, and most sex workers cope with a lot more awfulness than PUAs ever will.)

So when I told PUAs that I wanted to talk to their girlfriends and exes, I got pushback. Even PUAs who liked talking to me felt anxious about letting a feminist near their girls. Presumably, they're scared that feminism is catching. I tried looking for PUAs' girlfriends and exes through other means, like Craigslist, but I had no luck. Finally, one of my contacts in the community found me a coach who was willing to let me talk to his girlfriend.

To be sure, the coach felt anxious about it. When his girlfriend called me, I could hear him making indistinct noise in the background. She kept saying, "I'm sorry, can you hold on?" and then telling him to quit shouting so she could hear me. She agreed to meet me for coffee. The night before our coffee date, I missed several messages from the coach, demanding to talk to me before I talked to her.

I didn't screen his calls on purpose; I was busy organizing an event. I did, however, choose not to call him back before I met Tiffany the next morning.

Tiffany had bleach-blonde hair, perfect makeup, and a great smile. She was so pretty and fashionable that I immediately felt self-conscious. But once we'd sat down with our drinks and chatted for a few minutes, I realized Tiffany felt much more self-conscious than I did. I put off asking questions in order to make her feel more comfortable; we bonded while talking about our hair, and speculating about human meat consumption. She had a wonderfully evil way of raising her eyebrows while pondering cannibalism.

Tiffany's boyfriend was in his late twenties, and had one child with a previous partner. Tiffany herself was a 21-year-old marketing major. She seemed to feel no discomfort with pickup artistry whatsoever. "I have a lot of respect for the community," she told me. "I mean, if my boyfriend were going home with other women then I wouldn't like that, but he's not. He likes it when I go out into the field with him, and he wouldn't want me with him if the community were sleazy or sketchy."

She was such a lovely lady, it was obvious that Tiffany's presence would increase her boyfriend's credibility. I wasn't surprised he brought her out with him.

By the end of our conversation, Tiffany seemed totally relaxed. "My boyfriend was way too worried about you," she confided. "He kept telling me that I had to be careful about you... that you'd try to get me in a corner. I don't know what he was so scared of."

I heard a more negative tale after I published an article about PUAs in an online magazine. A woman read the article and emailed me to ask if she could tell me her story. She described herself as "late 20s, educated and attractive," and said that she'd recently realized that she was dating a man who used PUA techniques. She figured it out after she heard about the classic PUA curriculum *The Mystery Method,* and then picked up the book out of curiosity. That was when she learned that her beau had run many of Mystery's routines on her, verbatim.

She mentioned that she had already had misgivings about him before discovering *The Mystery Method*. As she wrote:

He told me several times that he might be dating other women, or maybe not... he was always ambiguous. He would also say that he could fall in love with me if I kept dating him long enough... or maybe not. This ambiguity was driving me completely insane. My close friends were asking me how it was possible that I could reduce myself to the state I was in, planning my life for his needs, always worried about losing him, as if he was the only man in the world. Whenever I tried to leave him, he would suggest that he could fall in love with a persistent woman.

The lady said that she'd never been so obsessive before; that she was ashamed of how obsessive she'd become. Once she found out about her partner's pickup artistry, she read more and more about the seduction community, and it was painful. She described the learning process as "draining" and "poisoning" her, and she said that she was constantly watching his behavior for PUA tells. She was always trying to figure out his game, but she didn't tell him she knew that he was a PUA... and she was ashamed of that, too.

Finally, she said that she really did stop chasing him. She concluded that part of the reason she'd fallen for him was that she had some issues, and she even went into therapy. At that point, he started coming after her. "It looked like the less I cared about him," she wrote, "the more he needed me."

In the end, she said that she was tired and discouraged and wanted to end the relationship. She sounded regretful, but she also sounded certain that it was the right thing to do:

I am going to tell him that I know about Mystery's book, and I just cannot live with it. I hope he doesn't get too aggressive with me... he has that issue, too. I like this man; he is charming and stimulating. But it is clear to me that he needs total control over women. In retrospect, he was kind of honest when he told me that he could fall in love with a woman who dated him long enough. I think I bound him to me, but I don't think this kind of bound is what I want. We have both manipulated each other, and I feel I cannot have a relationship that is based on a lie.

Then she asked for my thoughts. I wasn't sure where to start in advising her, so I just tried to support her decision to break it off and to give her some ideas about how to set boundaries with him. I also suggested that if she was afraid he might become "aggressive," she might have the conversation in a public place. That touch of anxiety about physical violence made me worry for her. I hope things worked out okay.

* * *

Lesbian, gay, bisexual, transgender, and queer folks very rarely participate in PUA discussions. Some lesbians read PUA materials, if forum posts are anything to judge by, but I never met a lesbian PUA in person. From glancing around at the various reactions on the Internet, it seems that some lesbians find PUA materials helpful, and others find them appalling.

One anti-feminist lesbian has written about pickup artistry under the pen name "Female Misogynist." My favorite post on her blog is the one where she calls women's right to vote an "unreasonable demand." She also explains that "women are allergic to responsibility," and "if women are going to be faithless sluts, men should take advantage of them." I'm not sure what to make of her perspective, but I figured she's worth mentioning. [2]

In general, anyone who has problems with traditional, heteronormative gender roles is going to have problems with the seduction community. Most of those people get so annoyed that they avoid pickup artistry from the start. This means that guys who want seduction advice and who don't want to deal with traditional, heteronormative stuff will either look for that advice outside the seduction community, or they'll try to adapt pickup advice for their needs.

Remember my goth-feminist-S&M-PUA friend Brian? The guy I described as a Type 1: Analyst *to the max?* Brian and I have discussed this extensively, because he prefers to date non-mainstream women. He's an S&M switch, meaning that he can take the dominant or submissive roles, and he prefers to date dominant women or other switches.

As Brian once said to me: "Picking up dominant women is largely uncharted territory, because male sexual and especially social submissiveness is taboo in the seduction community. Pickup focuses a lot on elements of traditional masculinity, such as dominance. But what if you don't particularly enjoy being dominant, or you prefer to date women who are dominant? You have to step outside the stereotypical pickup paradigm."

One PUA coach told me that he had a client who was an S&M submissive, but who wanted advice on picking up girls. The coach asked for my help because he wasn't sure what to say, so I told him the story of my ex-boyfriend who was most in touch with his submissive side.

When I met this particular ex-boyfriend, I was much less experienced than he at S&M, and I was basically unaware of my dominant side. I suspect that a lot more women than we think would be up for being S&M

dominants, but since cultural norms tell us that women aren't dominant, lots of those women simply don't recognize those feelings. [3] My ex-boyfriend agrees, and as a result he's specifically trained himself to surreptitiously draw out a woman's dominant desires.

With me, he started by offering me his fear. We saw each other around the S&M community a few times, and I guess he took note. Then one day, we were both at an S&M meetup. He was speaking to someone else nearby, and he remarked that I terrified him. He knew that I'd overhear.

I looked at him. He avoided my gaze. Eventually he worked his way around the crowd so he could speak to me, and that was when he met my eyes and said directly to me, straightforward, in a charming and casual tone: "I'm terrified." He was being so obvious: *You scare me, but I'm still talking to you, even though I'm sure you could hurt me real bad.* Yet there were so many tacit dimensions to what he was doing, and I had never quite seen anyone like him before. I was intrigued, and felt myself gain a predatory focus. Pretty soon, I was fantasizing about tearing him apart.

To the PUA coach who asked for my advice, I suggested that the key for a submissive man is to maintain his confidence while offering his partner small pieces of unspoken social power. Maybe submissive men could even mirror the "shit tests" that some women give during heteronormative adversarial flirting, although I'm not entirely sure how a man would ask a woman: "Are you a player?" Especially since "slut" is an unalloyed insult for women, but "player" is more of a mixed tease-compliment for men.

Aside from the question of dominant women, another interesting question is how much PUA tactics are optimized for women from particular cultures or subcultures. For example, I suspect that adversarial flirting behavior (including shit tests) is much more common in mainstream nightclubs than it is at science fiction conventions or street protests.

A lot of PUA advice is universal. Indeed, I've already talked about how women aren't the only ones who act in these ways... like in Chapter 4, where I told you about my ex-boyfriend whose behavior closely matched a PUA list of "compliance tests." Yet some PUA stuff is outright silly. Some of it is outright evil and designed to manipulate partners with low self-esteem, as I will describe in the next chapter. And perhaps some PUA advice is best suited to very specific contexts.

Brian once observed to me that: "Mystery, who was a huge influence on the modern seduction community, is biased towards Los Angeles extravert club-goers who have a very in-your-face, dog-eat-dog, power-oriented social and sexual culture. I fully agree that this style is often inappropriate elsewhere, and will be overkill and even harmful to many women and men. So many PUAs are miscalibrated due to Mystery-induced confirmation bias: Mystery revealed the norms of what was going on in LA, and now PUAs can only see LA wherever they go."

Brian added, "Other social models haven't been considered fully because Mystery's was so convincing and so close. You have to go into really unusual scenes, like the goth scene or fetish scene, to break Mystery's paradigm and finally realize that the model must be expanded." Later in the conversation, Brian also noted that he feels sorry for PUAs who are sarging in certain environments, because they put up with so much more snide behavior from women than he does.

Unfortunately, for a PUA who isn't as self-aware as Brian, he may not even realize that extravert club-going girls aren't what he wants until long after he's spent time chasing them and calibrating his social skills to them. The common advice in the seduction community is to practice in mainstream clubs, but Brian thinks this puts a lot of nerdy PUAs in a weird bind. After all, if they learn how to talk to girls from standard PUA material, they'll get used to environments and social groups full of women that they have little in common with.

Brian's two main suggestions were that nerdy introverted guys might consider practicing:

NERD ENVIRONMENT 1. Through online dating sites.

NERD ENVIRONMENT 2. During the day, like at libraries and laundromats and coffeeshops. As Brian observed, "The introvert girls are out during the day. They don't go to nightclubs."

Still, the problem remains that if the goal is to practice in-person social interaction as much as possible, then bars and clubs really are the best environment, because they're the easiest places to talk to lots of different people in a short period of time.

I did okay talking to Tiffany, but out in the field, I found that I was less interested in talking to PUAs' targets than to the PUAs themselves. Some PUAs seemed to think that because I'm a woman, I understood "what women are thinking." But usually, 5 minutes talking to the average mainstream clubgoer — of any gender — leaves me bored stiff.

A friend of mine suggested that one of the reasons I'm interested in the seduction community is that it's actually *a way of helping me understand mainstream women.* This could be true; I really don't know. Maybe my motivation for this project didn't just arise from being an ugly duckling in public school. Maybe it also came from being teased by the Mean Girls.

* * *

CHAPTER 9:
A Disease of the Mind... It Can Control You

In which the famous PUA Gunwitch attempts to seduce a girl at a party, and is rejected, and shoots her in the face. (Allegedly.) Gunwitch's teachings aren't even the most Darth Vader-esque that Clarisse has seen, though, and so Clarisse offers a whirlwind tour of an almost comically villainous PUA blog. The chapter title is from the song "Disturbia," by Rihanna.

* * *

I've been snippy about PUAs so far, but I've also tried to show you the positive side. Around early 2011, after quite a lot of research and interviews, I was feeling kinda okay about the community. Then a famous PUA guru shot a woman in the face. Allegedly.

The guru, Allan Reyes, went by the PUA name Gunwitch. He was mentioned briefly in *The Game,* and he had amassed a decent following of his own. His slogan was — wait for it — "make the ho say no." I am still not making this up.

Word on the street, and by "the street" I mean "the Internet," was that Gunwitch hit on the lady at a party. He (allegedly) groped her so aggressively that she (allegedly) pulled a knife on him. Then she (allegedly) left the room. She (allegedly) came back 15 minutes later, at which point Gunwitch (allegedly) shot her. By some miracle, she survived; thanks for asking. [1]

(Eventually, Gunwitch was not charged with the crime because the victim had a criminal history and her testimony was considered sketchy. This is like saying that nothing I write on my blog today is trustworthy because I lied a few times in high school. But it's no surprise to feminists that women with "questionable histories" are often considered fair game for violent assholes. This is a major aspect of the sex workers' rights movement, for example.)

Needless to say, the (alleged) Gunwitch shooting prompted much commentary. Feminist websites reported on the event with a bizarre mix of horror and glee. Countless "Blast Through Last Minute Resistance" jokes appeared on PUA fora; I admit that I laughed at some of them, because I'm a bad person. Gunwitch's remaining adherents insisted that Gunwitch must have had "a good reason" for shooting the girl. [2] Meanwhile, the blogger Hugh Ristik wrote a post ending with the phrase, "Fuck you, Gunwitch." [3]

Much of Gunwitch's stuff was typical PUA tactics, but it had a particularly violent edge. A straight male PUA-hating friend emailed me this amazing quotation from a Gunwitch manual:

Your initial state when seeing women you want is very important: the right one will cause you to approach them, the wrong one will panic and confuse you — preventing you from taking any action to ever meet them. If you do not meet them you almost certainly CANNOT have sex with them. Your internal state when you first see an attractive woman must be one of sexual enthusiasm, horniness, and unapologetic desire. NOT one of panic and wonder of what to do or what to say.... Ted Bundy, the infamous serial killer / sociopath didn't feel fear or panic when he saw a target. He felt rage, sexual perversion and desire to kill, hence NO fear to approach them, of course wanting to have sex isn't the same thing, but its still more effective than feeling fear or confusion about your desires and direction. [4]

I could kinda see where Gunwitch was going that paragraph: it's important to encourage socially anxious people not to worry about talking to strangers. Or at least, I could kinda see where Gunwitch was going... right up to the Ted Bundy part. Yes. Ted Bundy. *Forget* Casanova. *Ted Bundy* is who *I* call a seduction icon.

Let's all think like serial killers, guys! It'll be *great.* Trust me.

The Ted Bundy comparison is so instructive. It sums up the biggest problem I have with most of the seduction community: describing tactics in terms of effectiveness, while treating moral concerns as irrelevant.

Most PUAs obviously took great pains to separate themselves from Gunwitch. They portrayed him as an outlier. Gunwitch held an actual blood feud complete with death threats against another well-known coach, Adam Lyons, who's a much more reasonable fellow. And when I spoke to Neil Strauss in the interview that I included in Appendix D, Neil carefully described Gunwitch as an "unstable individual." When I said that lots of feminists disliked the community especially after the alleged Gunwitch shooting, Neil said: "That's like when a politician does something bad and people say all politicians are bad." He added, "I'm surprised it took this long for someone in the community to do something that stupid, but I would never have guessed it would be something that violent."

I didn't have much time to talk to Neil, and I was nervous about coming off as a so-called "humorless feminazi," so I didn't probe further. But I wondered how Neil would react if I pointed out that *his own book, The Game,* features pictures of men holding guns and knives while pursuing women.

It was only one event... but parts of the PUA community were reacting in really fucked-up ways. Given that a PUA guru had *actually just (allegedly) shot a woman in the face,* could I feel okay about a community full of guys using terms like "target"? I am a feminist who feels deeply about the problems of rape culture, and occasionally counsels survivors of rape and assault. Could I really feel okay about PUAs?

As much as I'd fight to the death for free speech — and believe me, I would — metaphors and culture and group dynamics *are not innocent.* The bottom line was the question: would a guy like Gunwitch have (allegedly) shot a woman in the face, if he didn't have a misogynist community backing him up?

I knew I'd never be sure.

* * *

There's an important concept from history of science that I thought about a lot while researching PUAs: the antique scientific theory of "phlogiston."

If you put a large container (like a tall drinking glass) over a burning candle and trap the flame inside without fresh air, it will eventually flicker out. Several hundred years ago, scholars believed in the existence of a substance called phlogiston. Supposedly, phlogiston was an invisible substance produced by fire. Too much phlogiston would suffocate fire. Scholars believed that flames without fresh air died because they eventually produced enough phlogiston that it filled up the available space, thereby suffocating the flame.

Today, we know that this is incorrect. Flames require oxygen. If they're trapped without fresh air, flames go out *because they use up the available oxygen,* not because they're suffocated by phlogiston. So, the phlogiston theory is wrong. But at the time, it fit reality better than previous theories about fire. It explained why fire wouldn't burn without fresh air, for example. People had observable reasons for believing in the existence of phlogiston. The theory persisted for over a century.

Phlogiston *seemed like a totally observable and obvious phenomenon.* Nevertheless, phlogiston *still did not exist.*

In the same way, pickup theory has a lot of assumptions wrapped up in it, especially stereotypes about women. PUAs have some good ideas about seduction, and they have made amazing observations about typical heterosexual dating. However, the Darth Vaders will try to convince you their tactics work because all women are irrational, dumb, childish, weak-willed, gold-diggers, inherently submissive, or whatever other gross stereotype you care to choose. Just because a PUA can show you how to flirt, that doesn't mean his assumptions behind his advice are reasonable.

A straight dude friend of mine, who is extremely popular with women, once remarked that: "Pretty much all I know about PUAs, practice-wise, seems evidence-based and sound. Pretty much all I know about it, theory-wise, sounds like the sort of thing you come up with when you're twenty and drinking in a dorm room at four in the morning."

Remembering this is particularly important when looking into the Dark Side.

* * *

When I think of the Dark Side of the seduction community, I don't just think about Gunwitch. Nor do I think about hypnosis or rape. My primary case study for how bad PUAs can get is a blogger who goes by Roissy, a.k.a. Citizen Renegade, a.k.a. Heartiste. [5]

In my Grand Typology of PUAs, "Darth Vader" is my final PUA type. I just spent way too long reading *Star Wars* arguments online, and I learned that I am not qualified to make assertions about who on the Dark Side is more powerful than Darth Vader. But whoever would be more evil and more powerful than Darth Vader, that's Roissy. Roissy is a good writer, an insightful social analyst, and an obviously smart person... and he is almost comically villainous. Perhaps it would be more appropriate to call Roissy "the one to rule them all, the one to find them, the one to bring them all and in the darkness bind them."

Anyway, some of you will read my description of Roissy, and be astonished that I don't sound enraged to the point of aneurism. So let me tell you this: Roissy encapsulates and personifies a tremendous amount of what I think is wrong with the world. However, I don't think I'll convince anyone by ranting about him. Therefore, I've tried to analyze his output as dispassionately as possible.

Let's start by talking about how unbelievably misogynist Roissy is. He describes women's genitals as a "fetid, humid mess." [6] One wonders why he wants to go anywhere near such a thing. In another post, Roissy tells us that "women are inherently amoral. They are de facto nihilists. They are sociopaths of convenience." [7] So he loathes both our bodies and our minds; I guess at this point we're basically symbols.

Roissy compares women's brains to predictable, pathetic "hamster wheels" so often that he's developed elaborate extensions on the metaphor. In fact, Roissy doesn't even explain that metaphor anymore. He simply assumes that his readers know what he's talking about when he says things like, "[With a girl who seems to have man-style game], cancel the first date. But give a quasi-plausible reason for doing so; just suspicious enough that it caffeinates her hamster." [8] Another good one is, "The hamster is in overdrive in this one, his wee tongue hanging out, gasping for breath, the axel on his wheel coming off." [9]

These metaphors are meant to describe women who seek to make sense of a man's actions, or rationalize their own actions. (As if men never rationalize their actions, or try to understand women.) But in fairness, the hamster wheel is a typical misogynist metaphor across the Internet, so maybe Roissy didn't come up with it himself. We must be fair. [10]

The "hamster" is classic phlogiston, and it's not even very clever phlogiston. It's not a real theory about women's behavior... it's just an excuse for feeling superior to women.

The blogger Hugh Ristik once called out Roissy for writing a post about how hitting women is okay. As Hugh Ristik later wrote to me,

I criticized Roissy for writing a post where he described slapping a girlfriend of his, said it was deserved, and argued that hitting women can turn them on in some circumstances. I asked him to clarify whether he really believed that non-consensually hitting women was acceptable or not, but he has never responded. Roissy's post was deleted in response to criticism. I made the same points in the comments on his blog more recently, and the denizens called me a "gender traitor." Unfortunately, some men are so starved of knowledge about masculinity that they idolize Roissy and overlook some of the more problematic things he has said.

Other favorite Roissy topics include how women shouldn't vote, women shouldn't work, etc. etc. etc. ad nauseam. In a post called "Is Female Careerism a Form of Infidelity?" he writes that "Women who place their careers front and center are committing a kind of betrayal of their sex's biological and psychological imperatives." [11] In a post called "Sexual Dystopia: A Glimpse at the Future", he writes that "the worst thing to happen to America was women's suffrage [i.e., the right to vote]." Roissy concludes that, because women can vote, "we are going the way of Rome": i.e., because women can vote, the USA is going to collapse. [12]

And Roissy, like many misogynist PUAs, compares feminism *itself* to a giant shit test. Yes folks, that's right... if only men would act sexydominant, feminists would forget all about equal pay for equal work. And voting. And abortion rights. And sexual double standards. And rape.

And generally having a voice in society at all. All those silly little thoughts would run right out of our silly little hamster-driven heads!

*　*　*

Here's an excerpt from one of Roissy's best-known blog posts. The title is, quite simply, "Dread." The post explains that:
There are two ways to guarantee a healthy relationship. By healthy, I mean the girl is in love with you and there is no threat of her leaving; you have all the leverage you need to assure yourself peace of mind and a steady sexual outlet.

*1. **Meet your soulmate:** If you are extremely lucky enough to cross paths with your soulmate this is the easiest way to live the kind of romantic bliss that Hollywood movies exalt. A soulmate connection is the Golden Ticket to happiness and a dreamlike existence. But it is rare. Don't live as if it will happen to you....*

*2. **Instill dread:** Women respond viscerally in their vagina area to unpredictability, mixed signals, danger, and drama in spite of their best efforts to convince themselves otherwise. Managing your relationship in such a way that she is left with a constant, gnawing feeling of impending doom will do more for your cause than all the Valentine's Day cards and expertly performed tongue love in the world. Like it or not, the threat of a looming breakup, whether the facts justify it or not, will spin her into a paranoid estrogen-fueled tizzy, and she'll spend every waking second thinking about you, thinking about the relationship, thinking about how to fix it. Her love for you will blossom under these conditions. Result: she works harder to please you.*

The key for the man is to adopt a posture of blase emotional distance alternated with loving tenderness. Too much of either and she'll run off.

Examples of effective doom inducement:
Cook her a romantic candlelight dinner at home. Make it a memorable experience, complete with jazz, chocolate, and rose petals. Then, do not talk with her for four days afterwards.

Ignore her calls for a week. When you eventually answer and she reads you the riot act, act as if nothing was wrong and accuse her of sabotaging a perfectly good relationship, "just like all the other women in this stupid city. I thought you were different." Hang up on her angrily.

[Lots more examples, primarily focused on making her feel jealous or anxious. And then....]

Thermonuclear Option:
Have an affair and make sure she finds out about it. Arrange the

confrontation so that it does not happen at your place. When she confronts you, don't get defensive. Don't speak at all. Let her vent. Let her punch you in the chest and scream obscenities. When she takes a breather, tell her she's never looked more beautiful and you will never stop loving her. Then without waiting for her response calmly walk out the door and break off all contact for two weeks. When she comes back to you... and she will... you will have a love slave for life. [13]

I'm so fascinated by this passage. For one thing, there's the paragraph on soulmates. Even when PUAs acknowledge the reality of emotional escalation, they very rarely acknowledge that emotional connection requires work. (Admittedly, the work of emotional escalation is often instinctive... the same way picking up girls is instinctive for some people.) PUAs may even talk about love, but they almost always discuss love like it's a lightning bolt. To PUAs, love is something unexpected; love "just happens." Simultaneously, PUAs complain that women expect sex to "just happen." They complain that women have no idea how much work goes into creating a fun date, et cetera.

Another fascinating bit is the idea that it's just women — not people of other genders — who respond viscerally to jealousy, unpredictability, mixed signals, danger and drama. Most PUAs constantly seek ways to blame women for the game. But of course, the above blog post *could never have been written* by someone with zero personal interest in mixed signals, drama, and so on. Roissy once wrote a different post on how to deal with women who use masculine game tactics. He noted that "girls who play a man's pickup game are drama queens who substitute the thrill of psychological manipulation for the emptiness of their gutted hearts." [14] Naturally, *men* who play a man's pickup game are *completely different*. Men couldn't ever be drama queens at all!

Another fascinating bit is how Roissy assumes you want a "love slave for life." Roissy eats egalitarianism for breakfast.

Mostly, however, the problem here is the incredibly negative and selfish frame.

A woman who used to work as assistant to a PUA coach once wrote an article in which she noted that the coach's clients seemed mostly like decent guys, who merely needed social guidance. She then added:

However, the tactics of the trainers and PUAs themselves were a different story — a far more sinister one. For them, manipulating women was often a game. They enjoyed seeing how far they could push the limits of their skills. I met girls that were being cheated on. I saw texts from women begging to be taken back.... There were stories you could tell a woman to make her panic about losing you every time you left a room, and while I never witnessed this in action, I don't have a hard time believing it's the truth. [15]

And don't forget the woman I talked about in the previous chapter, who wrote to me that:

This ambiguity was driving me completely insane. My close friends were asking me how it was possible that I could reduce myself to the state I was in, planning my life for his needs, always worried about losing him, as if he was the only man in the world. Whenever I tried to leave him, he would suggest that he could fall in love with a persistent woman.

This is the Dark Side: using strategic ambiguity to influence targets towards feeling confused, anxious, scared, and dependent, rather than helping them feel confident, loved, energized and free.

Roissy's insight doesn't excuse how terrible he is. An evil genius is still evil. But I must admit that he is very good at describing flirtatious strategic ambiguity. The problem is that his goal is never to facilitate mutual relationships — it's always to create adversarial ones.

* * *

Is it necessary for humans to organize ourselves into competitive hierarchies, where people on the bottom suffer? Is it necessary for human hierarchies to sustain themselves through violence... both physical and social?

Is it actually possible for everyone to get along?

Roissy certainly doesn't think so. In a blog post called "Diversity + Proximity = War", he writes:

People like to form into competing groups. This natural impulse is encoded in every human being's DNA. It is a deeply embedded encoding, and can't be excised. It can only be controlled by authoritarian measures, i.e. ultimately at the point of a gun." [16]

This absurdly overstated argument starts with a typical PUA claim about "biology," and gives a typically dark reading on it. Even if Roissy could prove that competing groups are "encoded in every human being's DNA" and "can't be excised," he would be unable to prove that competitive urges can "only" be controlled by violence. But while his words don't tell us much about the real world, they tell us everything about Roissy.

Roissy *believes* in competitive hierarchy. He *believes* with the force of a zealot or an evangelist. He *believes* that non-consensual violent dominance is both inevitable and necessary. This is most visible in his anti-feminist, anti-progressive posts, but it's also visible in everything he writes. The most absurd post might be the one where he posts a picture of a mixed-race gay couple holding up an adopted Black baby, then adds a picture of a thin man proposing to a fat woman, and titles the whole thing "The Folly Before the Fall." [17] (Translation: Roissy believes that the current political discussion of gay marriage, the value our nation places on ethnic diversity, and the fact that thin men are proposing to fat women are all reasons the USA is doomed.)

But there are other ridiculous Roissy posts to choose from. Because Roissy writes primarily about the game, he usually expresses his belief in non-consensual violent dominance through PUA advice. His preferred mode of violence is social rather than physical, but that doesn't make it any less violent.

There are two PUA terms that are the defining "PUA asshole words": those words are "alpha" and "beta." It's difficult to get a consistent definition for these terms, but the core concept is kindasorta comprehensible: an "alpha" is a person who rules a social environment; a "beta" is a person who occupies a lower social tier. Hypothetically, "alphas" are leaders and "betas" are followers. Hypothetically, "alpha males" get all the "best" women. Hypothetically, PUAs all want to be "alpha males."

Much of this "alpha male" stuff is based on questionable pop evolutionary psychology; it's another reason to remember what I said about phlogiston. I'm not really into evolutionary psychology myself, but it's worth noting that *even some people who care about evolutionary psychology* have written irate articles about why PUA "alpha male" phlogistonic narratives are stupid. For example, here's a ranty quotation from a long blog post by a True Believer in evolutionary psychology. The post is called "The Alpha Male Narrative Myth":

Evolutionary psychology and hunter-gatherer anthropology are ridiculously important and useful to a zillion things, and they continue to be held back by the pop-PUA bullshit that gets circulated endlessly. In other words, it makes my life difficult because I have to waste my time dealing with flak from people who object to the bullshit narrative — while I agree with their objections to the narrative. Darwin's baby gets thrown out with the bathwater because a few people want to sell an image and a bunch of poorly researched ebooks. [18]

Feel free to follow that footnote, read the post, and Google for similar posts if you care about why PUAs are wrong from an evolutionary psychology perspective. Personally, I don't; that's beside the point for me.

A lot of smart PUAs don't talk alpha and beta at all. The words don't come up in *The Game,* for example. When I noticed that, I began to wonder why certain PUAs use this "alpha and beta" framework — and why the PUAs who love it the most are usually jerks like Roissy, while reasonable PUAs are hesitant.

I've concluded that using the alpha/beta framework correlates so highly to being an asshole because *the alpha/beta framework is most useful for PUAs whose major goal is to gain and maintain power.*

Such PUAs are not as interested in connecting with women as they are in gaining power over women. They're not as interested in making friends with other men as they are in dominating other men. Of all PUAs, they are most invested in a clear hierarchy, because *they want a world where they can see themselves on top.* Not just on top of women... on top of *everybody.* Feminists have been known to say that: "Misogyny is usually misandry." In other words, dehumanizing women is often the flip side of dehumanizing men, and vice versa.

I think it's possible that there's some value to alpha/beta theory, as long as it's talked about in a nuanced way rather than a stupidly overblown way. I think "alpha" and "beta" are clumsy words that mainly express male insecurities, but as an S&Mer, of course I believe that power is sexy. Yet the great lesson of S&M is this: *even though power is sexy, it doesn't have to control our non-sexual lives.*

If power affects a situation, then we can acknowledge that power — we can even play with it — and *at the same time,* we can work to keep our relationships mutual and cooperative, rather than adversarial and hierarchal. Many S&Mers do this by compartmentalizing our violent power dynamics, and talking about S&M carefully when we're not actually doing it. And those of us who engage in adversarial flirtation know that there's a time when you stop issuing negs and shit tests, and start being open about how you feel.

Maybe humans are unable to *completely* escape adversarial hierarchies, and maybe we crave strategic ambiguity. But surely we can try to keep our relationships *mostly* mutual and cooperative, and compartmentalize power as much as possible. The great thing about humanity is that we get the better of our worst instincts *all the time.*

PUAs who are obsessed with alpha/beta theory have one key weapon other than game: *gender policing.*

Feminists use the phrase "gender policing" to talk about how gender is defined and enforced by culture. Different cultures have incredibly different perspectives on gender. In some cultures, for example, there are people who can live like the "opposite" sex as long as they wear the right clothes, or there are widely-understood categories of people who are seen as a "third gender." (If you're interested in more information on this, Google topics like "Samoa fa'afine" or "India hijra.") In contrast, other cultures — such as the USA — are more confused by people who don't fit into the traditional gender binary. The USA has very little traditional space for a person who is neither traditionally male nor traditionally female.

And regardless of how gender roles look, all cultures have definitions of "what makes a man (or woman)." Certain clothes are intended for each gender. Certain jobs are "more appropriate" for certain genders, and so on.

When a person steps outside a gender role, then many members of that culture will *police* that person. For example, if a USA man has long hair, or wears a dress, or works in a typically "feminine" profession (like nursing), or is gay, then he will be mocked for it... possibly even physically attacked by other men. Trans people — and genderqueer people, who identify as neither male nor female — are sometimes visible violators of gender expectations, and they suffer for it. For example, the statistics on how trans people are harassed, threatened and assaulted are mind-blowingly horrible. [19] But make no mistake: the purpose of gender policing is to keep *everyone* in their place.

Allow Roissy to tell you all about it. Or rather, allow him to tell his hypothetical future son:

To my son: You will learn how to say Hi to girls before the age of 16 if it kills you. There will be no Star Trek or Lord of the Rings posters in your room. You will instead have Helmut Newton [arty photos of thin naked girls] hanging on your walls and a copy of Mystery Method. *I will treat the family dog better than you if you major in anything that doesn't ensure a salary high enough to keep you from grubbing off me. Learn how to throw a punch. If you turn out gay, don't ever bring your "boyfriend" around me.* [20]

Men *must* know how to charm women. Men *must not* enjoy stereotypically-"geeky" pursuits, like science fiction and fantasy. Men *must* publicly show interest in stereotypically-"hot" ladies. Men *must* fight. Men *must* achieve a certain type of career success. Men *must not* be gay. In short, Roissy writes about gender policing better than I ever could. (In case you're interested, his main words of wisdom for his future daughter are that he'll disown her if she has sex with "losers," has sex for money, or majors in women's studies... but he'll gladly buy her plastic surgery "if necessary.")

Many alpha/beta discussions are classic examples of gender policing. Some PUAs actually go so far as to define "alpha" as "attractive to women": an amazingly circular notion. Roissy appears immune to the tautology of telling men to act alpha in order to get women... and then making statements like "Make no mistake, at the most fundamental level the CRUX of a man's [alpha] worth is measured by his desirability to women, whether he chooses to play the game or not." [21]

Of course, since Roissy is supposedly excellent at the game, his "alpha" definition has the self-serving side benefit of *making him alpha by default*. In his world, he not only gets to pass judgment on women and tell other men how to act; he straight-up gets to rule. Much of what Roissy writes is skillfully designed such that those who draw insight from his perspective are also likely to buy into his power. After all, why create a hierarchy, if not for the purpose of putting himself on top?

Given these cultural patterns and incentives, it's unsurprising that Roissy's alpha/beta writings often devolve in two directions:

A) *Labeling certain attractive or unattractive behaviors as belonging to "alpha males" or "beta males,"* and then using "alpha" or "beta" to talk about those things, rather than discussing the precise behavior. For example, supplication is frequently associated with betaness, and supplication is used as an example of beta males being unattractive. But we could just as easily talk about supplication, without bringing betaness into the picture at all.

Roissy had a Beta of the Month feature on his blog for a while, whereby he'd mock various overly-beta dudes. Such dudes include men in abusive relationships with their wives. (Because obviously the best thing to do for those guys is... to mock them? It might be funny if it wasn't so sad.) On a slightly less depressing note, Beta of the Month also includes men who make the mistake of writing supplicatory letters to ex-girlfriends with lines like "you were the most incredibly gorgeous and sexy young woman I have ever known." Upon finding this letter (and the ex-girlfriend's snide response), Roissy ripped that guy a new one for being such a beta. [22]

This is really too bad, because some PUA tactics are so smart. Most PUAs who talk phlogiston about alpha and beta are shortchanging themselves more than anyone else, because they could be breaking down the actual situation and coming up with tactics that work instead.

Roissy sometimes manages to express real insight despite his overuse of alpha and beta, but it's because he *defines* dealing with compliance tests, using negs, and even "flirty teasing" as alpha. Obviously, if "tactics that work" equal "alpha"... then "alpha" will equal "tactics that work." It must be nice to build a language that makes you king.

B) *Policing masculinity.* The above Beta of the Month entry also includes a picture of a man in an obviously submissive position. A favorite theme of masculinity-policers is that manliness equals heterosexual dominance. As Roissy delightfully puts it,

If [this submissive photograph is] a fetish, then this is proof that some fetishes are the domain of losers. If you must have a fetish, make it

something alpha like collaring your woman.

Roissy can count himself lucky if some of my favorite musclebound, badass male submissive friends don't find him before I do.

Gender policing is a widespread phenomenon; it's not something that only PUAs do. In fact, there are *anti-PUA fora* around the Internet *for men...* and these fora engage in a hell of a lot of gender policing, too. If I had a dollar for every Internet thread where angry men call PUA coaches "gay," then I could afford several dozen overpriced bootcamp tickets.

I really wish more PUAs would talk about gender policing. You'd think they'd see it clearly, since it's often used against them. Yet for a group of men with such masculinity issues, it's amazing how eagerly alpha/beta theorists will "prove their manliness" by mocking "less manly" other men. It's ironic, but I can't laugh at it — it's too sad. It's like how some women call themselves feminists, and complain about women's sexuality being limited or attacked... and then turn around and insult some girl by calling her a "slut."

One of my feminist male friends once read Roissy's blog and texted me to ask, "Do you suppose he got stuffed in the locker a lot by jocks when he was in high school?" It's a reasonable question. Bullies often become bullies because they have, themselves, been hurt. Bullies buy into the hierarchy that hurt them, because they can't let go of their pain.

Let me clarify, in the final analysis, that I'm obviously not the biggest fan of hierarchy. But we live in a world full of entrenched hierarchies. We can work against entrenched hierarchies, but we won't be able to dismantle them all right away. I believe that the world would be a better place if there was more emphasis on mutuality and cooperation. But *sometimes we'll just have to deal with power.* At those times, the question becomes: how do you get power, and *how do you use it once you have it?*

Let's say you have a lot of gendered power... for example, suppose you're a successful PUA. Do you use your power to hurt both women and men by building a framework that's both anti-woman and anti-man? Or do you seek metaphors and actions that are neither misogynist, nor misandrist?

What freaks me out about Roissy is not that he knows about social power. I'm more worried that he cares so little about responsibility.

* * *

There's an easy, pretty explanation for Roissy: he acknowledges that long ago, he loved deeply, and the lady broke his heart. From what he writes, he treated this woman about as well as he treats any other woman.

Unfortunately for him, when the lady wised up and left, he realized he was in love with her and tried to get her back. She wasn't dumb enough to fall for it, so Roissy concludes that *his love is what drove her away.* "If you want a girl to fall out of love with you," he writes, "shower her with love." Gosh, I can taste the pathos.

My favorite comment on that post is the fourth one, which says:
this explains a lot, roissy.

you're completely wrong about [the claim that "if you want a girl to fall out of love with you, shower her with love"]. you just showered her with love too late. she was probably hurt and had emotionally moved on by then, honey. you boys just don't realize that timing is everything. you weren't ready to settle down, and your last attempts to hold onto her were just too late. [23]

It would be charmingly romantic to believe that this experience made Roissy into what he is, but I doubt it. Don't get me wrong... I'm sure that Roissy is *partly* motivated by pain, and possibly vengeance. I'm also sure that he's mostly motivated by power.

Make no mistake: Roissy is on the worse end of the PUA continuum, but he's fairly representative of many PUAs. Roissy is famous in his corner of the blogosphere; some bloggers call it the "Roissysphere." His blog receives hundreds of admiring comments on every post, and other PUAs make similar points all over the place, although they're rarely as smart or eloquent as he. I've heard that the original Roissy doesn't even write the blog anymore. Supposedly, he now farms out his "Chateau Heartiste" to talented acolytes, and simply edits their words.

Truly, it can be difficult to find a more wretched hive of scum and villainy than Roissy's comment section. My #1 favorite comment on any Roissy post is this: "[Women] really are insipid, vapid airheads. If it wasn't for the pussy, there would be a bounty on them." [24]

Says it all, really.

The man who wrote those words doesn't merely disdain women. He doesn't merely hate women. He *fears* women. After all, you don't offer a bounty to hunt something down *unless the target is dangerous.* The most misogynist corners of the PUA subculture not only discuss ways to aggressively manipulate women. They also paint women as selfish, deceitful and hazardous.

Roissy's attitudes scare many guys away from pickup artistry, including guys that Roissy supposedly wants to help. What I find much more alarming, however, is that after being exposed to people like Roissy, *many guys start believing it is necessary to have awful attitudes if they want to attract lots of women.*

The blogger Hugh Ristik once wrote, "I don't like how people first exposed to writings on 'game,' 'pickup,' and 'seduction' through Roissy's blog will attain a skewed perception of what those things are all about." The coach Mark Manson once said to me, "Roissy is pretty much as bad as PUAs get." Of course I agree. But I'll add that Roissy makes an excellent warning sign.

* * *

More and more friends were curious about my "research," especially given that it was all I could talk or think about. One friend met a semi-famous PUA at a party: Herbal, from *The Game*. My friend texted me, "I thought Herbal was oily even before I knew he was a PUA. He now has a blog, wrote a PUA book and sold it chapter by chapter online, travels constantly, lives in an RV and blogs about it for the vicarious netizens, and is going to Japan for a few months. He feels frivolous, like a papier mache parody of an adventurer."

After I'd been back in the country for eight months or so, even The Dude sat me down one day and asked me to explain why PUAs are interesting. He heard me out, then shrugged. "I dunno," he said. "It sounds kind of... vapid."

My friends were correct. Frivolous. Vapid. I *finally* thought carefully about why PUAs interested me so much. Past the PUA fetish, past my desire for validation, past my ugly-duckling search for social power. In a way, I felt disgusted with myself for giving PUAs so much brain space.

PUA coach Mark Manson once told me that groupie girls get into pickup artistry because they have "intimacy issues": because their emotional walls are too strong for the average guy. When he said this, I worried that I saw myself within the description. But I've been in love. I've had relationships. I've had some really long relationships. No way do I have intimacy issues, right?

Right?

I have never entirely understood my own motives for being an activist, but I'm pretty sure that at some point I wanted to make the world a better place. Wasn't I a gigantic feminist? Didn't I have a deep-seated sense of morality, or something? Why was I wasting my time learning about PUAs, then wasting more time feeling anxious and sorry for myself afterwards?

Worst of all, why was I indulging my cynical and manipulative side? Shouldn't I be trying to defeat it... or at the very least, seek positive metaphors for human interaction rather than negative ones?

Honestly, I thought, *I might as well change my working title. Instead of*

"*Confessions of a PUA Chaser*," let's call it "The Terrible Angst of a White, Straight, Cisgendered, Healthy, Able-Bodied Middle-Class USA Girl Who's Never Had A Real Fucking Problem In Her Life."

I could claim that examining PUAs prepared me for a harsh dating world. I could claim that my research was a form of self-defense. Also, learning about PUAs often forced me to engage with my personal darkness: my worst opinions of men. In some ways this was bad, because it caused feelings of hatred and paranoia. But it could also be compelling. Reading Roissy's blog, and then talking about it with men I trusted, sometimes felt like an exorcism.

Some of the worst PUA stuff was bizarrely seductive and validating, because it put women in strong, admirable role... perhaps stronger than the writers understand. Roissy, for example, writes a lot about how men will become lazy and useless *unless* they have to accomplish things *in order to sleep with women*. This implies that it's women's responsibility to withhold sex from men who don't accomplish enough.

It also implies that women are the most stable, useful, forward-thinking and productive element of society.

And you know what?

Imagine me switching into a Dark Lord voice, right about... *now:*

Maybe women *are* the most stable, useful, forward-thinking and productive element of society. Maybe most men really *won't* ever do anything unless we force them to do it by the threat of withheld sex. Maybe male societal dominance has endured because women are so much *stronger* than men. By this, I don't just mean the strength to endure childbirth; I mean the strength to work hard at things that men often refuse to even acknowledge as "work," like emotional management.

Maybe women have always been the only ones strong enough to do what has to be done (like the emotional management and chores involved with a family), rather than whatever will get the most attention (like monuments and empire-building).

Maybe this is why society has historically repressed women's career aspirations, social power, and sexuality... because it actually *will* destroy society if we focus on our own fulfillment, rather than managing and rewarding those lazy fuckers. Plus, since men are way more violent than us, we gotta keep them occupied somehow. Otherwise the world would collapse in warfare.

So maybe women have the real strength, but feminism is a red herring, because women *should* spend our strength constructing lies about how weak we are, for fear that otherwise men will never get off their asses again.

And we really *need* men to keep devising new objects and competing for power. Because what this world really needs is lots of new stuff to consume, plus lots of competitive hierarchy.

Right?

No. Just... no.

Now imagine me switching out of the Dark Lord voice.

Folks, I did not come up with the above man-hating paragraphs after reading feminist theory. Those paragraphs came from investigating anti-feminists. And unless I'm associating with anti-feminists, I don't actually believe that stuff (much). It's the Dark Side, and it's not true. Remember: misogyny is often misandry. People who hate women usually don't think well of men, either.

Thanks for tempting me with the Dark Side, PUAs. I hope I someday recover.

In some ways, I loved the feeling of being "tempted by evil," hypnotized and sucked in. I also loved the challenge of trying to understand perspectives that feel so inimical. It hurt, but it was *fascinating*. I had to wade through tons of bullshit to deal with PUAs, but researching them also allowed me to confront my fears.

Many ideas I found in the seduction community initially felt like they undermined my ethics and feminism. Yet engaging with them also allowed me to engage with politically incorrect and potentially subversive philosophies. I believe that my ethics and feminism are stronger, more flexible, and more realistic today because of my exposure to PUAs. It took me a lot of mental processing to get here, though.

* * *

I had attended a few events with James Amoureux by the time of the (alleged) Gunwitch shooting. I told James about it as he dropped me off at home after the local Porn & Chicken club night. Then I watched his reaction. James gasped, his eyes flew wide open, and he looked horrified. "That's terrible," he said. "Oh my God, I hope that girl is okay."

I got the sense that he was performing his reaction a bit. On the other hand, don't we all perform reactions a bit, when we hear about horrible events?

"So did you hear about that male dominant down south? The guy who shot his girlfriend by accident?" James asked.

Indeed, I'd heard about the incident. A young gentleman named Arthur John Sedille had allegedly been playing around with his girlfriend, and had allegedly held a loaded gun to her head as part of a sexual fantasy. He then shot her dead, and was claiming that the whole thing was a terrible accident.

Obviously, most S&Mers distanced themselves from the situation as quickly as possible. There were raging threads on various online S&M fora, arguing about how stupid and unsafe the couple had been. There were also assertions that Sedille *must* be lying due to some fact about the gun, the body, etc. Some people thought that Arthur John Sedille shot his wife in cold blood, and was trying to use our community as a cover.

James was pointing out to me, gently, that the S&M community could be judged very harshly by our worst outliers. Perhaps we might be judged as easily as the PUA community.

"I get your point," I said, and gave him a hug goodnight before exiting his car.

He leaned out the window. "Are you coming to Porn & Chicken next week?"

"Maybe," I said. "I'll call you."

I climbed my apartment stairs thinking about my own S&M fantasies. It's unlikely that I'll ever write about some of the more out-there shit I masturbate to, because it is too out-there. And since we're talking about a gun-loving PUA guru, I might as well admit that I sometimes fantasize about guns. S&M tropes and imagery are sometimes as violent as anything you can imagine. But I get angry when those images are used to judge S&M. I get angry when people call us wicked and deviant because of those images: *they are only images.*

And yes, there are plenty of assholes in the S&M community who will say horrible, misogynist things. There are predators in the S&M community who will *do* horrible, non-consensual things... the same way there are predators in the mainstream. I would be angry if someone judged all of us, based on those people.

It's different, I thought. *Gunwitch was a famous, respected guru with lots and lots of followers, and he actually showed no respect for the women he pursued. Gunwitch un-ironically referenced Ted Bundy! S&M community leaders promote gender equality and discourage abuse. They encourage everyone to see people as people.*

How much was I willing to bet on that, though? There are probably famous S&M community leaders who have done really bad things. Is any community immune from bad leaders?

I poured myself a glass of water in the kitchen and drank it slowly, thinking about James. I was rapidly concluding that the best music is not available in Chicago's mainstream club scene. I was also concluding that Porn & Chicken was kind of boring. Much as I love "Technologic," I'd rather dance to Infected Mushroom or Nine Inch Nails. I wasn't sure I needed further observation from a PUA perspective, either.

Once again, I found myself wondering what kind of agenda James had with me. I still wasn't picking up Indicators of Interest, and my own attraction to him had mostly faded. Mostly, not entirely. I reckoned it would never fade entirely. Yet, hot as he was, I couldn't feel at ease with James. I kept trying to figure out his angle.

The thought was sudden, weirdly shocking, and hilarious: *maybe he just wants to be friends.*

With another man, that would have been one of the first possibilities I considered. With James, it took me months to come up with it. I had to laugh.

I remembered the girl who once told me that James "will lie to you until he gets you into bed." I remembered James himself counseling me, "It's not *you,* it's the game." It seemed like such a distant and insincere approach. I thought about the (alleged) Gunwitch shooting. I thought about James's reaction when I told him, and my impression that he was performing.

It wasn't that I thought James was a bad person, exactly. I didn't trust him. But maybe he just wanted to be friends. I wondered what that friendship would look like.

My close friends were starting to tell me that researching PUAs was bad for me. It seemed like in every discussion about unrelated topics, I'd bring up a new PUA vocabulary word. I examined my own social anxiety, and I agreed with my friends. I felt like my bitterness about romance, dating, and men and general was reaching unmanageable levels. This was screwing me up. I wanted out.

... Or at least, I was *pretty sure* I wanted out.

When I looked at my *actual behavior,* it wasn't inevitably clear that I was acting different from how I would normally act. But remember that metaphor study? The researchers asked their subjects what factors had influenced their decisions about what actions to take, and only 3% of the subjects noted the role of the metaphors in their decision-making. If I did something different, then *would I know that I'd done something different?*

I was getting to the point where I understood PUA vocabulary. I could get most PUA jokes, and interpret subtle critiques. I definitely wasn't an expert, but I could hold up my end of a conversation with an experienced PUA. Statements that once struck me as incomprehensibly bizarre now made a certain kind of sense.

It was possible that these metaphors weren't affecting me like I thought they might be. But the PUA community *certainly* didn't make me feel *good* about myself, or about men. Reading their fora, watching them in action, and talking so much about the game was obviously fun. Sometimes. But sometimes I felt like I'd overdosed on a bewildering, nauseating drug.

I would sometimes read a single PUA blog post, and then feel sick for hours.

Plus, what was arguably worse was that *my bad reactions were fading.* I'd gotten to the point where most PUA material didn't faze me. I was building up a tolerance for this poison.

I like to travel, and sometimes I like forcing myself to acclimate to new things. I've spent some time in deep culture shock, much deeper culture shock than I experienced in the seduction community. (At least my PUA circles spoke English.) I've mentioned before that some culture shock experts list "symptoms" of culture shock, and one of those symptoms is "not feeling like yourself."

It's very clever to list "not feeling like yourself" as a "symptom" of culture shock, *as long as your goal is to assimilate into the new culture.* But if you like yourself the way you are, then "not feeling like yourself" might be the point where you question the costs of your newfound cultural understanding. It might be the point where you consider going home.

I didn't feel like myself, and I felt on a gut level that I was paying an internal cost with my PUA research. Even if I hadn't quite tallied it yet.

What was it going to take? Was I going to wait until something really terrible happened, before I pulled back? Wasn't it a strong enough omen, that a PUA guru *had just shot a woman in the goddamn face?* (Allegedly, goddamnit.)

And as for James, I just didn't trust him. Whether my reaction was based on stereotypes or rumors or something else, I knew I didn't trust him.

In the end, I didn't call James, and I didn't head out to Porn & Chicken again.

* * *

***

CHAPTER 10:
I Want To Love But It Comes Out Wrong

In which Clarisse becomes so anxious about PUAs that she mistakes a random guy at a party for an undercover PUA, has nightmares, and drunk-calls a guy she dated to accuse him of trying to use her for sex. Also, there's a total breakdown in strategic ambiguity with Adam, and the emotional escalation Field Report concludes. The chapter title is from the song "Blood and Roses," by The Smithereens.

***

After I stopped going to Porn & Chicken, I decided that it was time to start writing this thing you are reading right now. I'd been planning to work on other projects first, but I had to get this crap out of my system. Seriously. I felt like I was way *past* that maxim about hammers and nails. I was measuring the game of all the naturals I knew, and giving them tips. I kept counting the shit tests in Lady Gaga songs. ("I Like It Rough": just listen to it. You'll see.)

One night, at a party, I became intoxicated and paranoid... I'm sure you know what I mean. Thus, I became convinced that the guy hitting on me was a stealth PUA. He went by the codename Zach Lash, which is a PUA handle if ever I heard one. His opener was shooting me with a squirt gun, and things got even better from there.

"You're like a beautiful statue," I said to Mr. Lash, after we'd been flirting for about an hour. "You're a fucking work of art."

He was bemused. "What are you talking about?"

I examined him with interest. "Is this all you do with your time? Go around to parties picking up girls?"

"No," he said. "Why would I? Do you think I should?"

Zach had spent years as a sailor; he'd just returned from Antarctica; and he rode a motorcycle. With each successive characteristic, I became more sarcastic. It was too suspicious! Everything he'd done with his life was *too* calibrated for adventure. Or picking up girls.

"Okay, seriously," Zach finally said. "Could you *stop* looking at me like I'm lying *every time I say anything?*"

In retrospect, I'm amazed he put up with it. He wasn't the greasy asshole I suspected him to be, but in a way, I guess he was flattered by my allegations. We ended up getting involved, and I eventually taught some of Zach's lines to a classroom full of PUAs. (He's the source of the "Describe yourself in 5 things you've done" routine that I mentioned when I gave you my Top 3 Routines in Chapter 6.) When I mentioned this to Zach, he howled. "You can't teach *them* my game," he cried. "You're ruining my mojo. You might as well cut off my hair, Delilah!"

I later confessed that I was actually having nightmares about being hunted by disgruntled PUAs. (Nightmares... or fantasies? Hard to say.) Zach thought this was hilarious... so hilarious that he wrote the first chapter of a story called "Somebody Fuck Clara." The main character is named Clara Rose, and she makes it her business to reveal the true identities of various PUAs on her blog.

"Somebody Fuck Clara" was never completed. Alas. I hereby present the opening scene of this unfinished masterpiece:

"This bitch just needs to get laid!"

Every head in the room turned to stare at Modus, who had just leapt up, his outburst punctuated by the exclamation point of his laptop slamming shut. The anger and indignation shook his every muscle, making his signature red bunny ears twitch like frightened prey.

Softly, DigaMe spoke to the crowd as he lay a comforting hand on Modus's shoulder. "It's Clara Rose. Her post today outed Taurine."

Modus collapsed into one of the red leather, overstuffed, brass-studded armchairs that filled each nook in the Player's Club. The room murmured uneasily. Taurine was a charter member, and like a father to Modus.

"Maybe he's right...." It was Boon. He was new and still clumsy with Game, but had turned the slur of 'Noob' on its head and claimed it as his own. "Maybe that's the answer!"

The gathered members of the Player's Ball didn't get the joke, and Modus's anger seemed to be finding a focus in the bucktoothed noob who dared to break the silence.

"No, no, listen! This feminazi is singling us out, driving us into the kind of publicity where Game just doesn't count anymore! Hopper can't get anyone who's ever heard of the Internet now that he's been Posted! He's living off second-hand cougars and Luddites! That shit gets old, guys!

"We've been going at this the wrong way! We can't fucking peacock our way out of a publicity shitstorm. We haven't been able to discredit her, too much of what she says is true. She needs to get laid. We have to combat this problem the only way we know how. Somebody fuck Clara Rose!"

* * *

At some point around this time, I apparently drunk-called a guy I'd dated a couple times earlier that year. At four in the morning. To accuse him of using me for sex.

I don't quite remember this call. I mean, I sort of remember it, but I don't remember any details. I only know enough to tell you about it because I heard about it later. You see, I'd gone on a few dates with this gentleman, and then he moved to another city. So the next time he visited Chicago, he called and said that we should hang out. Once we were together in person, he asked: "Hey, do you remember that time you called me earlier this year? It was hilarious. You were drunk, and you were extremely irate with me. You claimed that I had no interest in you except to fuck you."

I don't normally get so drunk that I can't remember things in the morning. Even my dad teases me about how little I drink. When I'm drinking a lot, it's a sign that I've either just broken up with someone, or I'm in some other form of emotional turmoil. It's also unusual for me to drunk-call people at all. My college friends tease me about how I never drunk-call people. I guarantee that some PUAs are going to read this paragraph and claim that I'm trying to preserve my "nice-girl image." But what I'm actually trying to do is show you how confused I was.

I suspect that this incident took place after one of my nights out with PUAs, during which the guys would network with club promoters to get tons of free drinks. Even after I decided that I needed to detox from the seduction community, there were still one or two events that I attended. I was having trouble letting go.

To their credit, many PUAs took a brotherly, protective approach to my physical safety. They always made sure that I got home in one piece. I think that this infamous drunk call occurred one night after I made it to my apartment. I think I remember grabbing a glass of water, and sitting on the couch with my head in my hands. And then picking up my phone.

"Oh, my God," I said, months later, when this gentleman told me about the accusations I threw at him. "I'm so sorry. I can't believe I did that."

"No way, don't apologize," he said. "I've been telling people about that call for months. Bragging about it, really. It's one of my favorite anecdotes! You were kind of incoherent when you called, so I calmed you down. While I was doing that, I realized that this PUA stuff is seriously messed up. But it's fascinating! So I did my best to get you into your analytical lecturer mode. Once you clicked into analytical lecturer mode, you started reeling off a ton of interesting information. I asked you questions for like

30 minutes, until you went to bed. Then I went and looked at some online PUA fora. After I read what those guys were saying, I completely understood why you were freaking out."

"Are you sure it's okay?" I asked. "I feel bad about doing that to you. I feel like this story shows how much I needed to detox from pickup artistry."

He laughed. "It's 100% okay," he said. "Seriously. It was funny and charming and, above all, it was *interesting*. Feel free to drunk call me ranting about PUAs anytime you like."

I'm lucky he had such a sense of humor about it. I hope I didn't do that to anyone else.

* * *

In fairness, one guy who hit on me did turn out to be a PUA. Or rather, he was a former PUA. I met him in a dungeon. He was fun.

"I loved *The Game,"* he told me, "because I had such a similar experience. I mean, I never pursued seduction to the point where I was living in a Hollywood mansion with Mystery and Courtney Love. But I did get really into it, and then I got disenchanted with it, just like Neil Strauss."

"Why did you become disenchanted?" I asked.

He shrugged. "I felt bad about the way PUAs treat girls. PUAs don't respect girls' time. Besides, the game got me girls I couldn't talk to. After a while I realized I didn't actually want that girl-around-town. I wanted something different. Someone more interesting. Like you."

"Am I so interesting?" I said, in a faintly ironic tone.

"That's girl-speak for 'flatter me more,'" he mocked. "Do other men fall for that?"

This gentleman was also the source of my favorite neg, ever. I mentioned it in the first chapter, but I want to tell you the story again, because it's my *favorite*. Ready? Here's my Field Report. It was our second date. We were chatting in a cafe (yes, he bought the drinks), and we arrived at a lull in the conversation. He gazed deep into my eyes.

"Wait a minute," he said slowly. "Are your glasses held together by epoxy? It looks like you had to repair them at the corners."

"Yeah," I admitted.

He grinned. "Everything about you just *screams* 'starving artist,' doesn't it."

This totally made me laugh forever. Unfortunately, he wouldn't take me home that night. He preferred to make out with me and play S&M headgames until I was panting with desire and pawing at his chest. "I like to tease," he said cheerfully as he kissed me at my door, then walked away. "Don't write anything too mean."

"Fuck you!" I shouted after him. I was laughing. "I will *not* write about you!" Except apparently I'm writing about him now. Oh, well. I guess I was shit testing.

He told me once that I was hard to read. "Really?" I asked.

"Oh, yes," he answered. "Hasn't anyone told you that before?"

But you see through me all the time, I thought.

Still, even if he could see through me, I figured that if he thought I was hard to read, I should up my game. Later, as we stopped at the curb before crossing a street, I decided to run an experiment: I gleamed up at him.

He glanced down at me and paused, then kissed me. "Sometimes you just look like you ought to be kissed," he said. His reaction was well within the parameters I'd been aiming for. I wondered if he'd seen the calculation flash behind my eyes.

I guess that sort of feminine body language is something the Mean Girls learn in high school.

* * *

That guy made a real impression. He made such an impression that, although I was about to visit San Francisco for a sex education conference, I was thinking about him more than I thought about Adam.

Adam and I hadn't kept up contact very well, partly because I'm not instinctively good at keeping in touch long-distance, and partly because he wasn't, either. I called him once, I mailed him some books, he called me once, we emailed a few times, and that was it.

So as I prepared to head back to San Francisco, I realized that I had absolutely no idea what was going on with Adam. Part of me thought: *Maybe it would be better for me to avoid Adam, let that relationship fade, and use thoughts of this new guy to preoccupy myself.* Another part of me thought: Don't be silly. Why am I even considering that? And I couldn't pin down a reason.

Seeing a long-distance partner again, when there hasn't been much contact, is always a little awkward. Yet it only took a few minutes of making out with Adam for the same old incredible attraction to surge through me.

It took a few hours for my emotions to follow. I remember the moment quite clearly: I was resting my head on Adam's chest listening to him talk about social justice... and I felt myself slip back into intimacy with a heart-quickening pulse.

It would be so easy to let go. It would be easy to fall head-over-heels in love with him, I thought. Part of me really, really wanted to. Another part of me sighed, and told me that someday I'll have to quit acting like an adolescent.

With me feeling so confused, it's no wonder S&M got complicated again. As I've said before, I suspect that relationship ambiguity intersects very badly with S&M, because there's so much strategic ambiguity in S&M already.

We had some extremely fun sex, and then we had some complicated sex. Adam watched my responses, got uneasy. And stopped.

"Sometimes we have these moments," he said, "when we're doing S&M, where I think everything is fine. But then I look again, and I don't know where you are."

His voice had a new kind of wariness to it: an analytical coldness. The tone alone made me tense up.

"Look, I can't deal with this," he said.

I tried to control my reaction to those words, but I couldn't hide it. I think I actually gasped. "I'm sorry," Adam said immediately. "I don't mean to sound... threatening. It's just..." he trailed off and made a helpless gesture with his hands. And I felt furious at myself.

For one thing, I was angry that I didn't feel able to talk more completely about my emotions. I understood Adam's position: having an S&M partner you can't read is both scary and frustrating. I was also angry at myself for being so vulnerable. For getting myself into a game that I suddenly felt I couldn't win. I felt like I'd overplayed my hand.

And I felt like these were rookie mistakes. They were rookie mistakes for a polyamorist, and they'd be rookie mistakes for a PUA. It's been years since I had a relationship that was so important to me, where I felt so insecure and had such unspoken limits.

I believed I was wiser than this, I thought.

* * *

Adam and I smoothed things over, spent a bunch more time hanging out, went to see some friends together, and parted on good terms. On the surface things seemed okay, but I felt more anxious than ever. I resolved to spend some time thinking about what I wanted from him, to see how things developed next time I saw him, to be patient and not to worry in the meantime.

Possibly this was the wrong decision. A few days later, Adam canceled our next date at the last minute. By text message. Because he was too drunk to meet.

With most guys, this would be an instant dealbreaker.

I was chilling out in a park with The Dude when I received Adam's text message. I felt like I'd been punched in the throat.

Adam warned me not to rely on him, I thought. But I hadn't expected something like *this*.

"Um," said The Dude. He clearly was not sure what to say. "Do you think Adam is taking you for granted?"

"I don't know," I said distantly. I remembered how last time I was in town, Adam had told me I was uncancelable. I frowned over my phone.

I was not yet sure how bad I felt. I tried not to focus on the worst-case scenario, but I knew exactly what it was. The worst-case scenario was that Adam wanted nothing more to do with me, and didn't have the guts to tell me directly. *Adam wouldn't end things this way,* I thought. *Would he?*

Or maybe the worst-case scenario was that Adam had done this to keep me in line because he felt like I wasn't pliant enough. I thought of the PUA who once told me, "Canceling is incredibly powerful." I thought of Roissy's post on dread. I shook my head.

Adam can't be gaming me on purpose, I told myself. *He's a total feminist! He doesn't know a damn thing about PUAs!* But everyone has some natural game, including feminists. Adam himself might not recognize his own game.

Maybe, I thought, *he's such a genuinely kind and sensitive guy that the only way he can allow himself to be manipulative is by being confused. Everyone plays the game. It's just a question of how we think about it, and how much we play.*

The Dude watched me compose a text response, then delete it without sending. "Are you enjoying how Adam is giving you drama?" he asked, in an I'm-just-curious tone. "Girls enjoy drama, right?"

"You're joking, right?" I said in exasperation. *"No,* I'm not enjoying this. What do you think I should do about it?"

"Pretend it never happened," said The Dude. He was serious.

Oh, Dude, I thought. *You are such a dude.*

I couldn't figure out what I wanted, so I finally texted Adam a neutral response (something like, "haha, drink lots of water"). I had no idea what to do.

I found myself seeing the situation as a compliance test... if I let this pass, then Adam would have a huge amount of unspoken power in the relationship. I found myself concerned that I'd already walked into Adam's frame by texting him a neutral response... I should have either taken control of the frame and made it clear this wasn't okay, or ignored him. I found myself obsessing over tactics ranging from freeze-outs to Demonstrations of Higher Value.

My instincts struck me as viciously manipulative. Maybe my instincts had always been manipulative, and I was only now identifying my game behaviors.

No. This isn't me, I thought. *Or... if it is me, then this isn't who I want to be. I have to actually fucking talk to him. If that means lessening our strategic ambiguity, then so be it. And if that means being vulnerable, then I have to be vulnerable.*

Adam emailed me the next morning to ask how my night went. I still didn't know what to do. I took a while to get back to him, during which time I talked to a few people about the situation. I was reality-checking myself through my social networks, and preparing my emotional fallbacks in case the worst happened. It's one of the most important functions good friends can serve: keep you reasonable about your relationships. It's one of the reasons it's important to have friends who understand your values.

Codename Zach Lash said, "I mean, it's possible that Adam is as confused as you are. He might have been drinking because he felt anxious about you. Honestly? It sounds to me like you haven't been letting Adam communicate with you."

"No," I protested. "I've given him plenty of chances to communicate," but then it was hard to describe what those chances had been. So much was unspoken.

One of my lady friends said, "Give Adam a chance to apologize before you take any actions. He already knows that he fucked up."

"He might not realize it," I said doubtfully. "Sometimes men are stupid about these things."

"Is *he* stupid?" she asked. "Some men are idiots. Is Adam an idiot? As long as he's not an idiot, he knows that he fucked up. Meet him in person, and *give him a chance to apologize before you say anything."*

I probably should have called Shannon. I guess I was scared that I already knew what she'd say: *Parking brake.*

In a strangely inevitable twist, I ended up discussing the situation with my favorite PUA, the polyamorous S&Mer Brian. Brian found me at a goth club, where I was leaning on a banister and watching the dancers moodily. Before I knew it, I'd told him all about Adam.

"I'm afraid of my instincts," I confessed. "I keep wanting to do manipulative things."

Brian leaned on the banister next to me. As always, his eyeliner was perfect. "I know you hate freeze-outs," he said. "With some justification. But they aren't always a tactic. They're a way of communicating. When you do a freeze-out, it gives information about how you're feeling. I'm not saying you should ignore this guy, but maybe you *should* be cold when you see him again; you could do a mini freeze-out. That's how you feel, after all. If you don't act a little bit cold and distant, then he might not understand how upset you are."

"I don't know," I said. "Maybe I just shouldn't see him again at all."

"Maybe," said Brian. "You've been anxious about him for a while. You should trust your instincts. On the other hand, it doesn't sound like you have anything to lose by talking to him. Like your friend said, you might as well give this guy a chance to apologize in person. But you have to be willing to next him if necessary." He stared at the dancers, and his voice hardened. "You *always* have to be willing to next people," Brian said.

* * *

I met Adam at a coffeeshop. We got through ten minutes of casual conversation. I started wondering what I would do if he didn't bring it up. I *really* didn't want to fish for the topic. Then we arrived at a pause.

"So yeah, sorry about the other day," Adam said, and smiled.

Right away, I could tell that this was a pro forma apology. He was saying it to get it out of the way, as if he'd burped at a polite dinner. Adam expected me to laugh, to change the subject.

I took a sip of tea to give myself a moment to think. "What happened?" I asked. My tone was neutral; I was *sure* it was neutral. I sounded like I was chatting about the weather.

He shrugged. "Oh, you know. I was hanging out with some friends right before I was supposed to see you, and time got away from me."

I nerved myself up for A Conversation. "I was pretty upset," I said levelly, and watched his smile fade. I read concern in the way he lowered his eyes, leaned forward. *Okay,* I thought. *Maybe this has a chance.*

We talked for a long time. He said, "I'm really sorry, I should have known better," and promised it wouldn't happen again. We talked about how much we'd lost touch; he said he'd call more. He laughed when I confessed that I felt occasionally anxious about calling him. "I'm *never* going to *not want to hear from you,*" he said.

But there were a ton of red flags, too. I mean, aside from him flaking so suddenly on me in the first place. When we talked about keeping in touch, Adam's eyes slid sideways from mine. *He'll never actually call,* I knew. *He's saying this because he thinks it's what I want to hear, even if it's not true.*

No, maybe I'm wrong, I argued with myself. *He's never lied to me.*

A more obvious red flag came up when Adam referred to me as one of his "friends": "I didn't worry about canceling on you," he explained, "because I cancel on my friends all the time."

Canceling on your friends because you got unexpectedly drunk is sketchy too, I thought. *Anyway, didn't "we both know" that this isn't "friends with benefits"? You were the one who said it was "more than that," Adam. But that was a while ago... and maybe you were just saying the right words to keep me in the fuckbuddy zone.* I felt suddenly cold, and I chose my words carefully.

"Do you remember that conversation we had in Golden Gate Park?" I asked. "The one where we talked about 'friends with benefits,' and you asked me to explain 'secondary relationships'?"

"Yes..." he said, and paused. "I guess..." he said slowly, "I'm not used to having important relationships that aren't monogamous."

At the time, I took this to mean that he thought he might adjust to the idea eventually. But maybe it meant that, for Adam, a non-monogamous relationship could never be important.

In the end, Adam sighed. "Help me not hurt you," he said. There was still genuine concern in his tone, but I detected a note of impatience.

I shivered. *The fact that you just said that,* I thought, *means that it's too late.* There's a word some PUAs use, for what a woman with good game can do to a man: she can beta-ize him, so he no longer makes any rules in the relationship. I felt like a supplicant. I felt like I'd been beta-ized. I felt like I'd fucked up his emotional compliance test. I felt like I'd lost control of the frame.

Uneasy, I dropped by The Dude's apartment, where he was working from home. "How'd things go with Adam?" asked The Dude.

"Fine, I guess," I said. "I guess he said all the right things...."

"Excellent," said The Dude, and went back to his computer. A moment later, one of his lady friends called.

Excellent? Well, maybe, I thought.

I ruminated over the situation for too long when I should have been working. One word seemed to fit Adam too well: *incongruent.*

* * *

The next time I slept with Adam, I felt brutally disconnected. It was fun... sex with Adam was always, at the very least, fun. But I was distant, even though I wasn't trying to be.

When he asked me how I was feeling afterwards, I simply said: "Satisfied," and didn't let him into my head. I couldn't bring myself to sleep over. I left early, telling Adam I had work to do. (In fairness, some of my most productive writing hours are the ones between 12-4 AM. As I write this sentence, it's 2.03 AM. So at least I was congruent.)

I remember that night, and wince. I can't believe I told Adam that I was, merely, "satisfied." I wasn't trying to be cold, but I ended up doing a mini freeze-out anyway. It makes me feel guilty to think about it.

Adam and I were supposed to see each other one more time before I left San Francisco. An hour beforehand, I ran into The Dude, who remarked that I seemed agitated.

"I don't want to go see Adam," I explained. "I thought all day about canceling on him." I thought for a moment. "I'm still thinking about canceling." I thought some more. "Maybe it's not a good idea to see him when I'm feeling so conflicted. If I want things to work out, then I shouldn't talk to him when I'm in such an unstable mood."

"You don't have to go see him," said The Dude, quite reasonably.

The Dude was wearing the you're-being-crazy expression, but of course he would never tell me out loud that I was being crazy. Unless I needed to hear it. That meant I was currently a little crazy, but not too crazy. Which was okay, right? Right?

I tried to pull my thoughts together.

"That's true," I said. "I don't have to go see him. And I kinda want this to be over. But it's 6.30, and I'm meeting him at 7.30. I'm leaving town soon, so I can't easily reschedule. If I cancel now, at the last minute, and I don't reschedule... then that'll be a pretty serious 'fuck you.' If I do that, then I'm tacitly saying that I never want to see him again."

And of course, I did want to see him again.

Except maybe I didn't.

"I'm making Indian food for dinner," The Dude said, after a quiet companionable moment. "In case that helps your decision."

"No, I'm gonna go," I said, "although I might come see you in a couple hours, depending on what happens." I sighed, and rested my forehead on his shoulder. "I'm sorry I'm so neurotic. Can I have a hug?"

The Dude gave me a hug. "Wow, are you okay? I didn't realize you were so upset about this."

I shook my head. "I don't know, man. ... Can you say that you still like me and think I'm a good person?"

Sometimes, I need to hear these things.

"I still like you and think you're a good person," he said. "You'll be fine. I'll save you some Indian food."

* * *

A PUA called me on my way to meet Adam: he let me know about an upcoming Chicago PUA Summit, where PUAs from across the USA would present their wisdom and train newbies in the field. *This I gotta see,* I thought, and asked how I could get in. He said my presence might be controversial, but he'd call back later with some ideas.

This (and Rilo Kiley on my iPod) put me in a bizarrely good mood. I had to calm myself once I met Adam. He wanted A Conversation right away, so we went for a walk.

"Look," Adam said, as we made our way towards the park. "I've been thinking about what I told you the other day, about keeping in touch and all that stuff. And I feel like a jerk, because I know I'm not going to do those things."

My heart sank, even though I'd guessed this to be true. *I've tried talking to him and telling him what I need,* I told myself. *He told me what he thought I wanted to hear. Now I have to be willing to next him.*

I can't remember most of what we said. We were both less than coherent, or maybe it was just me. I will say this: Adam was trying to be as honest as possible. And if all he'd wanted from me was sex, then he easily could have gotten it. Not everything is a compliance test. Sometimes, people just let you down... or you fail to have shared expectations in place from the start.

In the final analysis, I didn't feel like Adam was gaming me, or seriously trying to dominate the frame of our relationship. I just felt like he was confused. Unfortunately, a confused person can be just as bad for you as a player. And if you're emotionally invested, you have to protect yourself just the same.

"Maybe we're just done here," I said.

"Saying we're done sounds so *final,*" said Adam. And then he said things like, "I'm just not very reliable at this point in my life."

After we'd gone back and forth for a while, I said: "Look. I almost canceled tonight. I came to see you because I feel that, in the final analysis, this is too good to give up on. Even if I'm more into you than you're into me, I think you do care about me, and I think I can handle the difference in our feelings. So... do you want to stick with this? Or are you here because you wanted to end this in person rather than by email?"

Well... I tried to say something like that. My actual words were more forceful, frustrated and poorly organized. I don't recall them clearly. My emotions were taut as a wire.

I remember exactly how Adam answered, though: "Maybe I'm somewhere in between," he said.

In between? What the hell was "in between" breaking up and not breaking up? I felt like I was seeking Adam's enthusiastic consent for a relationship, and he was giving me Last Minute Resistance. Or shit testing me. If women have Anti-Slut Defense, maybe men have Anti-Relationship Defense. *Maybe Adam wants me to game him more,* I thought, *otherwise he'll feel like he's giving it up too easy.*

Except my position in the game was much weaker now: I'd lost all plausible deniability. Strategic ambiguity would be a lot harder, from now on.

Men don't fucking know what they want, I thought. *The first rule of men is, never listen to what they say.* I felt abruptly tired and cynical.

Adam officially ended it a few minutes later. "I know this is going to sound corny," he said, "but I hope we can still be friends. I know everyone says that, but I mean it."

I tried to resist the rush of anger. *He's saying this because he likes me as a person,* I told myself. *Not because he wants to hang out as "friends" and then seduce me into the fuckbuddy zone.*

"That's sweet," I said coldly.

Adam looked at me sidelong. "I try," he said gently.

* * *

Some PUAs claim that women aren't attracted to men who are really into them. Some PUAs will read this story and claim that I would never have been attracted to Adam if he didn't make me so uncertain. In the depths of my PUA obsession, I wondered if that was true.

But I knew how I felt about Adam from the first date, and I started suspecting that I should cut things off after the second date. I've had incredible first dates with guys before, where they were super into me immediately afterwards, and we had super intense mutual relationships as a result. I remember one date, for example, where the guy called me every day for a week after, and I didn't feel the slightest amount of uncertainty about whether he liked me... *and* I remained excited about him!

A delicious dose of strategic ambiguity can come from doing novel things together. It can come from compartmentalizing extremely intense ambiguities like S&M. It can come from adversarial flirtation that stops when the situation gets serious. It doesn't have to come from uncertainty about the relationship itself.

Indeed, I've had several long-lasting relationships with men who, as Roissy puts it, unwisely "showered" me "with love."

So girls can definitely be attracted to men who are totally into them. So there. *So there,* PUAs.

I suspect there will also be people who read this and claim it shows that polyamory (or S&M) is a bad idea. It's like clockwork: anytime someone tells a story about a confusing polyamorous situation, someone will pop up who claims that it proves polyamory "can't" work. Actually, though, this just shows that polyamory is complicated. It shows that secondary relationships require more careful choice and ongoing maintenance than I thought they required. *It does not show anything else.*

Long-distance relationships make a useful counterpoint here. Most people wouldn't read this tale and immediately think that it "demonstrates" that long-distance relationships can't work. That's because people aren't looking for excuses to discredit the idea of long-distance relationships the way people want excuses to attack polyamory. And really, all this shows is that long-distance relationships are complicated, too. It shows that long-distance relationships require more careful choice and ongoing maintenance than I thought they required. *It does not show anything else.*

Later, while finishing this book, I told the Adam story to the PUA coach Mark Manson. Mark said, "For what it's worth, I think your final reactions demonstrated strong healthy boundaries. Someone flaking on you is one thing. Someone flaking on you when you're trying to sustain some sort of long-distance relationship-type-thing is a big thing. And someone flaking on you because they're drunk in the middle of the afternoon is a huge red flag."

After reflecting for a moment, Mark added: "I think you got paranoid about thinking Adam was doing it intentionally, or to manipulate you. But after diving so deep into the PUA stuff, it's understandable that you worried about that. It's kind of like how guys in PUA start perceiving everything women do as shit tests, when really many women... hell, many people... are just disorganized or confused or inconsiderate. They don't mean to yank on your feelings, it just kind of happens because they're not making conscious decisions."

* * *

When I got back to Chicago, I visited Shannon for dinner again. She has a great bond with her husband. I felt mildly envious as I watched them together, but mostly it was beautiful to see.

PUAs rarely talk about how *choosing to commit* affects things, but in long-term relationships, that choice is key. A person who specifically decides to seek a committed relationship is a million times more likely to find one — whether that relationship is monogamous, polyamorous, married, unmarried, whatever. Movies and novels and hormones all team up to promote a myth of "The One": a soulmate, an ideal match. A person who will barrel you over, whether or not you're open to it.

But in reality, if you find a good match, then if you consciously commit to that person, your emotions will often follow your lead.

And if you wait for someone to strike you like a perfect brilliant lightning bolt, you might wait a long time. Or forever.

Shannon has obviously prioritized commitment. We talked about it as I did some post-breakup processing. "I've been rather cagey with the guys I meet," I said, "and I've been letting relationships develop in a fairly random way. But I should probably go in with more intentions."

"Maybe," she shrugged. "You know that I was nervous about committing to my husband. Eventually I figured that if I just bit the bullet and did it, I'd know soon enough if that was the correct choice. I didn't instantly know that he was the Right One, but I figured that he was pretty damn close... so if I chose to commit to him, he would probably become the Right One."

Later that evening, they went to bed and I sat in their living room with my laptop. I meant to get a few quick tasks out of the way before heading home, but I tend to get wrapped up in my work. I was still in her living room when Shannon returned an hour later, and sat next to me on the couch.

There was trouble with her husband, a certain ongoing problem. Shannon curled up under a blanket and we talked about it. She felt exhausted, she felt at her wits' end. She was ridiculously busy, she had a million things to do the next day, she couldn't afford to be awake, and now she was up late dealing with this....

"I'm so tired," she said. "I'm so tired." I took her hand, and put my head on her shoulder.

This is the scary part of commitment: being responsible for someone else. Dealing with someone else's inconvenient issues. Becoming unable to get going, when the going gets tough.

One side of the commitment divide is the super-religious idea of sleeping with only one person — marrying that person forever. That side claims that any sexual thoughts about others are a sin. But the other side is, "You always have to be willing to next people." And neither of these sides are fully human.

"You always have to be willing to next people" implies that you can always find a "better option." It implies that we should be able to make a list of a dozen fine-tuned characteristics, and choose from people who meet them. It also implies that there is no inherent benefit to commitment.

But human beings aren't factory-made. We can't be constructed to specified parameters. And sometimes commitment is what a relationship needs in order to flourish.

On the other hand, while I was writing this thing you are reading, I dated a guy who was so taken with me that he talked about marriage within the first couple weeks. "I've *never* felt like this," he told me. "I've never met someone I actually thought I could *marry.*" I felt a bit skittish that he seemed to be so all-in, so fast, but I was pretty into him, too. I thought seriously about whether he was marriage material, though it took me a while to admit it.

And then he broke up with me and said, "Sometimes I think men just aren't capable of the kind of commitment women are."

So. Should I be committing more quickly? More easily? Should I seek men who say that they want more commitment?

Well... maybe.

* * *

It was almost a year before I saw Adam again. We didn't talk at all for months, because I wanted time to get over things. Then we corresponded, occasionally, for more months. And then. He came to see me in Chicago.

"I used to think polyamorous relationships require less commitment than monogamous ones," he said to me. "But I think that in many ways, they require more."

I'll leave discussions of Anti-Relationship Defense, Last Minute Resistance, and freeze-outs to the peanut gallery.

If one of us is trying to win the game, then I'm not sure who's winning. I don't think either of us is trying to defeat the other, though. It's mutual, not adversarial. We've talked over the lessons learned. We'll see if we can figure out something that works for both of us, this time....

Anyway, this may be a story for the future.

* * *

* * *

CHAPTER 11:
The End Is The Beginning Is The End

In which Clarisse is unexpectedly designated a "coach" by some PUA organizers. She gives a talk and offers "coaching services" at a PUA Dating Skills Convention in Chicago, and reports every detail from the depths of the rabbit hole. The chapter title is after a song with the same name, by the Smashing Pumpkins; Clarisse prefers the Stuck In The Middle With Fluke Vox Mix.

* * *

Some Chicago guys were organizing a national Pickup Artist Summit, also labeled a Dating Skills Convention. The ticket price was steep for a starving artist, however. "I don't think I can afford that," I told Jonnie Walker. (He's my archetypal Type 4: Leader PUA, the one who told me that he wants to "make men better men through pickup.")

Part of me was relieved. *Maybe I'm finally climbing out of this rabbit hole,* I thought.

Then Jonnie called back several days before the convention. "We can get you in free as a speaker," he said. "Which is great! I've been telling the guys we should have you speak for ages. But you have to talk to Nathan. You haven't met him. He's in from New York, and he's the organizer."

Nathan's game was intensely adversarial, and it started before I even met him. He emailed me saying that we should get together for lunch that same day. I had a full schedule, but the summit was only two days away, so I agreed. Nathan was staying way across town from me. He texted a suggestion that we meet in his neighborhood.

"Let's meet in the Loop," I replied. "It's halfway between us." He didn't answer for a while, so to make things easy, I texted him a restaurant address and suggested that we meet there in 90 minutes.

"No," he texted back immediately. He suggested a different neighborhood that was still quite a hike for me.

I tried calling, and he ignored the call. "We're pretty far away from each other. Maybe we should talk on the phone instead of having lunch," I texted. Nathan didn't answer at all... even though he'd just texted me a minute before.

It was basically lunchtime. I started feeling irritated.

After Nathan ignored me for over ten minutes, I thought, *Fuck this. If this guy respected my time, he would have agreed to meet me halfway already, or he would at least answer my scheduling texts when I send them. I know he has his phone and he's getting my messages, because he responded to the first ones. So he's freezing me out, as if I were the one shit testing him. He's trying to intimidate me into going along with his meet-me-in-my-own-neighborhood compliance test.*

I was literally opening my planner, arranging my day sans Nathan, when he called. *Wow,* I thought, staring at my planner. *Is that luck, or excellent calibration? Or am I just completely paranoid?*

I answered, and we arranged lunch in the Loop.

* * *

Nathan had a shaved head and a sharklike grin. We chatted amiably about everything from upbringing to careers. "I used to work in politics," he said, "but I never cared much. I started out working for the Democrats, because that was the local political machine, but eventually I got big enough that Republicans would hire me too. I got to the point where I'd be on one line advising a pro-choice campaign, and then I'd switch phone lines to a pro-life campaign." He laughed. "I'm a whore."

My sex worker friends have more integrity, I didn't say. I saved my energy for when Nathan got down to business: he asked me detailed questions about both feminism and pickup artistry. I critiqued various PUA concepts, but I did it very gently. I offered various thoughts on masculinity and men's social roles.

When the bill came, Nathan turned to the waitress and gestured to me. "This girl's a feminist," he told her. "She'll be paying the whole bill."

I laughed, and smothered my annoyance. *I pegged this guy right,* I thought. *I wasn't being paranoid at all.* "Nice try," I said aloud. We split it, of course.

On our way out of the building, Nathan nodded at the door. "I know you're such a feminist," he said, "you'd love to open the door for me."

Honestly, I thought. *Is he going to test me all weekend?* I smiled tightly. Who knew... maybe he was testing to make sure I could handle the other guys at the summit.

"I thought you'd be a lot more radical," Nathan said when we finally made it out to the sidewalk. He shook my hand. "I must admit, I judged you too quickly for being a feminist. You've got a lot of good stuff to say.

Send me some ideas for your talk, and I'll put you in the schedule."

Nathan called the next evening to ask what I'd be selling at the summit. "I'm not selling anything," I said.

"You should be," he said. "I've been talking to the guys about this, and we've all noticed that there are no other female coaches in Chicago. There's a real gap there."

I'm a coach now? I thought. I leaned against a handy wall and closed my eyes, trying to think.

I can't do this regularly, I told myself. *It would destroy me.* On the other hand, starving artists don't make a lot of money, whereas successful PUA coaches make bank. I felt like I was pondering a deal with the devil.

"I don't think I've got the skills for this," I said honestly.

"Just by being a woman, you're already more calibrated than most men," said Nathan. "You should go for it."

* * *

I emailed my favorite PUA, the goth-feminist-S&M switch Brian, for advice. I added, "The dude in charge has been making me jump through hoops nonstop and really pissing me off (especially with douchy jokes about feminism)... so I'm still not 100% sure I'll do it."

Brian wrote back, "Too bad the organizer is miscalibrated. It seems that he is both interested and uncomfortable with feminism, and the combination of those things manifested as a shit test. I hope he doesn't turn you off from it. While his behavior is off-putting, I think it would be a shame if the lair missed out on your presentation because of it."

Brian's email made me laugh. He knew exactly how to influence me with a combination of flattery and PUA analysis. And it worked!

* * *

I dressed carefully for the first day of the PUA summit. I had to look attractive, but I wanted the guys to respect me, too. It was a fine line. I came up with a sexy-but-professional outfit that included both long sleeves and knee-high black boots.

Coaches in attendance included Jonnie Walker, James Amoureux, and some guys I didn't know. Most came in from out of town. Owen Cook, a.k.a. Tyler Durden from *The Game,* was slated to speak on the last day of the convention. He was the biggest name by far, but he only dropped by long enough to talk. I later mentioned this to Mark Manson, who is less famous, but still successful. Mark laughed. "I used to speak at these things all the time, but now I turn down 90% of them," he said. "The few occasions I do them these days, I usually make a point to show up an hour before I speak and then bolt about an hour afterward."

When I got to the convention center, James was already there. I went and sat next to him immediately. He was the perfect person to give me social proof among the assembled men. I felt like I'd walked into a lion's den, but I calmed myself by discussing sociology with James. (We tried to convince another coach to read Erving Goffman's classic *Stigma*, or possibly *The Presentation Of Self In Everyday Life*. We did not succeed.)

Lots of the guys explicitly refused to identify as PUAs, even some of the coaches. Overall, the emphasis was on natural game. One or two coaches tried to run routines on me, which was hilarious, but routines seem to be going out of fashion. This may be because the PUA community is becoming more and more mainstream... which means a lower percentage of incoming guys are social phobics. Or it may be because the community is finding better treatments for social phobia.

The group at this particular convention seemed pretty good, ethically, although I still had to bite my tongue and pick my battles a lot. Alpha/beta theory was at a relatively low ebb, thank God.

Most of the guys in attendance fit into my classic Type 2: Freaks and Geeks category, although there were strands of my other five types as well. You know how in my Grand Typology of PUAs, I designated Type 5 as the Sharks? If I could put a picture of Nathan the organizer next to Type 5, I totally would.

The convention went from a Friday evening through Sunday night, and each coach gave a talk of about 45 minutes (except Tyler Durden, who got several hours). Every night included expeditions to local nightclubs. I'll summarize what some of the coaches said:

#1: One coach talked about how you must express your emotions to be effective. "I went for a long time where girls would be uncomfortable because they said I wasn't emotionally available," he explained. "It took me a while to understand what they meant. Emotionally available just means you're conveying how you feel. Girls don't trust you if you don't emote."

Amen, I thought. *Nor should we.*

That coach didn't describe any specific emotional IOIs, though. I reckon that could be because he hadn't thought about "emotional IOIs" the way I think of them, but it also could be because his goal was to encourage guys to express their genuine emotions. Maybe he didn't want to provide scripts for fakery.

#2: Another coach discussed the social aspects of the community: how it was all about developing close relationships with his male buddies, and he'd become best friends with some of his wingmen. He also encouraged attendees to make friends with naturals, and learn game that way. "It's hard because it feels like you're making friends with the jocks who used to beat you up," he said, "but you gotta be humble. You gotta know that you can learn from everyone."

That guy confessed to weird feelings, as he realized that he is now like a lot of men he once resented. "We have become those douchebags we used to talk about," he said.

#3: His business partner talked mostly about logistics, like for example ensuring that the date always ends at a venue for sex. The coach noted that he had one excellent date he'd used 30 times. It started with sending the target a text saying, "Do you like chocolate, sushi and adventure?" After she inevitably said yes, he'd take her to a sushi place. Then they'd head to a place that served s'mores: he used the messy food as an excuse to get the first kiss done. And finally, home, where he had a trampoline in the backyard.

"I tell her that I don't know what the deal with this place is," he explained. "I say I know for sure that it has a trampoline, but I think it might be abandoned, and we have to be quiet. After we jump on the trampoline, we sneak into the house. Then she notices that I know where everything is, that the cats recognize me, and so on. Eventually she figures out that it's actually my place." By then, apparently, it was easy to hook up with her.

My favorite part of the chocolate/sushi/adventure date was that the coach once used it on 4 roommates. "The first roommate loved it," he said. "The second roommate realized I was taking her on the exact same date the first roommate experienced. She got mad. The third roommate hadn't heard the story from the first two roommates, so she was surprised later. And the fourth roommate went because she heard so much about it from the other three."

#4: Nathan's talk was all about self-improvement. He started by saying, "I'm going to use the dehumanizing 10-point scale, and I'm going to use it to talk about us. Most gurus won't tell you this, but the truth is that if you *really* want to start scoring HB10s, the easiest way is to *be* a 10." He went on to encourage guys to get their shit together, dress well, exercise, follow their passions, have good careers, etc. It surprised me... and made me like him more.

#5: When James Amoureux talked, he focused on S&M, and especially sexual communication. He emphasized safewords. He even used the words "enthusiastic consent," which made me smile, although I'm positive that I was the only other person in the room who knew he was referencing feminist theory.

Unfortunately, James also talked about dominance being a male trait and submission being a female trait. I sighed internally and raised my hand, because I couldn't let that one pass.

"Hey James," I said when he called on me. "What about male submissives?"

"Oh yeah," he said, and didn't hesitate. "If you're a guy and submission is your thing, then that's cool too. Men should feel free to own their desires."

"Hey James," I said. "What's a switch?"

"You," he said, and pointed a finger at me. Then he laughed and defined it: a person who can switch back and forth between dominant or submissive roles. We didn't have time to talk more about those ideas. Still, if I accomplished nothing else at that convention, at least I reduced the gender policing.

#6: My own talk was initially scheduled for Sunday morning, but Nathan came and sat next to me much earlier. "Can you talk in ten minutes?" he asked.

"What?" I said. "No! I haven't prepared it yet!"

"You'll be fine," Nathan said soothingly. "I'm sending you up in ten minutes."

So my talk was less organized than I wanted it to be. It also wasn't very aggressive; I didn't have time to calibrate my words precisely, so I decided to risk being too nice rather than too snide. I did my best to question concepts like "shit test" and to push back against aggressive Last Minute Resistance techniques. I encouraged the guys to build their social calibration with all kinds of random interactions, rather than focusing entirely on bedding women.

But I made it clear that I had no problem with random consensual sex. I also tried to frame everything in terms of effectiveness rather than morality: for example, "Aggressive LMR techniques appear really needy, which turns girls off," rather than "Aggressive LMR techniques might pressure a girl into doing something she hates."

A few audience members seemed restless, but a lot paid attention. One attendee sent me an email later thanking me for my talk. He wrote:

I really enjoyed your lecture, which I saw as a sort-of reality check on PUA philosophy. I was really getting turned off from reading the "tips" online, which are all about creating these routines that will get a hottie from Point A (stuck-up bitch) to Point B (the asshole's bed). It's a world where using Neuro-Linguistic Programming to get a girl all hot and bothered without her knowing it is considered a legitimate way to relate to another human being. Not my thing.

I can't be sure whether that guy was the exception or the rule, though.

When I was done, the guys applauded, just as they had for the other speakers. Nathan came forward with his sharklike grin. "What I like about Clarisse," he said, "is that she gets it."

* * *

The first sojourn to the local clubs involved all the coaches lining up at the front of the room, and each taking on three or four clients. The idea was that we'd all go off to the clubs, and each coach would offer an hour or two of advice to these clients for free, by way of advertisement. I was unprepared for this, so I tried to stay in back when Nathan lined up all the coaches... but he shark-grinned and gestured me up front. "Come on, Clarisse," he said. "You're helping us out tonight."

Nathan advertised me to the group as a kind of double agent: "she's got a woman's perspective." I felt unsure that I could relate to the perspective of the women these guys were aiming for, but I held my peace. I ended up with several very different clients: a beautiful Spanish dance instructor, a tall scrawny guy, and a hipstery skatery dude.

The nightclubs were just as I expected: an ocean of women with yards of straightened hair and pounds of lip gloss. The hipstery skatery dude definitely wanted more guidance than I was able to give. When I told him he should just go try talking to people, and added that I didn't have a strong preference about what he said, he became exasperated. "You're the fucking *coach,"* he said.

How the hell did I end up here? I wondered.

The tall scrawny guy had no interest in the club population at all. "I came to this convention because it seemed intriguing in an anthropological way," he said. "Honestly, I don't want to practice openers on these girls. I'd like to hear more about your writing."

The Spaniard was somewhere in between. He gave me impromptu dance lessons to Lady Gaga songs, and asked a lot of questions about my life. However, his major interest was still the targets around the club. He struck me as handsome and charming enough already; I mostly provided logistical help, like by distracting interfering friends.

Jonnie Walker had sent his clients off into the crowd, and was leaning up against a pillar. After an hour or so, I went and asked him for advice. "I wasn't ready for this, dude!"

"I thought you might not be," Jonnie said cheerfully. "But you dove in anyway, and you're doing fine. I knew we could rely on you to do what it took. You're a ballsy girl. I like that about you. Also," he gave me the once-over, "nice outfit. You dressed to look good, but also so we'd take you seriously." He nodded to me with professional courtesy. "Perfectly calibrated."

Another coach negged me a few minutes later. I flipped him off. "Don't beg," he said, and I had to laugh. "I'm stealing that one," I said.

Nathan had actually put a wire on one of his clients, and was listening to the guy's conversations at a distance. That may have been when I nicknamed him Mr. Shady. I am pleased to report that the other coaches and clients thought this nickname was perfect... although we also agreed that Nathan grows on you.

Indeed, one coach had been calling Nathan shady for years. The next day, Nathan passed us in the hallway while we were discussing how shady he was. Nathan flipped us both off, and kept walking.

"Don't beg," I called after him.

He cracked up. "Get over yourself," he called back.

* * *

After Friday, we weren't assigned to clients, but some of us went out anyway. I kept drinking enough to maximize drink deals, and we all kept club-hopping. Saturday night was patchy like a badly-edited montage.

At one point I got totally separated from the guys, and ended up in a clump of other women. I felt an irrational panic at this, like the ladies would detect the double agent in their midst and tear me to pieces. Luckily, none of them seemed to think anything was amiss. One told me they'd all evaded the cover charge to get into the club. "I love being a girl," she said, and winked. I nodded as if I felt like we had lots in common, and made my escape.

I should have asked *how* she evaded the cover, because I actually have no idea. Me, I got in free because one of the guys knew a promoter.

As I walked away from the ladies, a guy came up thisclose and murmured in my ear, "You look so *innocent.*" I glanced at him. He wasn't with our group. I resisted the urge to tell him to work on his opener.

I finally found one coach charming three girls in a corner. He grabbed my arm. "This is my best friend," he announced, and proceeded to perform ridiculous poses with me. I laughed on cue, then distracted one of the girls while the coach tried to get his target's number.

"Look at these cell phone pictures I took of your bestie," she said.

"Ooh, you should keep that one," I said excitedly as we scrolled through them. "He's a great guy," I added in a confiding tone, then thought,

I should probably feel worse about this than I do.

I ended up making out with a different coach, in a rather desultory way. "You're unique," he told me. *I'm bored,* I thought, and couldn't even bring myself to feel guilty.

Some time later, I ran into Nathan. "Where have you been all night, Mr. Shady?" I asked.

He shark-grinned. "Why must you call me that?"

"I've been discussing you with the guys," I said. "We might also start calling you Magneto. From the X-Men."

"I don't get it," Nathan said. He was still grinning.

"Yes you do," I said.

Nathan took my hand and pulled me towards him, then did a single ballroom-dance twirl. We call this the PUA twirl. "I think I've got a read on you, sugar," he said.

"Go for it."

"You have white-collar professional parents. You grew up in an affluent area. You're fascinated by subcultures... all subcultures." He did another PUA twirl and paused, as if he were about to pull a trump card. "This is your way of rebelling," he said.

I gotta admit, it's a thought I've had before. How does a feminist S&M sex educator take a walk on the wild side? When you look at it that way, my PUA obsession seems inevitable.

"You know," Nathan said thoughtfully, "in the past two weeks I've had two women tell me I'm either a nice guy pretending to be an asshole, or an asshole pretending to be a nice guy. What do you think?"

"I don't get the nice guy vibe from you at all," I told him, with perfect sincerity.

He laughed. I wondered if he thought I was shit testing.

Later still, Nathan and I stood chatting with two other PUA coaches on a streetcorner. A single streetlamp warmed us. One of the guys was telling us about a girl he really liked. He was truly, madly, deeply about her. He was using words like "love."

After a while, the lovesick gentleman departed. Nathan and the other coach set to gossiping. "I don't get it," said the other coach. "There must be something he's insecure or confused about."

"Well, the way he's behaving is incongruent," said Nathan. "He keeps saying he wants to travel and pick up girls all the time, but he thinks he's in love with this girl? Incongruent."

"Seriously," said the other coach. "I don't get it. I've seen him pull much hotter girls."

"She must have incredible game," said Nathan.

I couldn't contain myself. "Maybe he meshes with this girl on a personality level," I protested... then added slowly, "but I guess personality is part of game." I felt a sudden, strange moment of dizziness. *Like Alice falling down the rabbit hole,* I thought.

"Yes. Personality is game," Nathan said. He said it gently and patiently, as if speaking to a protegee.

The other coach wouldn't look at me. Maybe he was disgusted. "What the fuck is a personality?" he asked, but it didn't sound like a question.

* * *

I liked a lot of the guys I met. At the same time, throughout the convention, little moments made me want to cry.

Obviously, there were stories and jokes about women, especially fat women, old women, etc. Nathan mentioned offhandedly that, "I often think that every ten years, I should get another 20-year-old. Then, when she's 30, I'll ditch her and get another 20-year-old."

During one question-and-answer session, I told the assembled clients one story I've already told you, about how I tried to ask a boy out in my teens when I was a skinny nerd girl with weird pets. I explained that the boy answered my impassioned inquiry by informing me that I could shove one of the pets up my ass. I told this story because I was trying to reassure the guys. I was trying to show that everyone experiences horrible moments of rejection.

Later, a nerdy-looking client came up to me and explained that the story "just goes to show that women love assholes." I gritted my teeth. *Who the fuck does he think I asked out?* I thought. *Some "alpha" jock?*

"Actually," I said coolly, "the boy who rejected me was a huge nerd who loved the natural sciences." This was, in fact, true.

The look on the client's face was priceless. He'd definitely figured that I was cruelly rejected by his high-school enemies, rather than a "nice guy" like him.

During another question-and-answer session, a client addressed a classic question to all the assembled coaches. "Should we lie to women?" he asked.

I'm afraid I lost my temper while responding to that one. My answer was not coherent. I should have treated the question like the shit test it was.

Jonnie Walker answered, "Don't lie. If you lie to women, you're not much of a man."

James Amoureux answered, "I don't lie. Lying makes me feel like I'm not being myself."

Nathan answered, "Tell the truth." Then, of course, he shark-grinned. "But you don't always have to tell the *whole* truth."

The coach who once claimed I was his "best friend" was not present.

* * *

Tyler Durden was slated to speak on the final day. I took care of some errands in the morning, and then sat around at home. I felt exhausted. I got a glass of water and drank it, staring out the window.

I don't want to miss Tyler Durden in person, I tried to convince myself. *He's the villain of* The Game! *This should be fascinating.*

I drank another glass of water. I checked my email and wrote quick responses to unimportant messages.

I was late.

I changed into my favorite tank top. It's based on a design by the feminist artist Jenny Holzer. It's shaped like a wifebeater, and it says "Abuse Of Power Comes As No Surprise." I wondered if any PUAs would get it.

I checked my email again.

I played a few songs from Dougie MacLean's "The Search." I wondered whether I should be listening to "Point Of No Return" from *Phantom of the Opera,* instead.

I was really late. I realized that I'd missed Jonnie Walker's talk. A couple guys texted to ask if I was coming.

I thought about how I'd gone along with the coach's "this is my best friend" game. I thought about making out with the other coach, and feeling nothing. I thought about Nathan saying, "Personality is game," and the other guy asking, "What the fuck is a personality?"

At times, this stuff was entertaining and fun. I *loved* the game, and I wanted to be good at it. I wanted to master the art of strategic ambiguity... and to leave everyone in the world uncertain and fascinated. I wanted the power to spar verbally with jaded PUAs. I wanted to be able to assess a social situation with Terminator vision.

And I wanted to avenge myself on all the guys who ever rejected me. I wanted to avenge ten thousand years of oppression on behalf of womankind. Naturally, I also wanted to feel superior to girls who are far more beautiful than me.

I felt incredibly depressed.

Tyler Durden's talk was halfway over. *If Tyler Durden comes through town and I don't see him, I'm gonna be so disappointed in myself,* I thought. That's how I finally got out the door.

* * *

When I walked into the convention room, Tyler Durden — real name Owen Cook — stopped mid-sentence. I was, of course, the only woman in the room. "I hope you're not easily offended," he said to me wryly.

This infamous man was slim, mercurial and orange-haired. Apparently, when he began his PUA career, he was quite plump. He told the audience that he once took it as a point of pride that he could pick up women while fat... and then he encouraged the audience to lose weight. Owen's devilish, laughing eyes blinked through expressions at the speed of light. His charisma occupied the whole room.

Within ten minutes, Owen was talking about how guys should "never let a girlfriend wear makeup," because if she wears makeup, you won't be able to tell from her complexion whether she's eating and exercising right. Then he stopped short. "Wow, I sound really sexist right now," he said, "I'm saying you should control your girlfriend's makeup and lifestyle...."

To reassure him, I laughed very obviously. Owen didn't worry about sounding sexist again, at least not out loud. It wasn't long before he noted that "girls will cook and clean for you if they like you enough." Then he theorized that men who do chores around the house *cause women to be feminists.* "No wonder some women are crazy feminazis," he exclaimed. "It's because their husband's a little bitch!"

Remember, folks, feminism only happens because men are too beta. It has nothing to do with human rights or anything silly like that. I wonder how this squares with the theory that all women want is control.

The bulk of Owen's talk, however, was about congruence. He observed that you can get away with saying nearly anything, as long as you've got real confidence and it matches your mood. Apparently, he has picked up girls while saying things like: "If she's old enough to bleed, then she's old enough to breed."

Owen Cook's company, Real Social Dynamics, initially took a lot of cues from routine-based game and the Mystery Method. In fact, he lived with Mystery and Neil Strauss while they developed Mystery's business. *The Game* claims that Tyler Durden eventually started manipulating his clients by making the clients feel like they'd gotten more from his workshops than they actually had. It also claims that he callously manipulated other PUAs. For example, he pulled a long freeze-out on Neil Strauss. Other versions of this story float around the seduction community, and some make Neil into the villain rather than Owen.

Personally, I have no idea what's true, but I attest that Tyler Durden in person seems incredibly authentic and entertaining, despite the fact that he's something of a high-strung asshole. I liked Neil Strauss better, and I'd be more likely to trust Neil. On the other hand, I wonder what Owen would be like if I sat down with him personally, the way I did with Neil.

The session closed out with some exercises to practice natural game. For instance, Owen put us all in groups of four, and told us to take turns making up sentences based on a word that the previous guy used. So if the guy before me said, "I like electronic music because it makes me feel excited," then I could make up a sentence using "electronic" or "music" or "excited" or whatever. I've heard that this exercise has been popular in the community lately, and was originally inspired by improv theatre.

These, folks... *these* are the evil secrets of the PUA subculture.

The coach I'd made out with the previous night really wanted A Conversation. Through a combination of guile and willpower, I avoided this. He left town, then texted me several times in the next month. You might think he genuinely liked me, but I tell myself that he was just trying to keep me in his stable, like the cynical PUA he is. Right?

Well, wrong. I know. I'm sorry.

The anthropological tall scrawny client complimented my "Abuse Of Power Comes As No Surprise" tank top. No one else got it.

* * *

A big group went out for dinner that night. Nathan convinced me to come by promising to pay for my dinner. I couldn't afford it otherwise. After we got the bill, Nathan paid for the total but said, "You get the tip, sugar." Then he walked away.

Jonnie Walker was sitting next to me. He gave Nathan's back an annoyed look. "I gotcha," he told me. We'd been talking about relationships all evening. Jonnie was still involved with the lovely blonde woman, the one I once assisted him in jealousifying. By now, I felt like Jonnie and I were actual friends.

"Thanks," I said. I was surprised and touched by Jonnie's gesture. It takes a brave man to volunteer to pay a woman's dinner tip in front of PUAs.

"Jeez," one of the clients said. He was sitting on my other side. "I don't get the impression that Nathan values your opinion, Clarisse."

I shrugged. "He's just shit testing," I said.

* * *

After the summit was done, I could barely think or work for several days. It felt like an extended hangover. I tried to remind myself that I am a worthwhile human being and not a piece of meat. I tried to recall the PUAs who obviously like women as people... but I kept thinking of statements like "every ten years I'll trade my 30-year-old for a new 20-year-old." Or better yet, "What the fuck is a personality?"

I'm never attending one of those things again, I thought.

The coach Mark Manson emailed to ask how it went, and I gave him a capsule version. He wrote back, "The conferences are horribly toxic. It's like they somehow manage to combine all of the worst elements of the PUA (fanboyism, hero worship, screwed up teachings, a bunch of dudes coming together to brag about lays) and then celebrate it. I made the mistake years ago of planning to hang around the full 3-4 days at one of those things. It depressed me to the point that I almost gave up and got a day job. And what a disaster that would have been, hah!"

I called Brian for post-convention processing, which required approximately 90 minutes of rambling. "Are you going to keep giving PUA talks?" he asked.

"I don't know," I said.

On the day before he left Chicago, Nathan convinced me to meet him in his neighborhood. "I know a bartender up here," he texted. "She'll give you free drinks." We ended up sitting down for an all-you-can-eat taco deal, too.

"I love these all-you-can-eat deals," Nathan said. "I try and make 'em regret it, by eating as much as I possibly can." I glanced at him sidelong, and he shark-grinned. "I *am* shady, aren't I," he acknowledged.

We competed in taco-eating. I made it to 15 before calling it quits. Nathan ate one more serving, bringing him to 18. "I just wanted to beat you," he said cheerfully.

I picked up some new industry gossip, which is always fun. Then we moved on to PUA community critiques. I mentioned that I kept trying to dissociate from the PUA community, and failing. "Yeah, I know what you mean," Nathan said.

"Really?" I said. "But you're so into it."

"Sure, but I'd have to be an idiot not to see its flaws. Like calling women 'targets.' That's awful. On the other hand, I've been hanging out with a lot of naturals lately, and naturals are much worse than PUAs."

"What do you mean?"

"Naturals *lie,*" Nathan said. "And they lie about *big things.* Naturals lie about what kind of job they have, or what kind of car they have, in order to get laid. PUAs never lie about that stuff." He shook his head. "They're a bad influence on me," he said.

I've met plenty of honorable naturals, I thought. *This probably says a lot about the naturals you hang out with.*

After that, we talked about definitions of the community. "There are naturals who never read any pickup advice at all," I said, "but there are also guys who only need a little bit of a boost... who only read a little bit. I'm never sure what the boundaries of the seduction community are. When does a guy start counting as a community member? Is it when he reads his first forum? Goes to his first meetup?"

"I'd say that it's when he spends his first dollar," said Nathan.

The conversation meandered into coaching advice. "I've been meaning to talk to you about something," Nathan said. "When women get into this stuff, it fucks them up, but it fucks them up differently from guys. Female pickup coaches have a hard time relating to men. Eventually, they get to a point where every time they connect with a man, they can't even see the connection. All they can see is game. So they start measuring men on a really shallow level. They start dating men for nothing but looks, or money."

"I'll keep it in mind," I said, and I have. I still think of it occasionally.

Nathan wasn't throwing nearly as many tests at me. *Maybe he respects me a little bit by now,* I thought. He had one-itis for a young virgin, and I advised him about what she might be thinking. We discovered that we've both had some very long-term, committed monogamous relationships: my longest lasted 6 years, his 7 years.

Somehow, we ended up discussing my worst past relationship. I realized I was speaking angrily when Nathan laid a hand reassuringly on my arm.

I took a deep breath. *Wow, I'm totally bonding with Mr. Shady,* I thought.

"I was super young," I said awkwardly. "I had low self-esteem. I wouldn't get into a relationship like that now."

Nathan nodded. "That's one of the reasons I got into the community," he said. "To make sure I never got trapped in a bad relationship again."

Shockingly, Nathan paid for my tacos. Don't get too excited. They were $6, and paying for a cheap dinner is a common game tactic... but you're supposed to do it only once you've trained the girl not to expect it.

* * *

Around the time of the summit, there were several active discussions on my blog about PUAs and masculinity. Those discussions felt so stressful for me that I closed them down and disallowed further comments. Some of my dedicated readers noted privately that I seemed much more prickly than before.

Jonnie moved away from Chicago. He invited me to his going-away club night. I was out of town, but I wished him the best.

His message reminded me of James Amoureux. I remembered how James talked about consent at the PUA summit, and how he'd said that "Lying makes me feel like I'm not being myself." *I might have misjudged James*, I thought. I invited him to a party, but he never got back to me. I still spot him around the city sometimes, and he attended one of my events a few weeks before this book was published.

I went to a science fiction convention with some old friends. They hadn't seen me in ages, and I hadn't attended the convention in years. I had fun, but I also detected changes in how I dealt with people there. I realized that every time men talked to me, I currently assumed that they only wanted me for sex. And sometimes I also assumed that women who spoke to me were seeking some kind of social proof. Years ago, I never thought that way.

I no longer felt confident that I was interesting or that men might value my intelligence. In a weird way, my self-esteem was lower than it had been since high school.

Back in Chicago, I met yet another great activist guy. He asked me out. After dinner, he leaned back and gave me a measuring look. "You're so *authentic*," he said.

"I haven't felt very authentic lately," I said frankly, but his words stuck with me. My whole life, I've prided myself on honesty. Being recognized so clearly by someone I respected made me feel warm and fuzzy...

... even though the compliment came from one of those lying, conniving *men*.

Nathan emailed to ask if I wanted to be the official wingwoman for an upcoming Lollapalooza pickup event. I didn't reply for a week or so. Eventually, Nathan texted to ask again. I hedged. He pushed. I agreed. Then I spent several days feeling sick whenever I thought about it. *Why the hell am I doing this?* I asked myself.

Finally, I emailed Nathan again. "Hey, I'm sorry, but I'm just gonna have to back out," I wrote. "I can't be involved in this subculture anymore. I do appreciate the invitation and I wish you the best."

"I understand," Nathan replied. "Good luck in your endeavors, whatever they may be. Did something new happen?"

I thought about the activist who'd called me "authentic" over dinner. I suspected that if I wanted to save the shreds of my own authenticity, I had to run away from PUAs. But hadn't that been obvious all along? "No," I wrote back. "Nothing new."

* * *

* * *

CHAPTER 12:
At Last I Am Free

In which Clarisse presents her Grand Theory of The Ethical Game. The chapter title is after a song with the same name, by Pretty Lights.

* * *

A few weeks after the conclusion of the Chicago Dating Skills convention, one of my readers found some horrible PUA blog posts and emailed them to me. He felt especially upset by them, because he had personally learned useful things from the community. "I'm feeling particularly strongly now that it's important to separate out the good from the bad in the seduction community," he wrote. "It seems like it's really easy for a lot of guys to just fall into the whole thing, rather than taking the good and filtering the bad."

His statement confirmed my suspicion that it was time for a Grand Theory of the Ethical Game. But I thought back to the questions that the blogger Hugh Ristik once asked:

I think there are many questions we need to ask about the seduction community:

* What is it? What are its practices and assumptions?

* What drives men towards it? What are the experiences of these men? How do they see the world? What are their goals?

* To what degree do the practices advocated by the community work with women? And what does "work" mean?

* Is the seduction community damaging or sexist towards women? Does it have positive impacts on women?

* Is the seduction community damaging or sexist towards men? Does it have positive impacts on men?

* What is the relationship between the community and gender political movements [like feminism]? What are the areas of conflict, or overlap?

* Are the practices of the community ethical?

I put the last question last for a reason: although it's the question people like to jump to immediately, I think all the previous questions must be answered or at least considered before this one can be approached intelligently.

Ethics don't exist in a vacuum. To talk about ethics, we need examples and context.

So: What is the seduction community, and what drives men towards it? Well, I hope this book has taught you a lot about it. It's a surprisingly diverse country. The coach Mark Manson once wrote to me,

Every guy getting into this is in it for the same reason: to feel loved and less lonely. How they interpret that runs the spectrum based on their beliefs and their history with women. Some of them interpret it as a need to fuck everything that moves, others realize they just want a nice girlfriend. Some are divorced men who want to get married again. It's common for people to attribute "PUA Beliefs" to the vocal minority who are coaching and marketing when the silent majority of guys are actually seeking really basic successes.

For every guy who's posting and boasting about his 8 fuckbuddies, there's 10 guys who don't post who just really want to get a date with a nice girl, and when they do they disappear and are never heard from again. This is probably the first thing I noticed when I started doing a lot of market research when I expanded my business. It's why David DeAngelo and a product called Double Your Dating *makes literally 30x as much money as a company such as Real Social Dynamics which specializes in "lording clubs" and "banging 10s" or whatever it is they talk about these days. The market doesn't lie.*

But I don't believe that every dude in the PUA community just wants to feel loved and less lonely. Roissy, whose blog I toured in Chapter 9, is obviously in this for power, along with the other Darth Vaders. I never personally interviewed anyone as bad as Roissy, but if I did, I wonder whether that guy would say something like: "Every guy getting into this is in it for the same reason: power and revenge."

Hugh Ristik also asks whether the community's practices "work." Many PUA techniques seem to "work" very well, as attested by many success stories. Some men can, indeed, turn into dazzling Lotharios if they put in a lot of effort. But while a lot of the techniques and attitudes can be good for getting laid, a lot are no good for building a mutual long-term relationship. "The first rule of women is, never listen to what they say" is kinda the worst possible maxim if you want, say, a pleasant marriage.

And it's not always clear which techniques build attraction; there are too many variables per encounter. Is the target attracted because of the neg, or the shit test reframe? Is she attracted by neither the neg nor the reframe, but rather the PUA's congruent confidence? Or is she attracted for some reason that the PUA has not identified?

When we do have techniques that work — negs, reframes, and congruence all have something to them — it's *still* true that PUAs have no reliable idea of *why* they work. Not everything is a shit test. Sometimes women *do* know what we want. What the fuck is an "alpha"? Phlogiston, my friends. Phlogiston.

It's also not clear who can maximize which techniques. For every guru whose approach repels you, there's probably a guru you'd agree with 90% of the time. For every over-the-top success story like Neil Strauss, a thousand guys pay a thousand dollars for PUA products and never take a single girl home. On the other hand, Mark Manson once told me that PUA market research consistently shows that "like 80% of the guys, once they experience some success (they get laid a couple times, they get a girlfriend), they're never heard from again." So there's clearly a remedial aspect to the community's teachings that is frequently overlooked. A *lot* of guys get in, get some insight, and get out.

Is the community sexist? In some ways the answer is obvious. Many PUAs reduce women to hysterical, idiotic sex objects whose feelings don't matter. ("[Women] really are insipid, vapid airheads. If it wasn't for the pussy, there would be a bounty on them.") Many PUAs also reduce men to aggressive, sex-driven automatons whose feelings don't exist. ("I've seen him pull much hotter girls. What the fuck is a personality?")

In terms of rape culture, PUA metaphors often back up the commodity model by talking about women's "value." PUA metaphors blame the victim with phrases like "buyer's remorse" and aggressive "Last Minute Resistance" techniques. PUA metaphors reinforce adversarial gender roles, most obviously by making women into "targets." Which gets especially freaky when, say, a PUA guru shoots a girl in the face.

Plus, the seduction community is very heteronormative: it really buys into problematic gender standards. Back in the feminist chapter, a feminist acquaintance compared the game to the advertising industry and said: "The thing is, advertising isn't just a consequence of problematic norms... it's a creator of them, too. And PUAs aren't just working with the hand the universe dealt them, they're reinforcing those norms through their exploitative behavior."

However, a few positive impacts exist, and not just on men. If straight men are working hard to make themselves more attractive, then that's awesome for straight women, right? And since some PUAs promote careful sexual communication, and some PUAs tell guys not to push against Last Minute Resistance, those guys are opposing rape culture, right? And if some men are becoming more aware of their emotions through the community, then that's great. If they're finding themselves, and developing a sense of personal balance, and exploring their "inner game," then that's good for them *and everyone around them.*

And, of course, there's the immense amount of observation PUAs have done of human dating practices. Remember how Hugh Ristik once said that, "Pickup is a barometer of what's fucked up in wider society." There's a lot to learn from PUAs. Most of them imitate sexual behavior that's quite typical in the mainstream. And in terms of problems like aggressive LMR techniques or misogynist metaphors, it's not clear that asshole PUAs are worse than misogynists in the mainstream. This doesn't excuse Darth Vader PUAs like Roissy, of course. But it does give a sense of the potential big picture.

Hugh Ristik's last two questions were about the community's relationship to feminism, and whether PUA practices are ethical. I see these questions as overlapping. Yet there are so many PUA tactics and attitudes and effects that asking, "Are the practices of the community ethical?" makes no sense. PUA techniques are a collection of social tools: some are more susceptible to being used for evil, the same way a sword is more likely to be used cruelly than a table. But as Brian noted when my relationship with Adam was on the rocks, even the dreaded freeze-out can be a communication tool or an honest expression of desires rather than a weapon... as long as it's used carefully.

So the real question is: What is the ethical game? What does it look like?

As PUA ideas have hit the big time, various ethicists have sought to sell their own theories of Ethical Game. Feminist S&Mers and polyamorists do it by continuing what we've always done: we tend to emphasize direct and explicit verbal communication. We encourage people to talk about what they want, extensively, *before* they do anything sexually. We encourage explicit communication because we want to create sex and relationships that are both mutually hot and mutually well-understood.

Explicit, direct communication is hard. But it gets easier with practice: I know this from experience. I also know that *people are likely to develop a preference for explicit communication if it seems more necessary.* Many S&Mers and polyamorists develop these preferences because our desires are unusual and precise, and complicated words will help us get what we want. Feminists develop these preferences because explicit communication is the clearest way to ensure sexual consent.

Accordingly, some people react to criticisms of explicit sexual communication by saying that *we should make it necessary.* Here's an example exchange from the comments on an awesome, thoughtful feminist

S&M blog. A male commenter asks:

I once had an argument with a very good female friend of mine about kissing. She was perturbed about a date who asked her if he could proceed to kiss her. She said the man should just know. It should be instinctual and u lose the moment as soon as u ask. I said that was bs, the first move is one of the most nerve wracking things, the very fact that he asked shows his politeness and tact and frankly a lack of presumptuousness. ... What do you think? What's the line between politeness and passivity?

The feminist blogger, who goes by the name Holly Pervocracy, responds that:

I don't say this very often, but "you lose the moment as soon as you ask" girls really are ruining it for the rest of us.

As far as I'm concerned, they can go without ever being kissed until they wise up.

However, I think (or would like to think? augh) that most girls are not like that, and that you should not plan for girls to be like that. I'd definitely rather offend someone by asking than offend them by not asking. [1]

Holly implies that people who don't like explicit communication should effectively be banned from kissing: she says, "They can go without ever being kissed until they wise up." I think Holly's smart, and I generally like her writing. I have a certain cantankerous sympathy for her perspective here, and I have said similar things myself in the past.

Yet it's clear that lots of people aren't big on direct and explicit communication. In fact, many people say that direct, explicit communication *cannot possibly be sexy*. As Hugh Ristik once pointed out on my blog:

Men attempting sexual communication often run afoul of women's preferences for masculinity, because it looks wimpy or insecure. ... I googled "asking for a kiss," and found this discussion on an online dating site. [2] *I went through all 14 pages, looked for stated female preferences for men to ask or not, and added them up.*

- 142 women gave an answer
- 98 (69%) preferred that men not ask
- 11 (7.7%) preferred that men do ask
- 31 (21.8%) were fine either way, liked both, or said it depends. (Though many of these women still leaned towards men not asking.)
- 2 (1.4%) preferred to make a move themselves
Words used to describe men asking for a kiss:
awkward
nervous
wimpy

lame
limp
insecure
gross
dull
puss [3]

I think it would be interesting to contrast that list of words with, say, a list of words that men might use to describe a woman who wants a relationship, when that woman doesn't know how to "figure it out on her own" through skillful emotional escalation. I bet *that* list would include words like "awkward," "insecure," and "nervous." New female-specific slurs might include "clingy" and "crazy." Not all men would agree about this hypothetical list, but many — perhaps 69% of them? — would.

After posting the list of words, Hugh Ristik pulled out some quotations from women in the discussion who disliked being asked for a kiss. Those women said things like:

If you have to ask, then the answer is no... just kiss!!!

or:

Oh, God!!! Never ask! Just move slowly to her lips. If she wants to kiss you, she will. If not, she either catch you on the cheek or turn her head. And it REALLY annoys me if a guy asks me if I would like to have sex with him. If he can't figure it out on his own, the answer is always NO!

A discussion from an online dating site is not conclusive, and the women who commented in that discussion can't represent All Women Everywhere. Still, it's clear that some people will socially punish others for trying to talk explicitly about a sexual interaction. We are not merely dealing with a world where explicit verbal sexual communication is hard. We are dealing with a world where lots of people *actively dislike and resist* explicit verbal sexual communication.

When people protest that explicit communication is *really hard,* feminists often respond by saying something like: "Yes, it's hard. Suck it up and do it anyway." Or we respond like Holly did — by saying that we should be *more* afraid of potential harm than afraid of losing the moment.

But the reality is, *even we fuck this shit up.* Look how long the goth PUA Brian and I took to acknowledge what was going on between us, even though we're both feminist polyamorous S&Mers. Look at my relationship with Adam, where I was fairly explicit about a lot of things, but I was *totally not explicit* about others, even though I run workshops on explicit sexual communication.

Why are we fucking this up? Is it just because good communication is a challenging skill to learn? Communication is definitely a challenging skill! But I suspect that part of the problem here is also that it's actually, legitimately difficult to find the sweet spot where good communication meets tasty strategic ambiguity. Even those of us who promote explicit verbal sexual communication sometimes have mixed feelings about it, or have difficulty with it in practice.

Holly says that she thinks "most girls are not like that" — i.e., she thinks that most girls would prefer explicit communication. But we have no decent evidence one way or the other. And we do know that some people who dislike explicit communication are very aggressive about it: they say things like, "If he can't figure it out on his own, the answer is always NO!"

Perhaps people who say those things simply *like* implicit communication better than explicit communication. That's why they insist that the other person "has to figure it out on his own." What they mean is that they want the other person to communicate in their preferred mode. They want the other person to speak their language, sort of, except it's obviously not "speaking" at all. Maybe they even *test partners' implicit communication skills* by offering certain challenges... like shit tests, perhaps?

I would guess that people like this group together, and that this attitude is more common in certain cultures or subcultures — the same way different jargon, slang, and dialects develop in different cultures and subcultures. A lot of people who are familiar with the S&M and polyamory subcultures have remarked on how many nerds and geeks populate those subcultures. (I've been known to joke that I'm bound to marry a kinky software engineer.) But there are plenty of people who do sexual activities that look a lot like S&M, or who have relationships that seem quite polyamorous, but *who don't talk about it explicitly the way we do.*

When it comes to sexuality, there's really nothing new under the sun. For example, open marriages were once so common in France that open marriages were commonly referred to as "French arrangements." But historical French people certainly weren't reading books about what we now call "polyamory," and they weren't using jargon like "primary relationship." (If only because the word "polyamory" was devised in the early 1990s.)

I have often thought that the S&M and polyamory subcultures are less about the sex we have, and more about the way we talk about it. I would like to export ideas about explicit communication from S&M and polyamory, because on a feminist level, I've always thought that explicit communication is better for consent. Yet if people who come into these subcultures tend to be better with words than the average person outside these subcultures, then perhaps the verbal techniques we use within these subcultures are not well-suited to the average outsider.

I would guess that people who like explicit communication are more attracted to groups where explicit communication is valued, like the subcultures associated with polyamory or feminism or S&M. Whereas people who don't like it are more attracted to subcultures where it isn't, like mainstream nightclubs in Los Angeles. Where they are then deconstructed by Mystery and become a huge influence on modern pickup artistry.

Have you ever heard the Depeche Mode song, "Enjoy the Silence"? That's another good example of this phenomenon.

The feminist S&M blogger Holly says that given the choice, she'd rather "offend someone by asking than offend them by not asking." This is a reasonable perspective. I've said similar things.

But if a lot of people can't stand explicit verbal sexual communication, then a person who takes that attitude will be discarding a lot of people. And if *a really large number* of people are reluctant to use explicit communication, then refusing to interact with them may not be the best way to change the culture. After all, if there are a lot of them, and if they can't make out with us, they'll make out with each other, and nothing will change.

In other words, if we create a solution that no one will use, it's not a real solution.

I asked some big questions in Chapter 5 when I was talking about feminism, and here they are again:

* If lots of people seek strategic ambiguity from their sex and relationships, then where is the line where strategic ambiguity becomes non-consensual or cruel?

* What are the "bad" types of strategic ambiguity, as opposed to "good" ones that work better for consent?

If many people enjoy ambiguity or non-explicit communication, then my questions about how to promote strategic ambiguity and enthusiastic consent *at the same time* aren't just questions about how I can get what I want. They're also questions of how we can convince the world to think about consent in a feminist way.

Indeed, as I have thought about this and reviewed my experiences, I've realized something important that feminists don't grapple with: *Explicit communication can become its own kind of weapon against consent.*

Some people are better at some types of communication than others. For example, I have always been better at writing than most people I know. However, I suspect that I am not as good at non-verbal communication as most people I know.

What this means is that if I encourage people to use explicit and complex language, then I am attempting to move conversations into a sphere where I have more skill... and therefore, I am attempting to move conversations to a sphere where I have more power and privilege. We all play to our strengths, of course, and there's nothing wrong with that. But if I pull a maneuver like this with a person who is much worse at using words than I am, then that person may perceive my actions as a grab for social power. And in a way, that person will be correct.

So when people who are highly verbal — such as most feminists — attempt to create social standards that focus on explicit communication, we are trying to create social standards that benefit us.

In my relationships, I believe that I'm obligated to respect my partner's feelings. If I want a relationship to be harmonious, then I should try not to do things that hurt my partner unnecessarily, and I should try to pay attention to his signals. If I perceive that my partner is acting uncomfortable, then maybe I shouldn't force him to tell me verbally that he's uncomfortable before I change what I'm doing. That's what it means for me to respect his consent.

Now, if my hypothetical partner mostly communicates non-verbally, and I mostly communicate verbally, then we may not be a good match. Maybe we would be better off breaking up. But if I'm in a relationship with someone, then it's cruel for me to ignore his signals, as long as I can see them.

For example: even in S&M, where I take explicit verbal communication very seriously, I try to pay attention to non-verbal signals. I've got a crystal-clear memory of the first time I was in charge of hurting my partner, and I stopped *before* he called his safeword.

We were in bed. The room was lit only by candles. I'd left scratches all over my lover's body, and there were serious bruises developing, too. He was crying, and begging me to stop.

My sight felt sharpened. Everything *sparkled.* I was totally focused on my submissive. I knew I was pushing him to the limit, but he hadn't called his safeword, and I didn't feel like I was done yet. I thought about what I wanted to do next, and came to some very painful conclusions.

I stood up, and dragged him out of bed. He huddled at my feet, head bowed, shivering. Wrapping my fingers in his hair, I wrenched his head up to face me. His eyes were closed and tears leaked slowly down his cheeks.

Desire crackled through me. I wanted to hear him scream. But... he was much quieter than he had been over the last hour. His face was still. No more pleas poured from his lips. It seemed like my partner had gone way into the back of his mind, far from me.

I knew he loved me. I knew he might be reluctant to disappoint me. Maybe he was so reluctant that he couldn't look out for himself. He hadn't spoken the safeword, but I'd never seen him become so quiet and non-reactive, and I didn't feel confident to continue.

So despite my desire, I said his name. I said it gently, and then I asked, "Do you remember your safeword?"

My lover shuddered. It took him a moment to reply. "Red," he whispered: the safeword. "Red." I took in a deep breath, quieted my frustration, and then sat down with him as he broke into sobs. I put my arms around him and gave him the aftercare he deserved.

When we talked about it the next day, I asked my partner how he would have felt if I'd kept going. If I hadn't asked him about his safeword. He hesitated, then said, "I don't know."

My response sounded something like this: "I want to be able to trust you to call your safeword if you have to. I really need to know what I can and can't do."

He nodded and said quietly, "I know..."

... yet we both still felt edgy about where the limits lay.

(Years later, walking through Golden Gate Park with Adam, this moment would come to mind. I remembered it clearly when Adam said: "I want you to be clear about your boundaries. I really need to know what I can and can't do.")

I could have ignored my lover's unspoken signals. After all, he didn't use his safeword. He probably wouldn't have blamed me, later, if I seriously harmed him. I could have used the expectation of explicit verbal communication as a blunt instrument. I could have used the expectation of explicit verbal communication *to give myself the social power to push him too far.* But as frustrating as it was to stop, I'm glad I did.

That submissive was, by the way, one of the more articulate and self-aware men I've known. Intense S&M has a way of bewildering even the most self-aware people.

So this, too, must be part of the Ethical Game: No matter how skilled we become with words, *sometimes words just don't cut it.* Safewords and other types of explicit communication are incredibly useful and important. However, taken to extremes, *explicit communication can become a social weapon to disempower other types of communication that are just as valid.*

Obviously, I think that explicit verbal communication is really important. I am really glad that my life path has forced me to develop decent explicit verbal communication skills around sexuality. In particular, I firmly believe that a verbal "No" should always mean "No," unless safewords are involved.

My point here is *not* that I think we should abandon explicit verbal communication. My point is that communication is a varied set of skills. I think it's possible that explicit verbal communication is the *most important* communication skill. But it's not the *only* communication skill.

I've mentioned "kino," or physical escalation, and PUAs talk about it a lot more than I do. I've mentioned that PUAs value social "calibration" and emphasize practicing social interaction in order to calibrate oneself to non-verbal signals. I've talked about a lot of other PUA insights into tacit communication, from "shit tests" to "compliance tests."

Any theory of the Ethical Game must include these types of communication, not just explicit communication. I'd like to see more feminists and S&Mers and polyamorists talking deeply about different types of communication, and I've tried to add to that conversation with this book. Even if you accept nothing else I wrote — even if you think that all my theories are ridiculous — I hope you will think about these different types of social interaction, and what they mean for your own ethics.

* * *

So. Now that I've described the PUA context, and now that I've explained the problems with previous feminist ideas about the Ethical Game, it's time to start laying out the premises for my own Grand Theory of The Ethical Game. Ready?

First: I will acknowledge that those of us who try to be careful, intentional and ethical about love and sex will sometimes feel like we're "losing," or "getting less," than other people who are less ethical. In his brilliant short story "Brief Interviews With Hideous Men," the writer David Foster Wallace has a character say that:

I seem to be developing more of a sort of conscience [about falling in love]. Which a part of me finds terrifying, to be honest. ... I admit there's a kind of dread at the idea of having a conscience in this area, as if it seems as if it's going to take away all room to maneuver, somehow. [4]

Ethics can be painful. I think it's important to acknowledge that. Sometimes it's hard to do the right thing. Yet this doesn't make ethics any less crucial. And I suspect that in the long term, we ethicists get better relationships out of the deal.

In Chapter 5, when I was writing about feminism, I quoted the amazing essay "Towards A Performance Model of Sex" by Thomas MacAulay Millar. Thomas is another feminist S&Mer, and his analysis shows it. He offers a "performance model" as a metaphor for sexual interactions that's way better than the "commodity model":

Like the commodity model, the performance model implies a negotiation, but not an unequal or adversarial one. The negotiation is the creative process of building something from a set of available elements. Musicians have to choose, explicitly or implicitly, what they are going to play: genre, song, key and interpretation. The palette available to them is their entire skill set — all the instruments they have and know how to play, their entire repertoire, their imagination and their skills — and the product will depend on the pieces each individual brings to the performance. Two musicians steeped in Delta blues will produce very different music from one musician with a love for soul and funk and another with roots in hip-hop or 1980s hardcore. This process involves communication of likes and dislikes and preferences, not a series of proposals that meet with acceptance or rejection. [6]

To design a metaphor for the game that's beneficial for everyone, we want to encourage people to be creative together — whether they're speaking, "making music," or just gazing into each other's eyes.

The game can be adversarial, or it can be mutual. You can treat your date like a target or an opponent, or you can treat your date like another player. You and your date can be on the same team. If this is a roleplaying game, then your date is a Player Character rather than a Non-Player Character. If this is a first-person shooter, then the arena is set to co-op mode. Okay, I'll stop being a huge nerd.

And sex isn't everything. (Nor is marriage, Rules Girls.) And if you act like sex (or marriage) is everything, then you could lose a lot of friendship and love.

I already asked: *if lots of people seek strategic ambiguity from their sex and relationships, then where is the line where strategic ambiguity becomes non-consensual or cruel?* I think the line often falls if you stop caring about your partner's feelings.

Here's one idea that I like from the blogger Hugh Ristik: many pickup tactics seem more ethical as long as they work *on both parties.* For example, time dilation — where you schedule multiple venue changes over the course of the date — often works on the PUA as well as his partner. It's hard to claim that it's wrong to make someone else feel like they've spent much more time with you than they actually have, as long as you're making yourself feel the same way. If your tactics work on you while they work on your partner, then ethics become a matter of self-interest.

But not everything can affect you the same way it affects your partner. That's why communication is so important. There's some obvious non-consensual behavior, such as ignoring a partner who says "no," that is just plain wrong. Some lines are less clear, though, and that's where you want to pay attention to communicating properly — and respecting what your partner tells you. That's where you want to keep improving your calibration, so you can listen to non-verbal signals as well as verbal ones. In the S&M encounter that I just told you about, the strategic ambiguity of our S&M might have become cruel if I'd become unsure that my partner could take it *and continued to push him anyway.*

The ultimate example of a person who advocates *only* negative strategic ambiguity is the article on "dread" that I discussed by Roissy, the worse-than-Vader villain in Chapter 9. His goal is actually to leave his partners with a "constant, gnawing feeling of impending doom." I mean, he actually wrote those words. If you care about people, don't do that to them.

In Chapter 7, I also gave you a Theory of the Friend Zone and the Fuckbuddy Zone. I've talked about the ways those zones can be misinterpreted. I don't think everyone who finds themselves in those zones is being manipulated on purpose. But I've also outlined situations in which sending certain sexual or emotional signals can cruelly string people along. And *that* is not okay; that's using communication to hurt people, rather than being a true partner.

I also asked: *what are the "bad" types of strategic ambiguity, as opposed to "good" ones that work better for consent?* I strongly suspect that strategic ambiguity covers an awful lot of things. I suspect that many kinds of contrast, challenge, novelty, and unpredictability hook into similar places in our psyches. Some people want more of them, and some people want less: total certainty is on one end, total uncertainty is on the other. PUAs talk about "direct game" and "indirect game," but most of them acknowledge using a mixture of the two. The middle path is strategic.

In Chapter 2, I cited a Real Study that shows how going on novel, challenging dates could increase romantic feelings. I also talked about "shit tests" and harmless adversarial flirtation, and I've given you many examples of mutual S&M encounters and communication tactics throughout this book.

In Chapter 3, I discussed PUA "Last Minute Resistance techniques," and described some differences between "mutual LMR techniques" and "aggressive LMR techniques." Mutual LMR techniques are the ones where the PUA is most concerned about creating a mutual experience, like by using awesome foreplay, or by figuring out why the lady objects to sex and addressing that issue directly. Aggressive LMR techniques are the ones where the PUA steamrolls her objections and ignores her reality.

And in Chapter 4, I addressed "compliance tests." A negative compliance test is done entirely to gain power, or to gain some benefit that has nothing to do with a mutual relationship. An example might be a woman who goes to a bar and gets a man to buy her a drink just because she wants the drink, and who walks away from the man immediately after he buys it. On the other hand, positive compliance tests are issued by a person who actually cares about their target and wants a relationship, or who genuinely needs help. An example might be a woman who is having trouble getting something out of her purse, and asks a man to hold her drink for a moment so that she can use both her hands.

These, I believe, are all ways to think about the ethical game.

* * *

People often ask about my biggest takeaway from the seduction community. It's a question that I can't answer easily. Sometimes I describe the most vivid moments and personalities that I found there, or sometimes I give them my Grand Taxonomy of PUAs. While I learned a lot, picking a single Moral Of The Story wouldn't be right.

One of the moments I remember best happened at the Chicago Dating Skills Convention, when one of my favorite clients asked the assembled coaches: "What if you have one steady relationship, and you're frequently having sex? How do you keep up your motivation to go out and find other women?"

Several other coaches said things like, *"Never* abandon the game. *Always* keep yourself in shape socially." When I answered, I tried to keep my tone from sounding like a lecture.

"It's all about your priorities," I said. "So many guys get into this and think they want to bang all the hot girls in town. Maybe that is actually what you want, and if so, there's nothing wrong with doing it consensually. But maybe what you want is to have a long-term relationship, or to focus on a limited number of sexual connections. Or maybe your desires will change over time. Keep an eye on yourself. And focusing on one or two long-term relationships... that's how you get *good at sex*. If you want to be good at sex and not just picking people up, then that's the way to go."

I like to think my advice was worth their expensive summit tickets. It probably wasn't.

I once asked AnneBonney — another feminist woman who spent a long time reading and commenting among the PUAverse — how she would advise a newbie to the community. She said something similar:

A) Think very, very carefully about what your goals are, what you are willing to do to achieve them, and WHY you want them. I think a lot of dudes who are struggling with their interactions with women are unhappy in a lot of different ways, but see "getting better with women" as the way to fix all of what ails them, relatively easily. But just like a woman who thinks she'll be happier when she loses 20 pounds, there are a lot of cultural influences informing what "happy" means and what we want or need to get there that are bogus and bent to a system that doesn't have our happiness in mind.

B) Be very, very careful who you listen to and where you put your trust and resources. There were so many disgruntled ex-students of various gurus, who felt swindled or at least shortchanged, or who listened to a busted philosophy for years, continuing to be unhappy or just getting more and more angry at both the gurus and the women they weren't successful with. At this point, I mean, the seduction community is what, 15 years old, and there are hundreds of folks willing to take your time and money all with different "programs." I always found that most of the men I encountered were willing to put in a lot of effort getting reviews and that sort of thing before trying a new guru, but even that is flawed, because in such a diverse community there's going to be a few people who are die-hards for anybody. I think successfully picking people to listen to requires a big dose of point A here: if you don't know what you're looking for, all the guys offering "get-laid-quick" schemes are going to look equal, and you could be in a place you weren't anticipating very easily.

And while reflecting on his life as a PUA, the coach Mark Manson once described how damaged men get sucked into the seduction community:

Something deep down in their emotional fabric drives them much further. They excitedly accept the objectification and relish in the validation. I did. And I see other guys do it too. And really what it is is their way of sorting through their emotional baggage. Some guys it takes 10-15 women. Some it takes 50-100. Some guys are damaged too deeply and never get out. But the truth remains: you don't sell your soul to the devil unless part of you is already a little dead inside.

I am not an exception, just another casualty.

... You don't end up in the Pick Up Artist community unless you are incredibly unhappy or unsatisfied about something. It may be conscious, it may be unconscious. It may be short-term, or it may be deep-seated and long-term. But the fact is, the community acts for a lot of men as a diversion or scapegoat from dealing with their real issues — their emotional issues.

We're men, we're experts at rationalizing painful feelings away — we hate dealing with them. For a lot of men, all these eBooks and audio courses merely act as rationalizations — a way to escape for a little bit longer, a way to logically solve the unsolvable. Emotions aren't quantifiable or objective, so these men band together in attempt to quantify and objectify their emotional lives together, under the auspices of "improvement."

And by their shared metrics, improve they do. "I had my first Single Night Lay." "I banged my first 9 last night." Etc. But there's no yardstick for happiness, fulfillment, meaning or significance. This may sound lame and campy, but when you've met as many miserable guys with 100+ lays as I have, you may take it seriously.

Some PUAs forget... they forget that there's a whole life to these interactions behind the objectification and quantification. They enter the validation trap — where a cocaine-addicted stripper has more value than a Plain Jane with a Ph.D, where a threesome has more value than an engagement ring, where things like acne scars or B-cup tits suddenly become deal-breakers in a relationship.

... In the end, I suppose this article should be taken as a cautionary tale. There's a lot to gain from that whole movement, but there's also a lot that you can get trapped in and sucked under by. A friend of mine put it perfectly when he said, "You can judge a self-help movement by how many people leave it. If people are leaving it, then it's doing something right." Well, many people leave the PUA community, so it must be doing something right.

Just make sure you're one of the ones who leaves. [7]

I thought I had an epiphany for a while. I thought maybe a feminist PUA curriculum would be the best idea ever, and that I was totally the woman to do it. My feelings about PUAs became so knotted that I never went through with it. I did, however, talk briefly to a woman who independently came up with the same idea. Her name is Charlie Nox, and as far as I know, she's on her way to implementing her own feminist PUA curriculum. I asked Charlie some questions by email, and she wrote:

One goal of my book is to fill a need and want that exists in the pickup community. A lot of my guy friends are hesitant to read pickup books because they want to be decent guys. Even guys within the pickup community, like Nick Savoy, president of Love Systems, Inc. (formerly the Mystery Method) talks about why part of the reason they changed company names was to reflect that the desire to be successful with women is becoming more mainstream and that they don't have to refer to women as bitches and hos to date them. I think now is the perfect time to fill the void.

Another goal is to make feminism palatable, understandable, relatable and immediate for groups of people who have normally rejected it. Those of us already identified as feminists know that Feminism is For Everybody (thanks bell hooks). Now, how do we get everybody to listen while we talk about that?

She's got my endorsement, that's for sure.

I swear to God, I recently found the most amazing fortune in a Thai fortune cookie: "Love is a game that two can play and both win." I tried to seduce the cute waiter by handing him the fortune, but he haughtily denied me. Alas.

Maybe that means I'm no better at the game than I was when I started. But maybe that's okay.

These days, I feel pretty well detoxed from my PUA obsession... although I'm sure that if you're desperate for my wisdom and want to help a starving artist, you could convince me to take your money. I'll show up to our coaching sessions in knee-high boots and a tank top that says "Abuse Of Power Comes As No Surprise." If your philosophy is faulty, I'll make you bleed.

Actually... that sounds like fun.

Maybe someday I *will* offer private lessons in seduction.

But not today.

* * *

* * *

About The Author

* * *

Clarisse Thorn is a feminist, sex-positive educator who has delivered sex-related workshops at museums and universities across the USA. She created and curated the original Sex+++ sex-positive documentary film series at Chicago's historic feminist site, Jane Addams Hull-House Museum. She has also volunteered as an archivist, curator and fundraiser for that venerable S&M institution, the Leather Archives & Museum. In 2010, Clarisse returned from working on HIV mitigation in sub-Saharan Africa. Her writing has appeared across the Internet in many many places. She blogs about feminist sexuality with a focus on S&M at clarissethorn.com, and tweets @clarissethorn.

Links for connecting with Clarisse:
Blog: http://clarissethorn.com/blog
Twitter: http://twitter.com/ClarisseThorn
Facebook: http://www.facebook.com/clarisse.thorn
Become a fan of Confessions *on Facebook:* http://www.facebook.com/ConfessionsOfAPickupArtistChaser

* * *

Also check out Clarisse's awesome book
The S&M Feminist: Best Of Clarisse Thorn!

This is a selection of Clarisse's best articles, plus commentary on the context in which she wrote each piece, the process of writing it, and how she's changed since then. Plus "study guides" to help readers get the maximum mileage from each section!

Paperback copies: https://www.createspace.com/3878670

* * *

* * *

APPENDIX A:
Detrimental Attitudes You Can Pick Up Through The Seduction Community

This article was originally written years ago by a gentleman who has thoroughly investigated the seduction community. Chris's main interest is writing about remedial social skills and shyness, but in the past he also offered some basic dating advice. Part of that involved trying to warn guys off the weirder aspects of the pickup artist world, which is where this article originated. He's since moved away from giving advice in that area and is concentrating just on social skills. His main site is available at SucceedSocially.com.

Clarisse first encountered this article when she started researching pickup artists, and thought it was so interesting that she used it as part of a workshop. She was disappointed when the author took down from the site where it was posted, and asked if she could repost it on her blog. A heated thread ensued, one of several where Clarisse's commentariat has debated PUAs. [1]

When Clarisse requested this post for republication, Chris agreed but added: "One thing that seems good is that those old articles are getting more and more irrelevant by the day, since the seduction community seems to be catching on to how weird some of its advice can be. It has a ways to go, but I definitely see a trend towards it getting more grounded and healthy... well as healthy as a subculture about picking up girls can be, of course."

* * *

The Seduction Community is a strange subculture. Some of its odd ideas are just harmless quirks. I think some are plain counterproductive to your success though. Internalizing them will make you a less appealing person, and you may end up doing worse with women. The maladaptive ideas below can also appear in other subcultures which have members who are aiming to improve themselves along some dimension.

I can't claim credit for coming up with many of the points below. I'm just throwing them together into one cautionary list. Some of these are fairly well known pitfalls in the scene, even if some of the guys who are aware of them can't put them into words. Others you'll recognize from *The Game* by Neil Strauss, which was good about drawing attention to the Community's odder elements.

Feeling arrogant and superior just for being in the Community

In a general sense, many guys in the Community have that feeling of superiority that comes from believing you know better than most people. They think they're in an elite class because they have this special knowledge about how to get girls, and about how things really work. They feel above all the guys who don't possess the information they have.

This smugness has nothing to do with one's actual ability to get girls. Guys in the Community can have swell heads whether they're master pick up artists or complete virgins. It's that they know certain things that supposedly puts them above other people.

Well actually Community guys can also feel superior because they really are doing well for themselves sexually, and look down on men who aren't enjoying the same lifestyle. You'd think only successful guys could think this way, but inexperienced ones do as well sometimes. In their minds they honestly think that because they know how to get girls on paper, they really are players on some level. They'll do things like scoff at a friend who's having a dry spell, even though they haven't had sex in even longer.

Seeing almost all mainstream guys as AFC's

Community guys often see pretty much any guy that doesn't know about the scene as an Average Frustrated Chump to be looked down on. Except for the odd mainstream guy who is naturally good with women, it's a pretty Black & White distinction between enlightened Community guys who know the score, and the teeming AFC masses who make every dating mistake in the book.

Ironically many guys in the Community hardly get any girls, and many so-called AFCs do just fine with women, even if they are following traditional dating models that apparently don't work. Many of the AFCs end with genuinely cool partners as well. They haven't all settled for the first thing they could get because they don't have the PUA skills to get truly quality women. Community guys end up with so-so women as well. They're as likely to go home with a drunk, fugly girl from a bar as the next person. All types of men can do well, or not well, when it comes to dating.

The definition of what marks a guy as an AFC seems to depend on the situation as well. Even if a mainstream guy is doing well with girls on the whole, all he has to do is display one AFCish behavior to earn the label.

However, when Community guys make these same mistakes (and everyone makes them, no one's perfect) they don't consider themselves as falling into this category.

Trading one set of misguided ideas about women for another

Before they get into the Community, the typical guy has beliefs about women such as:

+ Women are special, beautiful creatures.
+ Women need to be saved and protected.
+ Women need to be loved and nurtured.
+ You need to make women feel special.
+ Women need to be wined and dined and romanced.
+ Women want nice guys.
+ Women don't like sex.

A little too naive and romantic in other words. Then they get into the Community and before long they've been exposed to ideas like:

+ Women are flaky and unreliable.
+ Women are emotional and illogical.
+ Women only live in the emotion of the moment, do what feels good at the time, and justify their actions to themselves after the fact.
+ Women are manipulative and use guys for free drinks and dinners.
+ Women are fickle and have short attention spans.
+ Women are self-centered and self-interested.
+ Women primarily go to clubs for attention and validation from men.
+ Women constantly test men, try to devalue them, and try to make them jump through hoops.
+ Women try to make men suck up to them and put them on a pedestal.
+ Women think their pussies are made of gold and sell them to the highest bidder.
+ Women don't know what they really want.
+ Women are confused and hypocritical. They'll profess to dislike whorish behavior then blow a guy in a bathroom that night.
+ Women are programmed to want to get knocked up by an Alpha Male then ensnare an unwitting Beta Male into raising the child for her.
+ Women will cheat on their partners coldly and unemotionally.
+ Women are slaves to how their friends and society sees them. They want to sleep around, but have to be discreet about it.
+ Society's expectations have given women all kinds of weird hang ups up about sex and hooking up. Their minds are full of strange rationalizations and justifications.
+ Women are powerless to resist the right type of guy. Even if they're married, they'll get sucked along.

\+ Women are easily manipulated by simple magic tricks and talk of new agey topics.

I'm not saying there's no truth at all in these statements, of course there's some. These statements do describe some women, or the way some women act in certain circumstances. But taken as a whole, you gotta admit this set of beliefs is pretty negative, misogynistic even. Just as all women aren't special creatures that need to be rescued, they aren't all fickle, emotional, and selfish either. The truth is probably somewhere in the middle, and it depends on the girl. Some girls are really normal and cool and easy to talk to.

Having too many misguided attitudes towards relationships

The Community isn't known for giving particularly good advice about relationships. You get the sense some guys are projecting their past (unsuccessful) experiences of relationships into their general advice:

\+ All long term relationships eventually become stale, boring, and unsatisfying.

\+ If a guy in the Community gets a girlfriend it means he's settling, giving up, betraying the scene, accepting he can't climb to the top of the mountain, etc.

\+ Girls become dissatisfied and antsy before long in relationships and constantly need to be kept on their toes by the man.

\+ The only way a guy can have a good relationship is if he first plays the field and dates around a lot.

\+ Relationships naturally work best when the man is running the show.

\+ If you really show you like a girl, or spend a lot of time with her, she'll think you're clingy and weak and get sick of you.

\+ Girls are instinctively programmed to try and whip, control, and tie down men.

\+ Overall, a lot of the advice is about power dynamics and who's controlling who.

\+ Women constantly test men in the relationship.

\+ If a woman seems unhappy with some aspect of the relationship you have to run some sort of game on her to make her calm down.

\+ Guys have to use various techniques to train their girlfriends and get them to accept various conditions that the man wants.

Like I was saying, do some of these points sometimes describe some relationships? Totally. But put together these points reflect an overly cynical perspective. With any lens you view the world through, you'll see some things accurately but completely miss the boat on others. A totally idealistic lens would be just as bad, in a different way. There are healthy relationships out there where none of the points above could describe them.

Feeling you have to abandon your past life

I've seen this message board conversation quite a few times over the years:

Poster: "Ever since I got into the community I can't relate to my friends anymore. I want to sarge but they just want to stay in and watch TV like AFCs."

Responders: "If you want to get good at this you have to turn your back on your old life. Your old friends aren't like you anymore."

I just think this attitude is wrongheaded. It's one thing to get into a new subculture and be keen to improve yourself. It's another to feel you have to jettison your previous life in its service. Some socially awkward people can be negative about others and have a bad habit of looking for excuses to drop their friends. I was one of them. This viewpoint may be rooted in that.

Then there's that common idea that the only way to get good at picking up girls is to drop everything and devote yourself entirely to it for a few years. After all, that's how such and such guru did it. There's probably a more balanced way to go about it though. Why give up your current friends? Why screw up your education or career? There has to be a less obsessive approach to take.

Interpreting everything you come across through Community concepts

I'll say that sometimes when guys do this it really is just a harmless quirk or an understandable part of the learning curve, but I've seen people go wrong with this thinking enough to edge it into this article. This point gets into that saying, "If you give a child a hammer, he'll find that everything needs hammering." The Community's ideas provide a fairly extensive set of advice for socializing with women, and other people as well. But its concepts don't cover everything that can happen in the world. Lots of times things happen that a Seduction Community concept doesn't address.

Guys can run into trouble when they unconsciously shoehorn every social situation they come across into the relatively small catalog of community ideas. As a result, they can often end up reacting to situations in a weird and socially inappropriate manner. Examples: Seeing a girl joking with you as a 'neg' or an attempt to make you lower value. Seeing every request from a girl as a test or a hoop she wants you to jump through. Seeing every joke or disagreement from guys as an attempt from them to 'out-alpha' you. Or just seeing all guys as competition and challengers of your status in general.

There are concepts from outside the Community that are useful too. Even mainstream dating or relationship advice has a lot to offer. Just

relying on the toolbox the Community provides isn't enough.
Being too down on mainstream society
At the center of its world view the Seduction Community has several beliefs that are negative towards society:
+ Society encourages guys to follow dating advice that doesn't work.
+ Society indoctrinates guys into an AFC, nice guy mindset.
+ Society gets guys to follow a model of dating that gives the advantage to women, allowing them to be spoiled and to do the choosing.
+ Society gets guys to follow a model of dating that rewards certain types of guys (good looking, rich, powerful), while screwing over others.
+ Society socially conditions guys to be afraid of things that are actually in their best interest, like being able to approach strange women.
+ Mainstream people are generally mindless, brainwashed sheep.
+ Mainstream people are unhealthy and gorge themselves on things like junk T.V. and drinking.
+ Society fears and misunderstands the Community. Even though the scene knows more about dating, the mainstream will never look upon it favorably, because that would mean giving up its hegemony over courtship.
+ Over played analogy: Society is like the Matrix, Community guys have taken the red pill and know how things really work.

I refer to my previous thoughts about how a particular point of view can be right in some regards, but inaccurate if you try to say it delivers the complete truth about something. I'd never deny society has problems, but I don't think it's this monolithic evil force out to make all guys into wussy losers either. Many people do just fine in it. I guess when I hear ideas like the ones above I think of the types of guys who would end up in the Community in the first place, and what their personal experiences of society must be like, and how well they probably feel they've done under the current system. When I mull over that question for a minute I'm not totally surprised this scene can be so down on the mainstream.

Community members can also use their disdain for the mainstream to justify some of their stranger behaviors ("It's fine that I'm doing this, I'm not plugged into the Matrix and know my actions are okay. I'm not going to be a victim of social conditioning.")

Focusing on nothing but getting women and valuing everything in terms of how it helps your game
If a guy is hopeless and desperate it isn't unreasonable for him to want to get over his issues. And I don't think there's anything inherently wrong with throwing your life out of balance temporarily. You write exams and your life is devoted to school for a few weeks. You have a baby and your

life is devoted to the newborn for half a year. But you can go too far with this. Some guys unnecessarily put their educations, social lives, or careers on hold. Going too far with anything isn't good.

When you focus on getting better with women too much you can end up judging everything based on how it helps you improve your game:

+ "Go to an art gallery? Art doesn't help my game. Oh, but maybe there will be girls to hit on there. Oh, maybe learning about art will help me hook up with artsy girls."

+ "Hang out with the guys? No, no girls there. That's not a good use of my time. Oh, but maybe I could learn some Alpha behaviors from them, so it may be worth a shot."

+ "I like hanging out with Phil because he's good with women. I don't like hanging out with Dan because he's an AFC."

+ "Read this pulpy thriller? No, it won't teach me any Inner Game concepts, so I'll pass."

+ "Should I drink? Well on one hand it will reduce my approach anxiety, but on the other, it will hinder my ability to remember my lines."

What about judging things according to different criteria, like will you have fun doing it? There's more to life than immersing yourself in learning how to be a player. The corny thing to say is that it's these extra things that you have going on in your life that are what truly makes you interesting and attractive. If you only focus on game you get odd and one dimensional.

Basing your entire identity around being a "PUA"

I'll remind you again here I never said I came up with all these criticisms myself. Guys in the Community are sometimes seen as lame and creepy by regular folk because their whole identities are based on their being players. It's all they think or talk about. Their long term goals all consist of hitting various milestones related to hooking up with girls. Some of them style themselves as Miyamoto Musashi-type characters, on a quest to "master the game."

If you get carried away with this mentality your life can get thrown pretty off-balance. It may also not be good for your mental health to have your entire identity wrapped up in how well you do with girls. If that's all your self-esteem is derived from what happens if you hit a rough patch with the ladies?

Seeing other people as tools to use toward your own improvement

I wouldn't say the Community directly encourages this per se, but I've seen it in several guys, myself included if I'm being honest. I've also heard other people complain about it. Some Community members can become so focused on their own improvement that they become selfish almost. They see other people as a means to the end of them getting better with women.

They stop considering how other people may feel in a given situation.

They'll see their guy friends as people to go out with so they don't have to hit up the bars alone, or targets to practice their AMOGing tactics on. They'll see other Community guys in the same way, people to grease the wheels of their own development. They'll see random strangers and women as subjects to practice and experiment on. They'll see other players as models to emulate, or to pump for advice. They'll be invited to a party and ignore their friend's request not to hit on the women there. They'll be selfish wingmen, or sell-out a buddy if they think it will make them look good to a girl.

Bringing a 'gaming' attitude into all your social interactions

A lot of the advice in the Community is about how to get girls through manipulating social dynamics in your favor. You choose your words. You monitor your body language. You plan everything out ahead of time and follow a repeatable formula. Ingrained in this mindset is the idea that when you're interacting with people, under the surface you have to wage all these little tactical battles, over who's "controlling the frame" or who has higher situational value. More than that, there's an attitude of finagling and beating the system, or of finding a hack.

This overall paradigm of interacting with people, that you have to 'game' others to get what you want, can take over and poison the way you get along with everyone, not just girls. You get overly calculating and Machiavellian. You think everyone is out to get you. You can't just relax and be yourself. You can't be sociable without a scheme or an agenda. You think the way to succeed in any situation is to trick and conquer people, not be the real deal.

Neil Strauss introduced the very similar idea of being a Social Robot, first in forum posts and then in his book. A social robot is someone who may be good with girls, but he's a hollow core surrounded by a shell of preplanned routines and responses, and tricks and strategies. And he thinks everyone else is a social robot too. He ends up acting much like the way I described above.

Here's an example of social robot/constant gaming thinking. Say you're on the phone with your friend and he implies he's got to go. Most people would go, "Okay, talk to you later." and think nothing more of it. A social robot's over analysis may lead him to think something like, "Oh, he's trying to lower my value and increase his own by hanging up on me and implying he has better things to do. Well I'll not answer him right away to show I'm indifferent and Alpha and make him qualify himself to me. Then the next time we talk I'll subtly put him down to reassert my dominance."

Thinking you can reduce all human interactions down to a

repeatable formula

The Social Robot concept gets into this. Other people have pointed it out too. It's the idea that it doesn't matter what you're really like as a person, or what you truly have going for you, if you have the right lines and actions memorized for every situation, you'll be able to hook up with girls. You just spit out the right words, and respond to situations as they come up with the right pre-planned solutions, and the woman becomes interested. Doesn't matter if you can't have a witty, spontaneous conversation to save your life, just repeat the lines that are shown to have predetermined effectiveness.

People usually say this type of thinking goes back to the fact that lots of guys in the Community are supposedly logical computer programmer types, and that they think, in their socially naive manner, that they can turn interpersonal interactions into an algorithm. Another popular comparison is of nerdy guys seeing conversing with women as a video game. They think they can beat the system and find an exploit, the same way they can discover how to get their characters up to level 99 before they're supposed to be. Not going to happen. Will make you seem weird. If you want to do better with the opposite sex you legitimately have to improve yourself.

Believing any of the weird ideas from particular schools of thought on how to get women

The points above covered general Seduction Community-wide counterproductive beliefs. The various methods and teachings in the scene may also contain odd or harmful assumptions. For example, one school of thought may presume women always act a certain, unflattering way. Another may expect you to adopt a certain odd attitude. They may be wrapped up in new age nonsense. Or they could prescribe that you do particular quirky behaviors.

* * *

The blogger Hugh Ristik added some cautionary thoughts when this was posted to Clarisse's blog:

In my experience, pretty much everything in this article is true. As someone with extensive experience with the seduction community, everything he talks about is familiar to me, and causes me to chuckle while reading. It's nice to see accurate and tempered criticisms of the seduction community from someone who understands it.

That being said, outsiders of the seduction community (particularly those who already have a beef with it), might get some skewed ideas about the community from this article. Chris didn't make any claims of prevalence about the attitudes he criticizes. Someone, particularly a biased reader, could walk away from this article thinking that most or all PUAs hold most or all of these attitudes. That's dubious.

The actual proportion of the seduction community who holds these attitudes depends on how you define "PUAs" and who exactly counts as a member of the seduction community. Do I count? Does my married ex-wingman count? Does Clarisse's dad who's read a David DeAngelo book count? Does Guestina — a woman posting on Clarisse's blog who has applied pickup knowledge — count? Does Chris himself count?

On Chris' old site where this article was posted, he talked more positively about the seduction community in his old articles. Specifically, he mentioned how much it had helped him, even though he felt that he has now moved past it.

* * *

***

APPENDIX B:
Towards My Personal Sex-Positive Feminist 101

This was originally posted simultaneously on Clarisse's blog and at the feminist group blog Feministe. Clarisse occasionally updates it if she thinks updates are needed, and there's an evolving list of relevant links at the end of the online versions. There are also plenty of links in the text that Clarisse didn't bother to footnote here; if you look at the online version, the links are all there. [2]

***

There's an aphorism from the early 1900s literary critic Andre Maurois: "The difficult part in an argument is not to defend one's opinion but to know it." Even though I identify as an activist and genuinely want to make a real impact on the world based on my beliefs... I often think that much of my blogging has been more an attempt to figure out what I believe, than to tell people what I believe. And sometimes, I fall into the trap of wanting to be consistent more than I want to understand what I really believe — or more than I want to empathize with other people — or more than I want to be correct. We all gotta watch out for that.

But I'm getting too philosophical here. (Who, me?) The point is, I am hesitant to write something with a title like "Sex-Positive 101," because not only does it seem arrogant (who says Clarisse Thorn gets to define Sex-Positive 101?) — it also implies that my thoughts on sex-positivity have come to a coherent, standardized end. Which they haven't! I'm still figuring things out, just like everyone else.

However, lately I've been thinking that I really want to write about some basic ideas that inform my thoughts on sex-positive feminism. I acknowledge that I am incredibly privileged (white, upper-middle-class, heteroflexible, cisgendered etc) and coming mostly from a particular community, the BDSM community; both of these factors inform and limit the principles that underpin my sex-positivity. I welcome ideas for Sex-Positive Feminism 101, links to relevant 101 resources, etc.

This got really long, and I reserve the right to edit for clarity or sensitivity.

***

Some Central Sex-Positive Feminist Ideas, according to Clarisse Thorn

1) **Desire is complicated, and people are different.** These ideas both seem basic and obvious to me as I write them, but I wanted to put them out there because I think they're useful anchors for all the rest.

2) **Gender is not a binary, and gender cannot be determined by a person's outer appearance or behavior.** Different people experience and display gender in a galaxy of ways. No woman in the world is perfectly submissive, perfectly hourglass-shaped, perfectly kind, etc, although these are stereotypes commonly associated with women. No man in the world is perfectly dominant, perfectly confident, perfectly muscular, etc. While many people reduce the idea of a person's gender to whether they have a penis or a vagina, the existence of trans people and intersex people proves that this isn't a valid approach. Individual people have all kinds of qualities that are attributed to the "other" gender... and the concept of an "other" (or "opposite") gender is weird in itself, because why does one gender have to be the "other", and what does that imply?

All this having been said, gender is frequently perceived as a binary, and many people fit themselves into the possibly-arbitrary system of gender that currently exists. There are ideas of "men" and "women" that are culturally understood, widely adopted, and socially enforced. Feminism has its roots in women resisting men's violent and social dominance, and in women resisting the cultural emphasis on stereotypical men's desires.

3) **Historically, sex has usually been defined in terms of two things: (a) reproduction, and (b) the sexual pleasure of stereotypical men.** Cultural sexual standards are based on these things. For example, the sexual "base system" (commonly discussed among USA schoolchildren) describes kissing as "first base," groping as "second base," oral sex as "third base" and penis-in-vagina sex as "home base." Why should this hierarchy exist? It only makes sense if we think of sex as being centered around reproduction. If we think of sex as being about pleasure and open exploration in ways that are different for everyone, then having a "home base" — a standardized goal — makes zero sense.

Another example: penis-in-vagina sex is often seen as "real" sex or "actual" sex, with all other sex considered "less real". How many arguments have you had over the course of your lifetime about whether oral sex "counts" as sex? (Hint: more than the subject deserves.) For a recent example, there's the Kink.com virgin shoot, wherein a porn model publicly "lost her virginity" notwithstanding the fact that she'd already had plenty of oral and anal sex on camera for years — she'd just never had vaginal sex.

As for sex being defined by the pleasure of stereotypical men: one example is how people usually think about orgasms. In my experience and that of people I talk to — and in the vast majority of porn — it seems commonly accepted that sexual activity ends with a man's orgasm, whereas women are commonly expected to continue engaging in sex after having an orgasm... despite the fact that many women seem just as tired and less-interested in sex post-orgasm as many men are. In part, this goes back to defining sex in terms of reproduction: men have to orgasm in order for reproduction to happen, so men's orgasms must (supposedly) be central to sex. It's all influenced by these other constructions, like how penis-in-vagina sex is "real" sex, or "home base": many people are confused by the idea that you'd shift sexual gears to (for example) manual stimulation if you've already "made it to home base." But it also arises from centering stereotypical men's desires — from a culture that just generally sees them as more important, more driving, and more necessary than women's. (Note that the majority of women don't achieve orgasm from penis-in-vagina sex in itself.)

When sex is defined in terms of reproduction and stereotypical male pleasure, the following things result:

+ People who aren't men have a harder time understanding their sexuality, because there are fewer models (for example: it's fairly common for women to figure out how to have orgasms much later in life than the average man — like 20s or 30s, if ever — and yes of course I've written about it)

+ Men who don't fit masculine stereotypes have a harder time understanding their sexuality (for example: there's a great essay by a former men's magazine editor in *Best Sex Writing 2010* in which he talks about how hard it was for him to come to terms with his desire for heavy women)

+ Even men who do fit masculine stereotypes feel limited from other types of exploration, and may derive less pleasure from sex than they would in a less broken world

+ Sex acts or sexual relationships that aren't reproductive are devalued, are seen as weird, or aren't even defined as sex (for example: stigma against gay sex, lesbian sex, many fetishes, etc)

4) **Women are expected to trade sex to men in exchange for support or romance.** Women who don't get a "good trade" (e.g. women

who don't receive a certain level of financial support or romance "in exchange for" sex) are seen as sluts. Men who don't get a "good trade" (e.g. men who don't receive a certain amount of sex "in exchange for" a relationship) are seen as pussies. (Yes, "pussies"... don't you just love that a word for female genitalia is a commonly used insult against so-called "weak" men?)

What this also means is that many people have trouble examining motivations outside this framework: women are always expected to be looking for more emotional or financial investment from a guy, whereas men are always expected to be looking for more (or more so-called "extreme") sex. Women who actively seek sex, or men who actively seek intimacy, are shamed and hurt and confused for it — often even within their own heads.

5) **Since stereotypical men have historically been much freer to explore their sexuality than people of other genders, the desires of stereotypical men have formed the pattern for "liberated sexuality".** As women have won freedom to act, work and explore outside the home more, we've been following patterns created mostly by men, and those patterns might look extremely different if women had created them.

When we talk about sexuality, I think that leads us to examine what "liberated sexuality" looks like. "Liberated sexuality" is often stereotyped as promiscuous, for example. "Liberated sexuality" is also stereotyped as being unromantic, never involving any of those pesky pesky feelings, etc. I write about this cautiously: I have no intention of telling anyone what "real" men do or feel, or what "real" women do or feel. However, it seems conceivable to me that most men are generally more likely to enjoy promiscuity and emotionless sex than most women are — if only for hormonal reasons. Here's a quotation from the brilliant trans man sex writer Patrick Califia on the effects of testosterone:

It's harder to track psychological and emotional changes caused by one's taking testosterone than it is to notice the physical differences. But I think the former actually outweigh the latter. It isn't that testosterone has made me a different person. I always had a high sex drive, liked porn and casual sex, couldn't imagine giving up masturbation, was able to express my anger, and showed a pretty high level of autonomy and assertiveness. But all of these things have gotten much more intense since I began hormone treatments. During the first six months on T, every appetite I had was painfully sharp. A friend of mine expressed it this way: "When I had to eat, I had to eat right fucking now. If I was horny, I had to come immediately. If I needed to shit, I couldn't wait. If I was pissed off, the words came right out of my mouth. If I was bored, I had to leave." My body and all the physical sensations that spring from it have acquired a piquancy and an immediacy that is both entertaining and occasionally inconvenient. Moving through the world is even more fun, involves more stimulation than it used to; life is more in the here-and-now, more about bodies and objects, less about thoughts and feelings.

... Casual sex has changed. When I want to get off, my priority is to find somebody who will do that as efficiently as possible, and while I certainly would rather have a pleasant interaction with that person, I don't think a lot about how they were doing before they got down on their knees, and I don't care very much how they feel after they get up and leave. It's hard to keep their needs in mind; it's easier to just assume that if they wanted anything, it was their responsibility to try to get it. I always preferred to take sexual initiative, and that has become even more ego-congruent. (pages 397-398, *Speaking Sex To Power*)

A trans woman friend once told me that not only did she get turned on more frequently pre-transition; also, she now has to feel more emotionally connected to her partner in order to enjoy sex. And she noted that she has to "take care of herself more" in order to feel turned on now — not just in the moment, but in life, and in the relationship.

If we accept that there is, speaking generally, a difference in sexual desires between men and women (although individuals will always be unique), then it leads to new questions. If women were socially and culturally dominant, what would so-called "liberated sexuality" look like? If people of all genders are following patterns set by stereotypical men, then what does that mean for attempts to think around those patterns?

6) Communicating consent is complicated, but consent is the only thing that makes sex okay, so we have to make every effort to respect it. All sex is completely fine with me as long as it's consensual. Seriously, I really don't care what you do — as long as it's consensual. (Try to find a consensual sex act that shocks me. I dare you.)

Communicating consent can, however, be complicated, and there are lots of different ways to do it. Many BDSMers are eminently familiar with this, as you can tell by the fact that some parts of the BDSM community have developed an extensive array of tactics for discussing consent.

Most people don't communicate directly about most things, and the stigma and high emotions around sexuality make it even harder for most people to communicate directly about sex. Hence, most sexual communication is highly indirect. Even among people who are accustomed to direct sexual communication — like many BDSMers — a lot of communication ends up being indirect and instinctive anyway; there's just no way to discuss every possible reaction and every single desire ahead of time. Everyone fucks up sometimes. No one in the world has a perfect track record on creating a pressure-free environment for their partners to express what they want... or asking their partners for what they want... or even knowing what they want in the first place.

So, yes, I acknowledge that communicating about sex and getting what you want consensually can be really hard. However, it's most important to not violate people's boundaries. No matter how hard it is, it's necessary to make a serious and genuine effort to measure and respect a partner's consent every time sex happens. Feminist ideas of enthusiastic consent are designed to help this process.

(Here's my attempt at a quick definition of enthusiastic consent:

The basic idea is simple: don't initiate sex unless you have your partner's enthusiastic consent. Not a partner who says, "Okay, I guess," in a bored tone, but doesn't actively say "no". Not a partner who is silent and non-reactive, but doesn't actively stop you when you start having sex with them. Not a partner who seems hesitant, or anxious, or confused. Enthusiastic consent means an enthusiastic partner: one who is responding passionately, kissing you back, saying things like "Yes" or "Oh my God, don't stop"... or a partner who talks to you ahead of time about what will happen, as many BDSMers and sex workers do, and knows how to safeword or otherwise get out of the situation if you do something they don't like.)

It's worth noting that there are critiques within feminism of the concept of enthusiastic consent. For example, some feminist sex workers point out that when they have sex for money, their consent is not exactly "enthusiastic," but they still feel that their consent is real consent, and that their choices must be respected. The same goes for some asexual people. Asexuality is commonly defined as "not feeling sexual attraction to others," but some asexual people have romantic relationships with other people in which they have sex entirely to satisfy their partner, and some of them have said that they don't feel included by feminist discussions of enthusiastic consent.

Hey, even some of my non-asexual, non-sex worker friends have problems with the idea that they aren't "really" consenting unless they're super-enthusiastic about the sexual act at hand. A married friend once commented wryly that if she and her husband always demanded 100% enthusiastic consent from each other, then the marriage would fall apart. But as we continued to discuss it, she and her husband both agreed that they have zero problem with the situation as it stands.

I don't want to sweep those critiques under the rug. I figure that as long as everyone's communicating about the situation openly, and working to keep things relatively low-pressure, then consent is likely to happen, even if it's not perfectly "enthusiastic." I've had extensive debates on the topic with other feminists, though, and I often seek more, because honing consent theory is one of my favorite things!

All this having been said: the concept of enthusiastic consent has been very helpful for me personally. I know that it's also been helpful for an enormous number of other people who are trying to understand boundaries in their sexual relationships. I absolutely believe that enthusiastic consent is an important and useful standard, and I do my best to observe that standard as much as I can in my own relationships. So, while I think some critiques are reasonable, I also think that the idea of enthusiastic consent is the best baseline assumption to start these conversations... if not to end them.

7) **In practice, as long as everyone involved is having consensual fun, criticism is secondary.** Practically speaking, consent is the most important thing; from a pragmatic standpoint, the question of whether sexuality arises from biology or culture doesn't matter nearly as much. (I find the question of whether BDSM can be categorized as a sexual orientation to be more politically and theoretically interesting than practically important.)

Understanding sexual biology or culture may help us grasp some of the complexities of consent. For example, people often have trouble saying "no" to things directly: when was the last time you explicitly said "no" when you didn't want to do something? Which of the following exchanges is more likely:

Person A: Hey, want to come over tonight?
Person B: You know, I'd love to, but I'm so exhausted from work, I really need to get some sleep.
or
Person A: Hey, want to come over tonight?
Person B: No.

People of all genders really don't like saying "no" to things directly. Grasping this important cultural concept is one step on the path of learning how to communicate effectively about consent. But in my book, it's really not as important to understand why people hate saying "no" directly, as it is to understand that people hate saying "no" directly. It's necessary to understand that because it means that very often, pushing someone until they say "no" can mean pushing them further than they wanted to go.

I believe that the most important role of social criticism — including sex-positive feminism — is not to tell people what to do. If you have sex that appears to be in line with ridiculous and oppressive stereotypes, I really do not care as long as everyone involved is consenting and having fun. I reserve the right to occasionally have consensual sex where a gentleman friend beats me up before fucking me, and I reserve the right to enjoy it.

But I want to offer sex-positive feminist analyses in order to help people understand themselves and their desires... and also understand their partners and their desires. I think that many people have sex they don't like, sex that's in line with ridiculous and oppressive stereotypes, because they haven't been exposed to anything they like better. I think many people have sex they don't like because they don't feel like they can look for something different — they think it's the best they can get. I think many people have sex they don't like because they think it's what their partner wants — and I think those people are frequently wrong, and I think most partners would genuinely prefer that everyone be having fun.

Which is why I try to deconstruct sexual norms and stereotypes. Which is why I encourage people to look for what they like. Which is why I always emphasize talking about it.

8) **Awesome, respectful, joyful, mutual sex means approaching sex as collaborative rather than adversarial.** Aside from solo sex (i.e. masturbation), sex always involves another person. And at its best, it's about having a good time with other people — understanding their reality, accepting it, playing with it. The best metaphors I've ever heard for sex were all about collaborative art, like a musical jam performance. Here's a bit from Thomas MacAulay Millar's totally brilliant essay "Towards a Performance Model of Sex" (please do read the whole thing someday):

The negotiation is the creative process of building something from a set of available elements. Musicians have to choose, explicitly or implicitly, what they are going to play: genre, song, key and interpretation. The palette available to them is their entire skill set — all the instruments they have and know how to play, their entire repertoire, their imagination and their skills — and the product will depend on the pieces each individual brings to the performance. Two musicians steeped in Delta blues will produce very different music from one musician with a love for soul and funk and another with roots in hip-hop or 1980s hardcore. This process involves communication of likes and dislikes and preferences, not a series of proposals that meet with acceptance or rejection.

... Under this model, the sexual interaction should be creative, positive, and respectful even in the most casual of circumstances.

("Towards a Performance Model of Sex" was first printed in *Yes Means Yes*, the brilliant sex-positive anti-rape anthology that I want everyone in the entire world to read. It was also reprinted in *Best Sex*

Writing 2010.)

9) **All people deserve equal rights, including sexual minorities.** As long as people are having consensual sex, they do not deserve to be stigmatized, harassed, or otherwise harmed for their sexuality. Period. No one should be fired for their sexual or gender identity. No one should have their kids taken away for their sexual or gender identity. Rape is still rape, even when it's perpetrated against a sex worker. I support decriminalizing sex work for a lot of reasons; for example, I'd love it if the law would quit harassing and jailing sex workers for having consensual sex, and I'd love it if sex workers could organize for better workplace safety. The bottom line is that people — all people — have rights. It's time to treat them that way.

* * *

In terms of actual ways to be sex-positive in everyday life, here are the three ways I usually encourage people to spread the sex-positive love:

A) **Avoid re-centering.** Sexuality shouldn't be societally "centered" on any particular norm, idea, or stereotype (except consent). It is frequently tempting to re-center "objective" ideas about sexuality onto ourselves, if we're different from the norm, or onto people we admire. But the truth is that — on a societal level — queer sex is just as awesome as straight sex; that BDSM sex is equally admirable as vanilla sex; that cisgendered people are not any more or less amazing than trans people. The decision to have sex is no better than the decision to avoid sex, and asexual people are just as great as hypersexual people who are just as great as anyone with any level of sex drive.

In alternative sexuality subcultures, one often encounters a kind of superior attitude, perhaps because we have to push back so hard against the norm. In polyamory, for example, some of us use the sarcastic term "polyvangelist": a person who insists that polyamory is "better" or "more evolved" or "makes more sense" for everyone, everywhere, than monogamy does. Neither monogamy nor polyamory is better than the other; they're just different. Polyvangelists are trying to re-center onto polyamory. Not cool.

B) **Start conversations.** One of the most damaging problems around sexuality is the overwhelming and constant stigma. It hurts people with certain sexual identities, preferences or pasts. It hurts them spiritually. It can hurt them societally, like when LGBTQ folks have difficulty adopting children, or former sex workers are not allowed to work at other jobs. It can even hurt them physically: 40 years after doctors started noticing the HIV pandemic, too many people are still refusing to talk about sex openly, or give healthcare to sexual minorities directly affected by HIV. To say nothing of people who are attacked or killed for their sexual minority status. Sexual stigma kills.

So when someone says something icky about sex and gender, or stereotypes a certain sex or gender identity, it's so great to challenge them — or at least to question them. ("Really? What makes you think all gay people are abuse survivors?") And some of the most powerful sex activism out there involves starting discussion groups, creating venues for discussion, hosting sexuality speakers or sex-related art, etc.

C) **Be "out" or open, without being invasive.** This can be tricky, because I don't want to encourage people to aggressively talk about sex at totally inappropriate times — and again, I'm against re-centering. On the other hand, the most powerful tool for destigmatizing sexuality appears to be coming out of the closet — whether a person is queer, BDSM, or whatever. Openly acknowledging, owning, and discussing your sexual preferences can help others respect those preferences — and can help others who share those preferences respect themselves. (Can you tell that I cried when I saw the movie *Milk?*)

* * *

***

APPENDIX C:
Mark Manson's PUA Taxonomy

***

I honestly don't even know where to start with a taxonomy. In my eyes, the industry is way too varied and complex. But if I had to start, here are some spectrums of beliefs/behavior I would look at as being fundamental among coaches/gurus:

1. WOMAN LOVERS VS. WOMAN HATERS — On one end, you have guys like Zan, Hypnotica, David Deida — men who glorify almost to the point of worship the feminine "essence" (whatever that is), and encourage men to seek it, enjoy it and revel in it. Despite buying into gender stereotypes, these guys see women as something to be enjoyed, respected, loved and reveled in. The haters are the misogynists. Roissy, Roosh, David X, etc. Notice both ends of this spectrum buy into gender stereotypes: one side just worships the feminine stereotype and the other hates it and seeks to exploit it.

2. OBJECTIFICATION VS. CONNECTION — On one end, the objectifiers see pickup artistry as a means to an end, and are willing to justify just about any behavior in order to get there. These are the guys who are willing to lie about their jobs or make up stories to get laid, or to push boundaries without any actual concern for the woman. Connectors are more concerned about forming and finding genuine emotional connections and compatibilities with women. A popular example of an objectifier would be Mystery himself. A popular example of a connector would be someone like Juggler.

3. MARKETER VS. PIMP — To become a successful coach/guru in the men's dating industry, you need to have at least one of two things: marketing savvy, or street cred. The guys with street cred are the guys who became popular purely from their exploits, by going out and getting laid constantly and doing it in such a way that other people noticed and wanted to start paying them. A good example is BradP. The marketers, on the other hand, got to where they are purely through excellent business tactics; they have little interest in credibility, and often don't have any. A perfect example here is John Alanis — a guy I'm sure you have never heard of,

who never posts on forums, but who makes more money than the two biggest PUA companies combined.

That's if you want to focus on gurus. If you want to focus on the community at large, the guys who actually read and use this stuff, well it's not nearly as exciting as you think. Marketing research (my own, and others') has shown repeatedly that for every guy posting on a forum, bragging about his exploits, or trying to memorize some guru's routines, there are 5-6 guys out there who are just reading casually and have very basic and humble goals.

I find doing a student taxonomy to be much simpler. Probably because I work with them daily, and have for years. But there are some pretty major and clear patterns:

1. VIRGINS — Usually 25 and under, but not always. These are the guys who are the last of their friends to lose their virginity and they're starting to get desperate and to seriously wonder if something is wrong with them. As a result, they're willing to try just about anything. More often than not, once they lose their virginity and get their first girlfriend, you never hear from them again. They're about 25% of the people who look into this.

2. YOUNG PROFESSIONALS — These are the overachievers. The guys who studied their asses off in college, got a good job and then started working 80-hour weeks to climb the career ladder. Typically in the 28-35 age range, these guys suddenly hit a point where they've become very successful professionally, but they look around and realize that all of their friends are married and that they haven't had time for a girlfriend in over three years. These guys usually improve quickly. Sometimes they sleep around for fun, but usually not. Again, once they get a girlfriend you never hear from them again. They're another 25% of the people who look into this.

3. DIVORCED MEN — Older men, usually 35+, fresh out of a divorce. They haven't been single in at least 10 years, and are terrified of it. Often (but not always) they got hosed by their ex in court and are a bit of an emotional wreck. Usually, for these guys, it's just about getting them back on their feet. More often than not, once they find a new girlfriend they like, you never hear from them again (notice a theme here). They're another 25%.

4. SELF-HELP JUNKIES AND RANDOM INTELLECTUALS — Read pickup materials mostly out of fascination. Whether horrified by it or intrigued by it (or both), they read it and follow it and think about it as some sort of hobby. They rarely put it to use, or if they do, they don't do it often. I think you, Clarisse, would fall under this one. Generally, these

people read recreationally and you never really hear from them at all. Typically, they're too smart to buy into all of the BS or don't get involved in the "community aspect" at all. Eventually they disappear. They're about 15%.

5. HARDCORE PUAs — These are the guys posting on forums, attending conferences, breaking down theories, arguing which guru is better, and becoming coaches. This is the vocal minority. If a guy ends up here, it's usually for one of a few reasons, none of which are good: 1) he's got some major emotional baggage with women, and obsessing about and fucking every single one of them is his way of processing and working through it (this was me, by the way); 2) he's got extremely low emotional intelligence, and for the first time in his life he's found a community that rewards his ability to objectify and behave strangely around others; or 3) he's got some sort of psychological disorder, whether it's a mild form of autism, Asperger's, Antisocial Personality Disorder, or whatever, and PUA is a useful intellectual way for him to understand and practice social interaction without being forced to connect with others on an emotional level. Most of these guys, once they get sucked in, they stay in for the long haul. It's hard for them to tear themselves away. This is the vocal minority. And the reason I don't go to PUA conferences anymore. They're 10%.

* * *

* * *

APPENDIX D:
Interview with Neil Strauss

Clarisse interviewed Neil Strauss in March 2011, then published the following article on the website for Time Out Chicago. *There are plenty of links in the text that Clarisse didn't bother to footnote here; if you look at the online version, the links are all there. [3]*

* * *

I'm extremely obsessed with pickup artists. I admit this freely. My obsession may or may not have reached fetish proportions; I can't tell anymore. This has been going on for years, but eventually I plan to write an article called "Confessions of a Pickup Artist Chaser: Long Interviews With Hideous Men". I am not lying. (If you're willing to publish it, call me.)

At this point, most people have heard about the pickup artist subculture; the primary reason for that is the 2005 bestseller *The Game,* written by rock 'n' roll writer Neil Strauss. Strauss chronicled his meteoric rise from a shy, lonely guy who could barely speak to women, to one of the world's most famous pickup artists. In the process, he pulled back the curtain on a community that until then had been largely underground.

It's hard to describe the community briefly, but briefly: it's a group of guys trading advice on how to pick up women, often selling tutorials on how to do so or beating their chests in classic (sometimes assholish) masculinity displays. On one end of the personality spectrum are super-shy guys, like how Strauss paints his former self: men whose extreme social anxiety leads them to seek advice for basic stuff, like having a conversation with an unfamiliar girl. On the other end of the spectrum are terrifying misogynists who I wouldn't want to meet in a dark alley — or, you know, ever. And there's not always a clean or obvious division.

My feeling is that there's good advice in the community for genuinely kind shy guys. But sometimes, it's so mixed with misogyny and cold-heartedness that wading through it can feel like panning for gold in a sewer. (And because some ethical guys are so desperate for advice that they'll wade through that, I've often thought that it could be good for feminists of all genders to try and develop our own pickup curriculum. Since there aren't yet any actively feminist pickup curricula, I've tried making a list of the least misogynist.)

Compared to many feminists, my stance on this community is positive. But honestly, I sympathize with feminist anti-pickup rage — sometimes I, too, pull back from my relatively positive stance. One such moment came at the beginning of this year, when famous pickup guru Gunwitch (who was briefly mentioned in *The Game)* actually shot a woman in the face. This occasioned much feminist discussion (a post I wrote on a feminist blog drew 322 comments), and some feminists drew parallels to the alarming 2009 murderer George Sodini, who was a passionate adherent to many pickup ideas as well.

After the Gunwitch shooting, I had to take some time off and remind myself that, in fact, I've talked to many pickup artists who specifically work not to be misogynist. There are even occasional pickup artists who actively seek to engage feminism; I don't always agree with them, but I give them points for seeking an ethical and gender-liberationist conversation about these dating tactics. Neil Strauss himself included a number of feminist quotations in *The Game*. (Which isn't to say that *The Game* gets a free pass from feminist analysis. Some of the tactics in there make my skin crawl.)

Strauss recently released a new book, *Everyone Loves You When You're Dead*. To write it, he went through his two decades of celebrity interviews to find moments of intimacy and truth. The thought of talking to such an accomplished interviewer was intimidating, but when the legendary pickup artist came through Chicago on promotional tour, I just had to request an interview.

Girls get social anxiety too. I was so nervous on my way there, I almost turned the wrong way down a one-way street and had to perform an incredibly dangerous u-turn in a busy intersection. By the time I made it to the Book Cellar, where Strauss was answering questions and signing books, the place was like a mosh pit. It was so full that I couldn't get in the door. I had to stand gazing through a crack as Neil Strauss, wearing an awesome sparkly purple tie and an engaging smile, chatted with his fans. The vast majority were male; almost all the questions were not about his latest book, but about *The Game.*

Notwithstanding the overt discussion of game, Strauss totally charmed me. He seems unconscious of his fame; he comes across as humble, kind, and genuinely curious about other people. He has friendly personal conversations with his fans, and freely admits it when he doesn't know what he's talking about. When we finally sat down to chat, he was totally chill about the fact that most of my questions weren't even about his latest book....

Clarisse Thorn: It seems like authenticity preoccupies you. I've heard your new book *Everyone Loves You When You're Dead* **is essentially a meditation on authenticity, is that right?**

Neil Strauss: The new book is like... I wanted to understand these people, who they are, where they come from, what made them, what drives them. Authenticity is the starting point, and then you start digging from that. First you have to wipe away the mask and the bullshit and the deceit and the self-deceit, and then you get to start.

In the book, for example, if you look at my Howard Stern interview for *Rolling Stone,* the first thing is you don't want his radio persona; you make sure he's giving you the persona his friends and his wife know.

What I'm trying to find out changes depending on where I am in my life. The interviews, to me, were as much about them as to answer questions for myself. So now I'm interested in intimacy, so I'm exploring intimacy in my interviews more. Even though it's really supposed to be about them, I'll ask whatever I'm naturally curious about. It's kind of a covert autobiography.

CT: I've personally been interested in how authenticity comes up in *The Game.* **It seems like a theme in the background; it's not overt.**

NS: We also call it congruence: when who you are on the outside matches who you are on the inside. I think one of the many misconceptions about *The Game* is somehow that guys are being taught to be fake — I know I'm more real and more honest than I ever was before *The Game,* when I was too shy to really express myself.

People go through a process of not being themselves. It's part of the journey. Through anything you have to struggle and get dirty in the mud and get to the other side and become yourself, and that's part of the process.

CT: This reminds me of pickup artist discussions around "inner game", where pickup artists try to develop personally by exploring themselves and their values and their life goals. I'm fascinated by the concept of inner game, because it's giving someone an opportunity to develop themselves, but it's doing it through the lens of pickup.

NS: What helps one's inner game, too, is just having some success: success breeds confidence, which helps your inner game.

To me there were two routes for *The Game.* One of them is that it becomes a funny blip on the pop-culture map where guys are wearing funny hats and coats and doing magic tricks. Or it becomes the beginning of a men's self-help movement — because self-help isn't emasculating anymore if you're doing it to get laid.

After getting into pickup, all of a sudden a lot of guys become more spiritual and do things they would never otherwise do. It's kind of ironic — I was just remembering the other day that before I did *The Game*, I made fun of a men's New Age group in a Beck video I was in. Then, a few years later, I'm kind of at the center of a men's support group.

CT: Yeah, speaking of emasculation... the reason I got into looking at pickup stuff was that I was thinking about masculinity, and the issues that men have with trying to be masculine and match up to those standards.

NS: My next-to-last book *Emergency* is about masculinity as well — the other side of masculinity. Being able to build a house and build a fire, protect yourself. One side is to be successful with women, and the other is to be a man and take care of things.

CT: I heard that recently you've been thinking of training women to be good with men. Can I ask how you might advise a woman to have good game? What kind of advice would you give her for picking up men, and what kind of relationship advice would you give?

NS: My main thing would be a deeper goal, which is to realize how many choices a woman might make based on low self-esteem. I think that there is some degree to which you can help women be more successful with guys. The real simple thing is that guys are attracted by sexual possibility; that doesn't mean you have to have sex with them, but guys are initially attracted by the possibility of sex. So you can be a really beautiful person, but if you're really uptight you'll be less attractive.

But the bigger choice is looking at what makes a woman sleep with a guy, looking at who she chooses to do that with, and seeing how much is based on a real connection with someone she wants to sleep with, and how much is based on self-esteem, whether it's being competitive with other women or — there are certain women hung up on guys, and they're only hung up on him because he didn't call. She fooled around with him a little bit, and he didn't call afterwards or was rude afterwards, and she wants that self-esteem back, so she's hung up on this guy.

It's a self-esteem thing. It's a different kind of self-esteem project with men.

Another thing that kills me about some women is that you should judge someone by their actions, not their words. I'll be like "Look, he did this," and she'll be like "But he said this."

CT: Don't you feel like guys do that too?

NS: Not as much as women.

I'm not an expert, but as far as relationships go, I do know this: in general, let a guy be a guy. A lot of women, not all of them, a lot of them feel insecure about men being men. Men get nervous about showing sexual interest, his full sexual side, because men's sexuality is seen as threatening. Also, a lot of women start trying to control a guy's freedom. I think you should give somebody their freedom anyway, but also, if you do that then you can find out by their behavior whether they're good for you or not.

CT: I noticed that you included a lot of feminist quotations in *The Game*, like Gloria Steinem and Jenny Holzer. Could you talk more about that?

NS: I felt like the main problem with the book, as I was putting it together, was that it needed more female characters. I couldn't invent another female character because there weren't any women giving advice in the community. So I thought, why don't I put in a female voice through these quotes.

Your intention for a book is never the same as the reception. You know the Simone de Beauvoir book *The Second Sex?* I wanted to do the equivalent for male sexuality. On some levels male sexuality is everywhere in society, but on the other hand it's completely repressed: men are afraid to show it because it will make them socially unacceptable as well as less sexually desirable. I wanted to write something that was honest about male sexuality, not like *Maxim* magazine or the billboards. *The Second Sex* is obviously a different book and much more philosophical than *The Game*, but my goal really was to do something like that.

CT: So how do you feel about feminism?

NS: I'm definitely not an expert, but it's splintered into so many things that I can barely define feminism. There can be people who are feminist, and people who hold the completely opposite view but are still feminists. It seems to me from the outside that there's a lot of people busy fighting each other rather than working toward their goals. It's a shame. Maybe you can tell me what feminism is.

CT: I think feminism is focused on providing positive choices and encouraging respect for women, but it's different things to different people. I'm on the sex-positive end of the spectrum, with a lot of focus on sexual freedom.

NS: Right, so there's sex-positive and then there's Catherine MacKinnon. Is Jenna Jameson a feminist? Is Catherine MacKinnon a feminist? I don't know.

CT: A lot of pickup artists talk about how much they hate feminism.

NS: Here's the deal. Anyone who hates something feels threatened by it. A guy who says he hates feminism (a) doesn't understand or know feminism, and (b) is scared of powerful women. Most attacks come from fear.

CT: You heard about the Gunwitch shooting earlier this year, right? How did you feel about that?

NS: I felt just devastated for the girl and her family. It was horrible.

He was an unstable individual. If you look in *The Game,* he's only mentioned as an extreme element — I mean, his philosophy was "make the ho say no". I'm surprised it took this long for someone in the community to do something that stupid, but I would never have guessed it would be something that violent.

CT: A lot of feminists came down on the community especially after Gunwitch shot that woman.

NS: That's like when a politician does something bad and people say all politicians are bad.

I think a lot of people say stuff about *The Game* who have never read *The Game.* Some people feel threatened by it. But when women have problems with the movement, I do understand. We still are a patriarchal society, as you know — men are dominant, and when the dominant group bands together, that's a threatening thing. So, to me, I can see that element of why it's threatening.

I understand, but I also think people should explore why they feel threatened and why they feel angry. All my books have been based on my fears. *The Game* was based on my fears of social and sexual rejection, and *Emergency* was based on my fears of what's going on in the world. *Everyone Loves You When You're Dead* is based on the idea that people are threatened by other people, so they shit talk people they see as competition.

CT: If you were to critique any one thing about the community, what would it be?

NS: My big critique is that while once the community was a free flow of ideas, and — I'm partly to blame for this, with *The Game* and everything — now it's been commercialized. If I got into the community now I wouldn't know what to do. It's splintered into these niche markets — a guy gets in, he's like, "What do I do? I only have so much money to spend." You have all these guys saying there's only one kind of game, and it kills me, because the game is all those things.

I think that show *The Pick-Up Artist* was good, but a long-term effect was to confuse the game with the surface elements. Wearing the feather boa and the fuzzy hat and the magic tricks isn't the game. But, that said, the game is about standing out from the average generic guy, and being unique and more interesting, but in a non-needy, non-desperate-for-attention way. The surface elements can change, but the deep principles are the same. It's about the social rules by which people operate.

CT: How do you feel you've developed during your journey from *The Game* to here?

NS: Bob Dylan said, "I'm never arriving, I'm always becoming." At these signings, people ask me what's it like to be perfect, and I'm like, "I'm not perfect!" I always tell them I'm not. I'm just a guy, I'm still on the path. I do feel like the insecurities I had about women have been cured and solved; it was like a two-year college for my social skills. I feel like I'm in a comfortable place; I've had adventures beyond what I thought was possible. But I know I have other challenges ahead of me.

My own little thing is, I've always tried to be honest, with no fear. With *The Game,* I thought about doing it under another name, because I was so scared of the reception. But I think it really worked because it was honest. I try to continue to do that.

* * *

APPENDIX E:
Brian's Kiss-Close Routine

After Clarisse met the goth-feminist-S&M PUA Brian for drinks, he dropped her off and she kissed him on the cheek. Later, when they were deconstructing their interactions together, he wrote her the following.

* * *

Actually, that kiss close pretty much is a routine, and it's one I'm very proud of. Here's how it works:

1. Hug goodnight. If she lingers in the hug, or lingers near me after it ends, proceed, else abort...

2. Point to cheek, and say "kiss goodbye?" or "kiss goodnight"? The more doubt I have about her interest, the more the phrasing sounds like a question. The more confident I am, the more it sounds like an order, but a light order. Yet in this circumstance, the order is really an implied question (like, "hey, come over to my house..." is a request), because she still has to take action herself. If I feel very confident of her interest (e.g. we have kissed before, or she has given me an SOI) then I might skip straight to pointing to my lips in the last step.

3. If she doesn't want to kiss, abort. If she says something in response that's not flirtatious, abort. If she does kiss, observe how she kisses. This will give a massive amount of information, if I have any doubt about her attraction or interest in acting on it. There are several main possibilities: (a) she kisses, but it's a quick friendly kiss, after which she pulls back, (b) she gives a sexual kiss, but pulls back, (c) she gives a sexual kiss, and stays in. If (a), say goodnight in a non-flirtatious way that ideally communicates that you got the signal that things are just friends. If (b), say goodnight in a flirtatious way. If (c), then continue.

4. Now it's time to take things to the next level. Depending on how she kissed my cheek, and how close she stayed in, I will either kiss her cheek, or initiate a kiss on the lips.

5. If I have doubt about interest in a kiss on the lips, I will kiss her cheek next, and see how she responds. I might preface kissing her cheek by saying "my turn" and watching her face for any discomfort. If I see any

discomfort or feeling her pulling away from the embrace, then abort.

6. If she has responded well to everything so far, then it's time for a kiss on the lips. Depending on the level of chemistry and any doubts I have, I would either point to my lips, or I would just move in for the kiss (while watching to make sure she is also moving in for it, and not away).

I like this routine because I think it covers my bases for many types of female responses. It has a great balance between asking for consent, but also confidence and flirtatiousness. It's also a yes-ladder, and someone responding to where I point is a powerful frame, but that's not the conscious reason I formulated it; my conscious motivation for the progressive steps was mutual confirmation of desire.

Here are the main potential responses I anticipate:

1. She isn't attracted to me, and doesn't want to kiss. That's no big deal; she will probably find my invitation innoffensive and easy to refuse.

2. She isn't enthusiastic about kissing, but does so out of people-pleasing. Since the request for a kiss on the cheek is so minor, it might be harder to refuse. First, I try to catch this in the hug stage. If she is lingering in the hug, then she is probably attracted to me. Of course, that doesn't mean she is ready to kiss me. She would only pass this screen without being attracted if she is very touchy-feely. Then even if she goes along with kissing my cheek, it's easy for her to pull away after, and she can just give me a peck, which tells me what I need to know. That should be the limit to potential issues with people-pleasing.

3. She is attracted and wants to kiss, but prefers men to ask explicitly. I asked, so we are good. I think the danger of this sort of woman finding my approach too presumptuous is low.

4. She is attracted and wants to kiss, but only likes men to ask explicitly if they are confident about it. I asked, and the pointing plus slight command tonality should cover the bases for confidence. After all, if I wasn't feeling confident, then it would hardly be necessary to point to the right place to kiss.

5. She is attracted and wants to kiss, but generally finds men asking to be wimpy. My approach won't be optimal, but I will still probably succeed, because the way I'm asking and pointing also has an element of a command, and it displays confidence. If I suspect a woman has this sort of preference, then I would use more of a command tonality. I am masking a request as a command, so that I am still making a request, but I'm not matching the pattern of the sort of wimpy request that she finds unattractive.

* * *

***

APPENDIX F:
The Much-Delayed Playette FAQ

This was written by Hitori, a lady who has posted a lot on PUA fora. Clarisse first mentioned Hitori while discussing emotional hookpoint during emotional escalation.

***

Q. HOW DO I GET HIM TO BE MY BOYFRIEND?

A. You are asking the wrong question. To start with, any dude who you get involved with will either be open to the possibility of a relationship on some level — or not. **You cannot control this.** Game affects how someone **reacts emotionally** to you, not their goals/values/personality.

That said, you can get a guy to be your boyfriend by:

1) Finding a dude who is at least marginally open to the possibility of the kind of relationship you want, and

2) Gaming him right

I will add, at this juncture, that if you game a dude right who is not open to the idea of a formal relationship, you can often still end up with a de-facto boyfriend — a relationship in all but name/rules/exclusivity. In fact, I'll say this now because it's important: the **practical reality** of your situation, i.e. **what you see in front of you**, matters much more to your **results** than any 'official designation' of relationship status.

All of this, however, begs the question:

Q. WHAT DOES IT MEAN TO GAME A DUDE RIGHT?

A. This isn't a 'system', but there are some ingredients that my experience **repeatedly** and **strongly** suggests make for "good" (effective, fun) game. This will be a STRATEGIC overview of the things you want to be looking out for.

1) He should be at emotional hookpoint before you sleep with him.

FORGET about making him agree to a relationship before you sleep with him. FORGET about establishing that you are "special" and "different" before you sleep with him through some sort of arbitrary ritual behavior like having him tell you so, or waiting three dates.

Do not bother trying to get him to appease your insecurity by asking him if he is like this with all the girls.

To the extent that you feel insecure, appease your OWN insecurity by doing what you can to be sure he's hit emotional hookpoint before you sleep with him. What do I mean by emotional hookpoint?

Emotional hookpoint is the intense, emotional, gut-level kind of attraction that most people think is required for a girl to spontaneously decide to fuck a guy. Guys feel this too — they just don't (usually) require it for sex. When guys are at emotional hookpoint, just like a girl in the same situation, they want to spend time around the person they're attracted to and have her think well of them and pay attention to them. EVEN IF THEY ARE PLAYERS. This as opposed to **physical** hookpoint, the quicker blink-fast assessment of whether a girl is doable.

Under the right circumstances, emotional hookpoint can happen very, very fast. It is important to be able to identify it when you see it, because as soon as you have it you've satisfied the first prerequisite for a solid close.

If you haven't hit emotional hookpoint it yet AND YOU WANT IT, don't put yourself in a situation where sex can happen and then refuse to have sex — just try to keep subtle control of logistics such that the rate at which you approach a possible hookup roughly corresponds to the rate at which his emotional attraction is growing. If you can't think of a smooth, natural way to delay isolation until you've hit hookpoint, then you have to weigh your options and make a quick decision: would you rather bail on the interaction, or go for it and risk the possibility that you won't hit hookpoint at all? I'd like to stress gently, here, that no matter **what** there are no guarantees. Some guys can hit hookpoint after sex. Some will immediately before. And some, no matter how long you have with them, never will. In either case, a smooth interaction is key — smoothly bail, or smoothly go with it. In general, I would avoid any kind of 'status of the hookup' talk or obviously artificial speedbump.

Emotional hookpoint can happen very, very fast. I've gotten this kind of attraction in a matter of minutes from dudes and — while I wouldn't act on it that fast — I have every reason to believe based on my other experiences that this could be a totally solid close. Usually once you give a dude the idea (see below) and the chance, it's a matter of hours.

If you don't care about whether you hook up with the same dude again or get a "solid" close, you don't need to worry about whether you have hit emotional hookpoint. This is purely contingent on your goals.

2) When it comes to first hookup, he needs to think it was his own idea

This will be in DIRECT contrast with much of the advice that you'll read (specifically, from MEN) about how to hook up with guys.

Do not go in direct.

I'll say it again: Do. Not. Go. In. Direct.

For sweet merciful Christ only knows what fucking reason, a close is not a solid close unless the guy feels (on some seemingly subconscious, half-submerged level) that it was his own idea. In my experience this even applies to guys who **know** better and can **tell** when you are down to fuck. You STILL should not aggressively initiate with them for the first-time hookup. After that, do what you want, but the first time he has to think it's his own damn idea.

This presents certain obvious challenges.

The most important tool in your arsenal, sad as it is to say this, will probably be what I think of as the "Whiff," as in "a whiff of pussy." In PUA terms this is more than an IOI, but less than an SOI.

The whiff: while you're talking, drop in some sexual content that DOES NOT REFERENCE him directly at all, but presents you as a sexual person. It can involve shit you like to wear, fantasies you have, your EFA, funny stories from your past... Whatever. Hell, it can be physical — things that you're wearing.

An example I KNOW I've given on this forum before: "So I was shopping, and lately I've been really into buying brightly colored panties because, you know, I wear all black all the time... And I guess it makes me feel like I have a **secret**."

Another actual example:

Him: I admit when I started dating my current girlfriend, I was kinda baffled as to what I could help her out with... Because she doesn't even own a computer! I'm used to meeting girls by making myself useful.

Me: You meet girls through work, eh?

Him: Busted, I'm bad. I think I met the last three girls I dated before her through work...

Me: Shame on you! Sleeping with clients! Tsk, tsk.

Him: Well, I didn't sleep with all of them... Some of them I just dated.

Me: See, I don't get that — dating without sex. I mean, to me, if I'm going to spend all that time listening to a boy talk... He might as well make himself useful, you know what I'm saying?

Him: Exactly!

In short, you want **sexually charged conversation** without any kind of implied intent. After you whiff enough times (and the required number varies drastically between guys, from "1" to "Am I gonna need to get you a map and a flashlight so you can find your dick already?") some switch in his brain will flip and he will go from thinking of you as abstractly fuckable ("I WOULD hit it...") to an actual prospect ("I COULD hit it...")

If you're any good at people, you can sometimes identify the exact second when this happens... Which is cool.

Sometimes, particularly if a dude is used to being able to get sex, this switch will flip before you ever even open your mouth. Other times, you can flip this switch even if you are normally the type of girl a dude wouldn't even consider (for example, and from experience, if you are not asian and your dude is ordinarily a rice-chaser).

3) Appropriate Sexual Tension Management

If there is any important personality factor you should be able to gauge about a dude to effectively game him, I would say the ABSOLUTE TOP OF THE LIST is what I think of as his "tension orientation."

If you take relationships and sex down to their simplest level, they really just have two ingredients:

1. Tension
2. Release

The satisfaction people get from sex, beyond the simple physical pleasure of it, comes from releasing tension.

Many guys, most typically guys who don't feel like they can get sex whenever they want... Are used to **sexual tension** without **sexual release**. If they think they can release sexual tension with you (read: get laid/get affirmation that you WILL or WOULD sleep with them/get validation that they are desirable), they will be interested in you because you can give them release from tension.

There is another category of guys — though this is more of a sliding scale than a binary thing — who are used to getting laid whenever they want. Often without realizing it, these guys will get progressively less thrilled with getting laid as time goes on because the certainty deprives them of tension. These guys will be interested in you if you can give them **tension to release.**

This is not the same thing as refusing sex — this is all about building sexual charge. In my experience, this is the most common mistake that girls make when dealing with player dudes: they want the dude, so they throw sex at him — which would work with guys who are release-driven, which is most guys. But what you really want to build with these guys is sexual charge! Tension!

It's worth keeping in mind that within this second orientation, guys have a tendency to become... Specialists. They may seek tension in the form of exploring kinkier and kinkier acts with the same woman, of seeking faster and more exhibitionist hookups, or simply of looking for sex with more and more or hotter and hotter women. Some of these will be compatible with your goals and others will not; don't expect him to change for you.

4) Be Touching Him

Kino matters as much for you as it does for dudes. Fucking pivotal.

Q. WHAT DOES IT MEAN TO GAME A DUDE WRONG?

As much as possible, avoid motivating people with feelings of obligation or guilt; inasmuch as you have goals, your goal is for them to want to do whatever it is that you want them to do. Obligation burns social currency.

Don't pay as much attention to the name of a relationship or "magic words" ("love," "commitment," "exclusivity") as you do to its form and function (level and frequency of attention paid, emotional intimacy, passionate attraction)

If you feel like you need a man to complete you, you're doing something wrong.

If you value what you want over what you need, you're doing something very wrong. This is something you should think about.

Q. HOW CAN I BE MEMORABLY GOOD IN BED?

Some general pointers:

Nothing makes or breaks sex more than your level of inhibition. This shouldn't need to be said, but it does: **move**. It is genuinely worrying how many women apparently think of sex as a spectator sport. Be willing to work up a sweat. Next: verbal feedback matters. Communicate, positively, what works for you and what he can do to make you feel good. One "I rub the right side of it, not the left" goes a long way. One "Fuck me, daddy, please, yes, God" or "Mmmmso good" goes even further. Develop your ability to talk dirty. Make noise. It's ok to be nasty and raunchy and raw, if you've picked a trustworthy guy. And if you haven't, what's the point?

Get over your body insecurity the moment you start to get it on. **Nobody** is perfect, and you are the female of the fucking species — the way you look, taste, smell is **designed** to get him hard. Let go of any worries about your looks when you have your clothes off. Seriously, if they start to rise just... Let the thought go. Don't try to argue with it, release it. Meditation might be helpful to learn how to do this, if you can't already.

Technique matters, but raw enthusiasm matters more. If you need tips on giving head, I wrote up a tutorial at some point — fish for it in my archive. I stand by it.

Be what Dan Savage calls GGG: "Good, Giving, and Game". Be willing to try things he's into, even if you don't initially think you'll necessarily like them. Does it make him so hard to suck on your toes that he could drive nails with his dick? Well, don't turn that down. Does he want to spank you? Give it a go. You will end up liking new things you try more often than you might initially assume — in part because, if you're picking the right guys, seeing them turned on by it will turn you on.

Finally, and most importantly: build sexual tension between sessions. In a way, your next sexual encounter starts the moment he gets off.

Q. HOW DO I GET OVER SOMEONE? I DON'T WANT TO GFTOM

Again, general pointers:

When most people say "I want to get over him/her" what they mean is "I want more leverage in my relationship with him/her". The latter is frequently impossible. Be clear on your goals: the objective is to be able to say "If I could sleep with him/her, I wouldn't." No "unless" allowed. No "until" allowed. When you can say this, and mean it, you're over it. There is no other meaningful measure.

Don't think about him/her when you masturbate. Ever. Hard and fast rule. Every time you break this rule, you are setting yourself back. Call it the JOSB, Jerk-Off Set-Back rule.

Cut contact until you achieve your goal, to the extent that that's possible. If you must, delete the person from your phone or leave their number for the future with a friend who will duly mock you if you ask for it back. Alternately, in less extreme cases, simply set their ringer to 'silent' and don't call back. You can do that, right?

Sleeping with someone else will help — a lot — but generally it will only help a lot if **you** hit emotional hookpoint for **them**. So if you don't have any prospects handy that that's true of, go out and meet people. Aggressively expand your social circle until you meet a good prospect, game, repeat.

Even if you're doing all this, give it about three months. At least, that's how long it usually takes **me** to shake a nasty crush.

* * *

APPENDIX G:
Footnotes

Clarisse last checked all hyperlinks in late 2011 or early 2012.

* * *

Chapter 1: **Come Jump In, Bimbo Friend**

1. The blog that was most significant for me, personally, has unfortunately not updated in years: http://sm-feminist.blogspot.com/
2. "Ms." Magazine editrix threatens to resign if S&M article is published: http://nymag.com/print/?/news/features/ms-magazine-2011-11/
3. 1980s attack on lesbian S&M club by radical feminists: http://glamourousrags.dymphna.net/reviewjeffreys.html
4. Radical feminist blogger encourages S&M sadists to commit suicide: http://rageagainstthemanchine.com/2009/02/07/please-somebody-come-and-defend-kinkcom/
5. Alice Schwarzer says "Female masochism is collaboration!": "Weiblicher Masochismus ist Kollaboration!" from *EMMA Heft 2,* 1991
6. "Ms." Magazine blog on *Feminism Is For Everybody:* http://msmagazine.com/blog/blog/2010/09/07/10-years-of-feminism-is-for-everybody/
7. Men's magazine editor on the narrowness of male sexual stereotypes: "What Really Turns Men On," by John Devore. Published in *Best Sex Writing 2010,* edited by Rachel Kramer Bussel. Cleis Press, 2010.
8. Treatise on the word "cisgendered": http://carnalnation.com/content/49458/1067/word-day-cis
9. PUA blogs that some fetishes "are the domain of losers": http://heartiste.wordpress.com/2009/12/13/november-2009-beta-of-the-month/
10. PUAs are assholes about non-"hot" women: http://www.feministcritics.org/blog/2010/02/02/open-thread-feminism-and-the-seduction-community/
11. Blonde women earn more: http://www.telegraph.co.uk/lifestyle/7552146/Blondes-paid-more-than-

other-women.html

12. Thin women earn more: http://www.huffingtonpost.com/2011/06/19/skinny-women-make-more-money_n_872799.html

13. Anti-feminist attacks the seduction community: http://lifestylejourney.blogspot.com/2010/02/pua-scam.html

14. Hugh Ristik on deconstructing the seduction community: http://www.feministcritics.org/blog/2007/03/07/what-is-the-seduction-community/

15. Negs: http://www.sosuave.com/articles/neghits.htm

16. As of late 2011, that page seems to have been closed to the public. Neil Strauss also sent the message with that quotation to his email list, which used to be available to all subscribers for free (but no longer is). If you're dying to see it, email me and I'll forward it to you. Here's where it was originally posted: http://www.neilstrauss.com/neil/what-separates-a-winner-from-a-loser-is-2

17. Tyler Durden on negs: http://www.bristollair.com/2011/pua-seduction-methods/examining-different-pua-methods-pt-2/

18. Pitiless blogger on negs: http://heartiste.wordpress.com/2011/09/26/the-subtle-art-of-the-insidious-neg/

19. Mark Manson left a comment on market research on this post: http://clarissethorn.com/blog/2011/04/18/guest-post-detrimental-attitudes-of-the-pickup-artist-community/

* * *

Chapter 2: You're A Good Soldier, Choosing Your Battles

1. Actual study on novelty and romance: http://www.nytimes.com/2008/02/12/health/12well.html

2. Clarisse's old blog post that mentions adversarial flirting as a proxy for S&M: http://clarissethorn.com/blog/2009/04/09/storytime-with-clarisse-have-i-always-been-a-domme/

3. "What are you thinking about" as a so-called shit test: http://heartiste.wordpress.com/2011/08/07/what-are-you-thinking-about/

4. Tactics used by abusers: http://www.dhs.state.il.us/page.aspx?item=38490

5. Mark Manson's post on "shit test paranoia": http://www.practicalpickup.com/shit-test-paranoia

6. Mark Manson's post that includes apologies:

http://www.practicalpickup.com/5-ways-to-deal-with-womens-tests

7. Token resistance: "Token Resistance to Sexual Intercourse and Consent to Unwanted Sexual Intercourse: College Students' Dating Experiences in Three Countries," by Susan Sprecher et al. *Journal of Sex Research,* volume 31, number 2, 1994. Pages 125-132. The study asked respondents the question: "Has this ever happened to you? You were with a person who wanted to engage in sexual intercourse and you wanted to also, but for some reason you indicated that you didn't want to, although you had every intention to and were willing to engage in sexual intercourse. Has this ever happened to you?" About 15% of both male and female respondents indicated that they had done this 4 or more times.

* * *

Chapter 3: **Underground Communication**

1. Raven Kaldera quoted on polyamory: http://sexgeek.wordpress.com/2007/06/10/10-realistic-rules-for-good-non-monogamous-relationships/

2. Tristan Taormino on polyamory: http://suicidegirlsblog.com/blog/red-white-and-femme-eeny-meeny-miny-polyamory-part-ii/

3. LMR Lay Report: http://www.abcsofattraction.com/community/hall-of-fame-f64/lay-report-used-1-lmr-tactic-starting-to-set-up-a-routine-t813.html

4. Really awful LMR Lay Report: http://www.fastseduction.com/cgi-bin/search.cgi?action=retrieve&grp=4&mn=106197420797828&refine=

5. Response to above: http://www.fastseduction.com/cgi-bin/search.cgi?action=retrieve&grp=4&mn=106197421598169&refine=

6. Response to above: http://www.fastseduction.com/cgi-bin/search.cgi?action=retrieve&grp=4&mn=106197421598173&refine=

7. The first two "no"s don't mean much: http://thesocialsecrets.com/2009/04/5-easy-ways-to-over-come-lmr-last-minute-sexual-reservations/

8. Freeze-out example: *Magic Bullets* version 1.0, by Savoy. 2007 eBook. Current website at http://www.magicbulletsbook.com/

9. Louis C.K.'s comedy sketch: http://www.youtube.com/watch?v=b4hNaFkbZYU

10. Token resistance: "Token Resistance to Sexual Intercourse and Consent to Unwanted Sexual Intercourse: College Students' Dating Experiences in Three Countries," by Susan Sprecher et al. *Journal of Sex*

Research, volume 31, number 2, 1994. Pages 125-132. The study asked respondents the question: "Has this ever happened to you? You were with a person who wanted to engage in sexual intercourse and you wanted to also, but for some reason you indicated that you didn't want to, although you had every intention to and were willing to engage in sexual intercourse. Has this ever happened to you?" About 15% of both male and female respondents indicated that they had done this 4 or more times.

    11. Mark Manson on LMR: http://www.practicalpickup.com/the-cheerleader

    12. David Shade on LMR: *The Secrets of Female Sexuality,* by David Shade. David Shade Corporation, 2007.

    13. Riker's Rules: http://arizonapua.com/forum/index.php?topic=3038.0

    14. Women are more likely to catch HIV from men than vice versa: "Heterosexual transmission of human immunodeficiency virus (HIV) in northern California: Results from a ten-year study," by Padian, NS, Shiboski, SC, Glass, SO, Vittinghoff, E. *American Journal of Epidemiology.* 1997; 146(4): 350-57.

    15. Study on gender differences and casual sex: http://yesmeansyesblog.wordpress.com/2011/03/03/gender-differences-and-casual-sex-the-new-research/

    16. Women list an emotional connection during sex as more important to them than men: http://www.iub.edu/~kinsey/resources/FAQ.html

    17. Kink.com virgin shoot: http://missmaggiemayhem.com/2011/01/12/virginity/

    18. Most women can't orgasm from intercourse: http://www.scarleteen.com/article/advice/i_cant_orgasm_from_intercourse_and_its_ruining_my_relationship

    19. Clarisse's post on orgasms not being her favorite part of sex: http://clarissethorn.com/blog/2012/02/02/orgasms-arent-my-favorite-part-of-sex-and-my-chastity-urge/ - comments

* * *

Chapter 4: **If You Knew How Much I Loved You, You Would Run Away**

    1. "If You'd Sleep With Her, You Can't Call Her a Slut": http://goodmenproject.com/featured-content/if-youd-sleep-with-her-you-cant-call-her-a-slut/

    2. Kate Harding on *The Rules:*

http://www.salon.com/life/broadsheet/feature/2009/11/17/rules_dating_advice

3. XKCD on *The Rules* and *The Game:* http://xkcd.com/800/

4. The dating manual *He's Just Not That Into You:* http://www.usatoday.com/life/books/excerpts/2004-09-08-hes-just_x.htm

5. Compliance test definition: http://www.puaforums.com/common-pick-up-terms/3758-compliance-test.html

6. Van Halen and the M&Ms: http://www.snopes.com/music/artists/vanhalen.asp

7. Athol Kay on shit tests: http://www.marriedmansexlife.com/2010/05/some-common-fitness-tests-and-what-isnt.html

* * *

Chapter 5: **He's A Ghost, He's A God, He's A Man, He's A Guru**

1. Feminists don't like Neil Strauss: http://www.feministe.us/blog/archives/2011/03/25/i-totally-interviewed-the-worlds-most-famous-pickup-artist/ - comments

2. Anti-feminists don't like Neil Strauss: http://www.inmalafide.com/blog/2011/04/12/kill-your-game-idols-part-2-strauss-schwyzer-and-spengler/

3. The "commodity model" of sex: "Towards a Performance Model of Sex", by Thomas MacAulay Millar. Printed in *Yes Means Yes,* edited by Jessica Valenti and Jaclyn Friedman. Seal Press, 2009.

4. Rape culture defined by Ampersand: http://www.amptoons.com/blog/2004/02/11/what-causes-rape-anatomy-of-a-rape-culture/

5. Rape statistics: http://rainn.org/statistics

6. Rape definitions and male victims: http://www.rolereboot.org/sex-and-relationships/details/2012-01-erections-arent-consent-what-the-new-fbi-definitions

7. PUA on his default opinion of women as "worthless dirty whores": http://www.rooshv.com/the-dark-side

8. Buyer's Remorse Field Report: http://www.theattractionforums.com/18-21-forum/130069-can-t-just-stop-buyer-s-remorse-if-sorta-buyers-remorse.html

9. "Discover" Magazine blog on the metaphor study: http://blogs.discovermagazine.com/notrocketscience/2011/02/23/is-crime-a-virus-or-a-beast-how-metaphors-shape-our-thoughts-and-decisions/

10. PUA who cites *Yes Means Yes:* http://www.fastseduction.com/cgi-bin/search.cgi?action=retrieve&grp=4&mn=1299480531648347

11. Asexuality and sex-positive feminism: http://www.feministe.us/blog/archives/2012/02/07/an-asexual-map-for-sex-positive-feminism/

12. Mark Manson's post on why he's not a feminist: http://postmasculine.com/why-im-not-a-feminist

13. Jaclyn Friedman on "consent is not a lightswitch": http://www.amplifyyourvoice.org/u/Yes_Means_Yes/2010/11/9/Consent-Is-Not-A-Lightswitch

14. Tracy Clark-Flory interviews Jaclyn Friedman: http://www.salon.com/2011/10/30/a_sex_guide_for_todays_girls/singleton/

15. Feminist commenter says "PUAs rape women" on this post: http://www.feministe.us/blog/archives/2011/03/25/i-totally-interviewed-the-worlds-most-famous-pickup-artist/

16. Paper on social phobia: http://www.homepage.psy.utexas.edu/HomePage/Class/Psy394U/Bower/12 Anxiety Disorders /CLARK-SOCIAL PHOBIA.pdf

* * *

Chapter 6: **Down The Rabbit Hole**

1. PUA coach on women who approach: http://www.alternet.org/sex/148990/why_are_men_always_expected_to_make_the_first_move_in_sex_and_relationships?page=entire

2. Hugh Ristik on women who approach: http://www.feministcritics.org/blog/2010/10/03/do-men-or-women-have-fantasies-of-dominance-and-submission-noh/ - comment-126142

3. The awesome PUA blog post Clarisse was reading before The Dude called: http://charismaarts.com/ten-phrases-to-keep-your-conversation-exciting-but-truthful

* * *

Chapter 7: **Tough Guy**

1. Lists of abuse tactics: http://www.dhs.state.il.us/page.aspx?item=38490

2. Emotional IOIs as poker chips: http://www.fastseduction.com/cgi-

bin/search.cgi?action=retrieve&grp=9&mn=1289446216634569&refine=

3. Clarisse and Hugh Ristik discuss emotional IOIs: http://clarissethorn.com/blog/2011/04/18/guest-post-detrimental-attitudes-of-the-pickup-artist-community/ - comment-47331

* * *

Chapter 8: **Ladies And Their Sensitivities**

1. Porn & Chicken club night: http://evil-olive.com/events/mon-porn-chicken/

2. Blog post by Female Misogynist on PUAs: http://femalemisogynist.wordpress.com/2008/04/16/pick-up-artists-and-feminism/

3. S&M blogger Bitchy Jones on dominance going unrecognized among women: http://bitchyjones.wordpress.com/2007/10/11/why-95-of-dominant-women-agree-with-everything-i-say/

* * *

Chapter 9: **A Disease of the Mind... It Can Control You**

1. Gunwitch (allegedly) shoots a girl: http://manboobz.com/2011/01/10/gunwitch-update/

2. Gunwitch's followers insist that he had a good reason: http://manboobz.com/2011/01/07/gun-loving-pick-up-guru-allegedly-shoots-a-woman-in-the-face/

3. Hugh Ristik writes a post that says "Fuck You, Gunwitch": http://www.feministcritics.org/blog/2011/01/08/did-a-pickup-artist-shoot-a-woman-noh/

4. Gunwitch's seduction manual: http://www.gunwitch.com/seduction/gwm1.html

5. Roissy moved his blog recently. This is a tactic occasionally used by pseudonymous bloggers who are concerned about being tracked down by real-life associates. As of late 2011, Roissy is available at http://heartiste.wordpress.com/. I have saved copies of all the posts I cite.

6. Roissy calls female genitals a "fetid, humid mess": http://heartiste.wordpress.com/2011/04/29/alpha-assessment-tasting-success-edition/

7. Roissy calls women "sociopaths of convenience": http://heartiste.wordpress.com/2009/03/03/february-2009-beta-of-the-

month/

8. Caffeinate her hamster: http://heartiste.wordpress.com/2011/08/03/how-to-deal-with-a-girl-gaming-you/

9. Hamster in overdrive: http://heartiste.wordpress.com/2011/06/19/an-alpha-male-and-his-women/

10. Hamster definition: http://manboobz.com/2012/01/17/rationalization-hamsters-or-hamster-rationalizations/

11. Women who work are "betraying their sex": http://heartiste.wordpress.com/2011/06/23/is-female-careerism-a-form-of-infidelity/

12. Women's right to vote will lead to society's downfall: http://heartiste.wordpress.com/2009/06/01/sexual-dystopia-a-glimpse-at-the-future/

13. Dread tactics: http://heartiste.wordpress.com/2008/03/27/dread/

14. Girls who play a man's pickup game are "drama queens": http://heartiste.wordpress.com/2011/08/03/how-to-deal-with-a-girl-gaming-you/

15. Testimonial from a former lady PUA assistant: http://jezebel.com/5499094/the-secret-world-of-men-a-pickup-artists-assistant-tells-all

16. Diversity + Proximity = War: http://heartiste.wordpress.com/2011/06/29/diversity-proximity-war/

17. The so-called Folly Before The Fall: http://heartiste.wordpress.com/2011/07/15/the-folly-before-the-fall/

18. Evolutionary psychology and the "alpha male narrative myth": http://evolvify.com/alpha-male-narrative-myth/

19. Statistics on injustices faced by trans people: http://www.thetaskforce.org/reports_and_research/ntds

20. Roissy does gender policing: http://heartiste.wordpress.com/2007/06/27/an-open-letter-to-my-hypothetical-future-kids/

21. Roissy defines the crux of alpha manhood as good with women: http://heartiste.wordpress.com/2007/09/19/defining-the-alpha-male/

22. Roissy attacks a guy who misses his ex: http://heartiste.wordpress.com/2009/12/13/november-2009-beta-of-the-month/

23. The lady who broke Roissy's heart: http://heartiste.wordpress.com/2007/10/25/dodged-the-same-bullet-twice/

24. A bounty on women:

http://heartiste.wordpress.com/2011/08/07/what-are-you-thinking-about/ - comment-267855

* * *

Chapter 12: **At Last I Am Free**

1. Exchange about asking for a kiss on Holly Pervocracy's blog: http://pervocracy.blogspot.com/2011/07/how-to-not-be-creepy.html?showComment=1310928149621 - c6917844665418677680

2. Dating site conversation analyzed by Hugh Ristik: http://forums.plentyoffish.com/datingPosts3087240.aspx

3. Hugh Ristik's dating site analysis: http://clarissethorn.com/blog/2011/04/18/guest-post-detrimental-attitudes-of-the-pickup-artist-community/ - comment-49381

4. The story quotation is from: "Brief Interviews With Hideous Men," by David Foster Wallace. Printed in the collection *Brief Interviews With Hideous Men*. Back Bay Books, 2007.

5. David Foster Wallace's obituary: http://www.nytimes.com/2008/09/15/books/15wallace.html

6. The "commodity model" of sex: "Towards a Performance Model of Sex", by Thomas MacAulay Millar. Printed in *Yes Means Yes*, edited by Jessica Valenti and Jaclyn Friedman. Seal Press, 2009.

7. Mark Manson on his life as a PUA: http://www.practicalpickup.com/pickup-artist

* * *

Appendix Footnotes

1. The guest post on detrimental PUA attitudes at Clarisse's blog: http://clarissethorn.com/blog/2011/04/18/guest-post-detrimental-attitudes-of-the-pickup-artist-community/

2. Clarisse's Sex-Positive 101: http://clarissethorn.com/blog/2011/05/08/towards-my-personal-sex-positive-feminist-101/

3. Clarisse's interview with Neil Strauss: http://timeoutchicago.com/sex-dating/12914409/neil-strauss-interview

* * *

APPENDIX H:
Glossary

This glossary defines most of the technical terms that come up in the book. In parentheses after each term is the community where Clarisse found it. Most of this jargon obviously comes from pickup artists (PUAs), but Clarisse made some of it up. There are also terms from:
  * feminism,
  * queer theory,
  * polyamory — a community based around the philosophy that one can have multiple lovers and be radically honest about it,
  * and BDSM (colloquially S&M) — a community based around a shared interest in bondage, discipline, dominance, submission, sadism and masochism.

* * *

adversarial gender roles (feminism): The assumption that men and women are deeply, inherently different and are eternally opposed in a "war of the sexes."

aftercare (BDSM): A cool-down period after an S&M encounter, which often involves reassurance and a discussion of how things went.

agree and amplify (PUA): A tactic for responding to *shit tests* whereby the PUA agrees with the *target,* then intensifies what she said to the point of ridiculousness.

agree and continue (PUA): A tactic for dealing with *Last Minute Resistance* whereby the PUA verbally agrees with the target's reservations about having sex, then continues initiating sex anyway.

alpha (PUA): A term that indicates a dominant man in a social setting, who hypothetically "gets all the girls." Introduced in Chapter 9, when Clarisse points out that PUAs who use the term most tend to be power-obsessed assholes.

Alpha Male on Guard, or AMOG (PUA): A gentleman who interferes while a PUA is trying to game a *target.* PUAs have a number of strategies for dealing with this.

Anti-Relationship Defense (Clarisse): See: *Anti-Slut Defense*

Anti-Slut Defense, or ASD (PUA): Since women are shamed for wanting sex by means of slurs like "slut," some PUAs claim that the only reason women resist having sex is shame, or *Anti-Slut Defense*. Clarisse notes ironically that since men are shamed out of wanting relationships by means of slurs like "pansy" or *beta,* one could claim that the only reason men resist having relationships is shame, and that men have *Anti-Relationship Defense.*

approach anxiety (PUA): The feeling of dread one gets before initiating a social interaction with an unfamiliar person.

attraction phase (PUA): A phase in the seduction process whereby the PUA gets the target to feel attracted to him, or at least like she respects him.

Average Frustrated Chump, or AFC; below-Average Frustrated Chump, or bAFC; reformed Average Frustrated Chump, or rAFC (PUA): An *Average Frustrated Chump* is a guy with no *natural game* who has not yet been exposed to the seduction community. A *below-Average Frustrated Chump* is a guy who's even more awkward than the average beginner PUA. A *reformed Average Frustrated Chump* is a guy who feels that he used to be an AFC but is now well on the way to excellence. Clarisse occasionally jokes about considering herself an "Average Frustrated Chick."

beta (PUA): A term that indicates a non-dominant man in a social setting, who hypothetically is constantly passed over for female attention. Introduced in Chapter 9, when Clarisse points out that PUAs who use the term most tend to be power-obsessed assholes.

bitch shield (PUA): A *target's* instinctive tendency to be cold and unfriendly to an unfamiliar man, in order to ward off unwanted attention.

blaming the victim (feminism): The assumption that a rape survivor caused or contributed to the rape.

buyer's remorse (PUA): The catch-all phrase to cover situations when a target feels bad after sex with a PUA. Introduced in Chapter 5, where Clarisse points out that it can all-too-easily be a form of *blaming the victim.*

calibration (PUA): The ability to recognize and work with tacit social cues. A person with good social instincts is *calibrated*, while a person without them is *uncalibrated* or *miscalibrated.*

cisgendered (queer studies): A term that means "not transgendered." For example, Clarisse is a cis woman or a cisgendered woman.

comfort phase (PUA): A phase in the seduction process whereby the PUA gets the target to feel like she can trust him.

commodity model (feminism): The idea that women trade sex to men in exchange for commitment or support.

compliance test (PUA): A tactic for detecting a target's interest level, or for shifting social power within a relationship. Sometimes referred to as *hoop theory*. Deconstructed in Chapter 4.

congruent (PUA): An action or statement is *congruent* when it matches how the person actually thinks or feels; it's *incongruent* if it doesn't match.

Demonstration of Higher Value, or DHV (PUA): Any tactic that shows how fun and/or high-status one is.

direct game (PUA): Seduction tactics whereby one is open about one's sexual or romantic intentions.

emotional escalation (Clarisse): The process of deliberately fostering an emotional connection. While men are usually handed the responsibility for *sexual escalation* within a relationship, women are usually handed the responsibility of *emotional escalation*.

emotional hookpoint (Clarisse): See: *hookpoint*

emotional Indicators of Interest (Clarisse): See: *Indicators of Interest*

enthusiastic consent (feminism): A standard for ethical sex whereby one is expected not just to have a consenting partner, but an enthusiastic and excited partner.

fake Indicators of Interest (PUA): *See: Indicators of Interest*

false time constraint (PUA): The claim that one has less time available than one actually does.

field; Field Report, or FR (PUA): Anywhere PUAs practice approaching *targets* is *the field*. Afterwards, many PUAs write *Field Reports* about their experiences — or, if they got laid, they write *Lay Reports*.

frame; frame control; reframe (PUA): A *frame* is a paradigm, or a way of thinking about the world. PUAs theorize that socially dominant people set the terms of social interactions by *controlling the frame*. A person can take control of a social interaction by *reframing* it to their advantage.

freeze-out (PUA): A strategy for getting through a *target's Last Minute Resistance* by withdrawing all sense of romance or intimacy.

friend zone (popular culture): See: *Indicators of Interest*

fuckbuddy zone (Clarisse): See: *Indicators of Interest*

gender policing (feminism): Gender roles are defined by culture, and when a person steps outside their gender role, that person will often be *policed* or attacked by other members of the culture. For example, a USA man with long hair risks being mocked or beaten up. Introduced in Chapter

9, when Clarisse discusses misogynist PUAs whose primary goal is control, and points out that they seek not only to control women but also other men.

Go Fuck Ten Other Women, or GFTOW (PUA): A strategy for ridding oneself of *one-itis.*

hookpoint (PUA): The point at which a target is no longer merely polite or amused, but is genuinely interested in what one has to say. Introduced in Chapter 6, when Clarisse discusses *emotional hookpoint* in the context of *emotional escalation.*

Indicator of Interest, or IOI (PUA): Flirtatious signals from the target that the PUA can recognize and use to determine when it's time to move things along. Clarisse introduces her own concept of *emotional IOIs,* or emotional signals that one can use to determine how open someone is to an emotional relationship. PUAs describe *fake IOIs* as coming from women who want a PUA's approval for some reason other than sexual interest. Clarisse later builds her Theory of the *Friend Zone* and the *Fuckbuddy Zone* by describing these phenomena as deliberately stringing people along with fake IOIs — sexual or emotional. IOIs are introduced in Chapter 4, when Clarisse talks about the lady-game book *The Rules;* you can find Clarisse's Theory of the *Friend Zone* and/or *Fuckbuddy Zone* in Chapter 7.

indirect game (PUA): Seduction tactics with a high degree of *plausible deniability.*

inner game (PUA): Genuine confidence and sense of purpose; contrasts with outer game, i.e. one's physical hotness and the behaviors one exhibits.

keyboard jockey (PUA): Someone who reads theory online and then acts like he knows what he's talking about, but never puts it into practice.

kino escalation (PUA): Body language used during seduction.

heteronormative (queer studies): A term used to describe the cultural expectations of "normal" heterosexual relationships. For example, the expectation that men are the ones to pursue women during romantic interactions is *heteronormative.*

hoop theory (PUA): See: *compliance test*

Hot Bitch / Hot Babe, or HB (PUA): A conventionally attractive woman. Often accompanied by a 1-10 numerical rating of her hotness.

lair (PUA): A city's local PUA headquarters.

Last Minute Resistance, or LMR; LMR techniques (PUA): Last Minute Resistance is a term for a target's actions when she expresses hesitance or unwillingness about having sex. Last Minute Resistance techniques are designed to have sex with a target despite the unwillingness she has expressed. Introduced in Chapter 3, which is almost entirely devoted to deconstructing LMR techniques.

Lay Report, or LR (PUA): See: *field*

managing expectations (PUA): Ensuring that a target doesn't get the wrong idea about one's commitment to the relationship.

miscalibrated (PUA): See: *calibration*

natural game (PUA): Social tactics that involve understanding underlying principles of social interaction. Contrasts with *synthetic game*.

neg (PUA): A remark, sometimes humorous, used to point out a *target's* flaws.

Neuro-Linguistic Programming, or NLP (PUA): A field of inquiry dedicated to getting specific reactions from human *targets* by means of particular gestures or word choices.

New Relationship Energy (polyamory): The obsessive, irrational joy one feels after starting a relationship with a new and awesome partner.

next (PUA): A term for walking away from a budding relationship or breaking off an ongoing one. "You always have to be willing to next people" is a common PUA refrain.

one-itis (PUA): An infatuation that arises entirely from feeling unworthy, or the fear that "I'll never find someone else like this again."

open loop (PUA): A tactic whereby one starts an interesting conversation that's worth coming back to later.

opener (PUA): A line for starting a conversation with a *target*.

outcome independence (PUA): Lack of neediness; lack of fixation on a goal.

parking brake test (Clarisse): A test for detecting bad ideas: if you will feel like an idiot explaining yourself later unless you take precautions now, then you should take precautions right now.

peacocking (PUA): Ostentatious clothing that's deliberately out of place in *the field*.

phlogiston (philosophy): An antique scientific theory that was incorrect, but which seemed to explain many phenomena that had been hard to explain until then. Introduced in Chapter 9, when Clarisse discusses evil PUA frameworks and points out that while those frameworks may appear to be supported by some PUA tactics, *phlogiston* also appeared to be supported by reality.

plausible deniability (PUA): The pretense that a flirtatious, romantic, or sexual interaction isn't about flirtation, romance, or sex.

primary relationship (polyamory): A relationship with more commitment and expectations than other relationships. For example, a primary relationship might be one where the participants live together and/or are married. Polyamorists sometimes disagree about whether relationship hierarchies are desirable.

qualification phase (PUA): A phase in the seduction process whereby the PUA gets the *target* to seek his approval.

rape culture (feminism): A culture in which rape is prevalent and is maintained through fundamental attitudes and beliefs about gender, sexuality, and violence, including *rape myths*.

rape myths (feminism): Cultural ideas that make it harder to recognize, prosecute, and heal from rape. For example, many people believe that rape usually happens to young, "hot" women ... but interviews with rapists show that they usually prioritize targets based on how vulnerable they are, rather than how "hot" they are.

reframe (PUA): See: *frame*

routine (PUA): A memorized set of social steps designed to get a specific result.

safeword (BDSM): A word that any S&M participant can say at any time to stop the action.

sarging (PUA): Going out in order to practice approaching people.

secondary relationship (polyamory): A relationship with less commitment and fewer expectations than other relationships. Polyamorists sometimes disagree about whether relationship hierarchies are desirable.

seduction community (PUA): A term for the pickup artist community.

sexual escalation (PUA): The process of deliberately fostering a sexual connection. While men are usually handed the responsibility for *sexual escalation* within a relationship, women are usually handed the responsibility of *emotional escalation.*

shit test (PUA): Many PUAs theorize that women are always "testing men for dominance," and this idea gives rise to the theory of *shit tests*. Clarisse suggests that while this idea offers some insight, *shit tests* are better understood as a framework for faux-adversarial flirting.

social circle game (PUA): Finding partners through community connections or events.

social proof (PUA): Using other people to demonstrate that one is safe, fun, and/or hot.

Statement of Intent, or SOI (PUA): An explicit notification of one's interest, given to the target to ensure that there are no misunderstandings about the seduction.

supplication (PUA): Being desperate for attention. Introduced in Chapter 2, in the context of the "no buying drinks" rule.

switch (BDSM): A person who feels comfortable in either the dominant or the submissive role.

synthetic game (PUA): Social tactics that use a lot of memorized or otherwise "artificial" material, like *routines*.

target (PUA): The person the PUA is trying to pick up.

time dilation (PUA): A tactic whereby many venue changes over a short period makes people think they've spent more time together than they actually have.

Too Long; Didn't Read, or TL;DR (Internet culture): A summary of a long piece of text, offered with the understanding that it might have been too long to hold the audience's attention. Clarisse offers TL;DR bullet-pointed summaries at the end of all her chapters except the last one, which you should just read.

uncalibrated (PUA): See: *calibration*

warpig (PUA): A cruel term for a woman who is not conventionally attractive.

* * *

Printed in Great Britain
by Amazon